STUDIES IN IRISH HIST

*edited by*

**T. W. MOODY**
*Professor of Modern History*
*University of Dublin*

**R. DUDLEY EDWARDS**
*Professor of Modern Irish History*
*National University of Ireland*

**DAVID B. QUINN**
*Professor of History*
*University College, Swansea*

VOLUME V

# PUBLIC OPINION AND GOVERNMENT POLICY IN IRELAND, 1801–1846

*in the same series*

\*

IRISH PUBLIC OPINION, 1750–1800
by R. B. McDowell

PROTESTANT DISSENT IN IRELAND, 1687–1780
by J. C. Beckett

THE LAGAN VALLEY, 1800–1850
by E. R. R. Green

THE IRISH PARLIAMENTARY PARTY, 1890–1910
by F. S. L. Lyons

941.58

# PUBLIC OPINION
# AND GOVERNMENT POLICY
# IN IRELAND, 1801-1846

by

## R. B. McDOWELL

*Fellow of Trinity College, Dublin*

WANDSWORTH PUBLIC LIBRARIES

## FABER AND FABER LTD

24 Russell Square

London

*First published in mcmlii*
*by Faber and Faber Limited*
*24 Russell Square London W.C.1*
*Printed in Great Britain by*
*Latimer Trend & Co Ltd Plymouth*
*All rights reserved*

241
941.58

# CONTENTS

# PREFACE

In the preparation of this work dealing with Irish politics during the early nineteenth century I am deeply indebted to my colleague, Professor T. W. Moody, for encouragement and assistance. I am also very grateful to the Rev. G. O. Simms for assistance in reading the proofs; to Dr Brian Inglis and Mr G. D. Sullivan for permission to use their unpublished theses; to Mr T. P. O'Neill for permission to use his unpublished paper on the Irish land question before 1849; to Captain J. L. J. Hughes for checking the lists on pages 293–4; to Mr R. B. D. French, Mr T. L. Lalley, Father J. A. Reynolds, and the staffs of the libraries and repositories in which I have worked.

For permission to use manuscript material, my sincere thanks are due to the Marquess of Anglesey, Lord Hatherton, Mrs Duffin, Mr G. Howard, Colonel O'Connell-Fitzsimon, Mr M. O'Connell, Mr E. Little and Her Majesty's Stationery Office. My thanks are also due to the Board of Trinity College, Dublin, for a generous grant in aid of publication.

R. B. McDowell

*Jan. 1952*

# TABLE OF ABBREVIATIONS

| | |
|---|---|
| *BNL* | Belfast Newsletter |
| *Comm Journ* | Commons Journals |
| *DEM* | Dublin Evening Mail |
| *DEP* | Dublin Evening Post |
| *DUM* | Dublin University Magazine |
| *EP* | Evening Packet |
| *UR* | Ulster Register |
| *FJ* | Freeman's Journal |
| *FLJ* | Finn's Leinster Journal |
| *H.O.* | Home Office |
| *IHS* | Irish Historical Studies |
| *MR* | Morning Register |
| *NW* | Northern Whig |
| *Parl. Deb.* | Parliamentary debates |
| S.C.P. | State of the Country papers |
| *SNL* | Saunders Newsletter |
| S.P.O. | State paper office (Dublin). |

# INTRODUCTION

The Union thrust on British statesmen direct responsibility for the good government of Ireland. Between the two countries there were striking differences in historic tradition, social pattern, economic development, denominational balance and intellectual tone. In any case Pitt's bold experiment was begun at an inopportune moment. During the early nineteenth century British politicians were being forced to cope with an overwhelming variety of urgent, complex and novel problems. The growth of the empire, the Napoleonic wars, their aftermath, and above all the tremendous changes brought about by the Industrial Revolution—which of course steadily accentuated the differences between Great Britain and Ireland—threw a heavy strain on British political adaptability and intelligence. And for decades ministers, M.P.s and officials, often ill-informed, prejudiced and overworked, struggled in unfamiliar conditions to devise remedies for Ireland. Moreover the premises for political action which were being evolved in Great Britain during the age of *laissez-faire*, a period of abounding achievement, were unlikely to provide the best basis from which to approach the problems of a community mainly dependent on an ill-adjusted and backward agricultural system. Inevitably then, lack of foresight and initiative, blundering, and much wasted effort, characterized government activity during the first half of the century. But it would be misleading to dwell only on the negative and unsuccessful aspects, for during these years a substantial amount was accomplished, particularly since there was perforce a greater degree of state intervention than was conceivable in contemporary England. And in a period when the criterion of rational efficiency was being ruthlessly applied to existing institutions, the foundations of the modern Irish civil service, municipal government, police, poor law and primary education were firmly laid.

Throughout, the Irish administration was handicapped by the general political situation in which it had to function. The long drawn-out series of battles required to secure for the catholics full civic rights, and the persistence and growth of a nationalist movement which on cultural and

13

political grounds demanded the repeal of the union, meant that large sections of the Irish public were unable at any time to believe that the government was willing or able to respond adequately to the wishes of the community. To many Irishmen, 'the Castle' (the Dublin equivalent of Whitehall) was associated not only with the splendid isolation in which bureaucracy frequently prefers to operate, but with the unsympathetic authority of an external power. Nevertheless to sum up Irish politics after the union as a long struggle for national independence, would, by singling out one element, destroy the contemporary emphasis. Though catholic emancipation dominated Irish politics for three decades and was succeeded by repeal, British political conflicts were continually reflected in Ireland, and the political energies of many Irishmen were absorbed by issues which were British or common to the whole United Kingdom. Since up to 1848 even the repeal struggle was conducted only by constitutional methods, the great social gulf usually created by the opposition of absolutes arising from national conflicts, was absent in Ireland—or at least bridged at an incredible number of points. The difficulty of finding neat formulas for historical situations is illustrated by the fullness and complexity of O'Connell's career. The hero of the catholic masses, he was also an outstanding exponent of political utilitarianism, and in addition to being a brilliant demagogue he was a shrewd parliamentarian. Though he was by far the most outstanding Irishman of his time, the forcible exuberance of his personality should not be allowed to obscure the limitations to his leadership. To the Irish whigs he was at the best a useful ally who might become a liability. To the Irish tories he was anathema. And both these groups carried considerable political weight. The Irish whig party, which included many influential catholics, represented in Ireland a powerful political force, and was bound to benefit when the whigs attained office. Irish toryism, to a great extent the embodiment of militant protestantism, was tied up with established privilege, political and economic. The vast majority of Irish protestants were either whigs or tories. Nationalism as expounded by O'Connell and the Young Irelanders, even when expressed in the most generous and comprehensive terms, captivated only a few Irish protestants. In so far as the national consciousness of the repeal movement and the *Nation* was a subjective feeling, they simply did not share it and were unresponsive to either romantic or rational appeals. Their political and patriotic emotions were canalized in other channels. In addition, for Irish protestants the repeal of the union meant a distasteful transformation. From being part of a religious majority in the United Kingdom they would become a minority in an independent Ireland.

# INTRODUCTION

Finally in the protestant north east where industry had been successfully revolutionized, the union was synonymous with progress and prosperity.

If Irish politics were confused by the play of several forces—divisions over domestic issues, the local repercussions of British party battles, sectarian dissensions and the long argument over Anglo-Irish relations —the intrusion of Irish problems added considerably to the complexities of British politics. Lord John Russell may have been guilty of a pardonable piece of parliamentary exaggeration when he asserted, in the Maynooth debate, that almost every major political crisis since the beginning of the century had been caused or complicated by Irish affairs. Admittedly during the first half of the nineteenth century no Irish question so decisively disturbed British politics as did Home Rule in the eighties. Still Irish issues broke up cabinets, absorbed official time and energy, promoted congestion in parliamentary business, and by introducing sharp social, religious and racial antagonisms, embittered public debate.

If the union is clearly the starting point for a study of Irish politics in the nineteenth century then 1846 is obviously a terminus or halt. In Irish social and economic life the Famine is the great divide, but this year is also marked by a crisis in both British and Irish politics. Peel and O'Connell, old rivals, both essentially moderate men, and in the respectable sense of the term, political opportunists, had each to face a party mutiny led by his younger followers. In England, Peel's *volte-face* on the corn laws—hastened at least by the Irish emergency—led to a split in the conservative party which distracted English politics for over a decade. In Ireland, O'Connell's failure to keep his party together permitted a breach to open between constitutional nationalists and those who were prepared to use physical force, which lasted for about three-quarters of a century.

Irish history then, for the first half of the nineteenth century, was characterized by failure. The union failed to win general acceptance; the repeal movement failed to obtain its objective; the economic system failed to provide the majority of the population with an adequate and secure subsistence. Naturally the politics of the period are depressing. The exhausting and embittering struggle for catholic emancipation, outbreaks of agrarian violence, the Irish radicals' vehement and often unproductive efforts, the government's repressive measures and fumbling attempts at reform, combine to make a dreary pattern. But there also can be seen significant trends which persisted into the second half of the century—the growing strength and political self-assurance of the catholic middle class, the reshaping of the Irish administrative framework; the emergence of Irish unionism—particularly in the north— and the development and enrichment of the nationalist tradition.

15

WANDSWORTH PUBLIC LIBRARIES *

# 1

# IRELAND IN THE EARLY NINETEENTH CENTURY

Ireland after the '98 rebellion presented an awkward and urgent problem to a British government engaged in a desperate struggle for survival. Distracted by rebellion, Ireland invited a French invasion, which, if successful, would place the enemy in a position to carry out a gigantic pincer movement. Ireland had to be tranquillized and secured, and the obvious solution to the British cabinet seemed to be a union with Great Britain which would reassure the protestant minority, permit it to adopt a generous attitude to the catholic majority, render Ireland a safe field for British investment and enable it to participate in British prosperity. It was a drastic remedy but a wartime atmosphere sometimes has a stimulating effect on legislation, and although in Ireland the union was fiercely fought over, it slipped through the British parliament after a few languid debates. Political liabilities as well as empires can be acquired absent-mindedly. The bulk of the opposition were sulking in ineffectual secession, public attention was riveted on the fate of the second coalition, and the deep-rooted peculiarities which distinguished Ireland from England were uncomprehended in debates dominated by Pitt's superb but colourless classical oratory. In the discussions on the union at Westminster, only Lord Minto showed a real if fumbling appreciation of a factor which eighteenth-century thinking tended to ignore, nationalism. Speaking in defence of the union, he admitted that patriotism, which he defined as 'a solicitude for the happiness of the people who inhabit our country', presented a problem. But he pointed out how fortuitously formed was the area on which this emotion might be centred, and he drew a distinction between 'fantastical' and rational patriotism, the latter preferring the solid, real happiness of a country to its 'metaphysical identity'.[1]

[1] *The speech of Lord Minto in the house of peers, April* 11, 1799 (1799), pp. 85–100.

B

17

But so English in outlook were the predominant sections of Irish society that British politicians could be forgiven for underestimating the strength of Irish nationalism, for regarding the opposition to the union as being merely the reaction of a privileged interest which saw its position threatened, and for believing that it would disappear when the advantages of incorporation were appreciated. This opinion was confirmed by a simple fact which would strike a practising politician. Those Englishmen who expected that the hundred Irish M.P.s which the union added to the house of commons—the largest single addition in its history—would be 'less pure, less rational, less dispassionate'[1] than the average run of British members, must have been pleasantly surprised. Far from forming a distinctive, disgruntled separatist faction, the newcomers merged easily into the life of the house. The Irish M.P.s for the first three decades after the union were men of essentially the same type as those returned for British constituencies. Many were related to the great British political families, and the ease with which they fitted into British political life is illustrated by the fact that in the post-union period a prime minister, a foreign secretary, a leader of the opposition, a secretary at war, and two of the most admired orators in the house were all sometime members of the Irish house of commons. It was not until after catholic emancipation and the first reform bill that Irish members disagreeably different from the average English M.P. made their appearance in the house, and it was only in the eighties that there arrived at Westminster a large contingent of Irish M.P.s who were both politically uncompromising and as a body rather different in social origin from the vast majority of the house.

Nevertheless the union was responsible for an important innovation in parliamentary routine. It made catholic emancipation a major issue at Westminster and for a quarter of a century a great debate on the catholic claims was a feature of almost every session. This was an eloquent reminder of how wide was the difference between Great Britain and Ireland in one vital respect. In England, though the distinction between church and chapel still loomed large in many spheres, theological dissensions were no longer of primary importance in political life. In Ireland, on the other hand, the main, in fact almost the only political issue was the struggle of the catholics to obtain civic equality, and sectarian feeling penetrated into almost every aspect of life. During the sixteenth century, the Irish administration's religious policy had been an almost exact reproduction of that pursued in England, and as the two islands differed widely in their social and political circumstances,

[1] *Speech of the Rt. Hon. Sylvester Douglas* (1799), p. 168.

the result was that at the opening of the nineteenth century Ireland possessed one of the greatest ecclesiastical anomalies in Christendom, an established church whose adherents in a religiously minded country numbered only about a tenth of the community. One might have expected that sheer necessity would have compelled it to be a vehemently missionary church. But instead the Church of Ireland shared to the full the Augustan calm which characterized eighteenth-century anglicanism. Comparatively little polemical theology was produced by its clergy, and the ambitious schemes for educational and missionary work, adumbrated by the generation which remembered the hectic days preceding the battle of the Boyne, languished. There were several reasons for this easy indifference. Though the penal laws failed to extirpate catholicism, they compelled the catholic clergy to be cautious, and so deprived protestant controversialists of the stimulus provided by opposition. In any case the Irish ascendancy in the eighteenth century was confident that protestant supremacy in all spheres would be secured through the influence of two potent forces, reason and property, without recourse to enthusiastic and tasteless methods of evangelicalism. Besides, the machinery of the Church of Ireland was defective and inefficient. Legally speaking at least, the establishment was the continuation of the medieval church, and this meant that its organization tended to conform to the medieval pattern. Consequently the distribution of the parochial clergy was ill-adjusted to the requirements of an evangelizing church. Also, since the church's revenues were strictly attached by law to particular offices and benefices the remuneration of incumbents was oddly proportioned to the duties they had to perform, and the startlingly high revenues attached to many of the bishoprics both attracted members of the great parliamentary families to the church (where their prospects of rapid promotion were good) and enabled several bishops to set their heirs on the road to a peerage. But along with these fantastic prizes for the fortunate cleric went a lack of the necessities of ecclesiastical life. At the beginning of the nineteenth century 60 per cent of the benefices lacked glebe houses and 18 per cent were even unprovided with churches. In some dioceses the position was farcical or tragical. Jobbery, easy-going standards, the absence of any provision for old and incapacitated clergy, the existence of small, uneconomic livings leading to pluralism, all promoted non-residence, just over 30 per cent of the incumbents on a charitable estimate being non-resident at the beginning of the century.[1] And though the canon law on the subject of clerical residence was satisfactorily

[1] *Papers relating to the established church in Ireland . . . ordered to be printed 1807*, pp. 5–376.

strict, bishops found that owing to the complexities of ecclesiastical law the process of deprivation was 'expensive, tedious, and uncertain'.[1]

The prevalence of clerical absenteeism was peculiarly unfortunate since it increased the unpopularity of tithe, which provided the maintenance of the parochial clergy. As an expert in ecclesiastical administration with a gift for meiosis put it, 'the tithe system from causes over which the tithe owner had no control has not infrequently formed the subject of complaint and has been the cause apparently of much dissatisfaction and discontent'.[2] If the purpose of this 'partnership of the church with the agriculturalists of the country',[3] had been to produce the maximum of friction, its details could not have been better devised. The misdoings and miscalculations of tithe-proctors, the weight of the impost on small men, the exemption of the great grazier, *dubia*, such as the correct definition of a mountain and the legal status of the potato 'not being originally a native of the soil',[4] led to continual litigation and personal squabbles. Above all, the great majority of the tithe-payers were catholics and presbyterians who had not only to maintain a church to which they did not belong but to provide for their own clergy.

Towards the end of the eighteenth century hostility to tithe in Munster had reached such a pitch that the successor of the philosophic Berkeley was driven to write a lucid, and to churchmen conclusive, pamphlet in defence of the church's property.[5] Throughout the nineties the abolition of tithe was one of the fundamentals in the radical programme; and in the early nineteenth century there were sporadic attacks on the system in the west and south. Many of the propertied classes were also critical of the tithe system, and frequently suggested that a substitute for it should be found. During 1807 and 1808 county meetings attended by the local whig peers, in Queen's County, Tipperary, Kerry and Clare, and the grand jury of County Armagh, called loudly for the abolition of tithe and the payment of the clergy in some other form.[6] And the question was repeatedly raised in parliament by Irish whigs.

Pitt had considered a reform of the tithe system as part of the union settlement, and Castlereagh drew up an elaborate memorandum in which he suggested a scheme of commutation, which would give the incumbent a less uncertain and invidious income and relieve the agricul-

---

[1] Ibid., p. 26.
[2] *An account of the ecclesiastical establishment subsisting in Ireland*, ed. J. C. Erck (1830), p. lvii.
[3] J. Finlay, *Law relating to tithe in Ireland* (1828), p. vi.
[4] Ibid., pp. 237–8.
[5] R. Woodward, *The present state of the church of Ireland* (1787), new ed. 1808.
[6] *DEP*, 29 Aug., 26 Sept., 22 Oct. 1807, 12 May 1088, *BNL*, 20 Apr. 1808.

turalist of a distressing burden.[1] His immediate successors, being occupied with administrative reform, postponed tackling the question. Grenville, however, when he became prime minister, was anxious to deal with the subject. He thought that 'there was no doubt that to reasonable men such a measure must appear no less beneficial to the clergy of Ireland than to the country at large, but men are not always reasonable when their interests and particularly tithe interests are in question'. Nevertheless he hoped that even some of the Irish bishops might be persuaded to accept a well-considered plan. His viceroy, the duke of Bedford, who as a Russell, a radical (for a duke) and a leading practical agriculturist was scarcely likely to be sympathetic to clerical claims, declared that tithe was 'a source of torment and irritation' and fostered a spirit of rebellion amongst the lower orders. After considering carefully two schemes—the exemption from tithe of holdings under four acres, or a commutation for an amount, fixed periodically 'so as to afford a reasonable probability of preserving the clergy in their present stations in society'—he decided that the best course was to commute tithe for land. He insisted that if this course were taken, regulations should be made to prevent the clergy indulging overmuch in agricultural pursuits 'and thereby producing habits not altogether suitable to their sacred character'.[2] Unfortunately almost on the very day on which the duke finished drafting his memorial the crisis began which destroyed the Grenville ministry and its Irish policy perished with it. And though the whigs in opposition continued to press for tithe reform, the irrepressible Stanhope declaring that 'the best means of securing the permanence of the Irish church establishment was by placing it on the rock of poverty',[3] nothing effectual was done until the early twenties, and it was not until the late thirties that tithe ceased to be a major grievance of most Irish farmers.

It is frequently tempting to linger on those aspects of a privileged ecclesiastical body which contrast ludicrously with its ideals. But there were aspects of the establishment's life which decidedly overshadowed its defects in the eyes of its adherents. The ecclesiastical bench at the time of the union included, besides that flamboyant tourist the earl of Bristol, at least five bishops distinguished in contemporary scholarship. The majority of the clergy were resident and included in their ranks Burdy, the biographer, Whitelaw, a pioneer in social statistics, Gordon, the historian, and Berwick, the classicist. The support afforded to

---

[1] *Memoirs and correspondence of Viscount Castlereagh* (1850), iv. 193–210.
[2] *Fortescue MSS*, viii. 486, ix. 9–14, 69, 82–97.
[3] *Parl. Deb.*, first series, xxxiii. 821.

hospitals, orphanages and dispensaries by the members of the establishment about the beginning of the century shows they possessed no contemptible share of the charitable benevolence so emphasized by eighteenth-century divinity, and it should not be overlooked that the early years of the century formed a great era of church building which dotted all over the country seemly, standardized, stone churches in an inexpensive modified Gothic.

Recognizing with regret that they were living in an age when 'a deficiency in the ardour of opinion is too frequently deemed indifference and where moderation is sometimes denominated lukewarmness', the members of the church of Ireland were confident that their tradition nourished a fervent and sure as well as an enlightened and sober piety.[1] Nor did they overlook its political virtues. The Irish branch of the establishment formed one of the strongest links between Great Britain and Ireland. Her clergy by inculcating principles of loyalty based on scripture, rendered a service to the community.[2] And when resident they often performed the neglected social duties of the absentee landlord. Laurence, coming, as a result of the Regent's intervention fresh from England to Cashel in 1822, saw in the resident Irish clergy one of the principal civilizing forces in the country, and Bishop Jebb, while admitting that the southern clergy had few claims on their time of a strictly professional kind, believed they could be unceasingly employed in what would now be termed social service, 'in supplying the wants, soothing the feelings, and promoting the comforts and improving the habits and softening down the animosities' of the poor. The acceptance by a clergyman of a commission of the peace, was defended on the grounds that it enabled him to restrain vice and relieve poverty.[3] And Magee, the Rupert of the episcopal bench, in one of his charges, having shown that anglicanism alone had the notes required by an establishment, summed up the church of Ireland as being scriptural, catholic, tolerant, social, loyal and protestant.[4]

Keen churchmen were less embarrassed by the attacks on the church's property rights than might have been expected. If tithe was not of divine appointment, to descend to a more mundane level it was a species of

---

[1] For a good exposition of the outlook of the Church of Ireland at the opening of the nineteenth century see the charge for 1810 of T. L. O'Beirne, bishop of Meath, in *Sermons preached on several occasions* . . . (1799–1821).

[2] For a clear exposition of this point of view see G. Miller, *The present crisis of the Church of Ireland* (1845).

[4] R. Laurence, *A charge* . . . (1822), p. 13, J. Jebb, *A charge* . . . (1823), pp. 37–9, and R. Mant, *A charge* . . . 1–24, p. 61.

[4] W. Magee, *A charge* . . . (1827).

property held by as good a prescriptive right as any in Ireland. To tamper with it was to admit the thin end of a wedge which would in time overturn all property rights. As the rather fussy bishop of Ferns put it, 'the Jacobin faction' would not be appeased by the abolition of tithe but would go on to destroy 'every institution connected with the venerable constitution of England—the religious establishment in all its departments—the political institutions from the magistracy of the capital to the master and wardens of the meanest corporations—the seminaries of education from the university down to the lowest parochial endowment, all shall be swept away'. If in Ireland the catholic majority had to pay tithe, in England the dissenters were in a similar position, and though admittedly the latter were in a minority the former should have found tithe less distasteful. For 'while the dissenters are inimical to every establishment . . . the Roman Catholic, averse as he may be to paying tithes to protestants, considers them rightfully due to the clergy'. And wide variations in clerical income were justified in that by equating the clergy with the various ranks of secular society 'from the respectable landowner to the royal duke' they made the influence of religion pervade all classes of the community.[1]

At the opening of the nineteenth century protestant dissent in Ireland was almost entirely presbyterian, of Scottish origin and concentrated in the north-east. The other great English dissenting bodies, the congregationalists and the baptists had never taken root in Ireland, and the Irish methodists still preserved an uneasy connection with the establishment. It was not until 1816 that the majority of Irish methodists finally cut adrift from the Church of Ireland, leaving however a minority, the 'primitive' methodists, in communion with it. The northern presbyterians were at the beginning of the nineteenth century described as 'an active, intelligent, frugal, honest and thinking body of men'.[2] Though landed families of presbyterian stock tended to slide into the establishment, this was to some extent compensated for by the fact that the presbyterians were most thickly settled in the most economically advanced zone in Ireland, and formed a fairly prosperous community of business men, professional men . . . and farmers.

The presbyterian clergy as a body were well educated, highly respected and poorly remunerated. The presbyterian system of a hierarchical series of assemblies rising from the congregation to the synod, in which

---

[1] T. Elrington, *An inquiry into whether the disturbances in Ireland have originated in tithes* (1822); T. L. O'Beirne, *A letter from an Irish dignitary to an English clergyman*, (1822); *An examination of Mr Parnell's arguments* (1812); J. Jebb, *A speech delivered in the house of peers . . .* (1824).

[2] T. Gamble, *Views of the society and manners of the North of Ireland* (1819), p. 366.

laymen and clergy managed all the affairs of the church, created an ecclesiastical democracy and knit the whole community together. But at the same time the absence of endowments, the frequent opportunities for debate and the Scottish aptitude for logic chopping, promoted schism, and in 1800 there were four distinct presbyterian bodies in Ulster, the Synod of Ulster, much the largest, with its appendage the Presbytery of Antrim in which were grouped the less orthodox of the Synod's congregations, the Reformed Presbytery and the Secession Church, divided into two synods, the Burgher and the Anti-burgher. The latter bodies had resulted from the labours of missionaries from the Covenanting and Seceding churches of Scotland who had been enthusi-astically welcomed by presbyterians in the north of Ireland who believed that the ministers of the Synod of Ulster had become too easy-going in life and doctrine. Though they obviously met the requirements of some in Ulster, the Reform and Secession churches had technically no *raison d'être* there. The questions relating to the connection of church and state which had compelled them to break with the Church of Scotland had not arisen in Ireland and schismatic tendencies were reduced to absur-dity when the Irish seceders, following the example of their mother church, broke into two bodies over the attitude to be observed to the Scottish burgher oath.[1]

In the early nineteenth century the tone and outlook of Irish protes-tantism underwent a great change, a fact which was to have a profound influence on the country's social and political life. Long before the close of the eighteenth century, it was clear that the theology and piety which were most fully characteristic of that age had failed to give universal satisfaction, and there arose the evangelical movement, an ecclesiastical equivalent of the romantic revival. The core of the evangelicals' faith was their belief in the vital necessity of a personal realization of the saving power of God. Along with this went the conviction that it was of the utmost value to comprehend and fully accept some systematic exposition of the Christian faith. Evangelicals differed widely and vehemently over knotty dogmatic points, but they were unanimous in condemning the eighteenth-century tendency to exalt reason so that even in the religious sphere it threatened to overshadow revelation. From this followed an intense veneration for the Bible, the repository of revealed truth, it being continuously and fervently asserted that through the eager and humble searching of the scriptures the Christian

---

[1] J. S. Reid, *History of the Presbyterian Church in Ireland*, ed. by W. D. Killen (3 vols., Belfast 1867), gives a comprehensive if biased account of developments in Irish presbyterianism.

would come to grace and knowledge, though it was expected that his apprehension of the latter would be in accordance with the formularies accepted in evangelical circles. Finally the very name of the movement suggests what to the outsider was its most striking feature, the anxiety of its members to transmit to others the saving truths which they themselves were fortunate enough to possess. At this point it must be emphasized that though divided by denominational loyalties most Irish protestants shared in many respects a common outlook. Admittedly a few high churchmen might view with distaste co-operation with dissenters, and criticize the Bible societies for putting the whole Bible 'from Genesis to Revelation, deep, intricate and voluminous as it is, into the hands of labouring peasants, who at the best owe nothing to education but the mere technical operation of reading'. And there were presbyterians who had not forgotten past persecutions, who considered that the establishment's property in Ulster had once belonged to their church, and who resented 'rectoral scorn and insolence'.[1] But in the theological and even in the political and social spheres the elements of agreement on the whole out-weighted the causes of dissension.

Although much of what was typical of evangelicalism was implicit in Irish protestantism, the movement in Ireland received its initial impulse from across the water. Well before the middle of the eighteenth century Cennick the Moravian was at work founding settlements[2] and preparing the way for Wesley who visited Ireland no fewer than twenty-one times. Methodism was bound to have considerable influence on Irish protestantism, for though the Irish methodists at the beginning of the century were a comparatively small community they were an energetic one, including in their ranks Wesley's successor, the polymath Adam Clarke, and his first biographer Henry Moore, whose own autobiography gives a moving account of his tortuous struggles towards spiritual peace.[3] And, as has been already said, they were for a long period in close contact with the establishment. About 1770 the countess of Huntingdon, whose social position and astute generalship had placed her at the head of the Calvinist wing of the evangelical movement, declared in the course of a long letter to a chaplain she had planted in Dublin: 'Poor wretched Ireland, I trust, shall yet have a gospel day. I

---

[1] For examples of interdenominational acrimony see A. O'Callaghan, *Thoughts on the rendering of the bible* (1816) and *The Bible societies against church and state* (1817); *Banner of Ulster*, 18 March 1845; *The first and second blast of the trumpet against the monstrous union of presbyterian and prelacy* (1835).

[2] *A short account of the work carried on by the ancient protestant episcopal Moravian church in Ireland* (1889).

[3] R. Smith, *The life of the Rev. Mr Henry Moore . . .* (1844).

can't yet see how or when—but it must be and till I find that opportunity my eye is only waiting darkily for its accomplishment.'[1] The countess did all in her power to encourage evangelicals of her way of thinking in Ireland. Amongst her Irish relations were her daughter Lady Moira and her cousin Edward Shirley, once famous as the author of hymns dripping with effusive pathos, a clergyman who was capable when his principles seemed to be challenged of telling even his bishop with Crawleyesque vigour to behave himself.[2] In the early eighties one of Lady Huntingdon's ecclesiastical allies, Peckwell, the evangelical rector of Bloxham, arrived in Dublin to supplement the labours of those whom he designated 'the dry, formal clergy'. The eccentric Philip Skelton, though (according to Peckwell) 'blind in spiritual matters', secured him some pulpits, and Lady Moira arranged for him to preach at the Magdalen Chapel, where his forcible denunciations of sin so shocked and insulted the fashionable congregation that furious theological squabbles split for a time a section at least of Dublin society.[3] Another of Lady Huntingdon's Irish protégés was Edward Smyth, the nephew of the archbishop of Dublin, whose conversion to methodism naturally created somewhat of a sensation. In 1784 Smyth's brother founded the Bethesda,[4] a proprietary chapel in Dublin, which for years was to be the great centre of Irish evangelicalism. At the beginning of the nineteenth century its incumbent was Walker, one of the few fellows of Trinity who encouraged the 'praying students'[5] there. A rigorous Calvinist, and an upright and contentious man, Walker quarrelled with both the establishment and the methodists, threw up his fellowship and his chaplaincy, and maintaining himself by academic hackwork, led for twenty years a small, schism-riven sect, the Church of Christ.[6] Walker was not the only Irish protestant who found the establishment too lax and comprehensive. At the beginning of the century there were in Dublin several small dissenting groups of earnest evangelicals, the best known of them being the Kellyites, led by Kelly the hymn-writer, and the small body led by John Parnell (the second Lord Congleton) and J. N. Darby, termed the Brethren, later often referred to as the Plymouth Brethren.[7]

Walker's successor at the Bethesda, Mathias, a sickly, sincere man,

---

[1] *The life and times of Selina Countess of Huntingdon* (1841), ii. 147. Chapters xxxiv-xxxvii of this work are the main source for the early history of Irish evangelicalism.
[2] Ibid., ii. 179–81.    [3] Ibid., 195–7.    [4] Ibid., ii. 189, 201–3.
[5] *Brief Memorials of the Rev. B. W. Mathias* (1842), p. 17.
[6] J. Walker, *Essays and correspondence chiefly on scriptural subjects*, ed. W. Burton (1884).
[7] H. Groves, *Memoirs of Lord Congleton* (1884).

whose sermons still display the strength derived from narrow convictions, tenaciously held, exercised a considerable influence on the Church of Ireland, both by his preaching and his connection with some of the numerous societies whose foundation marked the rise of the evangelical movement.[1] Other outstanding Dublin evangelicals in the early decades of the century were Alderman Hutton, at whose house religious meetings were frequently held, Thomas Parnell, 'a big solemn man, whose pockets bulged with tracts which he projected down areas and inserted under doors', and Lefroy, the tory politician and later chief justice.[2] Ten miles south of Dublin, Edward Daly was rector of Enniskerry. A robust evangelical, he 'preached, talked, catechized, disputed and controverted' until his throat was worn out, and in 1842 he was appointed bishop of Cork, being the first prominent evangelical to be placed on the bench.[3] Daly was encouraged and sometimes perturbed by the doings of his close friend and neighbour, Theodosia, Viscountess Powerscourt, who from time to time collected strange gatherings of evangelical ministers of different denominations to try and interpret biblical prophecy. Her letters, published by Daly after her death, dealing largely with the oppressive sense of sin which overshadowed her life, are, in spite of painful inadequacies of expression, one of the most poignant literary survivals of the movement in Ireland.[4] Near Limerick, John Hoare who often preached in the Bethesda was rector of Rathkeale. Down in Wexford Francis Lyte, after, as he put it himself, living 'comfortably enough . . . riding about, shooting, dancing and attending my curacy every Sunday', was suddenly shocked into earnest evangelicalism by a friend's death.[5] In Kilkenny, Peter Roe, whose ungainly austerity contrasted strangely with the gaieties of 'the Versailles of Ireland', set a high and unsparing standard of clerical duty. Continually catechizing, visiting, preaching, lecturing, he denounced theatrical performances, tried to substitute prayer meetings for card parties, and in spite of episcopal disapproval, struggled to keep a clerical society functioning.[6]

---

[1] For Mathias see *Brief Memorials of the Rev. B. W. Mathias . . .* (1842).

[2] W. Urwick, *Biographical sketches of the late Digges La Touche* (1868), p. 80; T. Lefroy, *Memoirs of the late Chief Justice Lefroy* (1871); R. S. Brooke, *Recollections of the Irish church* (1877); *Second series* (1878); J. B. Atkins, *Life of Sir William Howard Russell* (1911), i. 7.

[3] H. Madden, *Memoir of the late Rt. Rev. Robert Daly* (1875), p. 97.

[4] Theodosia, Viscountess Powerscourt, *Letters and papers*, ed. R. Daly (1838).

[5] *Evangelical Magazine*, 1818; *Remains of the late Rev. H. F. Lyte* (1850), pp. xvi–xvii.

[6] S. Madden, *Memoirs of the late Rev. Peter Roe* (1842). For an account from a more worldly point of view of Kilkenny life at this time see Lady Morgan, *Memoirs* (London 1862), ch. xiii.

# IRELAND IN THE EARLY NINETEENTH CENTURY

This summary account of the evangelical revival in the Church of Ireland may be criticized as being merely a series of disjointed notes on a few outstanding personalities. But in fact the advance of the movement in the establishment was a matter of permeation through personal influence, and was not marked by any decisive engagement. In Irish presbyterianism the course of events was very different; there the evangelicals only secured supremacy after a series of fierce battles. As might be expected Irish presbyterians adopted Scottish intellectual fashions. Now towards the end of the eighteenth century moderatism with its emphasis on toleration, benevolence and erudition, together with its comparative neglect of dogmatics, was on the decline, while evangelicalism was growing in strength. That Irish presbyterianism, which in the eighteenth century had been decidedly moderatist in outlook, was also changing, was shown by two decisions taken by the Synod of Ulster in the early nineteenth century, to supply bibles to the poor, and to take steps to promote presbyterianism in the south of Ireland. At the beginning of the third decade of the century the struggle between the old-established theological liberalism and the new conservatism began in earnest in the Synod of Ulster. The evangelicals had two great advantages. Their cause, which simultaneously emphasized the traditional presbyterian dogmas and the value of personal religious experience, had a wide popular appeal. And in Cooke, the minister of Killeleagh, who pushed to the front as the champion of orthodoxy, they had a leader who combined astute generalship, a ready if rather vulgar histrionic sense, an easy command of flamboyant oratory, and a fierce loathing of theological and political liberalism. The liberals on the other hand were handicapped by their natural lack of uniformity in outlook, some being decided unitarians (or as Cooke would say Arians), others being merely averse to doctrinal rigidity—as well as by the defects which almost automatically accompanied their virtues. If they were undoubtedly scholarly, broad-minded and philanthropic, their opponents declared they were often supercilious, cold, and self-complacent. There may be some exaggeration in the account of how one 'New-light' preacher maintained that when Saint Stephen exclaimed 'Lord Jesus receive my spirit' he was 'out of his wits or in such a state of excitement that he did not know what he was doing'; or in the story that another delivered a long discourse on the precise value of the Greek article when used before the word $\theta\acute{\epsilon}o\varsigma$,;[1] but there is no doubt whatever that Hamilton Drummond, a leading unitarian, when comparing his asso-

[1] W. D. Killen, *Reminiscences of a long life* (1901), pp. 17–18; *Life of Francis Power Cobb* (1904), p. 105.

ciates with their opponents was capable of declaring that the former were infinitely superior 'in all intellectual, moral and religious virtues'.[1]

The struggle in the Synod lasted five years, each meeting of the Synod of Ulster being marked by vehement debates which contributed little to theological thought, though the combination of *odium theologicum*, personal antagonism and contemporary taste produced some extraordinary oratorical effects. The discussions were prolonged by the efforts of the majority of the Synod to preserve the unity of the church, while asserting its orthodoxy, by gentle treatment of the extreme theological liberals. But Cooke pressed hard for stringent theological tests, and in 1828, after two checks, he persuaded the synod to decide that all candidates for the ministry should be examined on the Westminster Confession. In the previous year the synod had required its members to make a declaration of belief in the Trinity, in the following year a violent attack was levelled against a philosophy professor in the Royal Belfast Academical Institution whose orthodoxy was suspect. In these circumstances it was impossible for the more extreme liberals to remain in the Synod, and in 1829 a small group of 'remonstrants' led by Montgomery, after protesting that 'human tests and confessions in all ages have tended to encourage hypocrisy, to restrict the right of private judgment, to lessen the authority of scripture and to prevent that free inquiry and discussion that are essential to the extension of religious knowledge', withdrew to form the Remonstrant Synod. Within little more than a decade this schism was balanced by a *rapprochement* between the Synod of Ulster and the severely orthodox Secession Synod, the two synods uniting in 1840 to form the Presbyterian Church in Ireland, in which the evangelicals flushed with victory held unchallenged domination.

It is not so easy to sum up the balance of theological forces in the establishment. Since evangelicalism was a matter of tone and emphasis rather than a precise creed, and since no issue arose which demanded a clear-cut decision, it is hard to estimate its influence on the church as a whole. But after full allowance has been made for other currents of thought in the Church of Ireland, as well as for the remnants of presbyterian liberalism, it is clear from even a cursory glance at the enormous contemporary output of theological writing that evangelicalism was the predominant force in Irish protestantism by the middle of the nineteenth century. Many Irish protestants prided themselves on being evangelicals, and others who might have hesitated to adopt the label were deeply

---

[1] W. H. Drummond, *The Unitarian Christian's faith* (1830), p. 21. Drummond advised a minister to divest his sermons of all scholastic divinity and theological controversy (*BNL*, 17 April 1810).

influenced by the ideas associated with it. This meant that protestants had become far more conscious of their urgent religious responsibilities. During the eighteenth century they had tended to regard the conversion of their catholic fellow countrymen as something which was bound to be accomplished in time, given the obvious intellectual, moral and social advantages of protestantism. But the evangelicals were concerned with individual souls, to them it was theological treason to leave their neighbours in ignorance of the truth. Catholicism, with its array of false doctrines, its crafty clergy, and neglect of the scriptures seemed to Irish evangelicals a great barrier between the bulk of Irishmen and real Christianity. And if anything was needed to reinforce their theological loathing for Romanism it was their conviction that it was responsible for retarding the country's economic progress.

Kindness and self-assurance alike demanded active measures. The Irish protestants, members of a masterful governing minority had abundant political and theological self-confidence, and this, fused with the earnest activity—or as Alexander Knox complained 'busy benevolence'[1]—which was a prominent characteristic of evangelicalism, led to vigorous missionary activity in the Irish field. During the first thirty years of the century no fewer than five national societies[2] for supplying the spiritual needs of the Irish people were set on foot, the Hibernian Bible Society (1806) which in twenty-three years circulated 209,000 bibles, the London Hibernian Society,[3] the Irish Society (1818) for educating the Gaelic-speaking Irish and distributing bibles, the Religious Tract and Book Society (1810) which in ten years distributed 4,400,000 tracts, and the Sunday School Society for Ireland (1809) which in twenty years distributed 260,000 bibles and half a million spelling books. Then there was an inter-denominational organization, the Irish Evangelical Society, founded in 1814 to assist struggling congregations and itinerant preachers. This society trained its own preachers in Dublin and built chapels in southern towns.[4] There were also two somewhat similar organizations maintained by the presbyterians and baptists. The presbyterian Home Mission and the baptist Irish Society each had schools, scripture readers and itinerant preachers and strove to spread the knowledge of the bible amongst the peasantry.[5] All these societies played an immense part in Irish life. With their committees of clergy-

---

[1] R. S. Brooke, *Recollections of the Irish church: second series*, p. 73.
[2] See *Watson's or the Gentlemen's and Citizen's Almanack . . . for 1830*, p. 165 ff.
[3] Founded in 1806, the Irish Committee was set up in 1827.
[4] For the work of this society see *Evangelical Magazine and Missionary Chronicle*.
[5] J. Irwin, *The triumph of the bible in Ireland* (1832), and the reports of the Home Mission printed with the minutes of the Synod of Ulster.

men and zealous laymen—including a sprinkling of fervently protestant peers—their local branches, subscription lists, and annual general meetings at which the members could enjoy a deluge of encouraging oratory fortified by cheerful statistics, they drew Irish protestants together and imbued them with a consciousness of power and responsibility. Unfortunately their doings provoked intense hostility amongst Irish catholics and contributed largely to the communal bitterness which was one of the most prominent and ugly features in Irish life For while protestant feeling intensified and protestant activities developed, Irish catholicism was also changing.

The early nineteenth century was an age of rehabilitation for Irish catholicism, when by the long-sustained self-sacrifice of a poor community much was done to repair the material losses of the previous three centuries. In the forty-odd years between the union and the famine all over Ireland 'newly built slated chapels' replaced the low thatched barns or even 'mass rocks' and 'mass gardens' of the penal era.[1] Several cathedrals were begun, parish schools were started, new monastic houses, charities, diocesan seminaries, secondary schools, and societies for supplying the poor with religious books were founded, and the great national seminary of Maynooth steadily grew in importance until by 1850 about half the Irish secular clergy had been educated there,[2] and in spite of the precautions of the college authorities, were in sympathetic touch with the main currents of Irish politics. This still further strengthened the bonds between the Irish catholic clergy and laity. Both had suffered severely for their faith, and the parish clergy drawn mainly from the farming class were by economic circumstances doubly identified with their laity. They were maintained by the voluntary offerings of their parishioners, and their income level, though it freed them from cramping peasant poverty, was not high enough to cut them off socially from their flocks. Indeed Archbishop MacHale, who felt there might be a 'too familiar reciprocation of lay and clerical intercourse', warned priests against discussing ecclesiastical affairs and exchanging clerical gossip too freely with the laity.[3] Protestant politicians were of course afraid, particularly after catholic emancipation and reform, that the

[1] For 'mass rocks' and 'mass gardens' see P. O'Connell. *The diocese of Kilmore* (1937), p. 516 and *the Irish Catholic Directory for 1853*, p. 354. For a description of new chapels see *Irish Catholic Directory for 1840*, p. 244. *The Irish Catholic Directory*, an annual publication, compiled by W. J. Battersby, has a fund of information on contemporary catholic ecclesiastical activities.

[2] *Report of Her Majesty's commissioners appointed to inquire into the government and management of the college of Maynooth*, appendix, pp. 133–59, H.C., 1854–5 (1896, I), xxii. 205–31.

[3] J. MacHale, *Sermons and discourses* (1883), p. 454.

catholic clergy would be able to exercise undue influence over many Irish voters. How far this alarm was justified it is hard to say. Certainly the catholic clergy did not abstain from politics which were frequently concerned with sectarian issues, and one Maynooth professor laid down that a priest when dealing with an ignorant congregation was entitled to tell them, even from the altar, whom to vote for, and that it was the moral duty of an ignorant man to vote as the priest directed him. It must, however, be added that several of his colleagues, whose views seem to have been more conservative, were reluctant to see the clergy intervening in politics.[1]

Absorbed in a great effort to secure the basic necessities of ecclesiastical life, Irish catholicism was practical rather than speculative. When MacHale thought of literary work he was afraid that 'the care of refitting a portion of our national church, which alas, has not yet cleared away all the rubbish of its desolation, and gathering the scattered furniture of the sanctuary', would divert him from such pursuits.[2] And a Maynooth professor seems to have been justified by the college curriculum at this period in airing the perennial academic complaint that the burden of his teaching duties prevented him writing a book.[3] More theological literature seems to have been produced during the early nineteenth century by the much smaller English catholic community,[4] and the names of Wiseman, Charles Butler, and Milner are probably better known than those of any contemporary Irish ecclesiastical author. The outstanding figures for vigour and originality of purpose in Irish church history in the nineteenth century were England the missionary bishop, Theobald Mathew the apostle of temperance, Ignatius Rice a pioneer in the provision of facilities for primary education, and Catherine McAulay the foundress of the Order of Mercy, devoted to the care of the poor and sick. And the two outstanding Irish catholic publicists of the period MacHale, archbishop of Tuam, and Doyle, bishop of Kildare, though distinguished for the vigour of their polemic methods, made no permanent contribution to religious literature.

During the years while Irish catholics were slowly but successfully winning civil equality, resurgent catholicism collided violently with

[1] *Report of Her Majesty's Commission appointed to inquire into the management and government of the college of Maynooth, evidence*, pp. 14, 85, 36 H.C. 1854–5 (1896, I), xxii. 380, 402, 451.

[2] J. MacHale, *Sermons and discourses* (1883), p. 511.

[3] *Report of Her Majesty's commission appointed to inquire into the management and government of the college of Maynooth*, pp. 87–9, H.C. 1854 (1896), xxii. 159–61.

[4] Of the works advertised by a Dublin ecclesiastical bookseller in 1839 thirty can be identified as being by English writers and twenty-four by Irish (*Irish Catholic Directory 1839*).

protestantism revived by evangelicalism. As a result a great debate on the true interpretation of Christian doctrine was tangled up with disputes over government and professional patronage. *Odium theologicum* poisoned political life, and theological discussions were usually conducted with the boisterous crudity and vigorous vulgarity characteristic of contemporary politics. There was a vast output of theological literature, mainly in pamphlet form and usually on a low intellectual level, packed with the commonplaces of post-reformation polemics. A more spectacular form of controversy was the public dispute between protestant and catholic clergy, conducted before large audiences and regulated by a kind of Queensberry debating code. Earnest bishops, protestant and catholic alike, deplored these exhibitions, and it was rumoured that Whately had termed them 'spiritual cockfights'.[1] But the public revelled in the replies, rebuttals and learned taunts, hurled across the platform by champions of their respective faiths such as Father Thomas Maguire, regarded in Dublin as the British Bossuet,[2] and his inappropriately named opponent the Rev. Richard Pope. And the pitch to which excitement could rise is shown by the fact that when Crolly, later archbishop of Armagh, was said to have refuted in a series of lectures the objections to the catholic faith, the catholic peasantry of the north made songs in his honour.[3] Religious bad feeling played an important part in many zones of existence, influencing the picking of tenants, the selection of juries, the election of dispensary doctors, the appointment of civil servants, and the choice of a newspaper, a political party, a stage coach or an hotel. Theological loyalties, too, cropped up in unexpected places. At a race meeting a riot was caused by 'Protestant Boy' beating 'Daniel O'Connell'; in Carlow a squabble between the catholic curate and a group of protestant ladies over religious instruction in the gaol seems to have led to a battle between women prisoners with bibles in their pockets; and a quarrel between a parish priest and a rector over a sick man's removal to hospital ended in a strong detachment of the 5th Foot being sent for to preserve the peace.[4]

There were two important spheres in which sectarianism was a serious source of bad feeling, education and patronage. It is usually hard to distinguish precisely between secular and religious education, and in

---

[1] John West, *Remains of Charles Dickinson* (1845), liv; T. D'A. M'Gee, *A life of the Rev. Edward Maginn* (1857), p. 14; *Achill Missionary Herald*, ii.

[2] *From cabin boy to archbishop: the autobiography of Archbishop Ullathorne* (1941), p. 105.

[3] G. Crolly, *Life of the Most Rev. Dr Crolly* (1851), p. xlviii.

[4] J. Barrow, *A tour round Ireland* (1836), p. 136; *Letters of the Rev. James Maher* (1877), pp. xi–xvii; D. Massy, *The life and times of a faithful shepherd* (1855), p. 249.

Ireland during the early nineteenth century when private enterprise provided the former it usually tended to inculcate the latter. Hence the
trouble which frequently arose over schools founded by well-meaning,
strongly protestant landlords for their tenants. And when after 1830 the
state began to provide facilities for education on the primary and university level, each denomination was quick to safeguard its position and
to seize any opportunity of shaping state educational policy into a
favourable form. As for the effect a man's religion might have on his
temporal prospects, it was impossible to devise methods of selection
and promotion which would simultaneously promote efficiency, be fair
to the individual, and give each denomination its due quota of dignified
and lucrative posts. It is difficult to say what would have constituted
fairness. For instance, nearly all the Dublin hospital appointments in
1840 were held by protestants, and a catholic, while granting that nearly
all the celebrated Dublin doctors were protestants, pointed out that in
medicine it was scarcely possible for a man to obtain celebrity unless he
first held such an appointment. To this a protestant retorted that if you
took the membership of the College of Physicians (a cross-section of
the best qualified medical men in Dublin), the ratio of catholics to protestants was in proportion to their share of public appointments. But
a few years earlier in a similar discussion on legal patronage, Sheil had
explained that the reason why protestants greatly exceeded catholics at
the bar was that the government favoured them. 'They come to the
bar,' he said, 'not only with a view to rise in their profession by the exercise of their talents, but because the expectation of patronage allured
them to a profession to which so many places are annexed.'[1] An essential
factor of course was protestant predominance in those sections of society
from which the learned professions, the higher civil service and the unpaid local magistracy tended to be recruited. Moreover, as Peel when
considering the problem in the early forties realized, although the act of
1829 had placed catholics on an equal footing with protestants in civil
affairs, yet when any post in the government's gift fell vacant there
would be a protestant candidate with at least equal professional qualifications to any catholic, and with superior claims on political grounds,
since 'he had for a long series of years the advantage of monopoly and
privilege secured to him by the law. He has been thrown into constant
contact and intercourse with the government, and has been taught by the
law to consider himself and to look forward as a reward to the exclusive

---

[1] *Report from the select committee on medical charities, Ireland, evidence,* pp. 203,
289, H.C., 1843 (412), x. 217, 301; *First report from the select committe on the state
of Ireland,* H.C. 1825 (129), p. 101.

possession of the favours of the crown'.[1] Competitive examination of course provided an impartial method of selection, but it was slowly applied and only fitted to limited spheres. So during the first half of the nineteenth century, in a vast number of instances when an appointment or promotion took place, if theological considerations were not decisive, at least the denominational affiliations of the appointee were known and were often the cause of angry comment.

On the broader political field the sharpening of theological antagonisms and the reviving social vigour of Irish catholicism played a great part in determining the attitude of protestants to the major Irish political issue of the century. In 1800 Irish protestants were vehemently divided over the union, many, possibly the majority of them, being hostile to it. But when O'Connell in 1829 began his campaign for its repeal he secured comparatively few protestant supporters and protestant opinion as a whole strongly opposed him. This rally of protestants to the union can be partly explained as regards the north by growing prosperity, but protestants all over Ireland seem to have realized that though repeal legally meant only the restoration of the constitutional structure which existed before 1801, in fact with sectarian feeling harshening and the balance of social power inevitably if slowly altering, it meant they would find themselves in a much less advantageous position than they had enjoyed in the eighteenth century. So the maintenance of the union became a political tenet shared by the great mass of Irish protestants of every denomination.

During the eighteenth century it had been customary to attribute Ireland's economic ills to England's restrictive policy, and in the last two decades of the century Ireland's constitutional victories created the confident belief that with the restrictions swept away Irish industry, commerce and agriculture would all participate in a rapid advance. Economic optimism was in the air, and just after the union an Irish writer, having given a glowing picture of Ireland's economic potentialities, disposed of its one possible weakness, a lack of coal, by pointing to the admirable facilities for importation which Ireland enjoyed.[2] Englishmen shared with apprehension this view of Ireland's economic future. In 1785 hard-headed English industrialists were panic-stricken by the possibility that Irish manufacturers commanding abundant cheap labour and water power would become dangerous rivals; and twenty years later it was argued that the immense remittances dispatched from Ireland to absentee landlords living in England constituted a concealed

---

[1] Peel to de Grey, 22 Aug. 1843 (Add. MS. 40478).
[2] R. Fraser, *Gleanings in Ireland particularly respecting its agriculture, mines and fisheries* (1802), pp. 6–7.

danger to England's industrial strength, for as a result of these remittances a demand for Irish goods would be created in the British market
'in defiance of the skill and capital of the British manufacturer'.[1] These
fears were of course groundless. Excepting the north-east and a few
isolated enterprises scattered over the rest of the country, during the
forty years following the union, Irish industry steadily declined in the
face of British competition based on large-scale production, skilled
labour and easily accessible coal and iron, and by the thirties the south
of Ireland was strewn with industrial wreckage in the shape of unemployed artisans and decaying factories.[2] It is possible that the tariffs
which might have saved Irish industry would have been imposed by an
Irish parliament. Of course the Irish agricultural interest might have
selfishly and successfully opposed such a protectionist policy.[3] The
imperial parliament naturally did nothing, and could have justified its
refusal to injure British trade by the fashionable free trade arguments
of the day.

On agriculture therefore Ireland's prosperity and happiness depended.
But at the beginning of the nineteenth century Irish agricultural methods
were notoriously backward, inefficient, slip-shod and wasteful, and the
agrarian system, moulded and marred by centuries of civil strife, seemed
designed to discourage economic progress and to breed inequity and
dissension. Again an exception should be made for the north, and particularly the north-east. Over much of Ulster, tenant right, the prosperity
of the linen manufacture, and a coincidence in political and religious
views between landlord and tenant, created better social conditions than
were generally prevalent elsewhere. Visitor after visitor to the north of
Ireland reflected that here was an area resembling Great Britain. Lord
Henry Petty for instance spoke of County Down as 'the Yorkshire of
Ireland, the same universal appearance of wealth and industry and even
of neatness and comfort prevails'.[4] And Mant, a scholarly, rather
finicky English clergyman, after some years of exile in Killaloe, where
the peasantry frightened his English servants 'on whom he depended
for much of his domestic comfort and convenience', and laughed at his
gifts of shoes and stockings, was delighted to be translated to an area

[1] Lauderdale, *Hints to the manufacturers of Great Britain* (1805).

[2] See accounts of towns in the three southern provinces in S. Lewis, *A topographical
dictionary of Ireland*, 2 vols. (1839), and *The parliamentary gazeteer of Ireland*, 3 vols.
(1841).

[3] As early as 1810 a Dublin pamphleteer who was an aggressive free trader asked,
'if England can supply the various wants of Ireland on cheaper terms than our
manufacturers can, is it not in our evident interest to purchase where the article is
cheapest?' (*A short inquiry into the causes of the present distresses* (1810)).

[4] *The Creevy papers*, ed. H. M. Maxwell (1903), i, 143.

where 'everything... conveyed the idea of industry, neatness, good order, tranquillity and security'.[1] Outside Ulster, and in a mitigated degree even in that province, the Irish agrarian system was an economist's nightmare. Agriculture being the sole industry of any importance, the landlord had almost a monopoly of the means of existence, so rents tended to be high and the conditions of tenure hard, the tenant, who was usually left to carry out all the necessary improvements, having no right to compensation for his labour when his lease expired. High rents were among the factors responsible for the excessive degree of subletting and subdivision, 'the hacking and hewing of the land',[2] which character-ized the Irish agrarian system. It was the quickest and laziest way of making the soil pay, and was practised by all grades of landowners. If the great magnate disposed of huge blocks of his estate on long leases, the peasant provided for his children by splitting his farm, even if that meant the holding 'dwindled away to a cabbage garden',[3] or made a few shillings by letting potato patches to hungry labourers. Subdivision and the potato created (if for the moment they helped to solve) Ireland's major problem, the pressure of population on the means of subsistence. The Irish labourer or small farmer, once he had secured his holding, threw up a rude cabin and managed to exist on a diet of potatoes and milk or potatoes and water.[4] Such a low standard of living led to early marriages and large families, and in spite of emigration and disease the population rose from about five million in 1800 to over eight million in 1840.[5]

In the period of post-war depression which followed Waterloo and which hit Irish agriculture hard, the apprehension arose that Mal-thusian mathematics might prove sound in Ireland, or at least that an influx of starving Irish into the British labour market might force down British standards. The alarm was sounded by several parliamentary committees, which pointed out that there was in Ireland a redundant and growing population for whose labour there was no effective demand;[6]

---

[1] E. Berens, *A memoir of the life of Bishop Mant* (1849), p. 90; W. Mant, *Memoirs of the Rt. Rev. Bishop Mant* (1857), p. 158.

[2] *Report from Her Majesty's commissioners of inquiry into the state of the law and practice in respect to the occupation of land in Ireland*, evidence, Pt. I, p. 189, H.C., 1845 (606), xix. 251.

[3] Ibid., *Pt. II*, p. 266, H.C., 1846 (616), xx. 273.

[4] *First report from the select committee on the state of Ireland, and the minutes of evidence*, p. 49, H.C., 1825 (129), xx.

[5] K. H. Connell, *The population of Ireland, 1750–1845* (Oxford 1950).

[6] *Second report from the select committee on the state of the labouring poor in Ireland*, H.C., 1819 (409), viii. *Second report from the select committee on emigra-tion from the United Kingdom*, H.C., 1826–7 (237), v.

and in 1822 a member of the house of commons in the course of an exhaustive survey of Irish conditions, referred to 'what I must call a "vicious increase" in population'.[1] Even economic optimists such as Bishop Doyle, Whitley Stokes and John Finlay, who denied that Ireland was over-populated, agreed that steps must be taken to develop its resources—Doyle being sufficiently optimistic to expect that 'the legislature might in a single session pass such laws as would in the course of a few years render the poor of Ireland . . . beyond the reach of want'.[2] Three remedies were frequently suggested. Emigration,[3] the effect of which in any case would have been temporary, bringing more land under cultivation, and better farming methods. But Irish landowners lacked the capital required for large-scale reclamation schemes, tenants were slow to carry out improvements from which their gains would be uncertain, and English investors were reluctant to risk their money in areas where there were incessant outbreaks of agrarian crime. Consequently large areas remained agricultural slums, and the Irish peasant's economic future was menaced by ill-health, failure to obtain a potato patch, inability to scrape together his rent and worst of all a failure of the potato crop.

In addition to the remedies most frequently recommended—large-scale capital investment and emigration—a number of other panaceas (most of which required capital) were referred to from time to time—an Irish poor law[4] on the English model; tithe reform;[5] agricultural colleges;[6] loan societies;[7] farming societies;[8] the instruction and strict supervision of tenants';[9] the elimination of middlemen; 'a fungus

---

[1] *Parl. Deb.*, 2 series, vi. 1508.

[2] Malthus's views on Ireland were challenged by W. Stokes, *Observations on the population and resources of Ireland* (1820); W. Richardson, *Simple Measures by which the recurrence of famines may be prevented* (1811); Rev. J. V. Doyle, *Letters on the state of Ireland*, by J. K. L. (1825). Another economic optimist was James Cropper, author of *Present state of Ireland with a plan for improving the condition of the people* (1825).

[3] In North America, it was said, 'the duties of domestic life may be enjoyed without the revolting apprehension of bringing into existence a progeny to augment the dismal catalogue of misery' (*Emigration recommended*, by A retired officer (1822), p. 19).

[4] *A method of improving the condition of the Irish poor* (1810) and *A letter to the prime minister on the deplorable state of the helpless poor of Ireland* (1828); J. Edwards, *Interests of Ireland* . . . (1814); Sir W. Hillay, *A Sketch of Ireland* (1825).

[5] R. Bellew, *Thoughts and suggestions* . . . (1808).

[6] *Considerations addressed to the landed proprietors of County Clare* (1831), p. 21.

[7] *On the encouragement of the peasants in Ireland* (1825).

[8] Ibid., p. 54.

[9] *Considerations addressed to the landed proprietors of County Clare* (1831); W. Stokes, *Observations on the population and resources of Ireland* (1820); *An impartial review of the true causes of the existing misery in Ireland* (1824); Statement of J. H. Jephson on state of Tipperary, 1814 (Add. MS. 40238).

breed';[1] drastic diminution of taxation;[2] the promotion of temperance;[3] the encouragement of fisheries;[4] the cutting of canals; the use of the army under a specialized staff in road building;[5] the granting to poorer tenants of farms rent-free for seven years;[6] the foundation of large co-operatives, uniting farming and manufacture,[7] and the formation of a company to purchase estates which were to be sold in small portions to the tenants who would purchase their farms by terminable annuities.[8]

Most of these suggestions demanded action either by the government or by the Irish landowners. But as will be shown later the government was timid in tackling Irish social problems, and the Irish landowners as a class were inert and inefficient. Admittedly intelligent and improving landlords were by no means unknown, and where they were active it was noticed that 'the face of the country looks cheerful, healthy agriculture thrives, the peasantry are employed and have become industrious, happy, contented, manufactures are introduced, and all the advantages of civilized life are sought after'.[9] And the landlord might find himself surrounded by 'the interesting, the intelligent, the grateful Irish peasants'.[10] Of course he might not, for the well-meaning landlord could find himself like his tenants, the victim—admittedly in a less cruel sense —of the Irish agrarian system. Improvement by early nineteenth-century standards often implied rearranging and enlarging farms and dispossessing incompetent or superfluous tenants. To do this in a way which would be regarded by all concerned as intelligent and fair was impossible, and the operation was bound to arouse bad feeling. From one point of view Irish landlords might be dismissed as agrarian profiteers exacting the maximum advantages from a monopoly. But Irish opinion until at least the forties rarely condemned Irish landlords as a body— after all many of the most vocal reformers were landowners—and carelessness rather than harshness seems to have been their chief defect in the eyes of contemporaries.

[1] *An impartial review of the true causes of the existing misery in Ireland* (1822); Sir R. C. Hoare, *Journal of a tour in Ireland* (1807), pp. 338–40.

[2] W–T–, *Plan for the improvement of the condition of the people of Ireland* (1824).

[3] There are a large number of contemporary pamphlets advocating temperance.

[4] R. Fraser, *Sketches and essays on the present state of Ireland* (1822).

[5] Joseph Hardy to Lord Whitworth 1814 (Add. MS. 40237); *General view submitted to the government on inland navigation*, 1808 (H.O. 150).

[6] J. P. Kennedy, *Instruct employ, don't hang them* . . . (1835).

[7] *Mr Owen's plan for the amelioration of the population of Ireland illustrated* (Dublin 1822). An Irish Co-operative society was founded but seems to have accomplished little. (See F. Podmore, *Robert Owen: a biography* (1906), i. 277–82, ii. 377).

[8] *Statement of some of the causes of the disturbances in Ireland* (1825).

[9] *Remarks on the evils of Ireland* by A protestant inhabitant (1825).

[10] Lady Chatterton, *Rambles in the south of Ireland* (1839), ii. 170–1.

But frequently an Irish landed gentleman was either non-resident or financially hamstrung or both. The prevalent low conception of a landlord's duties encouraged absenteeism, and absenteeism bred negligence. Admittedly some of the great absentees, who were kept away from their Irish estates by their English commitments and who could afford to spend money on their Irish property, were represented by intelligent and well-meaning agents. But other absentees merely thought of what they could draw from their land, and often left their affairs in the hands of agents who were themselves absentees, 'giant' firms[1] in town, which handled a number of estates, and whose primary, or indeed sole function, was the extraction of rents. Moreover many Irish landowners, resident and absentee, were financially embarrassed, reduced to being little more than receivers for their creditors,[2] and thus, as a friendly critic put it, 'prevented from indulging the natural bias of their minds' when dealing with their tenantry.[3] Irish agriculture, unlike English, did not benefit from a steady flow of commercial and industrial profits seeking a secure and dignified investment, and with the business community unimportant and unassertive, the standards of a landowning aristocracy reigned socially unchallenged. The Irish landed gentry, the descendants of successful soldiers, pioneers, land speculators and Gaelic dynasts, were distinguished by their reckless high living and unthinking extravagance. Early in the nineteenth century a viceroy observed the great consumption of claret and champagne in Ireland, and Ponsonby in 1814, when appealing to the house of commons not to over-estimate the taxable capacity of Ireland, rather tactlessly pointed out that normally an Irishman consumed more wine than an Englishman with the same income.[4] Moreover these notions of conspicuous expenditure were not confined to a narrow group, for Anglo-Irish society if proud was not exclusive. Or rather, to put it more accurately, a large number of Irishmen felt themselves entitled or obliged to live like landed gentlemen. It was said that in Ireland every man until you came down to your shoemaker was an esquire, and that every tradesman sent a son to the university 'to become a gentleman'. And it was noticed how in country towns the local landowners looked down 'with sovereign contempt' on business people.[5]

---

[1] *Report from Her Majesty's commissioners of inquiry into the state of the law and practice in respect to the occupation of land, evidence Pt. I*, p. 165, H.C. 1845 (605), xix. 227.        [2] *Parl. Deb.*, 2 series, vi. 1509.

[3] See speech of Smith O'Brien in *Considerations addressed to the landed proprietors of the County of Clare* (1831), p. 34.

[4] Richmond to Whitworth, 18 June 1813 (Richmond papers) and *Parl. Deb.*, xxix. 489.

[5] *Glimpses across the Irish channel* (1824) and *Thoughts on the present disturbances* (1824).

The anomalous and inharmonious nature of Irish society was reflected in early nineteenth-century Dublin, still in the eighteen-twenties the second city in the British Isles.[1] No doubt much of its fashionable glory and political distinction had disappeared with the union. But though parliament no longer brought the nobility and great county families regularly to the capital, though the vice-regal court was said to be less select and though some of the great aristocratic mansions housed public offices, Dublin remained an important legal, administrative and ecclesiastical centre, a big garrison town and a university city. The eighteenth-century stately and spacious architectural tradition had not snapped with the union, and in the decades immediately following, in addition to sedate new residential quarters, a number of impressive public buildings and monuments were erected. If Brocas's Dublin was less consciously a capital than Malton's, nevertheless it was full of bustling vitality, of what a contemporary called 'enlivening eclat'.[2] But visitors were startled to find extravagance and acute poverty in close proximity. It was, one of them remarked, a 'patchwork' city.[3] It may be added that the intellectual life of Dublin was also extraordinarily uneven in its standards. If by the thirties Dublin medicine and mathematics were justly famous, every attempt to start a literary journal had failed[4] and the religious and political controversy which kept the presses busy was conducted with a narrow stridency which is unpleasantly remarkable.

Moreover it was often emphasized that much of the social display was deceptive. An intelligent observer, after commenting on the 'jaunting car, pleasure taking, careless look' of the Dublin streets, added that an outstanding characteristic of the inhabitants was a 'contented, self-satisfied mediocrity'; the primary ambition of the shop-keeper being to possess a carriage and of the professional man to be able to hunt.[5] After a corporation dinner in Dublin, a good-natured chief secretary remarked that the business men he had met, though they probably carried far less weight in commercial circles than their London equivalents, far more closely resembled in bearing the vice-regal aide-de-camps.[6] Thackeray described the same phenomenon more harshly, when he declared that in

---

[1] In 1821 Dublin in population came next to London; by 1831 it had been outstripped by Manchester; in 1841 it came fifth after London, Manchester, Liverpool and Glasgow.

[2] T. Cromwell, *An excursion in Ireland* (1829), p. 57.

[3] J. Barrow, *A tour of Ireland* (1837), p. 378.

[4] The success in the thirties and early forties of the *Dublin University Magazine*, the *Citizen* and the *Nation* all of which maintained serious cultural standards was probably largely due to their forcibly expressed politics.

[5] T. C. Foster, *Letters on the condition of the people of Ireland* (1846), p. 588.

[6] Morpeth to Lady Carlisle, 19 Oct. 1836 (Castle Howard MSS.).

Ireland 'if a gentleman has £100 a year to leave his family, they all become gentlemen, keep a nag, ride to hounds and swagger about the Phaynix and grow tufts to their chins like so many real landocrats[1]

[1] W. M. Thackery, *Book of snobs*, ch. xvii.

# 2

# POLITICAL ACTIVITY IN THE
# PRE-REFORM ERA

Local politics which to many Irishmen were the most strenuous form of political activity, were unaltered by the union. In each county the parliamentary representation rotated amongst a few great landed families, the returns being strictly correlated to the number of freeholders registered by each landlord.[1] The success of these families in monopolizing local political power and the part played by hereditary custom in Irish politics is shown by the fact that in 1830 no fewer than thirty-four of the county M.P.s belonged to families which had represented a county in the eighteenth-century Irish parliament, and another seven to families which had sat in that parliament for borough constituencies. As for the newcomers, whose slow influx did little to disturb the consistency of the pattern, eight were catholics, seven of whom belonged to families which but for the penal laws would probably have had a share in the parliamentary representation during the eighteenth century.[2] The one exception, Daniel O'Connell, was not perhaps so exceptional as he seems on the first glance. Though he owed his return to unorthodox methods, it had not been unusual for a successful and ambitious Irish lawyer to invest in land and build up a political interest which finally secured him a county seat. The Fosters before the end of the eighteenth century accomplished this in Louth, the Lefroys in the thirties struggled to do it in Longford, and the Fitzgibbons, led first by the earl of Clare and later by his widow, became the most powerful

[1] In eleven counties one member and in sixteen both members were usually returned by the great landed interests. The remaining M.P.s were returned by coalitions of the minor landed families (G. D. Sullivan, 'Irish parliamentary representation, 1800–32').

[2] The catholic members returned in 1830 were William Browne, Sir John Burke, Lord Killeen, Daniel O'Connell, The O'Conor Don, Richard More O'Ferrall, The O'Gorman Mahon and Thomas Wyse.

interest in Limerick, though after 1820 they had to share the county with a newer legal family the O'Gradys.

Turning to the boroughs, only five constituencies, returning seven members, Dublin, Cork, Downpatrick, Londonderry and the University (Trinity College), were decidedly open. The first two with fairly large and politically alive electorates were often keenly contested. Londonderry's political history was humdrum. Downpatrick had an electorate of five-pound householders and Croker, when contesting the borough in 1812, declared that the result 'absolutely depends upon pounds sterling'. And though he had 'the greatest repugnance to bribery' (as well as not much money) he begged Peel for a few small places in the gift of the government for his supporters.[1] In Trinity academic politics and a candidate's reputation and connections played a great part. Carrickfergus with a large electorate of freemen was an arena for contending interests and notoriously grossly corrupt. In Waterford, which in the eighteenth century might have been regarded as relatively 'open', political life was finally suffocated in 1808 when the two great interests there, led by Newport and Alcock, entered into a carefully drafted compact by which all the city patronage from the parliamentary seat down to the meaner municipal offices was shared between them. In Wexford there was a similar compact dating from 1798, but a quarrel between the allied interests led to a contest, a petition, an exposure of local politics before an election committee, and a decision that only resident freemen could exercise the franchise.[2] Ten years earlier after a long, hard battle, Limerick was added to the 'open' constituencies, an election committee deciding that only residents could be admitted to be freemen and so exercise the franchise. This decision destroyed the power of the local oligarchy which controlled the corporation as regards elections. In Kilkenny where the corporation was dominated by Lords Ormonde and Desart, the situation was similar, but it was not until 1830 after three defeats that the 'independents' wrested the seat from the corporation.[3] In Drogheda the independents, though they tried on several occasions, did not defeat the corporation candidate until October 1831 when the victory had already been almost secured on a wider field. The position in twenty-one of the remaining twenty-three boroughs can be summed

[1] Croker to Peel 8, 9, 13 Oct. 1812 (C. S. Parker, *Sir Robert Peel* (1891), pp. 48–50). Croker was trying to secure help in his contest from Peel to whom the cruder aspects of political life were repugnant, and his letters show a skilful blend of disgust at election tactics and requests for help.

[2] W. E. Hudson, *A treatise on the elective franchise* . . . (1832), pp. 422–33; *DEP*, 13 July 1830.

[3] *FLJ*, 25 Mar. 1820; *DEP*, 17 July 1830.

up simply. Each with a small hand-picked electorate was absolutely and securely under the control of its patron, who nominated the member, and in almost every case the same family held the patronage from the union to the reform act.[1] The other two, Newry and Lisburn had a comparatively large electorate, but were each under the control of a local peer. In the general election of 1830 when the political atmosphere was highly charged, in six boroughs regarded as 'closed' attempts were made to challenge the corporation's monopoly of the franchise. In five of these the attempts were unsuccessful, but in Coleraine some freemen and inhabitants who demanded to be admitted to the freedom of the borough turned up at the election and claimed to be allowed to vote along with the aldermen and burgesses who composed the corporation. After a petition which failed on a formality they won their case in 1831. In Galway where the freemen were fairly numerous the candidate supported by the dominant Daly interest was only successful after a hard struggle, and in Armagh where a corporation largely composed of clerics, and under the primate's control, elected a tory minister, the townsfolk hissed the burgesses and cheered the citizens of Paris.[2]

It goes without saying that the factors which usually decided an election in an Irish constituency were family influence, local interests and personal reputation. Occasionally, however, wider political issues played a part. The catholic question, as will be seen, affected some contests, and the government tried to increase its parliamentary strength by intervening in Irish elections. But the administration's electoral power, though diffused throughout the country, was relatively slight. As early as 1807 Arthur Wellesley, the chief secretary, when conducting an election campaign, deplored how little patronage was at his disposal and, like his whig predecessor Elliot, he found the Irish boroughs on the market (about eight in number) far too dear.[3] Ten years later Peel was also troubled by the problem of dealing with the more mercenary Irish borough owners. However he reflected that whatever happened, 'the friends of the government will not be the less returned, the only difficulty will be that the government will have difficulty in providing for those individuals whose return the government are more anxious for than ordinary supporters'.[4] Besides trying to purchase boroughs to dispose of

[1] Ennis and New Ross had joint patrons. In Youghal a strange political upheaval occurred about 1822. The earl of Shannon was the patron but following a law suit which gave the duke of Devonshire control of a number of valuable tenements in the town the patronage was transferred to him.      [2] DEP, 31 July, 10, 12 Aug. 1830.
[3] Mem. relating to Irish boroughs (Add. MS. 38359); Elliot to Grenville, 21 Oct. 1806 (Fortescue MSS., viii. 393).
[4] Peel to Liverpool, 29 Sept. 1813 (Add. MS. 38195).

to friends, the government could usually exercise some pressure in a contested constituency. Though its backing by no means ensured success, the Irish administration was often pestered with requests for assistance. Such requests, though naturally accompanied by effusive offers of future friendship, could be embarrassing to the government, for intervention might antagonize another interest. For instance in 1817, Lord Shannon, a potentate in the south, was so highly incensed by the Irish government 'interfering in the local politics of Cork' by supporting Hare for one of the county seats, that he sulkily refused a piece of patronage put at his disposal.[1] When the ministry of All the Talents were in office Grenville and Elliot were placed in an awkward predicament by the eagerness of Ely and the Beresfords to join them—in return for a pledge of government support at the coming general election. Unfortunately the parliamentary ambitions of both families clashed at several points with those of the Ponsonbys, the great pillars of the whig cause in Ireland. After tiresome negotiations the government were able to hammer out a compromise between the Beresfords and the Ponsonbys but Ely had to be left to fight for his own hand.[2]

Once elected, a member had a definite inducement to support the government. Convention decreed that patronage in a constituency—including county offices and revenue appointments—should be distributed in accordance with the wishes of the prevalent interest (which in practice meant the sitting member or his patron) if it was behind the government. And even a county member who merely intimated that he intended to support the administration as far as was consistent with his reputation for independence, thought he had 'a claim to some compliments of a minor nature'.[3] It was not always easy for the government to decide between competing interests in the same area. For instance Day, who headed a great connection in County Kerry, was indignant to hear that the patronage of the county had been handed over to Colonel Crosbie, who, he alleged, had been foisted on it by the freeholders of a single great interest; in County Cork, Lord Carbery, a government supporter, was annoyed when he discovered that he could not secure a tide-waitership at Baltimore except through Lord Shannon; and Lord Rosse on one occasion complained bitterly that the government had underestimated his importance in King's County relative to that of Lord Charleville, 'a man of much show who lives at great expense'. 'It is not',

---

[1] Correspondence between Peel and Shannon, Oct. 1817 (Add. MS. 38195).
[2] References to the government's negotiations with Ponsonby and Beresford are to be found scattered through *Fortescue MSS.*, viii.
[3] Sir Frederick Flood to Peel, 3 Jan. 1814 (Add. MS. 40218).

Rosse remarked, 'what a man spends, but what he has that matters.'[1] Any infringement of the conventions governing patronage aroused intense indignation. Peel as chief secretary was the recipient of a furious letter from Lord Clare, then *in statu pupillari* at Oxford, complaining that his right to nominate the high sheriff of County Limerick had been disregarded. And a later chief secretary discovered suddenly how, in an Irish county M.P., pride could accompany importunity. Littleton records in his diary that just after he took office, French, the member for Roscommon, called and asked for a living worth about £2,000 per annum for his brother. When Littleton informed him there were no livings of that value, French retorted 'Phoo, there are deaneries and bishoprics'. On French going on to demand a commissionership under the Irish church act for his brother, the chief secretary suggested he had better write to the prime minister. At this French flamed up. 'Sir', he replied, 'the Frenches have represented their county for seven hundred years. They do not write letters, they demand audiences'.[2] An emphatic and reasoned ungrammatical defence of the system by which government patronage was farmed out to the great county influences was advanced by a prominent county member, Denis Browne when he was asserting his right to a small piece of patronage (for, as he remarked, 'the humble walks of public life must be filled as well as the great ones'). 'Give me', he declared, 'the Mayo patronage and I will be able to do your business there, get you soldiers when you want them as in the case of the army of reserve, support your revenue by influence, preventing the extensive sea coast of this county being the resort of excise smugglers, supporting your excise revenue, when the province was disturbed quieting the disturbances, everywhere supporting the laws and keeping up the standard of loyalty.'[3]

It would be hard to exaggerate the place occupied by patronage in the day to day political life of Ireland during the early nineteenth century. British politicians were struck by the pertinacity with which Irishmen pursued official appointments and promotion. Fox remarked you would as soon find an Irishman without a job as without a brogue.[4] Peel, after thirty years of Irish politics warned a new lord-lieutenant that 'I have never yet met with a man in Ireland who has not either himself refused honours from the crown, or was not the son of a man who had, or who

---

[1] Day to Peel, —; Cahir to Peel, 12 Jan. 1815; Carbery to Peel, 28 Mar. 1815; Desart to Peel, 22 Nov. 1815; Rosse to Peel, 20 Mar. 1815 (Add. MSS. 40234, 40251, 40244, 40216).
[2] Littleton diary, 27 July 1834 (Teddesley MSS.).
[3] D. Browne to Peel, 6 Mar. 1815 (Add. MS. 40217).
[4] Fox to Bedford, June 1806 (*Correspondence of C. J. Fox* (1853–7), iv. 143).

had not married the daughter of a man who had been hard-hearted enough to refuse the solicitations of the government. . . . You will become very familiar before you leave Ireland with the expression: "My father over and over again refused a peerage." [1] Probably English politicians were rather quick to detect the mote in their neighbour's eye, but there may have been something in Redesdale's theory that the methods which the government had been compelled to employ in the pre-union era had 'given a corrupt character to the whole people of Ireland, and behaviour which in England would have excited surprise and indignation was not considered lamentable. It was considered a fair advantage'. [2] In any case in a poor country, where social pride was rampant, a hankering after genteel employment in government service was naturally prevalent. For at least the twenty years following the union about half of a chief secretary's correspondence related to personal requests, an incredible amount of time and energy was absorbed in mediating between the different interests involved, and an anthology could be composed of the varying modes of approach, ranging from the restraint practised by Colonel Bruen 'who professes never to apply for anything, but who nevertheless does drop into the Irish Office as often as most people' to the stormy tactics of another county member, who always retired from the chancellor of the exchequer's room declaring 'I think myself the most ill-used man in Ireland'. [3] Admittedly the administrative reforms which marked the period following the union steadily diminished the importance of patronage in Irish political life or at least cut down the number of available jobs. As early as 1802 the viceroy was complaining that the reorganization of the Barrack board would deprive the Irish executive of 'the means of obliging many Irish interests'. Ten years later Richmond, his successor, argued that the lord-lieutenant must have all the Irish patronage at his disposal, since even so he would hardly have enough to carry on the government, and by 1829 the chief secretary was driven to explain to an applicant that 'the patronage of the lord-lieutenant has been put on a footing which leaves me no prospect of being able to serve anyone in whom I take a personal interest. The fair claims upon every vacancy so surpass the number of vacancies that there is in fact only an apparent freedom of selection in most cases.' [4]

[1] Peel to de Grey, 23 Nov. 1841 (Add. MS. 40477).

[2] Redesdale to Liverpool, 18 Oct. 1821 (Add. MS. 38290).

[3] Leveson-Gower to Singleton, 13 Aug. 1829 (Leveson-Gower letter books); Littleton diary, 27 July 1834 (Teddesley MSS.).

[4] Hardwicke to Yorke, — (Add. MS. 35702); Leveson-Gower to G. Murray, 6 Apr. 1829 (Leveson-Gower letter books); Richmond to Peel, 5 Apr. 1816 (Richmond papers).

It is hardly surprising then, that from the union to the reform act the majority of Irish M.P.s supported the government. Convenience and probably conviction aligned them with the majority of the house. Nevertheless throughout this period there was a small section amounting to about one-fifth of the total which acted with the whig opposition. Survivors of the whig party in the Irish parliament, such as Grattan and the Ponsonbys, provided a nucleus for the group which in adverse conditions upheld toleration and moderate reform. Only at the very end of the period did it grow abruptly in strength. Early in 1830, when the Wellington administration was enfeebled by schisms in the tory party, two leading Irish whigs, Spring Rice and Newport, managed to array a majority of the Irish M.P.s against the government on a popular issue—a protest against taxation.[1]

During the latter half of the eighteenth century the Irish radicals, with a coherent political programme—parliamentary reform, administrative efficiency, the abolition of aristocratic privileges, catholic emancipation and Irish independence—with able pamphleteers and several newspapers advocating their views, and with a variety of organized activities, had become an important element in Irish politics. During the nineties their ranks had been reinforced by a mass of discontented peasants, and after a period of hesitancy the Irish radical leaders decided that only direct action could overpower an intellectually impervious opposition. The rising which ensued in 1798, ill-planned, ill-equipped, ill-co-ordinated and practically unaided, was an absolute failure, and the consequences for Irish radicalism were catastrophic. In addition to the discredit normally attached to unsuccessful rebellion, the loss measured in personal terms was drastically severe. During the nineties there were five outstanding men of ideas amongst the Irish radicals, Tone, Arthur O'Connor, Thomas Addis Emmet, William Drennan and William James McNevin. At the start of the new century Tone was dead, O'Connor was a general in the French army, Emmet and McNevin had been forced to carry on their professional careers across the Atlantic, Drennan, fertile-minded, upright and sensitive, with an acute eye for the defects of his associates, had dropped out of active politics. Until he left Dublin for Belfast in 1807 he seems to have been socially rather isolated, being engaged in the tiresome tasks of trying to build up a medical practice, and bring up a young family on an unsatisfactory income.[2] But the

---

[1] *DEP*, 6 May 1830. An indignant cabinet minister spoke of this protest as a move of 'the basest electioneering character' (Fitzgerald to Peel, 24 May 1830, Add. MS. 40523).

[2] *Drennan letters* (1931), pp. 320, 321, 377, and frequent references in the unpublished letters.

extent of the losses sustained by Irish radicalism can perhaps best be grasped by examining two acts of 1799 which between them expelled from Ireland over a hundred and forty persons. The long list of names, including as it does, half a score of gentlemen, half a dozen lawyers and as many doctors, a leading Dublin bookseller, more than a dozen substantial business men, a priest and a presbyterian minister, a civil servant, a bank clerk and an army officer, as well as artisans, farmers and labourers drawn from seventeen counties, offers an interesting sample of Irish radicalism and helps to explain the political torpor of the following years.[1]

But in spite of the long radical casualty lists, the government remained for decades haunted by the fear of a repetition of 1798 and 1803. Determined not to be caught napping the Irish administration employed a number of agents to keep a careful watch on Irish public opinion. These functionaries presumably were anxious to justify their cost, but despite their painstaking attention to every alarming detail their reports taken as a whole show the weakness of the radical cause so far as it can be distinguished from agrarian or industrial unrest. In the north only a few faint glimmerings of the movement can be discerned. In 1805 it was reported to the Castle that a communication from France had produced a great bustle amongst the contemptible remnant of the rebel party in Belfast.[2] During the following year it was reported that in County Antrim meetings were being held at which disloyal toasts, such as 'Union between true Irishmen', 'William Orr' and 'Henry Munro' were drunk. About the same time meetings of people from Down and Antrim were being held in Belfast, at which disappointment was expressed at the lack of news from France. At the end of the year it seemed that a deserter had stumbled on a large-scale conspiracy in the north. He heard that lodges were being formed throughout Down and Antrim, preparations for co-ordinating with a French landing were on foot, and cannon were available buried under ground. But the most easily tested part of the story turned out very intangible. For when digging operations were carried out, no cannon were found.[3]

At the other extremity of Ireland, down in County Cork, the doings of William Todd Jones who had been prominent in radical politics since the early eighties were closely watched. But all that turned up was that he was said to have been disseminating the doctrines of Paine on

---

[1] 38 Geo. III, cc, 78, 80 (Irish).

[2] A. Marsden to J. King, 19 July 1805 (H.O. 100/128).

[3] R. Haughton, Belfast, to ——, 18 Dec. 1806, —— to Marsden, 13 Feb. 1806 (S.C.P. 32); General Mitchel, Belfast, 3 May 1811 (S.C.P. 38); Bedford to Spencer, 23 Dec. 1806 (S.P.O. iv. 16, 2).

property, and even this information came from a biased source—a local landowner with whom Jones had been involved in a tavern squabble.[1] From Dublin a large amount of inconclusive gossip poured up to the government. In 1804 it was said that letters for the disaffected had arrived from France and that Dublin working-men were talking about the French coming.[2] Two years later it was noticed that a large number of '98 figures of the second rank were to be seen about, and that in societies such as furniture clubs they were talking about 'the business'. Still a few years later a number of men with '98 records were reported to be meeting in the Brazen Head, 'where all the principal rebels used to meet', and the disaffected in Dublin were said to be in a confident mood, having heard that Bonaparte had recognized the importance of Ireland. And the lower orders were saying that the French defeats in Spain and the stories of Bonaparte's ill-treatment of the pope were all English fabrications. But a government agent, after reporting a good deal of this stuff, adds, 'they have not shown any signs of a conspiracy in Dublin more than wishes and commonplace conversation'. In 1810 another spy listened expectantly to the conversation of about forty genteel-looking people in a Dublin public house. 'At first they seemed rather reserved but at the end of the evening that reserve almost vanished.' Nevertheless though they praised Bonaparte highly, their political aims were unsensational—parliamentary reform and lower taxation. As for the exiles in France, as early as 1803 the government was informed that most of them had no intention of attempting to renew the rebellion in Ireland, their conversation turning principally on the means of providing for their subsistence and the establishing themselves in foreign countries.[3] Nevertheless even after Waterloo the government was uneasy, and Sidmouth in 1820 transmitted to the Irish administration news reminiscent of 1798. From a reliable source he had heard that the English radicals had been assured that preparations for a rising in Ireland were complete and that the disaffected in Ireland were in touch with the liberals on the continent. Unfortunately Sidmouth's informant could not supply the names of the Irishmen concerned.[4]

[1] Heuston to ——, 3 Aug. 1807, D'Arcy Mahon to A. Wellesley, 20 Dec. 1807 (S.C.P. 33 and 34).

[2] A. Marsden to J. King, 13 June 1804, information dated 9 July 1804, and E. Nepean to ——, 5 Oct. 1804 (H.O. 100/22, 100/23).

[3] Informations dated 7 Dec. 1806, Sept. and Oct. 1808, Feb. 1809, 10 June 1810 (S.C.P. 32, 35, 36, 37).

[4] About the same time a Parisian offered the government full information relating to a projected Irish rising with 'reform as the word'. The Irish government were very

These subterranean grumbles so sedulously reported may be regarded as the last dismal reverberations of 1798. But before that explosion Irish radicalism had expressed itself through a variety of societies and public meetings, and these proceedings if unproductive of any immediate effect were at least stimulating. One of the most striking facts about Irish political life in the decades following the union is the decrease in activity of this kind. In the south it almost vanishes—if one excepts the long and strenuous campaign for catholic emancipation which absorbed the political energies of catholics and liberal protestants, such as Magee of the *Dublin Evening Post*. Only in 1817 when there were clamorous demands for reform from all over the British Isles, did undiluted radicalism for a moment display itself again. Reform meetings were held in Cork and Dublin and the reformers in the latter city formed a club which sometimes met for dinner.[1]

The importance attached to the catholic problem explains the lack of interest in other political issues in the three southern provinces. But the political apathy of the north, the forcing house of eighteenth-century Irish liberalism, the province identified in the past with the volunteers, the parliamentary reformers of the eighties and the United Irishmen, the area where presbyterianism and tenant right were potent forces, is far more surprising. Still it is explicable. Even Drennan had been shocked by 'the savagery of the lower catholics' in the rebellion, and the Rev. William Bruce, a leading figure in the cultural life of Belfast, was probably not the only man in the town, who might be politically described as 'an alarmed whig'.[2] Then in the years following the rebellion, Belfast, the centre of Ulster's intellectual life, entered on an age of rapid expansion and substantial prosperity at least for the bulk of the business class. Between 1791 and 1830 the population jumped from 18,000 to over 50,000.[3] Industries, with shipbuilding and cotton added to linen, and with the advent of steam and the factory system, developed steadily. In the early twenties three successful banks were founded. After intricate engineering controversies, prolonged parliamentary battles and com-

sceptical as to the value of this information. (S.P.O. iv. 13, 18.) Seven years later the government were informed that the French were taking steps to survey the Irish coast and collect officers with Irish experience, and as late as the great reform year of 1832 the home secretary was worried about a Frenchman in Dublin who was corresponding upon Irish affairs. (Goulburn to Wellesley, 19 Mar. 1827, W. Stuart to Peel, 12 Mar. 1827 (Add. MS. 37304), Melbourne to Anglesey, 2 Jan. 1832 (Plas Newydd MSS.)).

[1] *DEP*, 9, 14, 18, 23 Jan., 7 Aug. 1817.
[2] *Belfast Literary Society*, 1801–1901 (1902), p. 31, *Drennan letters* (1931), p. 311.
[3] *Historical account of the town of Belfast* (1819), and D. T. Owen, *History of Belfast* (1921), p. 379.

plex negotiations with the lord of the soil and other interests involved, the channel was deepened and the port provided with extensive docks. Though the corporation was an inert oligarchy, the citizens managed in the early part of the century to provide themselves with a decent water supply and an adequate police force. And in the midst of all these activities the charities of the town were so carefully attended to that according to a Belfast source their methods were copied in Dublin.[1] All these manifold and pressing activities helped to divert men from politics, and if the marquess of Donegall was rather too optimistic when 'he flattered himself that the town of Belfast particularly in the flourishing state it is at present would never again have entered into the politics of the nation',[2] his opinion of the north at this period is endorsed by Drennan, who declared a few years earlier that 'the north seems dead and rotting like their flax when sleeping in holes and ditches owing I think in a great measure to the literary talents of Belfast displayed in their vapid newspapers, etc.'[3]

As the above quoted outburst of Drennan shows, if politics languished in Belfast after the union there was plenty of intellectual activity. Theological controversy, particularly amongst the presbyterians, grew steadily brisker. The Belfast Literary Society (whose first publication significantly enough was on the linen and hemp manufacture) was founded in 1801, the Historical Society (a debating club) in 1811, the Anacreontic Society in 1814, and the Belfast Natural History Society in 1821. In addition, in 1806–10 an important educational scheme was launched by the foundation of the Belfast Academical Institution which consisted of two sections, a primary or school department, and a collegiate department, which was meant to be the germ of a northern university catering mainly for the presbyterians. All these educational enterprises, set on foot at a time when the enlightenment of the eighteenth century was merging with the earnestness of the nineteenth, evince a sincere if somewhat priggish eagerness to extend the boundaries of knowledge and raise the cultural level of the community. Drennan caught the contemporary mood when, at the opening of the Academical Institution in 1814, he declared that 'the general improvement and ultimate perfection in the plans and practice of education must in a great degree be brought about by the efforts of individuals—zealous and active individuals, persevering and

[1] For the development of Belfast during these years see D. J. Owen, *History of Belfast*, G. Benn, *History of the town of Belfast*, 2 vols. (1877–80), E. R. R. Green, *The Lagan valley* 1800–50 (1949) and T. Bradshaw, *Belfast general and commercial directory for* 1819 (1819), p. xix.

[2] *BNL*, 2 May 1809.

[3] Drennan to Mrs. McTier, 17 Apr. 1807 (unpublished Drennan letters).

even indefatigable in working out an object they know to be of public utility'.[1]

The shift in the balance of interests in Belfast intellectual life can be seen in the case of several individuals who had been active in northern politics in the late eighteenth century. The Rev. William Bruce, an urbane scholar, and a masterful minister, whose imposing presence attracted the admiration of George IV on his visit to Ireland, had played a leading part in the Volunteer movement, advocating vote by ballot at the convention of '83. But after the union his energies were completely absorbed in his school, his Homeric studies, the Belfast Literary Society and expounding his exceedingly liberal theological system. John Templeton, Russell's devoted friend, was busy accomplishing pioneering work in zoology, botany and geology. Of the proprietors of the *Northern Star*, Caldwell and Tennant were leading merchants and bankers, Robert Simms was a director of the Lagan Navigation Company, McIlveen remained an active member of the Belfast Society for Promoting Knowledge, William Magee, the bookseller, a few years after the catastrophe of '98 was investing heavily in landed property, and Henry Hazlett was a leading member of the Chamber of Commerce. Though these interests did not necessarily exclude politics, they obviously would compete with them, and offered alternative forms of public-spirited self-expression.[2]

In Belfast the town meeting summoned by the sovereign was the usual means through which public opinion manifested itself. Usually these meetings were concerned with municipal or charitable problems, but in several cases the liberal section of the community tried to carry political resolutions. In May 1809 a vote of thanks was passed to Colonel Wardle, the celebrated parliamentary muck-raker.[3] In 1813 after a riotous 12th of July when the military had to be called out, the liberals demanded a town meeting to inquire into the cause of the disturbance. The sovereign first put off summoning it, and then, when it assembled tried to adjourn it as quickly as possible. A genteel riot arose and a scuffle between Tennant and the Rev. Mr May led to the former being charged with assault.[4] Shortly afterwards the Friends of Civil and Religious Liberty of Belfast, with Drennan in the chair, held an in-

---

[1] Address of Dr Drennan printed in *Royal Belfast Academical Institution: centenary volume* (1913), pp. 203–7.

[2] J. Anderson, *History of the Belfast library* (1883), p. 35; *Belfast Literary Society 1801–1901* (1902); Benn, *A history of the town of Belfast*, ii. 217, 222–4; T528 (8) (P-R.O.N.I.).

[3] *BNL*, 2 May 1809. The inhabitants of Keady accompanied their address to Wardle with a gift of linen (*BNL*, 2 May 1809).

[4] *BNL*, 13, 20 Aug. 1813. Peel in a letter to Liverpool dated 15 Oct. 1813, spoke of 'some of the old leaven of "98" ' appearing in Belfast (Add. MS. 38195).

dignant meeting which adopted a petition to parliament calling for the suppression of all illegal associations, since party outrages were making Ireland more dangerous than the woods and savannahs of the American savages.[1] And a few years later when the conservatives got up a town meeting to vote an address severely reprobating an attack on the regent, the liberals led by the studious John Templeton, were able to secure the omission of a paragraph reflecting on the supporters of reform.[2]

In 1816 there was serious trouble over the Belfast Academical Institution. An educational institution supported by presbyterian dissenters, and numbering amongst its founders several well-known radicals including Drennan, was bound to be suspect by the government. Still, since it was backed by many leading Belfast business men and countenanced by the great northern magnates, it managed in 1814 to secure an annual government grant of £1,500. Two years later at a dinner held in Belfast on St. Patrick's eve, attended by a couple of teachers from the Institution and several of its governing body, radical toasts were drunk, and this, the chief secretary was informed, could not be attributed to uncalculating conviviality, as they had been approved in advance by a committee. The episode, which was made the basis of a parliamentary attack on the Institution by Sir George Hill, placed its directors in an embarrassing situation. Lawless, the exuberant catholic journalist who at that time was working in Belfast, issued a pamphlet calling on the 'boards' which controlled the Institution to stand firm. But even Drennan, who held that 'the boards' should not dismiss their officials on the orders of the government, thought they should express regret for what had occurred. To Castlereagh the incident offered an opportunity to check an undesirable development. He argued that the arrangement of 1802 by which the *regium donum* had been increased, had been based on the understanding that the presbyterian clergy would be educated 'at one of the established universities of the empire'. And he was sure that 'Drennan and his party' had been busy intriguing 'to destroy the effects of the settlement of 1802 and replace the synod in the ranks of democracy'. A threat that the annual grant might be withdrawn and the *regium donum* withheld from any minister lacking a university degree, might, he thought, be used to reduce the Institution to a school by getting rid of its professors. Peel was more cautious. He infinitely preferred conservative presbyterian ministers to radical ones, but if he had to deal with the latter, he 'would rather have them stipendiaries than independent'. In the end the government demanded a voice in the man-

---

[1] *DEP*, 2 Sept. 1813; *Trial of the Belfast Orangemen* . . . (1813).
[2] *UR*, 1817, pp. 16–18.

agement of the Institution, and since the proprietors would only concede a government veto on appointments, the Institution lost its grant.
But in spite of the government's attitude being plainly indicated, the
Synod of Ulster promptly took steps to appoint divinity professors in the
Institution whose certificates it would accept as a qualification for the
ministry.[1] This episode, which incidentally shows that the *regium
donum* had not had the effect expected by some of its supporters and
its critics, reveals the prevalence of sturdy independence rather than
radicalism in the north.

About this time the citizens of Belfast were greatly concerned over
two somewhat dissimilar matters—the burden of the window tax and
the wrongs of Queen Caroline. Two meetings were held to prepare
petitions to parliament against the first of these, and though Lawless
wanted the petitioners to use forcible language, the sovereign reminded
them that parliament should be approached with respect, and a reference criticizing the union was deleted from the petition. In August 1820
the sovereign severely snubbed a group of radicals who requested a
town meeting to consider the queen's case. So they themselves summoned a meeting which assembled in a dissenting meeting house, and
which was, according to Lawless, one of its promoters, marked by
'solemnity, decorum and propriety'—qualities rather lacking in the
object of their commiseration. An address was voted to the queen,
who, the irrepressible Lawless declared, was 'a widowed, solitary,
friendless, helpless woman'. A year later when the queen was triumphant, another meeting of the same kind, called on the king to remove
his ministers and demanded parliamentary reform. A few months later
when the queen died, a disorderly vestry meeting ordered that the
mourning with which the churchwardens had draped the pulpit of the
parish church and which the curate had removed should be replaced.[2]
A couple of years later in 1823 the Friends of Parliamentary Reform in
Belfast met at the first reform dinner to be held in the town since 1782.
It proved such a successful function that the second annual reform
dinner was held before the year was out.[3]

[1] For this episode see *The book of the Royal Belfast Academical Institution* (1913),
ch. v.; John Lawless, *A letter addressed to the proprietors of the Belfast Academical
Institution* (1816); *The Drennan letters*, pp. 385–97; Castlereagh to Peel, 9, 12 Nov.,
10 Dec. 1816; Peel to Castlereagh, 13 Nov., 2 Dec., 1816 (Add. MS. 40181); R.
Hamilton to Peel, 5 Apr. 1816 (Add. MS. 40253).
[2] *UR*, 1818, pp. 396, 1816, p. 300; *Irishman*, 25 Feb. 1820, 21 Feb. and 14 Sept.
1821. It may be added that the rector, a strong tory, returned to Belfast in time to
remove 'the mummery' before the service on Sunday.
[3] *Irishman*, 11 Apr., 28 Nov. 1823. At the first dinner James Mumford, a prominent

As can be seen from the activities outlined above—with the exception of the Academical Institution affair—Belfast politics conformed closely to the contemporary British pattern. Excepting Lawless's unending attacks on the union (and his stay in Belfast was comparatively short), the speeches delivered by radicals and liberals in Belfast were almost identical in tone and content with what one might hear at the same time in England. And at the great Belfast reform meeting held in December 1830, while a radical reform of parliament was vehemently urged by speaker after speaker, the statement 'the closer the union the greater our happiness and prosperity' was loudly cheered.[1]

Both Drennan and Lawless founded, during their years in Belfast, publications through which they could express their political views. Drennan, as has been mentioned, returned to Belfast in 1807, and in 1808 helped to launch the *Belfast Monthly Magazine* which ran for six years. Primarily a literary journal, most of the essays and verse which it printed were commonplace, stilted and imitative. But the magazine in its occasional comments on politics reflects Drennan's unaltered political and social opinions. Its fervent advocacy of educational progress and catholic emancipation, its glowing nationalism, and its admonitory tone to all groups in Ireland, were typical of its editor. He shuddered at the idea of Ireland 'ever being so melted down and merged into the British empire, as Wales and Scotland are', 'for there is a self-valuation, there are inherent rights, there is an inseparable sovereignty of nature and geographical distinction . . . which ought to be held and never parted with'. 'The perfectibility of a people', he stated, 'depends upon the free nature of its government, which inspires in the body of the nation generous and noble sentiment.' On these grounds he condemned the union, for 'when Ireland lost her political existence nothing of a public nature was left to produce any full development of intellectual powers, nothing to interest or occupy the generous affections of the heart'. Ireland, he bitterly exclaimed, was no longer worth living in, 'men of genius and talent will henceforth be as thinly scattered in this country as in modern Greece', and though Ireland's productive powers as regards pigs and potatoes might increase, in regard to scientific, literary or political eminence they were lost. The only thing which had checked Ireland's fall into 'a petty and insignificant provincialism' was the catholic question. Drennan hoped that the catholics when emancipated, 'would not forget the little island in the great empire . . . and part

figure in the political and philanthropic life of the town announced that on the day forty-five years back he had joined the Belfast Volunteers.

[1] *Report of the proceedings at the town meeting held at Belfast*, 1830.

with the independence, or if you will, insularity of character, which without being inconsistent with the union will guard them from neglect.'[1]

Lawless, besides being a generation younger, was temperamentally very different from Drennan. Impetuous and voluble, courageous and inclined to political exhibitionism, for a decade he played a prominent part with obvious gusto in Belfast politics. Not only was he compelled to say at least a few words at every political and vestry meeting he attended, but even at a complimentary dinner to the marquess of Donegall he became the centre of attention by standing on a table and trying to make a speech when the memory of Castlereagh was proposed.[2] A catholic, he was incensed by the inequitable treatment meted out to his religion in Ireland, and he poured out his opinions in over-emotional, vulgarly coloured, torrential prose. For some years he edited in Belfast first the *Ulster Register*, a monthly filled largely with selections from the English radical press, and then the *Irishman*, a weekly newspaper whose outstanding features were catholic news and radical politics. In both journals, it may be added, an agreeably egotistical editorial policy ensured that Lawless's own doings were adequately reported.

Shortly before Lawless left Belfast, staid, orthodox, presbyterian liberalism secured a newspaper by the foundation of the *Northern Whig*. Founded by Finlay, a local self-made man, its standards were well above the average, some attention being paid to literature as well as to market prices and shipping news, and its editorials were well knit, thoughtful, restrained, and relatively free from personalities. As might be expected, it was in favour of catholic emancipation, a moderate measure of parliamentary reform, the repeal of the corn laws, and intervention on behalf of the Greeks. It was quick to denounce with full details road-jobbing and rack-renting, calling upon the government to intervene between the heartless landlords and their tenantry. In ecclesiastical affairs it demanded the radical reform of the establishment and the abolition of tithe, reminding Irish presbyterians in a long series of articles of the prelatic persecutions inflicted on their ancestors. But its zeal was tempered by moderation. It advocated joint education so that the young should be taught 'that rational and genuine piety is the property of no particular sect but that the rays of true religion while they contain an assemblage of distinct colours . . . afford light and heat to the world by their intimate coalescence'. It censored the Catholic Association and the Orangemen as two of the greatest nuisances in the country. Repeal of the union was dismissed by the *Whig* as romantic and impracticable,

---

[1] *Belfast Monthly Magazine*, x. 251. 498; xi. 335–6.
[2] *Irishman*, 30 Aug., 6 Sept., 1822.

and on one occasion it remarked that the lives of such men as Newton, Boyle and Arkwright were more likely to interest Belfast mechanics than those of Emmet, Russell and Tone.[1]

The activities we have been describing concerned directly only a small proportion of the population. The participation of the ordinary Irish peasant in national politics was usually restricted to voting according to his landlord's wishes and occasionally rioting at elections. But during the earlier decades of the century many of the poorer classes were continually trying to maintain what they conceived to be sound standards of social behaviour by methods, which though undoubtedly illegal, were regarded by those who employed them, as a crude form of politics, by which the will of the community was enforced and evils ignored by the legislature redressed. Every year brought a crop of agrarian outrages, and the Irish administration was regularly engaged in diagnosing the state of the country, observing bad patches with concern, or thankfully expecting a quiet period. It would be a weary task to describe in detail the geographical distribution and the temporal fluctuations of outrage and disturbance between 1800 and 1830. Throughout the period Tipperary probably suffered most and Ulster least from agrarian trouble, though in the north religious animosity compensated for the absence of other forms of ill-will. The trouble in Tipperary seems to have started at the beginning of the nineteenth century with attempts to prevent strangers securing farms over the heads of their old tenants. About the same time in County Limerick labourers taking the jobs of men dismissed were flogged, and farmers were being deterred by 'corporal punishment' from employing labourers from other counties.[2] In 1806–7 there were serious anti-tithe troubles in Mayo and Sligo. 'Night battalions' shook out the corn which the canters had collected, and moving to secular grievances attacked and cruelly beat the local weavers to make them reduce their rates.[3] In 1813–14 Roscommon, Limerick, Tipperary, King's County, and Kildare were all disturbed, and in 1820 the operations of the organized peasantry and the military in county Cork resembled a miniature civil war.

The aims of the various illegal rural organizations, Threshers, Carders, Rockites, and Ribbonmen, varied slightly from time to time, but essentially they were direct and simple. Often they were hostile to tithe and sometimes to the dues demanded by the catholic priests. For instance

---

[1] *NW*, 22 Jan. 1824, 8 and 15 Dec. 1825.

[2] J. Traill to ——, 27 Apr. 1808, Report from Limerick, June 1801, Hardwicke to Pelham, 18 Dec. 1802 (H.O. 100/148, 100/103, 100/110).

[3] Bishop of Elphin to Lord Ellenborough, 5 Sept. 1806 (S.C.P. 32).

'the bandetti' round Ballymore (Westmeath) had as their programme, the regulation of the fees paid to priests and the abolition of wake offerings to the clergy as well as the fixing of conacre rates.[1] The peasantry were continually trying to prevent rents rising and farm labourers' wages falling. Auctions of land were forbidden. New tenants were sometimes compelled to quit farms. In Kerry 'land pirates' from 'foreign baronies' were warned off.[2] 'The bluebells' of Tipperary tried to prevent anyone save the previous occupier bidding for land when the lease had lapsed, until three years had elapsed.[3] In county Limerick attempts were made to fix labourers' wages.[4] In Cashel, two years later a notice was posted on a cabin door directing that no stranger should lodge there, that no labourer should work on a road for less than 2s. 6d. per day, and fixing the price of potatoes.[5] And in several cases in times of scarcity attempts were made to prevent provisions being moved.[6]

The methods employed to attain these aims—'the frequent administration of oaths, regular requisitioning of horses, the sounding of horns, the lighting of signal fires, the appearance of armed parties, and the unremitting robbery of arms'—were calculated to bind together the members of the illegal societies. Threatening notices were frequently stuck up, and people who offended against the agrarian societies' code were warned, beaten, shot or 'carded'.[8] Many instances could be given of the way in which the countryside could be terrorized, but a few culled from the dreary mass of reports will suffice. In county Kilkenny in 1810 publicans were warned not to supply a man who had recovered land through the sheriff.[9] A landlord, residing in the tranquillity of Bath, wrote indignantly to the Castle complaining that not only had he not received a penny of rent from his Pettigo estate for two years, but that the tenants had destroyed the manor pound, thus seriously handicapping his bailiffs, and boycotted the masons whom he had had to bring from fifty miles away to repair it.[10] In county Waterford an attempt was made to deter J.P.s from being over-busy by introducing their names

[1] Richard Willcocks to W. Gregory, 27 May 1813 (S.C.P. 40).
[2] Paper dated 21 Oct. 1807 (S.C.P. 35); J. Traill to ——, 3 May 1808 (H.O. 100/147).
[3] E. B. Littledale to J. Beckett, 13 June 1810 (S.P.O. iv. 16. 2).
[4] W. Ponsonby to E. B. Littledale, 10 Sept. 1808 (H.O. 100/148).
[5] Report from Cashel dated 24 July 1810 (S.C.P. 37).
[6] R. Kennedy, Philipstown, 9 Mar. 1812, report from Portaferry, 8 Feb. 1812; report from Skibbereen, 28 Apr. 1812; report from Kilkenny, 8 June 1817 (S.C.P. 38, 39, 41, 44).
[7] John Cooke to Sir R. Peel, Tipperary, 28 Aug. 1814 (S.C.P. 41).
[8] For an instance of carding see report from Cashel, 24 July 1810 (S.C.P. 37).
[9] Report from Kilkenny, 1 Nov. 1810 (S.C.P. 36).
[10] C. P. Leslie to ——, 10 Feb. 1817 (S.C.P. 44).

into ballads.[1] And in county Limerick a Captain Rock issued a notice, warning 'any gentleman that is to make a corps of yeomen that he might as well have his ears cut immediately'.[2] But the landed gentry were relatively safe. The victims of agrarian terror, which, operated in secret by desperate men, was bound to be often malicious and brutal, were usually farmers or labourers.[3] An alarming, if in its outcome not particularly tragic experience of a Kilkenny farmer illustrates the terrors of the night for the law-abiding. One night a party of men came to his house, compelled him to come out in his shirt, kneel down and swear he had no arms. Then 'the party went into his house, smoked a pipe of tobacco and told deponent that they were taking a great deal of trouble for him and other people and that they were Captain Rock's party'.[4] Understandably, 'the universal answer of the common people' in county Kilkenny when asked to assist in preserving the peace in 1813, was, 'how can we venture to do anything when we live in a lonely thatched house'.[5] Sometimes respectable men found themselves caught between two fires, for instance when the local magistrates meeting at Castlemartyr in 1815 resolved publicly 'not to let lands to any person who from terror or menace held out by the turbulent or lawless may surrender farms they have lately taken, further when their leases shall expire they shall not be reinstated and their names shall be published'.[6]

Local feuds as well as economic warfare distracted the Irish countryside. In many areas the peasantry grouped themselves in factions 'the Shavanats and Cravats' or 'the Fitzgeralds and the Hogans' for instance, which fought hard, apparently from sheer *esprit de corps* and alcohol. In the midlands for instance the peasantry were divided into two great factions, the Darrags grouped round Roscrea, and the Cummins about Parsonstown, which fought one another at fairs and markets. Their quarrels frequently arose over the renting of farms and their weapons were 'stones which they are very expert at throwing', and loaded sticks capable of smashing a skull, which could be hidden in a sleeve.[7] Like so many other aspects of Irish life, faction-fighting had theological implications. In the south the Ribbonmen seem sometimes to have identified their cause with the catholic faith, and in the north there were the Orange

[1] W. G. Paul, Waterford, to Sir C. Saxton, 29 Apr. 1811 (S.C.P. 38).
[2] Report from Co. Limerick, 1 March 1822 (S.C.P. 46).
[3] e.g. see a report from Newtownbarry, 24 June 1813 (S.C.P. 39).
[4] Information c. 1822 (S.C.P. 46).
[5] Desart to Peel, 20 Oct. 1813 (Add. MS. 40216). See also the archbishop of Cashel to the lord lieutenant, 25 Aug. 1814 (Add. MS. 40238).
[6] Printed papers from Castlemartyr, 14 Apr. 1815 (S.C.P. 43).
[7] Report from Co. Waterford, 27 Dec. 1808 (S.C.P. 35), J. Miller, Tipperary, to R. Willcocks, 11 Dec. 1825 (S.C.P. 48), Lord Rosse to ——, 10 Oct. 1827 (S.C.P. 49).

societies. The two groups naturally sometimes clashed. In Donegal, the playing of what 'some people call party tunes, such as God save the king' led to trouble; at Newry it was said in 1813 'seldom a night passes without the two parties trying their strength' and two years later at a fair in Tyrone, a fellow calling himself 'the Bonaparte of Ireland' led a rush at the protestants.[1]

In the manufacturing centres too, sections of the working class were organized, and often used direct action to enforce their standards of economic behaviour. In 1811 the weavers round Lisburn who had formed a combination with a handsomely designed ticket of membership were seizing and destroying webs. A few weeks before Waterloo some 'deluded workmen' in Belfast, weavers who insisted on regulating their wages, were sent to gaol. A year later intense indignation was aroused amongst the Belfast middle class by an attempt to blow up the house of a muslin manufacturer in North Street who was quarrelling with his workmen. Ten years later the journeymen and apprentices at a Carrickfergus calico printing works '"struck" as it is termed' for higher wages. The apprentices were at once committed to prison. During the same year the Belfast cotton spinners went on strike assisted by money from Glasgow. After some months the mill owners decided to reopen with new hands and the *Northern Whig* had a leader attacking 'combinations' for interfering with the laws of economics and for winning support by terror.[2] Nevertheless in the following decade there was another serious strike in the calico printing trade over the engagement of apprentices, one firm being compelled to close down.[3] The proprietor of the *Northern Whig* soon experienced unpleasantly the working of trade unionism in his own concern. Finlay, a vigorous, self-made man, a strong reformer, and a severe critic of landlordism, became in 1836 involved in a fierce dispute with his employees when the union interfered with the management of his establishment, refusing for instance to permit 'a person employed in a literary capacity' to handle a compositor's stick when business was brisk. In spite of threatening mobs Finlay imported men from Dublin, and when these were seduced into the union, being determined not to be beaten by 'the harassing uneasiness, unpleasantness, and misery' to which he was subject, he adopted 'a rather novel

[1] John Boyd, Lifford, to ——, 22 Aug. 1808; Report from Newry 9 Aug. 1813. Information from Tyrone, 1 Oct. 1815 (H.O. 100/148, Add. MS. 40229, H.O. 100/184).

[2] Hawkershaw, Lisburn, to General Michel, 23 May 1811 (S.C.P. 38); *BNL*, 7 May 1815, 1 Mar. 1816, 10 Jan. 1820; *NW*, 2 Feb., 9 Mar., 20 Apr. 1826.

[3] *First report from the select committee on combinations of workmen with minutes of evidence*, pp. 235–40, H.C. 1837–8(488), viii.

plan'. He fitted up, unknown to his men, a printing house, then he collected some charity school children, and 'put them into the secret printing office, slept them upon the premises, fed them upon the premises, and privately at night took them out to give them air and exercise', and on Sunday sent them down to his farm to take gymnastic exercise. With the aid of these little boys 'some not more than ten years of age whom I perched upon stools', a few personal friends, and Mrs. Finlay who assisted 'in a literary point of view' he defied the 'mighty combinators', published his paper, and in the end secured journeymen.[1]

In Dublin several trades of skilled and highly paid men were well organized, insisted on regulating their conditions of work, and were prepared to use rough methods to get their way. Moreover the Dublin working class were, intermittently at least, linked up with the country labourers through the Ribbon societies, a kind of proletarian underground, about which little definite information is available. However for a couple of short periods 1821–4 and about 1840, it is possible to get a fairly clear view of their activities. In the latter period a leading Ribbonman was brought to trial. For the former, we have a series of reports to the government many of which were painstakingly summarized by Major Sirr, the Dublin police magistrate who used the material so assiduously collected to secure the conviction of a leading Ribbon organizer.[2] There was in the early twenties an organization of Dublin working men, grouped in lodges under 'masters', with ill-defined aims though clearly disaffected and dissatisfied. Much of the energy of the society was consumed in talk, swearing in recruits, drinking toasts, 'No king', 'Downfall of heresy', 'Rights of man' and 'The major in a boghole with his heels up and we all laughing at him', and speculating about the future, it being rumoured in the Dublin slums that if the king, who was said to be a bastard, came to Ireland he would never go home again, and that 'all the Romans were going to fight against England who would be reduced to an alliance with the Turk'. However some practical work was accomplished. Plans were made to beat up a jaunting-car manufacturer who had discharged a couple of Ribbonmen, an attempt was made to shoot a master carpenter who had shot a man when a party of strikers were trying to force his employees to join them, at Castleknock, just outside Dublin, a gallows was erected on the lands of a farmer who had employed 'strangers' to get in his potatoes, it was decided to boycott

---

[1] *Second report from the select committee on combinations of workmen with minutes of evidence*, pp. 82–96, H.C. 1837–8 (646), viii.

[2] See two volumes of abstracts of information relating to Dublin societies 1821–2 in the Sirr papers, and informations dated June, July, April 1823 and June and August 1824 (S.C.P. 47).

the proprietress of a public house who out of jealousy had complained to the police about the way in which a rival establishment patronized by Ribbonmen was conducted, it was agreed that a farmer who had given information regarding an illicit still should not be shot but compelled to quit the country, and the possibility of blowing up William III's statue in College Green was discussed, a scheme being prepared for making the man who kept the key of the enclosure drunk.

The Dublin Ribbonmen were of course connected with their brethren in the country and even in Great Britain. For instance in 1821 delegates from Waterford, Limerick, Newry, Armagh and Belfast met in Dublin. Shortly afterwards seventy-two delegates met in Armagh and it was proposed to form a general board in Dublin, and at the end of the year there was a second Armagh meeting at which were present delegates from Leitrim, Louth, Longford and Dublin as well as the northern counties. This gathering decided not to permit any robber to join the society and fixed the 'signs'. In February 1822 there was a meeting of Irish delegates attended by representatives from Liverpool, and in June 1823 'one of the most explosive meetings ever held' took place in Bolton Street, counter measures against Orange demonstrations being discussed, and in June 1824 it was suggested that a committee of representatives from every Leinster county, known as the Independent Congress of the Most Holy Order of the Knights of St. Patrick, should be set up to receive monthly returns of men and arms.

As is customary in subterranean political organizations the Ribbon societies were riddled with dissension, fierce personal squabbles frequently breaking out. Finance often led to awkwardness. Sometimes there were complaints that nothing could be shown for the money collected, and when the Derry men wrote to their Dublin brethren for 'a trifle of money to carry on the war against the Orangemen', there was a bitter argument over whether £25 recently collected should be sent or used to carry on the struggle in Dublin. In June 1823 an informer sent in a vivid account of Ribbon society internal politics. When at a gathering of about 1,200 Ribbonmen assembled by night near Kilcoole, 'the masters' asked if there were any complaints, 'the cottage fellows from the Glen of the Downs' complained that their master kept his papers in a teapot where his wife could read them and was always drinking with protestants. He was promptly deposed. At a meeting of local masters the following night it was decided not to send any more money to Dublin, and to inform the Dublin men that though they were willing to abide by the decision of the organization many of them were too poor to provide a weapon which would keep off a dog. At the close of 1821 and the beginning of 1822 the disputes amongst the Dublin Ribbonmen centred round Michael Keenan, an overbearing, voluble, tough coal-porter. There were rumours, apparently unfounded, that he was a robber and an informer, and in December the examination of his accounts led to unpleasantness. Keenan insisted on remaining the link between the Dublin men and the national meetings of delegates, and claimed the right to veto the election of a co-delegate who had promised to tell his constituents all that had passed. After several angry meetings of masters had discussed Keenan's doings, a committee of inquiry was appointed, and 'Mr Keenan sittled his business, satisfactorily'.[1]

A couple of years later there was a schism in the Dublin Ribbon organization between the city Ribbonmen and the Fox and Geese men who seem from their meeting-places being at Harold's Cross and Kilmainham to have been drawn from the suburbs, but who were said to include forty-two city masters. Allegations of embezzlement and giving information were thrown to and fro, but after negotiations lasting some months the factions appear to have been reconciled in the summer of 1824. It may be added that about the same time there seems to have been a breach between the northerns and the Leinster men.

The same pathetic story of poor, untrained men trying to manufacture a political organization for themselves was unfolded at the trial of Richard Jones, charged with being a member of an illegal society in 1840. The society, known as the United Irish Sons of Freedom and Sons of the Shamrock was also called the Ribbon Society. It had branches in England and Scotland and various Irish countries and an elaborate time-consuming constitution. According to the attorney-general, its primary object was 'to spread the connection of the society and increase the number of its members . . . there being no contemplation of any direct proceedings of a seditious nature . . . though there were many expressions in its correspondence indicative of no satisfaction with the existing state of things'. In fact the 'friendship' money seems to have been spent on official expenses, feeing counsel and attorneys for 'friends prosecuted on account of friendship', and assisting persons to fly the country. As in the twenties the membership of the society was working class, with a sprinkling of small shopkeepers, and there were frequent wrangles over the behaviour of officials, charges of selling information being bandied about.[2]

[1] P. Roe to ——, 4 Apr. 1822 (*A report of the trial of Michael Keenan*, 1822). Keenan was arrested, charged with belonging to an illegal society and sentenced to seven years' transportation (*Report of the trial of Edward Browne and others*, 1822).
[2] *Report of the trial . . . on 23, 24, 25, 29 June 1840 of Richard Jones*, H.L., 1840 (241), xiv.

# 3

# ADMINISTRATIVE REORGANIZATION,
## 1801–30

During the early nineteenth century the Irish administration was inhibited by several factors from embarking on large-scale schemes of reform. The dulling pressure of daily routine was intensified in Ireland by the important part played by patronage and the continuous recurrence of disturbance.[1] Up to about 1820 the outlook of ministers and officials was coloured by the war and the post-war depression and cabinets were composed of men who were resolutely opposed to change in any form, or who conceived the defence of the existing order to be their primary duty. Moreover in respect to Irish affairs there was a division of power which was bound to undermine responsibility and liable to cause confusion. Two members of the cabinet supervised Irish affairs, the prime minister who corresponded with the viceroy on general policy, and the home secretary who was kept informed on Irish matters by the chief secretary, and who gave a final decision on major issues. And as the treasury stretched its tentacles through administrative life, the lords of the treasury, or the chancellor of the exchequer, began to have a say in the many matters in which financial considerations were involved. In Ireland the viceroy and the chief secretary formed a, sometimes uneasy, partnership. Theoretically the former was the superior, but the secretary was not only in charge of his own department (which was analogous to the home office in London) but also represented the Irish government in the house of commons. This meant that he could claim to be consulted on any subject which might be debated in the house and on patronage matters which might influence the attitude of

[1] Shortly after becoming home secretary Peel contrasted the work of his department 'where it frequently happens that no day passes without a letter to the secretary of state' with the burdensome duties of the chief secretary (Peel to Goulburn, 26 Dec. 1822, Add. MS. 40328).

Irish M.P.s to the government. It is to the credit of human nature in politics that the viceroy and the chief secretary often formed a harmonious team. Admittedly the absence of the latter from Dublin for about six months in the year helped; also, while the chief secretary was usually a young politician beginning his ministerial life, the viceroy was frequently a middle-aged nobleman at the apex of his career. And luckily several of the strongest and most intelligent chief secretaries were coupled with acquiescent lords-lieutenant. When however there were political or personal differences relations could be strained. Shortly after the union Hardwicke, the lord-lieutenant, was greatly irritated by the slackness of Nepean, the chief secretary, who loitered in London, blundered in Dublin, neglected his work, 'failed to take a liberal view of any subject, dwelt on trifles', and finally without resigning his Irish office accepted a seat on the admiralty board.[1] His successor Vansittart also failed to give satisfaction, for he did not back up the viceroy with sufficient vigour in his struggle with Foster, the Irish chancellor of the exchequer, who, taking advantage of the novel conditions created by the union and his own position, was making a bold attempt to become 'the efficient minister of Ireland'. This attempt to destroy the predominance of the viceroy and chief secretary in the Irish administration was soon checked. After a sharp struggle, in which Redesdale, the Irish chancellor, one of Foster's most persevering opponents, manipulated the procedure of the house of lords to hold up Irish finance bills, Foster, finding he would have to submit legislation in advance to the lord-lieutenant, resigned.[2] Returning to the relationship between lords-lieutenant and chief secretaries, Goulburn and Wellesley who represented opposing views of the catholic question were rather uneasily coupled together as part of the balancing policy on which the Liverpool administration depended. Anglesey and Stanley, who took office together at the end of 1830, rapidly evolved divergent Irish policies, and the consequent strain was not lessened by Stanley's admission to the cabinet, even though the lord-lieutenant was assured that Stanley remained subordinate to him in Ireland.[3] As for Eliot and De Grey who held office together during Peel's second administration, they were utterly and vocally antipathetic in temper and outlook.[4]

[1] Hardwicke to York, 8 Feb. 1802 (Add. MS. 35701).
[2] Redesdale to Vansittart, 24 May, 17, 20 June 1805 (Add. MS. 31330); Redesdale to C. Long, 7 Nov. 1804 (Chatham Papers, 330).
[3] Grey to Anglesey, 13 June 1831; Holland to Anglesey, 29 June 1831 (Plas Newydd MSS.).
[4] Sixty years later, Balfour, referring to the system as 'that practical paradox', compared the relationship between viceroy and chief secretary to that of a constitutional sovereign with his prime minister (Balfour to Dudley, 15 Aug. 1905, C. Petrie, *Walter Long and his times* (1936), pp. 95–7).

Even at its best the system was clumsy and Pelham, just after the union, proposed that most of the powers and patronage of the 'local administration' in Ireland should be transferred to the home secretary, the lord-lieutenant being left responsible merely for co-ordinating and directing the policing of the country. Naturally the 'local administration' reacted vigorously, both the lord-lieutenant and the chief secretary writing long counter-memoranda justifying their own official existence. The former contended that in the unsettled state of Ireland, a viceroy with 'contracted and enfeebled powers' could not soothe party animosities and maintain the authority of the crown. The latter argued that it would be impossible for the home secretary, if a peer, to handle Irish business in the commons, and that an under-secretary would not carry enough weight with the Irish country gentlemen. On receiving these remonstrances Addington's cabinet laid aside Pelham's proposal and no further attempt was made to remodel the Irish administration on carefully considered principles.[1] A little while later indeed, Hardwicke, who was a busy viceroy, concluded that the chief secretary was superfluous, and forty years later, Eliot, then chief secretary, exasperated by his position, argued that the lord-lieutenant, 'supposing him to be an able man', could manage Ireland with the help of an under-secretary, Irish parliamentary business being left to the home secretary.[2]

The evil of divided responsibility—almost inevitably leading to weakness and loss of initiative—was increased by frequent changes of personnel. Between 1801 and 1830 there were eight prime ministers, eight home secretaries, eight viceroys and fifteen chief secretaries. As a result it was sometimes felt that the 'permanent' officials, the under-secretary, and the law officers, exercised an overgrown and pernicious influence, forming, as Spring Rice eloquently expressed it, 'a small knot of men, powerful with the arts of counteraction and conversant with official details of business, active and energetic in mischief but from want of sympathy and common interest with the mass of the people (Lord Norbury would read this "the people of the mass") incapable of doing good'.[3] But their importance was probably exaggerated. Admittedly Gregory (under-secretary from 1812 to 1831) and Saurin (attorney-general from 1807 to 1822) were determined upholders of the protestant ascendancy. But while they may have strengthened the convictions of superiors who agreed with them, there is no evidence that they managed

[1] *Diary and correspondence of Lord Colchester* (1861), i. 278, 303–19, 321–30.
[2] Hardwicke to Yorke, 8 Feb. 1802 and Eliot to Peel, 7 May 1844 (Add. MS. 35701 and C. S. Parker, *Sir Robert Peel*, iii, 111).
[3] Spring Rice to Col. Shaw, 29 Nov. 1826 (Add. MS. 37304).

to convert a viceroy or chief secretary. In any case they were to some extent counterbalanced by liberal officials such as Plunket or Bushe. Saurin was dismissed abruptly by Wellesley, and Gregory, whose duties as he himself said were largely those of 'a thief taker', when a policy to which he was opposed was adopted, was snubbed and reminded 'that when he has stated his objection he has gone to the very verge of his duty, and that nothing then remains for him but to execute his orders or *tenues vanescere in auras*'.[1]

Only for a short period in the three decades immediately following the union did it appear as if an era of bold reform was about to begin in Ireland. This was when the whigs came into office in 1806. Fox considered that Ireland was 'the country to which the application of liberal principles and what I will call *our* system of policy is most required', and he pressed vigorously for the promotion of liberals in church and state, arguing that if one could not be impartial it was better 'to risk offending those attached to the old system than our real friends'.[2] The new government was anxious to conciliate the catholics, reform the establishment, remodel the tithe system, arrange for the payment of the catholic clergy by the state, introduce compulsory vaccination and provide for scientific instruction at Maynooth.[3] But this liberal programme was unrealized. Grenville's ministry lasted barely a year, and much of its energy was consumed by the general election of 1806 and in trying to prevent its catholic allies pressing their claims with unreasonable vehemence. Finally its efforts to produce a palliative for the catholics led to its dismissal, and no administration from 1807 until 1830, when the whigs after their long exile returned to power, attempted to carry out a comprehensive programme of reforms for Ireland.

What the whigs' successors regarded as the main problems to be dealt with in Ireland can be gathered from a memorandum drawn up in the early days of Portland's administration. The construction of a planned system of fortifications was to be undertaken immediately, steps were to to be taken to render Maynooth less suspect and to increase the 'respectability' of the clergy of the establishment, and the tithe question, a subject of 'great delicacy', was to be examined, 'for if nothing can be done

[1] Gregory to Peel, 12 Apr. 1813, Leveson-Gower to Singleton, 28 Feb. 1830 (Add. MS. 40196, Leveson-Gower letter-books). Gregory noticed after Wellesley had been for weeks in Dublin that he had never had a private conversation with him. He concluded that the viceroy wanted his resignation and resolved not to be provoked into offering it (Gregory to Peel, 2 Feb. 1822, Add. MS. 40334).

[2] Fox to Belford, 13 Apr. 1806 (*Correspondence of C. Fox*, iv. 133). Fox to Grattan, 17 Mar. 1804 (*Life and Times of Henry Grattan*, v. 243).

[3] *Fortescue MSS.*, viii. 97-8, 120-1, 128-32, 175-7, 224, 486-8.

respecting it, it is better to be able to say that the subject has been thoroughly considered'. Finally a vigorous police force, in the larger cities directly controlled by the executive government, was to be formed, since the lamentable condition of many areas was thought to be due to the absence of an efficient police.[1] Peel, when chief secretary (for the comparatively long period of six years, 1812–18) was particularly impressed by this last point, the necessity of strengthening the forces of law and order, and in 1814 he set up the Peace Preservation Force, detachments of which could be stationed in disturbed districts to reinforce the inefficient county constabularies, appointed by the grand juries. He also began the appointment of stipendiary magistrates, who, combining judicial and executive functions, supplemented and stimulated the justices of the peace.[2]

Gifted with administrative ability and eager to root out official abuses, Peel was prevented by a strong distrust of the unconventional from initiating a comprehensive and original Irish policy.[3] Orthodox British economic theory, which was steadily exerting increasing influence in political circles, continually dwelt on the value of unhampered individual effort, and the danger that government intervention might prove ineffectual or even upset the harmonious and productive working of economic forces. And, in spite of the differences between Ireland and Great Britain, Peel and his colleagues tended on the whole to apply these principles when dealing with Irish problems. After more than fifteen years' experience of Irish affairs, Peel explained that, though he was quite ready 'to give the fullest consideration to any measures which may be suggested for promoting the employment and improving the condition of the people of Ireland,' he had 'too much experience of proposals made for effecting these objects through the direct intervention of the executive government and by the application of public money not to feel very strongly the policy of strict inquiry and mature deliberation before such proposals be adopted'. When the quick if injudicious Anglesey sent him schemes prepared by the Society for the Improvement of Ireland, he coldly pointed out that 'this erroneous society' had over-

[1] Memorandum drawn up as basis for communication with A. Wellesley (Add. MS. 38359).

[2] H. R. Addison in *Recollections of an Irish police magistrate* which is based on the career of T. P. Vokes, gives a lively picture of the adventures of an energetic and resourceful stipendiary stationed in disturbed areas.

[3] During his period as chief secretary Peel, with typical thoroughness—and possibly with a rather over-optimistic trust in printed sources—employed Shaw Mason, the well-known Irish topographer, to collect for him a carefully planned library of books relating to Ireland (see N. D. Palmer, 'Sir Robert Peel's "Select Irish library"' in *IHS*, vi. 101–13).

looked the legislation which embodied its proposals. When Anglesey suggested that the government should assist Irish economic development by guaranteeing the owners of 'manufacturing establishments' against malicious damage and by subsidizing the construction of roads and canals, Peel replied that grants for public works discouraged individual effort, and that it would be most inadvisable for the state to relieve business men of their insurance costs and local districts of their duty to pay compensation for outrage.[1] On another occasion when, while still chief secretary, he was approached by a deputation of Dublin merchants with the request that the government should employ 5,000 men in removing the snow which was blocking the streets, he told them 'he was heartily glad they were punished for their want of exertion or that of the parishes'.[2] Goulburn, Peel's *alter ego* took a similar line in 1826 when a fever epidemic was raging in Dublin. Though it was said that the epidemic was largely due to under-nourishment, he refused to arrange for the distribution of bread, on the ground that it would undermine voluntary local efforts by encouraging the opinion that the government would provide for everything. But to show that this decision was based on principle and not on indifference to human suffering, he advanced money for emergency hospital accommodation.[3]

Nevertheless stark necessity on several occasions compelled the government to come to the rescue of large masses of the Irish poor. In 1817 £30,000 was advanced in small sums to supplement local subscriptions for the relief of the peasantry in areas where the potato crop had failed.[4] Five years later, in 1822, when there was a widespread failure of the potato crop, the government acted, as Peel put it, with a disregard for financial calculation and the strict rules of economics. There was not a general shortage of food, but the peasantry who relied on their potato plots had no purchasing power. The government solution was to provide employment by encouraging public works (generally road-making) on a large scale. £50,000 was voted for road-building under the direction of an engineer appointed by the lord-lieutenant. The lord-lieutenant was also empowered to make advances on the security of the county rates for the immediate undertaking of works sanctioned by the grand juries, and to subsidize local committees which were endeavouring to provide employment. In nine counties local committees were formed to collect subscriptions and set the poor to work, and a central committee was

[1] Peel to Anglesey, 26 July, 14 Aug. 1828; Anglesey to Peel, 27 July 1828 (Add. MS. 40334).
[2] Peel to Sir C. Flint, 1813 (C. S. Parker, *Sir Robert Peel*, (1891), i. 119–20).
[3] Goulburn to Peel, 11 Oct. 1826 (H.O. 100/216).
[4] Peel to Sidmouth, 21 July 1817 (C. S. Parker, *Sir Robert Peel*, pp. 244–5).

appointed by the lord-lieutenant, consisting of the under-secretary, an ex-county court judge, a well-known banker and a couple of military men, to supervise and subsidize these local committees. This central committee dispersed during a few months grants amounting to over £65,000, and formulated the basic principles on which it thought relief should be administered. Necessity alone, it insisted, could justify 'artificial interference with the regular order of Providence and society'. If it was imperative for the government to intervene, then it should be careful to give relief only by providing employment, to regard the employment of the poor not the value of the work undertaken as being of primary importance, and to pay low wages so as not to interfere with the ordinary demand for labour. One of these precepts was vigorously violated by Nimmo, the energetic Scotsman who was appointed by the lord-lieutenant 'Engineer for the west'. Misunderstanding the government's intentions, he embarked on work less calculated to relieve immediate distress than 'to promote what appeared to him great national improvements'. Thus, the chief secretary grumbled, he created the expectation that the government intended to spend large sums on works which ought to have been undertaken by the counties.[2] Nimmo, however, persisted, secured further grants and worked steadily for ten years improving communications in the west of Ireland.

Only one economic question was tackled with some spirit. When early in 1822 very serious agrarian trouble in the south forced the government to decide to renew the insurrection act, Liverpool pointed out to the lord-lieutenant that they must be prepared to face searching parliamentary criticism of their Irish policy. And since they believed that 'the disturbed state of the south of Ireland does not originate in what may be called political or even religious grievances but in circumstances connected with the complicated relation of society and property', they ought to outflank their critics by dealing with the tithe question. Liverpool himself was ready to consider measures for leasing tithe or for its commutation. And referring to the abolition of tithe on potatoes, he remarked that rarely could, 'so formidable a reason be stated for a qualification of the strict right of property'. However all the government managed to achieve during the session of 1822 was the enactment

---

[1] See reports of central relief committee to lord-lieutenant, 16 May, 13, 22 June, 1 July 1822; printed list of grants made by committee; report from central committee in Cork for relief of poor; R. Griffith to Wellesley, 8 June 1822; R. Wilcocks to ——, 15 June 1822 (H.O. 100/204, 205); *Parl. Deb.* 2 series, vii. c. 1125; *Correspondence and accounts relating to the different occasions on which measures were taken for the relief of the people suffering from scarcity in Ireland* (H.C. 1846 (734), xxxvii).

[2] Goulburn to Wellesley, 23 May 1823 (Add. MS. 37301); *Gent. Mag.*, 1832, i. 370.

of an ineffective measure for facilitating the leasing of tithes.[1] Shortly after it was passed, a meeting of Irish peers and M.P.s at the Thatched House tavern demanded a commutation of tithe. According to the chief secretary this stimulated the agitation. Threatening notices which had previously mentioned tithe, taxes and rent, began to refer exclusively to tithe, and in some areas the clergy in their efforts to defend their rights did not receive 'very active and cordial support from the gentry'.[2]

In the following session (1823) the government pushed through a major measure, the tithe composition act, which provided machinery by which an incumbent and his parishioners could substitute a fixed money payment, settled by arbitrators, for the tithe due from the parish. This measure was attacked from one quarter as conferring unfair financial and legal advantages on the clergy, and from another as 'an invasion and subversion of the ecclesiastical establishment'. An indignant petition backed by the primate and signed by the archbishops of Dublin and Tuam and fourteen bishops was addressed to the government, expostulating against the bill on the grounds that hitherto 'the estate of the church had been incorporated and identified with the mass of private property'. The government's tithe proposals menaced the unity of the churches of England and Ireland, and were that destroyed, 'there would be no security for the preservation of the identity in doctrine, worship, discipline and government which in both countries were the bulwark of the reformed catholic faith'. But Laurence, the archbishop of Cashel, perhaps the ablest man on the bench, refused to associate himself with this protest and even published a pamphlet in support of the bill, and Liverpool explained to the primate that if the government had not brought forward a tithe scheme the house of commons would certainly have appointed a committee, on which 'the predominant power . . . must have been that of the landowners of Ireland who would all from self-interest and some from faction have endeavoured to impose upon the clergy the most disadvantageous terms'.[3]

The tithe composition act of 1823 was rather slow in taking effect, for it dealt with a number of conflicting interests, and its complicated clauses baffled many parish meetings in spite of the fact that the government distributed widely an explanation of its provisions in non-technical terms. Nevertheless by 1832 over half the parishes in Ireland had

[1] Liverpool to Wellesley, 22 Mar. 1822 (Add. MS. 37298). For the ineffectual nature of the act see *Parl. Deb.* 2 series, vii. 1029 ff.

[2] *DEP*, 13 June, 22 Aug. 1822, Goulburn to Peel, 7 Sept. 1822 (H.O. 100/206).

[3] *Parl. Deb.*, 2 series, ix. 602, 1434; *A letter to the Rt. Hon. J. Abercromby* (1824); G. Beresford to Liverpool, 15 Feb. 1823, petition of the Irish bishops, Liverpool to G. Beresford, 24 Feb. 1823 (Add. MS. 37300).

adopted a composition and if the burden of the tithe was not lessened the element of uncertainty and other causes of parochial friction were removed.[1] The government also seems to have thought of introducing a permissive measure to enable landlords to pay the tithe of their occupying tenants, adding of course a proportionate sum to the rent. But the cabinet was afraid to add to the Irish landlords' burdens and was daunted by the degree of sub-letting in Ireland.[2]

To cope with this latter problem Sir Henry Parnell, a leading Irish whig suggested in 1825, and the government introduced during the following session, a drastic sub-letting act which subjected to severe legal disabilities a tenant sub-letting without his landlord's permission. The act was bitterly attacked, particularly by O'Connell, and vehemently defended. From the evidence collected by the Devon commission, it seems to have been completely ineffectual. Another prominent Irish whig, Sir John Newport, was mainly responsible for the only other major measure dealing with Irish agrarian conditions enacted in the three decades after the union, the tenements' recovery act of 1816.[3] It enabled a landlord to evict a defaulting tenant—whose rent was under £50 per annum—by taking proceedings in the assistant barrister's court.[4] Contemporary progressive opinion aimed at cheapening and hastening the working of the law. In this instance an apparent improvement in legal procedure was definitely to the disadvantage of the Irish peasant.[5]

If the government was exceedingly cautious in dealing with Irish economic problems, it was afraid to tackle educational questions. Education on sound lines it was widely believed would prove a potent panacea for Ireland, and in 1812 a strong commission having surveyed the existing educational facilities, recommended the creation of a government department which would build up a system of elementary education by providing schools, books and trained teachers. Religion, the commission recognized, would form an awkward element in any scheme for general education. But it felt it had devised a system, which 'by keeping clear of all interference with particular religious tenets may induce the whole to receive its benefits'. A selection of scriptural excerpts acceptable to all parties was to be used for general instruction, and the clergy

---

[1] First report from the select committee on tithes in Ireland, p. 167, H.C. 1831–2 (177), xxi.

[2] Wellesley to Liverpool, 18 Sept. 1822; Liverpool to Wellesley, 9 Dec. 1822 (Add. MSS. 37299, 37300).

[3] 7 Geo. IV. c. 29; Comm. Journ., lxxxi. 147; Parl. Deb., new series, xii. 521, 1151 ff., xviii. 573; 3 series i. 386 ff., x. 570 ff.

[4] The assistant barristers which were instituted in 1796 were roughly equivalent to the modern county court judge.

[5] 56 Geo. III, c. 88 (amended by 1 Geo. IV. c. 41); Parl. Deb., 2 series, xxxii. 1025.

of the different denominations were to give religious teaching to the children of their own creed. The apprehensions, immediately voiced, of leading protestants as to the way the catholics would work the scheme, must have warned the government that it was toying with an issue which might arouse violent sectarian strife. And in May 1813 after consultations between Peel, Liverpool, and Sidmouth, it was decided to do nothing.[1]

The government, shrinking from the difficulties inherent in a large-scaled comprehensive plan, limited itself to subsidizing lavishly private organizations which aimed at providing elementary education for the Irish poor. Generous parliamentary grants had been made to the Charter schools from the middle of the eighteenth century, and to the schools of the Society for the Discountenancing of Vice from the beginning of the nineteenth. In 1815 the Kildare Place Society (or the Society for Promoting Education in Ireland) began to receive a parliamentary grant which rose to £25,000 per annum. The first two bodies were definitely protestant and their schools were protestantizing in tendency. The Kildare Place Society, in many respects an intelligently managed organization,[2] was theoretically non-denominational, but it was under protestant control and regulations regarding the reading of the Bible met with the disapproval of the catholic clergy. In response to catholic pressure in 1824 a commission, and in 1825 a select committee of the house of commons, investigated the Irish education question,[3] and both these bodies recommended that the grants which were being made should be abolished or greatly reduced and that the government should encourage a system on the lines laid down in the 1812 report. By the time the tories left office steps were already being taken to implement the negative part of this programme—the withdrawal of the grants.

In the summer of 1829 the simultaneous existence of political agitation, religious excitement, and agrarian trouble, forced the cabinet to consider whether emancipation should not be followed by a programme of positive measures for the improvement of Ireland, and in July 1829 a cabinet committee of three, Peel, Goulburn and Fitzgerald was

[1] L. Foster to Peel, 27 Mar. 1813 (Add. MS. 40223); Bishop of Meath to Peel, April 1813 (Add. MSS. 40226); Peel to Richmond, May 1813 (Richmond papers) and Whitworth to Sidmouth, 19 Feb. 1814 (H.O. 100/177).

[2] For a eulogistic sketch of its work see H. K. Moore, *An unwritten chapter in the history of education* (1904).

[3] For Irish educational organization at the beginning of the nineteenth century see *Report of the select committee on foundation schools and education in Ireland*, H.C. 1837-8 (701), pp. 3-12; vii. 347-56; *First report of the commissioners on education in Ireland*, H.C. 1825 (400), xii; *Report from the select committee on education in Ireland reports*, H.C. 1828 (341), iv.

appointed to decide what Irish measures should be prepared for the coming session.[1] The prime minister, Wellington, was characteristically chiefly concerned with the preservation of order. And he was anxious to see the Irish absentees attending to their estates instead of 'balling and brawling' in London. 'We want in Ireland', he wrote, 'the influence of manners as well as law. How are we to get the former in the absence of nearly all the landed proprietors is more than I can tell?' With his customary shrewd, narrow grasp of essentials, he realized that a failure of the potato crop was bound to deprive the labourers, who were rewarded for their services by potato plots, of their wages, 'so that even if the markets of Ireland were filled with food for sale these unfortunate peasants could buy nothing as they have nothing'. He wondered whether it would be possible to forbid by legislation the payment of rent in labour and to enforce the money payment of wages. But, completely pre-occupied by his multifarious activities, he did not press this suggestion on his colleagues.[2]

Peel, after the wearisome debates on emancipation were over, was anxious in spite of his instinctive caution to produce 'a series of measures for the permanent civilization of Ireland'. His policy was the same as Salisbury's half a century later—twenty years of resolute government— except that Peel believed half that span would suffice. The enforcement of the law he considered a necessary preliminary to the success of any scheme for the amelioration of Ireland, and he eagerly advocated the formation of a unified police force, carefully chosen, well disciplined, and animated by a keen *esprit de corps* (which he was sure would be stimulated by the 'peltings' it would have to endure). Possibly indeed, the police could, he thought, be granted small plots of land and so form 'a trustworthy yeomanry'. He also considered the appointment of additional stipendiary magistrates, though the cabinet were afraid that this might weaken the resident gentry's interest in local affairs. Peel at this time also examined three other major projects for the improvement of Ireland, local government reform, an Irish poor law and a new system of primary education. The chief secretary warned Peel that while the protestants would be excited if the Kildare Place Society was abandoned, nothing would satisfy the catholic clergy. Peel himself was well aware of the difficulties surrounding an Irish poor law. When he turned to local government reform, which for him connoted checks on local extravagance, he doubted if it were possible for a board in Dublin to supervise effectually county finance, and he was afraid to take steps which might

---

[1] Ellenborough, *A political diary 1828–1830* (1881), ii. 64.
[2] Wellington, *Despatches . . . 1819–32*, i. 241; iii. 387, 390–1, 437; vii. 112.

weaken the Irish gentry's connection with local affairs or expose them to the attacks of 'provincial demagogues'. Still he was willing that the right to initiate expenditure on local works should be transferred to baronial sessions composed of J.P.s and the higher ratepayers, and he was prepared to consider Fitzgerald's suggestion that trained engineers should be appointed by the government to supervise the works carried on by the grand juries.[1] Leveson-Gower, the chief secretary, who was volatile and quick-witted, while agreeing with Peel that police reform was urgently needed, suggested that the government should tackle the question of tolls, 'a glorious field for the exertion of mischief-makers throughout Ireland', and consider amending the vestry act[2] which permitted a protestant minority to tax their catholic fellow-parishioners, 'for what I should term a religious luxury'.[3]

In fact the conservatives were very slowly evolving the programme the whigs were to implement during the thirties. By the beginning of the session 1830 they had prepared several Irish bills of some significance. A couple were measures tightening up the administration of justice by regulating the sheriff's duties and the compilation of jury lists. More important were a constabulary bill which placed the recruitment of the police throughout Ireland in the lord-lieutenant's hands and gave him a wide measure of control over the movements of the force, and a drainage bill which enabled the lord-lieutenant to set up local commissions with wide powers to carry out extensive drainage schemes. Both these bills were attacked on the ground that they dangerously enlarged the powers of the state. The police bill it was said trenched on the rights of the country gentry, the drainage bill was described by a hostile critic as 'an invention of commissioners, surveyors, clerks and officers at high salaries'.[4]

In retrospect the most important work accomplished by the government in the thirty years or so following the union was the unobtrusive reorganization and rationalization of the Irish civil service which had developed unsystematically from the middle ages, its anomalies, redundancies and sinecures being regarded not only as inevitable, but as positively useful when it came to procuring parliamentary support. In

[1] Peel to Leveson-Gower, 30 July, 19 Dec. 1829, 9 Jan. 1830 (Add. MS. 40337); A rough draft of Memorandum by Peel, 23 Oct. 1830 (Add. MS. 40309); Peel to Leveson-Gower, 23 Nov. 1829 (H.O. 100/249); Fitzgerald to Peel, 20 Nov. 1829 (Add. MS. 40323).

[2] 6 Geo. IV. c. 72.

[3] Leveson-Gower to Peel, 22 Nov., 4, 6, 11 Dec. 1829 (Leveson-Gower letter books).

[4] *Parl. Deb.*, 2 series, xxiii. 1111–14; M. Fitzgerald to Wellington (Wellington, *Despatches . . . 1819–32*, vii. 63–4). All four bills failed to pass.

England towards the close of the eighteenth century the spirit of reform and the exigencies of war alike stimulated a desire for efficiency and economy, and Abbot, the first chief secretary appointed after the union, was deliberately selected as an experienced administrative reformer, and during his short stay reorganized the revenue board and the board of stamps.[1] To the alarm of the old school of Irish officials, an overhaul of the public offices was begun, the first to attract attention being the board of works, which had been spending public money on doing up houses for people of influence, and whose accounts were singled out by a parliamentary committee as 'a curious specimen of official dexterity in manufacturing a statement by means of which a true return may be rendered as to figures, while the result must lead to a false conclusion'.[2] During the early years of the nineteenth century the attack upon the shortcomings of the Irish administrative machine was led by three bodies, the house of commons' committee upon public offices, another committee upon sinecures, and a statutory commission to inquire into the emoluments of the civil officers in Ireland, appointed in 1804 with the object of discovering 'a more effectual and less expensive mode of managing the revenue'. Following the reports of these bodies a number of offices which had no duties attached or the duties of which were discharged by deputies, were abolished, and salary scales, fixed hours of work, and promotion by merit were introduced into the revenue department. At the end of the war there was a determined economy drive which resulted in an effort initiated by the treasury to reduce the cost of managing every department. A number of Irish departments were in the next ten years or so amalgamated with their British equivalents. In 1816 the public revenues of Great Britain and Ireland were consolidated under the management of the United Kingdom treasury.[3] This meant that the establishment of the Irish exchequer was drastically reduced (with the abolition of several impressive semi-sinecures),[4] and during the next few years the boards of customs and excise of the two countries were fused and put under treasury supervision (1823), the boards of stamps were united (1827), the duties of the commissioners of public accounts in Ireland were transferred to the British commissioners (1832), the auditing of army accounts in Ireland was transferred to the secretary at war, and the auditing of barrack and commissariat accounts

---

[1] *Diary and correspondence of Lord Colchester*, i, ch. xiv.

[2] Hardwicke to Yorke, 6 Nov. 1801, 18 Jan. 1802 (Add. MS. 35701); *Seventh Rep. from the committee on public expenditure*, p. 160, H.C. 1810 (370), ii. 530.

[3] 56 Geo. III, c. 98.

[5] As Hardwicke had suggested in 1803 (Hardwicke to Pelham, 8 Feb. 1803, H.O. 100/112).

to the ordnance office in London.[1] In 1831 the two post offices were amalgamated, and in the same year the staff of the chief secretary's office was reduced and the viceregal court deprived of some of its glory and jobbery by a scaling down of salaries and the abolition of a host of decorative appendages—such as the Battle Axe guards. As ancient offices were annihilated new departments were being founded—the commissioners of endowed schools (1813), the national education board (1831), the Irish branch of the poor law commission (1838) and the revived Irish board of works (1831) which swallowed three or four existing boards.[2] But the new departments were severely functional in their organization, and managed with remarkably small staffs.

Moreover, before the middle of the century a quiet, persuasive, powerful force strongly favouring the new administrative standards was making itself felt throughout Irish official life. It is apparent from what has been said that the treasury controlled several Irish departments, but in addition there was another salutary check on inefficiency and jobbery. Annually the estimate for every Irish department had to be submitted to the treasury, and every increase justified by an explanatory minute.[3] This control was on the whole salutary, but it is doubtful whether the treasury tradition, with its emphasis on economy and caution, developed in the bracing atmosphere of a prosperous commercial country where the government was expected to restrict itself to a very limited range of functions, was altogether suitable for Ireland where bold state intervention might have had fruitful results.

Simultaneously, efforts were made to put local government on a sounder footing. In this sphere the difference of standards between the Irish and English landed classes is clearly perceptible. The English gentry, performing as justices of the peace executive and judicial functions,

---

[1] 57 Geo. III, c. 84 together with 3 Geo. IV, c. 56 and 6 and 7 Will. IV, c. 83; *Reports of the committees of inquiry into public offices* . . ., pp. 316–17, H.C. 1854 (1715), xxvii. 348–9.

[2] There were vested in the board of works the powers of the commissioners for the assistance of trade and manufactures, the commission for the issue of money constituted by the 57 Geo. III, c. 34, the directors of inland navigation, and the powers of the last-named body when sitting with additional members for dealing with Irish fisheries.

[3] *Report from the select committee on miscellaneous expenditure* . . ., pp. 190, 294, 407, H.C. 1847–8 (543), xviii, pp. 254, 388, 471. For instance after 1830 treasury sanction was required for tenders for the clothing of convicts and printing of school textbooks, and the fees of revising barristers, and the treasury was asking the Irish law officers to explain the cost of state prosecutions, drafting a scheme for accounting in Irish boroughs, supervising the revenue staff for Ireland and controlling the clerks' salaries in the chief secretary's office (S.P.O. iv, 16, 10, H.O. 100/245; Spring Rice to Morpeth, 15 Sept. 1838, Monteagle papers).

made a valuable contribution to English life. Their Irish equivalents' work as grand jurors and J.P.s was often sharply and deservedly criticized. The grand juries were shockingly careless when dealing with road contracts, and the excellent Irish communications system resulted largely from the facilities afforded by road-building for using public money primarily for private purposes.[1] As for the justices of the peace, the continuous references in government correspondence to the failings of the unpaid magistracy suggest at least that their standards of public duty fluctuated. Inertia and partiality were the faults of which the Irish justices of the peace were usually accused, 'a want of sustained activity, of mutual confidence and co-operation, a constant desire to find fault with the government and to complain instead of bestirring themselves'.[2] And there seems little doubt that in the early decades of the century, owing to the varied composition and indefinite boundaries of the Irish landowning class, some highly unsuitable persons were placed on the bench. Many J.P.s, it was said, were upper servants who were making money by rack-renting. In one disturbed area (County Cork) it was reported that the bench was 'filled by brewsters, maltsters, distillers and blackrent landlords'. And since the first three categories would not offend their customers, and the tenants of the last were the rioters, it was difficult to restore order.[3] Occasionally, too, a scandalous individual case cropped up. For instance there was the magistrate in Tipperary who used his powers under the insurrection act to clap into gaol for three days a half-pay officer with whom he had a public altercation on a private matter, there was the magistrate in Donegal who appeared from his correspondence with the government to be almost illiterate, and there was the Galway J.P. who was removed from the commission when it was discovered he was working an illicit still, though 'it went to Lord Manners's heart to punish a man who had such good cock shooting'.[4]

From the beginning of the century attempts were made to improve matters. Ponsonby when chancellor began a revision of the magistracy,

---

[1] T. Rice, *An inquiry into the effects of the Irish grand jury laws* . . . (1815); H. L. Lindsay, *The present state of the Irish grand jury law* . . . (1837); T. Jephson, 1814 (Add. MS. 40238).

[2] Peel to Leveson-Gower, 29 Nov. 1829 (Add. MS. 40332).

[3] Thomas Flynn to Peel, 30 Apr. 1816 (Add. MS. 40253); R. L. Conner to W. Gregory, 22 Aug. 1814 (S.C.P. 41).

[4] *First report from the select committee on the state of Ireland*, pp. 86–90, H.C. 1825 (129), viii; *Minutes of evidence taken before the select committee of the house of lords appointed to inquire into the state of Ireland*, pp. 94–5, H.C. 1825 (181), ix; Leveson-Gower to the lord chancellor, 29 Dec. 1829; Peel to Leveson-Gower (Leveson-Gower letter books and Add. MS. 40337).

asking peers and privy councillors to make confidential reports on persons they considered unsuitable to be placed in the commission of the peace, but he only managed to deal with two counties before he fell from office.[1] Ten years later Saurin tried to discourage Peel from making a fresh attempt to purify the magistracy by pointing out that it would be 'very wounding to the feelings of many loyal good men' to lose their seats on the bench, and that in any case though some low and unqualified men might be dismissed, much of the mischief was caused by those 'whose rank and fortune makes it impossible to leave them out of the commission of the peace'.[2] Nevertheless in 1822 Peel, in a 'desultory letter rather than a dispatch', suggested that an attempt might be made to improve the magistracy, possibly by a complete revision of the commission, though he admitted that if only fit persons were allowed to stay on the bench some areas would be bereft of justices of the peace.[3] The lord-lieutenant, Wellesley, accepted his suggestion; in the autumn of 1822 a general revision of the magistracy began; and within a few months Wellesley noticed that 'the mere knowledge of the existence of a plan of revision has produced salutary consequences by increasing the diligence, accuracy and careful conduct of the magistrates'.[4] About the same time a check was imposed on individual failings and eccentricities by the development under strong government pressure of the practice of holding petty sessions. This substituted for 'the arbitrary and irregular discharge of his functions by a single magistrate'[5] the joint action of at least two and probably more J.P.s acting publicly, and, after the petty Sessions act of 1827, sitting at fixed times and places with a clerk, records and fixed fees.

When in the year after Waterloo, English M.P.s learned, that in Ireland 'the sheriff appoints the grand jury, that the grand jury tax the country, that the sheriff has considerable influence at elections and that the sheriff is openly appointed on the recommendation of the member supporting the government', they were 'startled not a little'; and Liverpool, the discomfited chief secretary reported, could scarcely credit

[1] *Parl. Deb.*, xxix. 489. Peel remarked ten years later: 'I wish I could think the peers and privy councillors of Ireland so much above the influence of party feelings and personal hostilities as to entitle their representations on such a subject to implicit credit' (Peel to Wellesley, 12 Apr. 1822. Add. MS. 37298).

[2] Saurin to Peel, 4 Apr. 1816 (Add. MS. 40211).

[3] Peel to Wellesley, 12 Apr. 1822; Wellesley to Peel, 27 Sept. 1822 (Add. MSS. 37298, 37299).

[4] Wellesley to Peel, 29 Jan. 1823 (H.O. 100/208).

[5] J. O'Donoghue, *The Summary jurisdiction of magistrates in Ireland* (1855). R. Nunn and J. E. Walsh, *The powers and duties of the justice of the peace in Ireland* (1841), pp. 14 ff.

that such practices could exist. So Peel, rather reluctantly, for it meant surrendering 'a most convenient patronage', directed that henceforth the sheriffs should be chosen in the English fashion from short lists submitted by the assize judges.[1]

In the following year (1817) the first of a series of acts introducing a system of checks and balances into local government was passed. It provided that the justices of the peace should investigate and express their opinion on presentments for local works before they were considered by the grand jury. Many difficulties in drafting had to be surmounted, before a satisfactory scheme was evolved (the act of 1817 being repealed and remodelled in the following year), but by the act of 1836 which set up baronial committees of justices of the peace and ratepayers to examine and sanction presentments before they were voted by the grand jury and which provided an elaborate procedure for preparing plans and estimates, corruption was largely eliminated from county administration. In addition several acts fixed the salaries and qualifications of the county officials, and a striking departure was made in 1833 when it was decided that county surveyors should be appointed after a competitive examination conducted by a board of engineers of a high professional standing. These examiners at first found their novel task highly disagreeable, one unsuccessful candidate, a well-known agitator, threatening to have his examination discussed in parliament.[2]

---

[1] C. S. Parker, *Sir Robert Peel*, i, 221–2.
[2] *Papers on the reorganization of the civil service*, pp. 69–71, H.C. 1854–5 (1870), xx. 71–3, and J. T. Burgoyne to Littleton, 9 June 1834 (Teddesley MSS.).

# 4

# THE STRUGGLE FOR CATHOLIC
# EMANCIPATION

The struggle for catholic emancipation had entered on its last and longest lap before the nineteenth century began. From about 1770 onwards both in Great Britain and Ireland the catholic disabilities were being swept away, and after the great Irish relief act of 1793 the only remaining serious legal disabilities were exclusion from parliament and from the higher posts in the service of the state and the law. Admittedly these exceptions were important, humiliating and embittering, particularly to those catholics who from position or ability might expect a successful career in politics or at the bar. But it was tantalizingly obvious that one more major relief measure and they would be abolished. Pitt had of course intended to combine catholic emancipation with the union. He saw the problem as a mathematical one. The catholics were a majority in Ireland, therefore the protestants could not risk granting them civic equality. In the United Kingdom they would be a minority and the protestants could safely afford to be generous. The whole problem was a novel and tiresome one to British politicians who at the close of the eighteenth century were not highly conscious of theological issues. It was nearly a century since British politics had been greatly influenced by religious disputes and the prevalent atmosphere was characterized by a distaste, amounting at times to contempt, for complex and elaborate doctrinal systems. But in the last decade of the century the government almost simultaneously found that the Irish question, in which religious dissensions played a vital part, demanded sustained attention, and became aware that catholics might be considered a conservative and therefore anti-French force. Burke, with his accustomed ardour emphasized that the Irish catholics were the natural allies of a government fighting for order and decency against the revolution. And from about 1793 a much less impressive figure, Sir James Hipplesley, was urging the government to make a fresh approach to the catholic church. Hipplesley with his multifarious activities, plotting a revolution in South America, acting as a paymaster in India, managing the queen of Wurtemberg's finances, planning a settlement in Darien, meddling in ecclesiastical politics and trying to get an Irish peerage, was rather an asinine personage, but he knew Rome well, and as a self-educated and self-confident expert on catholic canon law he held a distinctive if not distinguished position in English public life. Writing to Windham in the early nineties, Hipplesley emphasized that the catholics were quite different from the other dissenters whose 'clerical democracy' accorded so ill with the British constitution; the pope, he explained, was a liberal-minded prince, anxious to conciliate the protestant powers, and he deluged members of the government (particularly Castlereagh when chief secretary) with letters and memoranda in which he advocated an amicable arrangement with the catholic church, by which, in return for emancipation, the state would acquire supervisory rights especially over ecclesiastical appointments and correspondence with Rome.[1]

Pitt and Castlereagh intended that the union should be accompanied not only by emancipation but by an augmentation of the incomes of the poorer incumbents of the establishment, by an increase in the *regium donum* (the government grant to the presbyterian church), and by 'a provision for the Roman catholic clergy that would render them more respectable in station, more independent of their flocks and more disposed to the support of the established government'.[2] A crude critic might describe these measures as an attempt to cope with theological differences by borough-mongering methods. A sensitive churchman might be shocked by their aggressive Erastianism. Perhaps the fairest view would be that the government's proposals reflect the attitude of conservative statesmen, who, terrified by the revolution, were striving to identify every influential element in the community with the existing order.

Only one of these subsidiary measures accompanied the union; the presbyterians were offered and readily accepted an increase in the *regium donum*, which radicals complained jeopardized the independence of their church. Admittedly presbyterian discontent ebbed during the early

[1] For Hipplesley's activities see his numerous letters in Add. MSS. 37848, 37849, and Hipplesley to Liverpool, 31 Aug., 2 Sept. 1814 (Add. MS. 38259).
[2] Grenville to Buckingham, 2 Feb. 1801 (*Courts and cabinets of George III*), iii. 128-9, *Memoirs of Lord Castlereagh*, iii. 161 ff.

nineteenth century, but this was probably due to economic and political changes which affected the outlook of Ulster protestants rather than to a crude financial cause; and on the one occasion when the government attempted to use the *regium donum* as a lever it was ignominiously defeated.[1]

The catholic bishops seemed willing in 1799 to accept a provision for their clergy and to allow the state a veto on episcopal appointments,[2] but the king's prejudices (which he shared with a substantial section of his subjects), together with his naïve conception of his constitutional obligations, inspired him to offer a stubborn resistance to Pitt's proposals before he had even seen them. Pitt resigned, and though Castlereagh, who remained in office, urged Addington 'to secure the government additional principles of authority and connection'[3] by arranging a provision for the catholic clergy, the government procrastinated until it was replaced by Pitt, who at the beginning of his second administration talked about granting salaries to the catholic clergy, but took no steps in the matter.[4] Meanwhile, apparently, the catholic clergy had come to the conclusion, that 'it would be discreditable to them and unbecoming their character if they embraced a separate exclusive advantage for themselves while the catholic laity were smarting under the disappointment of their expectations'.[5]

An immediate effect of the union was the transformation of the catholic question into a major issue in British politics. Year after year a petition from Ireland forced the subject on parliament's attention, and kept alive a Brobdingnagian debate, which, stretching over quarter a century, fills hundreds of columns of *Hansard*. Two cabinets collapsed when attempting to cope with the catholics' claims, every political crisis was complicated and embittered by dissensions between parliamentary 'protestants' and 'catholics', and finally the settlement of the question split the tory party at one of the most critical moments in its history.

From the intellectual point of view the great debate is disappointing. For one thing the two sides were too unevenly matched. Pitt, Fox, Canning, Castlereagh, Brougham, Grattan, Plunket and Wellesley were pitted against Peel, Abbot, Duigenan, Bankes, Eldon and Yorke. For another, within a few years nearly all the arguments had been exhausted and members were reduced to frequently apologizing for the repetitive-

---

[1] *Belfast Monthly Magazine*, ix. 195, 266; *Drennan letters*, pp. 303, 310, 325, 356, 364. And 55–6.
[2] Rev. A. Cogan, *The diocese of Meath . . .* (1870), iii. 230–1.
[3] Castlereagh to Addington, 21 July 1801 (*Castlereagh correspondence*, iv, 233).
[4] E. Nepean to King, 25 Oct., 18 Nov. 1804 (H.O. 100/123).
[5] *Parl. Deb.*, xxvi, 154–5.

ness of their orations. Lastly if the issue had clearly been between the confessional and the liberal state the discussion would have been one of fundamental significance. But the existence and legal status of the Scottish presbyterians, the annual indemnity acts, the considerable concessions, including the franchise already made to the catholics, blurred the issue, and reduced it to a question of degree and expediency. The debates resolved themselves into a prolonged controversy over whether, judged by their past behaviour and present principles, the catholics might be assumed to be loyal subjects, and the less easily dramatized problem of how the catholic community with its far-reaching claims on issues such as education could adapt itself to the life of a protestant state was scarcely appreciated let alone thrashed out.

The opponents of catholic emancipation argued that in spiritual matters catholics owed obedience to the pope, and since in practice it was impossible to separate spiritual and temporal concerns, their allegiance was divided. But while English speakers on the subject relied mainly on history and theology, some of the Irish opponents of the catholics' claims explained in concrete terms what they were convinced would be the consequences of permitting the catholics to return members to parliament. The catholic church in Ireland, they argued, was a great *imperium in imperio* composed of an ambitious gentry, an intolerant and arrogant clergy, and a people disposed by poverty and superstition to be their tools. Now granting that 'it is of the nature of every great corporation to infuse a strong zeal into its members for the advancement of its interest and power', it was impossible that a catholic could remain satisfied to see 'every protestant institution rolling in wealth and splendour while his own are in poverty and distress'. A struggle for ascendancy was bound to follow. And Peel explained that therefore emancipation would mean violent election contests in Ireland between catholics and protestants, a distinct catholic party in the house, and an attack on the Irish church establishment.[1]

Early in his official career, Peel, the most impressive opponent of concession, was briefed by Saurin, the Irish attorney-general, an able lawyer and an ultra-protestant-ascendancy man. To Saurin, the main cause of Ireland's evils was the catholic church, with its priesthood full of *esprit de corps* and determined to restore their church to its ancient splendour, and its ignorant and fanatical laity, nurtured on hostility to 'the British settlers' or in other words the protestants. Ireland, Saurin believed, was bound to be either a protestant or a catholic state; it was

[1] Examples of the arguments used can be found in *Parl. Deb.*, xxxvi, 307-9, 2 series, iv. 1003, 1841, 2 series, xiii. 40.

absurd for the supporters of emancipation such as Grattan to argue that it could be both or neither. The whigs would be consistent only if they proposed 'to give up the established church to the Roman Catholic laity, and that the British settlers or in other words the protestants should withdraw or make terms as well as they could'. 'How', Saurin asked, 'could the wit of man furnish an argument by which the existence of an exclusive protestant establishment could be defended in a country in which the population was more than two to one catholic if the government of that country was as protestant as catholic.' The whig policy was fantastic, but if the government took a strong line, insisted on obedience to the best parliament on earth, and compelled the lawless by justice and education to be tractable, the agitation for emancipation would soon die down.[1]

While their parliamentary champions strove on their behalf the Irish catholics themselves were not idle, and in their long pilgrimage through the political wilderness they invented or improved many of the methods for putting pressure on parliament which were employed in other great nineteenth-century agitations. At first their proceedings were conventional, unexciting and ineffective. 'Paragraphs in the public prints, or sentences in letters or exclamations in drawing-rooms'[2] led in October 1804 to a committee of leading catholics assembling in Dublin to consider whether they should petition parliament.[3] Between then and February several meetings were held, anything up to thirty persons being present, including Lord Fingall, Sir Thomas French, Corbally of county Meath, who was said to have a rental of £12,000 a year, Scully the barrister, McKenna the pamphleteer, and a number of Dublin merchants, Ryan, O'Brien, and Randall McDonnell. Fingall both acted as chairman and kept in continuous touch with the government. A dignified, well-meaning man, he was landed by circumstances in an awkward and anomalous situation. By status and instinct a conservative, he found himself at the head of an agitation of the under-privileged. With a foot in each camp he endeavoured to make the catholics acquiesce in the government's wishes. At the same time he made clear to the government the difficulty of restraining the catholics. The increased wealth and consequence which many catholics had acquired in trade, he explained, made them resent their disabilities, particularly when the French, Spanish and Austrian services 'no longer afforded a wide field for the sons of Roman Catholic families'. Also, he pointed out, 'the mercantile influence among

---

[1] Saurin to Peel, 16 Mar. 1813, 23 Mar. 1815, 15, 19 Apr. 1816 (Add. MS. 40211).
[2] T. Wyse, *Historical sketch of the late Catholic association* (1829), i. 136–7.
[3] Proceedings of the Roman Catholic meeting, 27 Oct. 1804 (H.O. 100/99).

the Roman Catholics had increased so much of late that the weight formerly enjoyed by the nobility and gentry had much diminished'. Fingall spoke from experience, for at the second meeting of the committee he was compelled to withdraw his motion that catholic relief be left to parliament, and in addition sustained a severe rating from Keogh for his behaviour in 1792. At the third meeting he met with a fresh rebuff. For when he remarked that it was unnecessary to send a deputation to interview Pitt, since Lords Kenmare and Trimblestown were in England, the committee insisted that someone to represent the mercantile interest should be sent over.[1] Before deciding to petition, the committee tried to discover what Pitt's views were, and 'whatever tended to throw light on Mr. Pitt's intentions was sought for with avidity'.[2] The uncertainty did not last long, for Pitt with a cold sense of proportion (infuriating to the victims) decided that emancipation must be subordinated to other considerations. In the middle of November the viceroy was informed that Pitt would oppose emancipation if the question were raised under existing circumstances, and Hardwicke passed this on to Fingall. The catholics hesitated between persisting with their petition or merely issuing a statement of their case. At the beginning of December Fingall thought the petition would be dropped. On the 10th a committee of five to petition 'in moderate language and general terms' was formed, but on the 15th the full committee decided, in spite of two gentlemen from Cork and Kerry who were 'disposed to be violent', to postpone the consideration of the petition to February—and Fingall was confident that this meant a further postponement.[3] It should be added that Fingall's conviction that it was not yet seasonable to approach parliament was shared by Lord Hutchinson, a sincere friend to the catholics in touch with English opinion, who at the beginning of 1805 emphatically declared that the catholics must wait until the next reign; an immediate move would only strengthen opposition, for 'the king, the church, the old women and the mob are powerful enemies in England'.[4]

Nevertheless the impetus in favour of petitioning grew. Letters were circulated from Fox and Petty, who—Hardwicke was convinced solely with the aim of embarrassing the government—were pressing the catholics to dispatch their petition over.[5] Then about the middle of

[1] Hardwicke to Hawkesbury, 11, 26 Nov. 1804 (Add. MS. 35709).

[2] Catholic meeting, 17 Nov. 1804 (H.O. 100/99).

[3] Hawkesbury to Hardwicke, 15 Nov. 1804; Hardwicke to Hawkesbury, 18, 20, 26, 28 Nov. 1804 (Add. MS. 35709).

[4] Hutchinson to Donaghmore, Jan. 1805 (D. Plunket, *The life, letters and speeches of Lord Plunket* (1867), i. 289).

[5] Hardwicke to Hawkesbury, 10 Dec. 1804 (Add. MS. 35709).

January, the new chief secretary, Nepean, whose attitude to his duties was rather cavalierish, suddenly intervened in what his colleague and critic the viceroy pronounced to be a most tactless fashion. He requested Scully the catholic barrister to let him have a copy of the petition to show Pitt. After that it was useless for him to stress the inadvisability of petitioning, for the catholics jumped to the conclusion that Pitt wanted to get the petition into an acceptable shape.[1] Early in January Marsden, the under-secretary, an able civil servant, tried to effect a compromise. He had meetings with Randall McDonnell, whom he could 'get hold of by vanity', and induced him to suggest that the catholics should present their case to the lord-lieutenant for transmission. On this plan being submitted to Downing Street, Pitt and Hawkesbury agreed that it could be followed if the catholic case was 'drawn up in decent and respectful terms' and if the viceroy held out no expectations it would be supported by the government. At the end of January, MacDonnell put this 'middle course' before the catholic committee, arguing that the cause would be damaged if it became a party question in parliament. But he was unsuccessful. The catholics were impatient, their hopes had been raised by Nepean's behaviour, and there were, as Fingall explained to the government, too many men of active and mischievous disposition in their ranks for him to keep control; so at a meeting in the middle of February it was decided to petition.[2] And the ensuing discussions resulted in the first catholic defeat in the united parliament.

In spite of the fact that the whigs came into office at the beginning of 1806 the events of 1806–7 were merely a more rowdy repetition of those of 1804–5. Ryan, a Dublin man, having met Fox in England as a member of the 1805 deputation, wrote him in November 1805 asking for his opinion as to what course the catholics should pursue and for a good piece of government patronage for himself. Fox with typical lack of discretion replied to both requests in the same letter, begging the Irish catholics to refrain from embarrassing their friends by pressing their claims. The ministry, he declared, if pressed, would support emancipation, and as a result would almost certainly be defeated and thrown out of office. Ryan, anxious to oblige his distinguished correspondent, summoned a gathering of influential catholics to sanction a policy of acquiescence. His attempts to select a suitable group to speak for the

[1] Hardwicke to Hawkesbury, 20 Feb. 1805 (H.O. 100/128); Hardwicke to Yorke, 6 May 1805 (Add. MS. 35706).
[2] Marsden to lord-lieutenant, 17 Jan. 1805; Hardwicke to Hawkesbury, 28 Jan., 20 Feb. 1806; Fingall to Marsden, 30 Jan. 1805 (H.O. 100/128); Hardwicke to Hawkesbury, 20 Jan. 1805; Hawkesbury to Hardwicke, 26 Jan. 1805 (Add. MS. 35706).

Irish catholics, led to violent disputes between those summoned to the meetings and those who attended uninvited. In the end, after a series of meetings in Dublin, the catholics in the spring of 1806 decided to rely for a time on the Grenville ministry's goodwill. Within a few months, however, they began to show signs of impatience, and the whigs had to perform the tiresome task of simultaneously expressing sympathy and demanding restraint. Even before this fresh agitation began, the cabinet had come to the conclusion that nothing would be gained by raising the catholic question again in the near future in parliament; nevertheless the government felt something ought to be done for the catholics not 'as a price of forbearance' but as a measure of justice. This feeling as well as the wish to encourage recruiting inspired the cabinet to make the attempt to open further the commissioned ranks of the army to catholics which led to its disastrous clash with the king.[1]

But while the cabinet was attempting to manœuvre this concession past the king and parliament the catholics in Ireland began to move. After a deputation had interviewed the chief secretary and discovered that the Irish administration would have to consult the cabinet about concessions, and that in any case there was very little hope of a relief bill, a meeting attended by many country gentlemen and farmers appointed a committee of twenty-one to draw up a petition as 'a measure of precaution', Keogh vigorously urging that if it was presented to parliament their friends would be bound to support it. Fingall, Gormanston, Bellew and their associates, who had, as Fingall explained to the chief secretary, in the past 'manifested just moderation', stood aside for about a month, and then joined the Dublin catholic agitation. Bedford, the liberal lord-lieutenant, hoped for a time that three concessions, the abolition of all restrictions on promotion in the army, and the admission of catholics to corporations and the office of sheriff, might prevent the catholics presenting a petition for emancipation to parliament. And in the middle of February the chief secretary informed a catholic deputation that all military commissions would be opened to catholics. Bedford felt that during this period the government ought to abstain from interfering in any way in catholic politics, and he would not allow 'the wishes of the Irish government to be blended with Lord Ponsonby's efforts to dissuade the catholics from pushing their claims'. Grenville was less aloof. He openly avowed his disapprobation of the line the catholics were taking, and was responsible along with Howick (the future Lord Grey) for sending Ponsonby over to Ireland to put a brake on the agita-

[1] For the whigs' policy at this time see M. Roberts, *The whig party, 1807–12* (1939), ch, i.

tion. And his brother, the voluble Buckingham, begged Fingall 'to lead Irish opinion that has run wild to the steady, dignified situation in which the catholic body stood before that mischief'. Fingall replied that it was impossible for him to resist public opinion. In fact a few weeks earlier in the middle of February he had made two unsuccessful attempts to delay matters, but at the end of the month the catholics adopted a petition which was entrusted to Fingall to present to Grattan. This exciting burst of agitation closed with an anti-climax. After the dismissal of the Grenville ministry in March 1807, Grattan and the ex-ministers decided that it was inadvisable to present the petition. When this opinion was communicated to a catholic meeting in Dublin, Keogh was for deferring action, while others resented retreating. Daniel O'Connell, however, successfully intervened in the conciliatory role he was often to play during the next decade. He successfully suggested a dignified compromise—to leave the management of the petition to the committee.[1]

The fall of Grenville's ministry destroyed for twenty years the possibility that emancipation would be carried by the government, for Grenville's three successors, Portland, Percival and Liverpool were all opponents of the catholic claims. But as not only the whigs but many of the government's supporters, including, indeed, members of the cabinet, were in favour of emancipation, it always seemed possible that it would soon be forced through parliament, and until 1829 the catholics conducted a long political siege in which various tactical devices were employed to wear down the hostile majority. In 1810 the Irish catholics tried to increase the weight of their agitation by giving a representative character to their committee. This brought them up against the Convention act of 1793 which had been passed to prevent any assembly claiming to be representative competing with parliament, though the catholics tried to conform strictly to the letter of the law, or, as the lord-lieutenant put it, 'to infringe the law without becoming subject to its penalties'. Since the agitators were men of substance, and since lawyers took a prominent part on both sides, the contest though verbally stormy was

---

[1] For the events of 1806–7 see Plowden, *The history of Ireland, 1801–1810* (1811), ii. 286–542; *An accurate copy of the petition finally agreed to at a general meeting of the catholics of Ireland* . . . (1807); *A sketch of the speech of Mr John Keogh at a meeting of the catholics of Dublin* . . . *24 Jan. 1807* (1807); *Proceedings of a general meeting of the catholics held on 18 April 1807*; Report catholic meeting, 19 Apr. 1807; Bedford to Spencer, 8, 10, 11, 13, 17, 28 Feb. 1807 (H.O. 100/141); Bedford to Grenville, 7 Mar. 1807; Grenville to Bedford, Dec. 1806, 11 Mar. 1807; Elliot to Grenville, 18 Jan., 9, 10 Feb. 1807; Fingall to Grenville, 2 Mar. 1807; Fingall to Buckingham, 4 Mar. 1807; Buckingham to Fingall, 10 May 1807 (*Fortescue MSS.*, viii. 491–4; ix. 20–22, 31–3, 65–79).

conducted with extreme decorum. For instance the lord-lieutenant in ordering the dissolution of a catholic meeting in February 1811 emphasized that the magistrate should try to attain his objective by 'formal' arrests, and a police magistrate who attended a catholic meeting, reported that the chairman's conduct was 'exceedingly polite and respectful' and that he did all in his power to secure the magistrate a hearing.[1]

The outcome of a sensational series of events, including several trials, was that the catholics substituted for the representative committee a committee nominated by an aggregate meeting in Dublin, but time and energy were wasted, and bickering began again between the 'forward' party and the moderates, on whether Lord French had shown sufficient firmness when a meeting over which he was presiding was dissolved, on whether they should vote an address demanding the removal of the viceroy and the chief secretary, on Lord Fingall's intellectual adequacy, and on whether a petition should be sent over in the spring of 1811. And repeatedly O'Connell had to intervene as a robust mediator.[2]

The legal attacks launched by the government checked the development of new machinery for conducting the agitation, and compelled the *Dublin Evening Post*, the leading liberal newspaper to moderate its tone.[3] The end of the European war rendered obsolete the argument continually employed at catholic meetings, that it was absurd by refusing emancipation to weaken the country in the face of an enemy who dominated the continent, and the post-war agricultural depression must have left many Irish catholic gentlemen with little time or spirit for politics. Finally there was the veto controversy, which distracted and divided the catholic leaders.

The idea that the government should have a negative control over catholic episcopal appointments was, as has been mentioned, current at the time of the union. In 1808 it was revived by the catholics' friends in parliament who suggested that the removal of the disabilities should be accompanied by 'securities', which their advocates seem to have regarded partly as a protection against papal aggression, but mainly as a means of mollifying the opposition to emancipation.[4] Liberals as a rule

[1] Richmond to Ryder, 21 Feb., 1811 (S.P.O. iv. 16, 2); Paper dated 23 Dec. 1811 (S.P.O. iv. 13, 18).

[2] *DEP*, 7, 21 Feb., 16 Mar., 23, 25 Apr. 1811.

[3] For the government's attack on the *Dublin Evening Post* in 1813 see B. Inglis's 'The freedom of the press in Ireland, 1784–1842'.

[4] Schemes which attempted to combine emancipation with 'securities' were produced in 1813, 1821 and 1825. Each scheme provided that the catholics should be permitted to sit in parliament and hold civil and military offices, and set up boards of commissioners in Great Britain and Ireland, respectively. In the first two schemes the boards were to be composed of catholic bishops and catholic and protestant

were inclined to dismiss as archaic the idea that the catholics might form a disloyal or even disharmonious element in the community. But they admitted that in spiritual matters catholics were subject to a foreign superior, and that with the expansion of Napoleon's power the papacy might fall under French domination. In any case emancipation was well worth a few concessions. It was awkward but understandable that the parliamentary supporters of the catholics' claims were unlikely to comprehend the reaction of fervent catholics to their proposals. For the parliamentary liberals, who sincerely believed in toleration, were inclined to depreciate the political importance of theological issues and to dismiss the laboured deductions from catholic teaching produced by the anti-emancipationists as much ado over theological niceties. 'I avoid', Grattan once declared when urging the catholics' claims, 'the dungeon of theology, the mad house of casuistry, and the noisy tub of the sectarians, nor do I dwell on their bookish ignorance, nor on their vulgar turbulence.'[1] Moreover the catholics themselves were not unanimous regarding the extent to which a protestant government might be permitted to interfere in ecclesiastical matters. A section of the English catholics influenced by Gallicanism were prepared to make considerable concessions.[2] And as shall be seen the Irish catholics were violently riven by disputes on the question. As for the government it took surprisingly little interest in the matter. At the close of the Napoleonic wars there was close and continuous contact between the British government and the papacy.[3] But Castlereagh's negotiations with Consalvi related mainly to the European territorial settlement, and the question of a concordat, though discussed, was soon dropped. Occasionally the British government intimated to Rome its wishes on ecclesiastical appointments—at least once more or less at the request of an Irish candidate. And at the end of 1814 Liverpool wrote to the pope expressing 'without reserve' his sentiments on the behaviour of the Irish catholic

laymen, and were to sanction the appointment of catholic bishops and deans and inspect ecclesiastical documents received from Rome in their respective areas. In the third scheme the commissions were to be composed of catholic bishops and the British commission was merely to examine documents from Rome (*Parl. Deb.*, xxvi. 271–95, and House of Commons papers, 1825, iii, 441–60; 1821, i).

[1] *Parl. Deb.*, xviii. 29.
[2] For the attitude of the English catholics during these years see W. J. Amherst, *The history of catholic emancipation*, 2 vols (1886); and B. Ward, *The eve of catholic emancipation*, 3 vols (1911–12).
[3] For the British government's relations with the papacy at this time see Ellis, *Castlereagh and Consalvi* (1942); C. K. Webster, *The foreign policy of Castlereagh, 1815–1822* (1925), pp. 112–13; Castlereagh to Consalvi, 30 Apr., 11 Dec. 1817; Cooke to Castlereagh, 18 Mar. 1815 (F.O. 43/10, 43/8); Wellington, *Despatches . . . 1819–32*, i. 24–35, 472–3.

leaders and on the restoration of the Jesuit order, and he was highly gratified that 'the answer of His Holiness evinces at least that he has received my representations with temper'.[1] In short, the British government during the early nineteenth century, though ready to accept the assistance of Rome in dealing with unruly subjects, shrank from formal and complex schemes for regulating its relations with the catholic church.

In Ireland the suggestion that the government should be given a measure of control over catholic episcopal appointments aroused alarm and anger. The veto, it was said, would twine the faith round the sceptre of an anti-catholic king. It would encourage the tendency of bishops to keep in close contact with the Castle. Priests would be turned into spies and informers. The type of priest likely to become a bishop if the veto was granted, it was said, was the man 'of family connections, of electioneering interest, a keen sportsman, or gambler, a jolly toper, a hearty fellow who sings a good song', and the people would be exasperated by seeing the man they preferred 'cast off, reprobated, scouted and dishonoured by the government'. The veto, according to Dromgoole, was only the thin edge of the wedge. In time, he suggested, the *congé d'élire* would be introduced, and priests would be compelled to seek permission to perform their duties from Orange magistrates. All confidence between priests and people would be destroyed and the Irish catholics turned into protestants or rebels. Nationalism immensely stimulated the theological objections to the veto. Clinch, addressing a catholic meeting, declared 'catholics of Ireland—you are bound to assume the national voice'. And O'Connell, a strenuous opponent of the veto, declared that he loved his religion because it was catholic and because it was Irish.[2]

Nevertheless there were Irish catholics who supported the veto, arguing that the whole matter was far less significant than its opponents asserted. As early as 1808, a group of catholic gentlemen in Louth asked the archbishop of Armagh whether the Irish bishops regarded a crown negative as inadmissible. The primate cautiously replied that such a concession was not forbidden by doctrine or canon law but that it might be dangerous. In the same year, Lord Fingall declared at a catholic meeting that he wished some means could be discovered for quieting the fears of their protestant fellow countrymen, and five years later Sheil, next to

---

[1] Liverpool to Castlereagh, 10 Nov. 1814 (Add. MS. 38260).
[2] *Royal veto . . . By An Irish catholic clergyman* (1809), p. 12; *DEP* 24 Dec. 1810; 18 May 1813; *Proceedings of the catholic committee* (1811); *Answer to Lord Fingall's letter*, by A. Fingalian (1810), pp. 25, 37; J. T. O'Flaherty, *Thoughts upon the catholic question and the veto* (1810), p. 17.

O'Connell the most stirring orator in the catholic camp, said that 'concession would disarm prejudice'—adding that he had compassion for the prejudices of everyone but especially of Englishmen.[1]

Up to 1812 with parliament adamant, the idea of conceding a veto received little support in Ireland. The Irish bishops twice, in guarded terms, condemned the proposal, and it was unconditional emancipation which was demanded by the great series of county meetings held during the summer of 1812. But when in 1813 the house of commons approved of the principle of emancipation with securities, the Irish catholics had to take careful stock of the situation. The catholic board moved cautiously, leaving the proposed ecclesiastical regulations to be dealt with by the episcopate. And Dr. Dromgoole, a narrow-minded amateur theologian, failed to get the board to declare that it would not consent to government interference in episcopal appointments. Almost immediately afterwards the Irish bishops announced that the securities were incompatible with the discipline of their church and that they could not assent to the bill without incurring the sin of schism. The catholic board backed up the prelates. Nevertheless there was a substantial minority, who in the words of Sir Edward Bellew, 'did not want the catholic laity to sacrifice their political interests to a nice point of ecclesiastical discipline'.[2] By the end of the year it was noticed that some of those who had been willing to concede securities were ceasing to attend the meetings of the board, and down in Cork dissensions between vetoist and anti-vetoist reached such a pitch that a new county catholic board was appointed to which the old board refused to surrender its books.[3]

In the spring of 1814 Quarantotti, secretary of the Propaganda, issued a rescript declaring that catholics should receive with gratitude the bill of 1813. It was easy to challenge the validity of this rescript on the grounds that Quarantotti was a subordinate official acting *ultra vires*, and the Irish bishops promptly declared it was not binding. It was awkward however for the anti-vetoists, when in the following year a letter from Cardinal Litta was published, stating that the pope was willing when a see was vacant to permit the electors to submit a list of candidates to the government, which might delete names before transmitting it to Rome. The catholic bishops promptly declared that to grant such powers to the crown would seriously injure the church in Ireland, and a great meeting of the laity in Dublin drew up a strongly worded remonstrance

---

[1] *DEP*, 5 Nov. 1808, 9 Dec. 1813; Paper dated 6 Jan. 1808 (H.O. 100/147).
[2] *The address of the Irish Roman catholic prelates . . .* (1810); *The address of the Irish Roman catholic prelates . . .* (1811); *DEP* 4, 18, 20, 25 May, 1 June 1813.
[3] *DEP*, 16 Nov., 4 Dec. 1813.

addressed to the pope, warning him, 'with less ceremony than is usual', that if this pernicious measure was persevered in it would lead to 'such a state of distrust and dissatisfaction as might end in the dissolution of that confidential connection in spiritual concerns' which subsisted between Ireland and the Holy See.[1]

The veto controversy slowly petered out, for the British government did not move and parliament steadily refused to consider emancipation. Moreover during the discussion there were constant references to a method of episcopal appointment which might conciliate those who feared foreign influence and at the same time strengthen the power and prestige of the Irish catholic clergy. In 1810 the catholic committee and in 1816 the catholic bishops pronounced firmly in favour of domestic nomination, that is to say that when an Irish diocese was vacant its chapter or clergy might transmit a short list of names to Rome. And this arrangement was authorized by a papal rescript in 1829.[2]

The veto dispute, by aggravating the differences which were bound to exist in so large and heterogeneous a body as the Irish catholics, during some years dissipated their energies and crippled their organizations. It would be an over-simplification to suggest that the line of division was purely social, for if the bulk of the catholics were anti-vetoist there were country gentlemen and lawyers on both sides. Nevertheless persons of property having a natural predilection for authority were more ready to make concessions, and Charles O'Conor, an erudite and excitable advocate of the veto, drew a parallel between contemporary conditions and the period of Rinuccini's mission, when 'the rude ignorance of the mass of our people placed them beyond the knowledge of that *genuine* catholicity which distinguishes the gentry of Ireland beyond those of any catholic country in Europe'.[3] On the other hand the strongly anti-vetoist *Dublin Evening Post* enunciated that the landed interest was usually to be found opposed to freedom and that 'the son of the merchant was for the most part more liberally educated than the son of the squire'.[4] In the summer of 1814 the Catholic Board, which had been weakened towards the close of the previous year by the secession of those who were willing to consider concessions, was proclaimed by the government, and when at the end of 1814 an attempt was made to reconstruct a catholic organization, Lord Fingall stood aloof.[5] When at

---

[1] *DEP*, 5, 28 May 1814, 14 Oct. 1815; *Thoughts on the veto*, by A Roman catholic (1817), p. 20.

[2] *DEP*, 17 May 1814, 29 Apr. 1816, 21 Nov. 1829.

[3] C. O'Conor, *An historical address on the calamities occasioned by foreign influence in the nomination of bishops to Irish sees* (1812), pp. 115, 127, 199.

[5] *DEP*, 25 May 1813.          [5] *DEP*, 29 Nov., 1 Dec. 1814.

the beginning of the new year (1815) a small meeting was held at his house to try and agree on the terms of a petition, Sheil produced a draft which used 'in his opinion the language of earnest prayer from which every intemperate phrase had been carefully avoided'. O'Connell said it was far too flattering to England, and a few days later when the anti-vetoists by nine votes to three secured the insertion of the word 'unqualified' before 'emancipation', the minority broke off negotations.[1] In the following year (1816) two petitions were produced, one by the Catholic Association founded by the anti-vetoists in 1815, the other by a group led by Lord Trimblestown, an *émigré* from France. The former demanded unrestricted emancipation, the latter expressed a willingness to submit to regulations, not incompatible with the catholic religion, which might render emancipation 'satisfactory and unobjectionable' to all classes of His Majesty's subjects.[2] The Catholic Association was not a success and though O'Connell tried to reconstruct the board in 1817 it ceased to meet at the end of the year, apparently being unwilling to assume responsibility for the debts of Father Hayes, who had been sent to Rome with the remonstrance drawn up in 1815 and whose efforts to express the Irish anti-vetoist viewpoint had led to his deportation from the papal states.[3] Some years later in 1821 the disputes on the veto flamed up again when Plunket carried through the commons a bill based on that of 1813. O'Connell was enraged by 'the vetoistical matter' contained in the scheme, and said that it would mean that in the future the catholic bishop would be selected by the county patron, but a meeting of the catholics of Dublin, which he does not seem to have attended, thanked the M.P.s who supported the bill.[4] O'Connell himself was not however completely intransigent, for at the end of the year he was trying with the help of Dr Michael Blake, a leading Dublin parish priest, to evolve a compromise; in the event of a vacancy either three names should be submitted by the electors to the government of which at least one should be submitted to Rome, or the government, should be given an opportunity of making a specific charge of disloyalty against a bishop elect which would be examined by the catholic archbishops of Ireland.[5]

As the reverberations of the discussion on Plunket's bill were dying away the rifts in the catholic ranks began to close. In 1821 and 1822 the two sections of the catholic body united to present addresses to George IV and the marquess of Wellesley on their arrival in Ireland. And in

[1] *DEP*, 12, 19 Jan. 1815.
[2] *Comm. Journ.*, lxxi. 311, 367–8.
[3] *DEP*, 19 Mar. 1816, 13 Jan., 5, 19 Feb., 25 Apr., 12 July 1818.
[4] *DEP*, 29 Mar., 10 Apr. 1821.
[5] *Correspondence between Daniel O'Connell and the Rev. Dr Blake* (1822).

1822 O'Connell issued a lengthy manifesto calling for the formation of a new catholic board to petition for emancipation and to devise a scheme for domestic nomination. Since dealing with the latter question would have involved beginning with a thorny subject, it was perhaps as well that it was not until a year later after conversations between O'Connell and Sheil that the Catholic Association was founded.[1] Its beginnings were not promising for it had difficulties over collecting subscriptions and a quorum. But the hard core of keen members amongst which O'Connell was prominent persisted, and by appointing committees to inquire into tithe and the Dublin corporation the association showed that it meant business. The peers and country gentlemen who had been members of the Catholic Board were asked to attend, and at the end of 1824, after two years of well-advertised if unproductive activity, the association took an important decision—a committee was appointed to study organization and tactics. O'Connell was chairman, and the report, which was obviously his handiwork, advocated a striking innovation in political technique, the creation of a large fighting fund by numerous small, regular subscriptions. The scheme in fact was based on the now well-known fact that the payment of a subscription often encourages people to identify themselves with the organization demanding it. O'Connell fixed the ambitious target of £50,000 per annum for catholic political and religious purposes, and though this was never reached, the catholic rent, with a minimum subscription of a farthing a week, local collectors, and frequently published subscription lists, was a potent force inspiring the movement with a sense of unity and power. To pay the rent, it was said, the poor gave up tobacco and snuff, pig dealers put aside the luck penny and even attorneys taxed themselves at the rate of a penny per case. As O'Connell said, the rent 'gave a unity of sentiment to the people from one end of Ireland to the other'. It also provided the catholics with a well-filled war chest, the association at the end of 1825 having funds amounting to £15,000 invested in government securities.[2]

The association's leaders successfully surmounted two hurdles which had seriously hampered the catholic cause in the past, dissensions in their own ranks and legal obstacles imposed by the government. The conservatives in the association did not cause much trouble, though they were so scared by some of O'Connell's phrases in the celebrated

---

[1] T. Wyse, *Historical sketch of the late Catholic Association*, i. 192–200.

[2] *DEP*, 15 June, 27 May 1824, 3 May, 29 Nov. 1825, 6 Dec. 1827. In 1813 a plan had been proposed for meeting the expenses of the catholic agitators by parochial collections throughout Ireland, each householder paying 10d. (Printed paper, 20 Oct. 1813, Add. MS. 40233).

report of 1824 that they tried to prevent it being printed, and they managed to defeat a proposal to hold an inquiry into the police.[1] Extremists of the other sort were more of a problem, for an ill-timed display of radicalism might have divided the association, frightened moderates and supplied material to the opponents of the catholic cause. Naturally parliamentary reform was mentioned from time to time, Lawless arguing that it was a necessary preliminary to emancipation. But it was not until August 1828 that the association decided to support 'constitutional' (Lawless attempted unsuccessfully to substitute 'radical') reform, including an extension of the franchise and shorter parliaments.[2] At the beginning of 1826 several members wanted the association to pass a strong vote of thanks to the Friends of Ireland in the United States (a body which included two well-known figures of the '98 epoch, Sampson and McNevin) for an address to the people of Ireland, which not only fervently supported emancipation but advocated the repeal of the union and the abolition of the establishment. The moderates were nervous and wanted the vote toned down but when a reckless supporter of the original motion declared that Ireland would be more prosperous without the British connection, O'Connell quickly intervened and backed by an overwhelming majority, swept the whole matter off the board by carrying 'the previous question'.[3]

The most dangerous threat to the association's unity arose in 1825, when Burdett attempted to weaken the opposition to the catholic claims by adding to his emancipation bill measures for disfranchising the Irish forty-shilling freeholders and granting a state provision to the Irish catholic clergy. O'Connell, who was in London at the beginning of the parliamentary session as a member of an Irish catholic deputation and as a witness before select committees, agreed to both these measures. He considered that the existing system which enfranchised hundreds of nominal freeholders merely played into the hands of the great county interests, and he thought that state salaries would contribute to the comfort of the clergy without diminishing their independence. Lawless and George Ensor, a well-known protestant radical, rushed into print as violent opponents of both measures. The obvious remedy, they pointed out, for the defects of the electoral system was the ballot, and a state provision for the clergy would ultimately subject them to government influence and deprive them of the respect of their flock. On the other hand Sheil exclaimed, 'We are sinking, and at the very moment we are going down we wisely determine never to enter the harbour by a

---

[1] *DEP*, 19 Feb., 27 July 1824.      [2] *DEP*, 7 Aug. 1828.
[3] DEP, 13, 26 Sept. 1825, 28 Jan. 1826.

tack'; to which Richard O'Gorman retorted that it was the forty-shilling freeholders not Sheil who were to be sacrificed. Signs of a schism appeared but the rejection of Burdett's emancipation bill by the lords called a halt to the parliamentary proceedings on the subsidiary measures. Irish catholics were on the whole hostile to the 'wings', but they were grateful to O'Connell, who during the latter half of 1825 not only displayed vigorous dexterity in defending his views but took the lead in devising daring and skilful counter-measures against the government's legal attack on the association. Moreover, seeing he was in a minority on a question which, owing to the attitude of the upper house, was for the moment an academic one, with a shrewd sense of political proportion, while refusing to acknowledge he was in the wrong, he agreed that for the future they should demand unqualified emancipation. And the association at the beginning of 1826, after rejecting a motion of Lawless's strongly condemning the wings, agreed, with some reserves on the part of the conservatives such as Gormanston and Sir Edward Bellew, that it was undesirable to introduce into parliament any measure tending to restrict the elective franchise or interfere with the independence of the catholic church in Ireland.[1]

As for the government it watched the association's development with baffled apprehension. The lord-lieutenant, Wellesley, complained that it was a self-elected, permanent council continually supervising and criticizing the administration of justice, that the collection of the rent 'would produce all the evil consequences of moral compulsion and force', that if the agitation continued he was afraid there would be a 'sudden ebullition of fanaticism' in some areas, and he even mentioned the possibility of a rebellion.[2] The chief secretary, Goulburn, was equally alarmed. In October 1824 he observed that the association was growing rapidly, and it was cold comfort to hear that several of its upper-class members, such as Lord Fingall and Sir Edward Bellew, disapproved of its activities, for 'they did not conceal that they would not dare to set themselves against it'. The whole country was being organized, party feeling was being inflamed, and Goulburn foresaw that at the next general election the peasantry would be encouraged to vote against their landlords.[3] The English and Irish law officers who were consulted at the end of 1825 agreed that it was impossible to proceed against the society under 33 George III c. 29 (the Irish convention act) or 60 George III c. 6 (an

---

[1] *DEP*, 19 Mar., 30 June, 3, 10, 12, 25 Nov., 15 Dec. 1825, 17 Jan. 1826; *MR*, 22, 28 Apr. 1825; John Lawless, *An address to the catholics of Ireland* (1825).
[2] Wellesley to Peel, 10, 14 Dec. 1824 (Add. MS. 37303).
[3] Goulburn to Peel, 7 Oct. 1824 (Add MS. 40330).

act for more effectually preventing seditious meetings). Only the Irish chancellor, whose opinion on legal points carried surprisingly little weight, was in favour of proceeding against the association under the convention act.[1] Peel's summary of the situation was clear and his conclusions pessimistic. They might denounce the association in parliament but it would beat them in a 'scolding match', if they waited for it to commit a breach of the law it would steadily grow stronger, and if they tried to check it by legislation it could easily take evasive action and bring the government into contempt.[2] Nevertheless in 1825 the government carried an act relating to unlawful societies in Ireland, which it thought would put a stop to the activities of the association. The results were ridiculous. When the bill was passing, a catholic committee was set up to see whether, 'without any violation of the law', a permanent body could be formed to manage catholic affairs, and O'Connell promised that as soon as parliament rose he would produce his scheme for a new catholic association.[3] In the event their successful efforts to evade the act's intentions strengthened the catholics' organization. The new catholic association, with aims carefully limited to those for which a permanent body could legally be formed, met frequently. Then every six months a catholic association was convened for fourteen days, and in addition there were aggregate meetings in Dublin and provincial gatherings in other centres. The government alarmed by 'the organization of physical strength and . . . well aware how difficult it is to limit the application of that strength to the ostensible object which in the first place it may exclusively profess to attain', considered taking further steps. When the catholics at the beginning of 1826 began to plan their first fourteen-day convention, the cabinet advised the lord-lieutenant to wait and see if the meeting, then proceeding, contravened the act of 1825, and not to proclaim it, lest the catholics by studiously avoiding in consequence of the proclamation those acts which they might otherwise have committed and which would have been the chief and most satisfactory proofs of its illegality, put the government in a public quandary.[4] In December 1826 the Irish law officers, though prepared to prosecute the Catholic Association, emphasized that the result would be uncertain since

---

[1] Goulburn to Peel, 10 Nov. 1824, enclosing opinion of Irish law officers, English law officers' opinion, 20 Dec. 1824, Manners to Wellesley, 2 Dec. 1824 (Add. MS. 37303).

[2] Peel to Goulburn, 6 Nov. 1824 (Add. MS. 40330).

[3] *DEP*, 30 June 1825. A dismal legal opinion explaining how the catholics could evade the act was given to Peel in 1828 by the Irish attorney-general (R. Peel, *Memoirs* (1856), i. 46–54).

[4] Peel to Wellesley, 3, 5 Jan. 1826 (Add. MS. 37304; H.O. 100/106).

the question would have to be left to a jury. In February 1827, just ten days before Lord Liverpool's collapse, the English law officers decided that the new catholic association was an illegal body, and at the end of 1828 Peel directed the lord-lieutenant to ascertain 'from the best authority what is the exact relation in which the law of the land and the catholic association stand towards each other'. The Irish law officers at once replied that the association had assumed a representative character thereby violating the convention act, but added that of course the issue would have to be decided by a jury.[1]

The government during this period was handicapped by its efforts to stand aloof from Irish party strife and avoid identifying itself with the protestant conservative party. In 1821 Lord Wellesley, a strong supporter of catholic emancipation, and the most outstanding figure since Cornwallis to hold the post, was appointed viceroy. His appointment reflected the gradual liberalization of Liverpool's ministry, and having liberal views and an autocratic temperament he thoroughly enjoyed the role of a conciliatory, detached, impartial administrator.[2] Besides being ready to fight the catholic association he was also anxious to squash another manifestation of extreme Irish politico-religious opinion. In July 1822 he tried to persuade the Orange leaders in Dublin to abstain from decorating the statue of William III in College Green, a focus for political rowdiness, and in November to avoid a breach of the peace he prevented the statue being decorated. As a result there was a vulgar and violent demonstration in the theatre against the lord-lieutenant, and the Irish administration (in fact the lord-lieutenant and Plunket, the newly appointed attorney-general) by charging the rioters with treason gave a grand jury selected by an Orange high sheriff, an excuse for rejecting the bills.[3] Two years later when the Irish government showed its impartiality by simultaneously prosecuting O'Connell for making a seditious speech and Sir Harcourt Lees, an eccentric clerical baronet, for publishing inflammatory articles, the Dublin grand jury displayed its animosity to the administration by rejecting both bills.[4] In spite of these setbacks Wellesley managed to inflict a severe check on his conservative opponents. In 1822 he pressed the government to extend to Ireland the British act of 1799 against illegal societies so that he could

[1] Opinion of the law officers, 4 Dec. 1826, 7 Feb. 1827 (Add. MS. 37304); Peel to Anglesey, 23 Oct., 17 Nov. 1828 (Add. MS. 40326).

[2] For an exposition of Wellesley's Irish policy see a long memorandum printed in *The letters of George IV*, iii. 297–312.

[3] W. C. Plunket to Wellesley, Jan. 1825 (Add. MS. 37303); Peel to Wellesley, 10 Mar. 1823 (Add. MS. 40324).

[4] *SNL*, 3, 6 Jan. 1825.

employ it against the Orange order. But his colleagues were averse to this course, which they felt would be both ineffectual and likely to stir up bad feeling.[1] But in 1825 probably as a result of Plunket's persistence, the act against the Catholic Association contained a clause which rendered societies composed of branches corresponding with one another illegal.[2] And about this time Peel, writing to Gregory, the Irish under-secretary, like himself a strong opponent of emancipation, emphasized that 'in this age of *liberal* doctrine we shall find it difficult to contend against emancipation as they call it unless we can fight with the advantage on our side of great discretion and forbearance'. Irish protestants should realize that their real strength lay 'in a conviction on the part of England that their cause is a just one and that the hostility which threatens them is the result of sheer religious bigotry and hatred and not the offspring of insulted and irritated feelings'. This was sound advice but unpalatable to angry and frightened men.

Impervious to legal attacks, the catholic agitation continued with increasing force. Its leaders wisely decided not to limit the activities of their organization merely to petitioning. Their object was not, as O'Connell put it, to force on parliament an annual farce, but to deal with discrimination and corruption at home, and he wanted the society to receive information about every local grievance.[3] The importance of this need scarcely be stressed. Increasing the association's scope was bound to increase interest in its proceedings; by becoming a perpetual committee of grievances it was able to amass material for propaganda and avoid the monotony which is bound to invade the proceedings of an organization devoted to a single objective during a prolonged struggle. In addition to the preparation of petitions and manifestoes, a number of matters, education, tithes, a religious census, church rates, the administration of justice, and the sub-letting bill, were discussed and in some cases referred to committees, and the association's activities, reported at length in the *Dublin Evening Post*, its 'declared gazette'[4] could compete at least in Ireland with those of parliament.

At the general election of 1826 the association advanced from petitioning to putting more direct pressure on M.P.s. As early as 1803, at the first normal general election after the catholics had secured the franchise, in several constituencies gentlemen found it necessary to court the catholic

[1] Wellesley to Peel, 15 July, 27 Oct. 1822; Peel to Wellesley, 22 Feb. 1823; Goulburn to Wellesley, 23 Feb. 1823 (Add. MS. 37300).

[2] Goulburn to Peel, 20 Apr. 1824 (Add. MS. 40330); Wellesley to Peel, 19 Jan. 1825 (Add. MS. 37303).

[3] *DEP.*, 22 May, 21 June 1823, 11 Mar. 1824.

[4] Wellesley to Peel, 2 Dec. 1824 (Add. MS. 37303).

vote.[1] Four years later the catholics of Meath told Bligh, one of the candidates for the county that he would not get their votes unless he pledged himself to oppose the government. The chief secretary urged Blight to fight unpledged, or at least to retire defiantly, declaring he woudl not be 'the tool of Lord Fingall'. Bligh however preferred a third, less dignified, course, to desert the government and get returned.[2] In the general election of 1812 which occurred at a crisis in catholic affairs the catholic vote played only a small part. O'Connell claimed that it was responsible for the defeat of Bagwell in Tipperary, but he regretted that in Cork many freeholders had failed to register. In any case in several constituencies the catholic vote was divided. After the election Lawless, at the catholic board, carried against O'Connell (who was probably influenced by personal reasons) a resolution to the effect that catholics who voted against the friends of the people were unworthy of the confidence of the board.[3] When the next general election (1818) came round the catholics were distracted by internal disputes, though in one or two constituencies the catholic vote played a part. At Drogheda the catholics backed Wallace, the defeated 'independent' candidate, and in Cork where they had been active registering freeholds, several leading catholics, including the celebrated England, spoke in favour of Hutchinson at the hustings.[4] Two years later, when the death of George III led to an unexciting general election with comparatively few contests, the catholic vote was not a noticeable factor. But in the following general election, that of 1826 the association went into action. At the beginning of the struggle the *Dublin Evening Post* called on the catholic clergy to exert themselves on behalf of supporters of emancipation, an aggregate meeting recommended catholics to vote for candidates who favoured emancipation, and the association became a centre of electioneering activity. A number of prominent catholics backed the successful candidate in County Dublin, and Hamilton who was defeated strongly resented the intervention of the catholic clergy; in Kilkenny O'Connell spoke against Butler Clark who was nevertheless returned, and Lawless, according to himself, conducted a highly successful oratorical tour on behalf of the liberal candidate for county Louth. In Roscommon it seemed at first as if the catholic vote would be split, but 'the great catholic interests' of the county coalesced, and one candidate who received their support was returned. It was thought that both the county seats would have been

[1] Hardwicke to Yorke, 24 Aug. 1803 (Add. MS. 35703).
[2] Wellington, *Civil correspondence and memoranda . . . from 30 Mar. 1807 to 12 April 1809* (1860) p. 55.
[3] *DEP.*, 8, 17 Nov., 8 Dec. 1812.
[4] *A full report of the proceedings at the election for the city of Cork* (1818).

won by emancipationists, but General Mahon, the probable second liberal candidate, cried off at the last moment. In Longford if the attitude of the catholic clergy had been appreciated in time, a liberal candidate would have appeared. But the most dramatic events occurred in Louth, Waterford, Westmeath and Monaghan, where the freeholders bolting from their landlords' control, and, inspired by the association and their clergy, managed to return local landowners who favoured emancipation.[1] In Louth it may be added that the revolutionary quality of the election was emphasized by the fact that the successful 'independent' candidate, Alexander Dawson, was a comparatively small landowner. Indeed, Sir Edward Bellew, the head of the catholic interest in the county, was reluctant 'to relinquish' by voting for Dawson, 'old associations and intimacies for it must be admitted that the general demeanour of the protestant nobility and gentry of the county was courteous, kind and conciliatory when not soured by religious prejudices'.[2] At the close of the election O'Connell publicly declared that he had changed his opinion of the forty-shilling freeholders, since he had seen their spirit and patriotism, and he founded the 'New catholic rent', to compensate freeholders who had been victimized by their landlords for voting liberal. 'The catholics of Ireland', he said, 'form a nation —they should have national resources.' It was suggested that the 'old rent' should also be used for this purpose, but O'Connell declared that to do this was illegal and Dwyer pointed out that it would discourage subscriptions for the new fund. Critics of the scheme such as Lawless and Conway argued that some landlords might start looking to the catholic funds for their rack-rents, but according to regulations drawn up by the committee which distributed the fund, relief was only to be granted after full details had been furnished by either the clergy or a local committee.[3]

Six months after the general election Lord Liverpool had to resign, and during the next year with predominantly pro-catholic cabinets precariously in office the association refrained from vigorously pressing its demands. But on Wellington becoming prime minister the agitation revived with increased vehemence, and the reconstruction of the government which followed the Canningite resignations provided the association with an opportunity for giving a dramatic demonstration of its strength. Vesey Fitzgerald, the new president of the board of trade, had

[1] DEP., 25 May, 13, 15, 17, 20, 22 June, 6 July 1826.

[2] W. Brett, Reminiscences of County Louth (1913), pp. 16-22. Brett was not certain whether Bellew died heartbroken by this breach with his order or from a neglected cold.

[3] DEP., 6, 8, 11 July, 2, 5, 12, 19, 28 Sept., 26 Oct. 1826.

to seek re-election in Clare, and after some hesitation O'Connell came forward as a rival candidate.[1] 'The strength of the agitatorarchy of Ireland shot from Dublin to Ennis',[2] and though Fitzgerald was backed by 'the gentry to a man',[3] the fear of eviction or 'the *esprit de corps* about voting with his estate'[4] failed to prevail with the forty-shilling freeholder against the influence of the catholic clergy and the association, with the result that O'Connell was returned by a resounding majority.

O'Connell's election challenged not only the protestant ascendancy but the great landed interests' traditional control over county politics, and provided a disturbing illustration of the power which could be wielded by a popular organization managed by middle-class liberal politicians. No longer, as an indignant conservative put it, were elections to be decided by freeholders voting as directed by 'generous benefactors, steady friends, extended information and superior judgement'.[5] To Wellington it was clear that if the government could not find a remedy, they would suffer all the consequences of a democratic reform of parliament. 'The Irish gentlemen have at present' he pointed out 'none of the influence which belongs to men of property in a well-regulated society'. Two factors in the situation profoundly impressed him, the immense influence over the mass of the Irish people possessed by the association, and the existence of a definite majority in the house of commons in favour of emancipation.[6] The association he was quite aware would prove a slippery antagonist in a legal tussle. Wellington also was well aware that it would be futile for the government to begin the battle without parliamentary backing, and that, Wellington realized, could only be secured after a conciliatory policy had been tried without success. Still, he was sure that the strength of the association was derived from the disabilities, and, looking to realities rather than names, he argued that emancipation would strengthen the state and the established church.[7] Five years earlier in a clear memorandum Wellington had drawn atten-

[1] The association tried to secure a protestant candidate before selecting O'Connell (*DEP*, 26 June 1828).

[2] DEP, 5 July 1828.

[3] Fitzgerald to Peel, 5 July 1828 (R. Peel, *Memoirs* . . .,i. 113).

[4] This euphemistic phrase was used by a large landowner in 1825. (*First report from the select committee on the state of Ireland*, p. 32, H.C. 1825 (129), viii).

[5] *A letter to the landed proprietors of Westmeath* (1828).

[6] Peel about 1828 noticed that in the debates on the catholic question 'it very rarely if ever happened' that the list of speakers against emancipation was reinforced by a young member even of ordinary ability (R. Peel, *Memoirs*, i. 102).

[7] Wellington's views on the situation are set out in Wellington to Peel, 12 Sept., 14 Oct. 1828, Wellington to the King, 14 Oct., 16 Nov. 1828, Wellington to Rutland, 7 Feb. 1829, A Memorandum 1 Aug. 1828, Wellington to Phillpots, 18 Oct. 1828, (Wellington, *Despatches* . . , *1819-1832*, v. 43, 138, 133-6, 252-4, 491, iv, 565-70).

tion to the increasing weight of the forces favouring emancipation, and had argued with unpractical realism that emancipation should be granted, accompanied by an onerous and humbling system of securities —which it was certain the Irish catholics would have rejected out of hand.[1] Now during the autumn of 1828 he impressed on the king the serious nature of the Irish situation, and in January he obtained permission to lay the catholic question before the cabinet. It was almost immediately agreed that emancipation had to be conceded, but at first the prime minister and the cabinet contemplated minimizing any dangers that might arise by devising elaborate ecclesiastical securities similar to those which had been proposed and argued over during the last couple of decades. State salaries were to be paid to the catholic clergy, catholic priests were to be licensed and registered, and catholic bishops were to be licensed before being permitted to exercise ecclesiastical functions in the United Kingdom. The government was to have power to remove a priest from the register and to refuse to license a bishop. But when the cabinet began to discuss these ideas in detail gusts of political realism swept through the room. It was decided it would be impossible to get parliament to give a grant to the catholic church. As for an effectual licensing system it was argued that it would be a complete innovation, create a fresh grievance, and produce general resistance, martyrs, and annual petitions. Ellenborough, who has preserved in his diary an account of the cabinet's efforts to formulate safeguards, after wasting a considerable amount of energy drafting unacceptable schemes, wearily concluded that it was impossible to control effectually the catholic church without recognizing it in a way which protestants would bitterly resent and imposing restrictions on it which the catholics would strongly resist.[2] The suggested safeguards were steadily whittled away, and in the end emancipation—admission to parliament and official posts—passed accompanied by only 'little securities', the prohibition of religious orders of men, the wearing of ecclesiastical habits in public and the use of territorial ecclesiastical titles, which merely proved ineffectual and irritating.

O'Connell was naturally exultant. 'Great and glorious triumph', he wrote 'as far as the emancipation bill goes. . . . No veto, no payment of clergy, no ecclesiastical arrangements. . . . Every mercy in short, every mercy.' Admittedly his fear that there would be 'a freehold wing' was justified. Emancipation was accompanied by an act amending the elec-

[1] Wellington, *Despatches . . . 1819-32*, ii. 592-607.
[2] Memoranda, 7 Aug. 1828, 29 Jan. 1829 (Wellington, *Despatches . . .*, v. 254-68, 475-6.

tion laws which raised the freehold qualification in the counties from forty shillings to ten pounds. O'Connell, when Brougham asked him to support the whigs who accepted the bill, refused in the strongest terms 'to turn my back on the poor fellows in Clare', and he described the bill as an act of mixed injustice. However he privately expressed the opinion that the new franchise might in fact give more power to the catholics.[1] The other 'wing' which accompanied emancipation was almost a tribute to O'Connell's legal acumen. An act was passed suppressing the Catholic Association by name, and, since previous legislation with this object had been evaded (to quote the act) by 'various shifts and devices', the lord-lieutenant was empowered for a year to suppress any association deemed to be a danger to the public peace.[2]

---

[1] O'Connell to his wife, 3, 5, 6, 7 Mar. 1829 (O'Connell Fitz-Simon MSS.); W. J. Fitzpatrick, *Correspondence of Daniel O'Connell*, i. 172-3 *DEP*, 12 Mar. 1829.
[2] 10 Geo. IV. c. 1.

# 5

# IRISH POLITICAL PARTIES IN THE
# AGE OF REFORM

D uring the reform era three parties dominated Irish politics, the
tories, the whigs and the repealers, the two first being offshoots
or local emanations of the great English parties, the third corresponding very roughly in its position and outlook to the English radicals
or more extreme liberals.

The roots of Irish toryism were deep set. But it could be argued that
the Irish tory party, as distinct from strong 'protestant' supporters of
the government, only emerged at the end of the twenties, when it began
to dawn on upholders of the protestant ascendancy that the government
might not be sound in its attitude on emancipation. Wellesley, a pro-
catholic viceroy, was a portent, Canning's ministry was an alarming
symptom, and towards the end of 1828 the Brunswick club of Ireland
was founded with branches throughout the country. Its aim was to
mobilize protestant 'rank, respectability and numbers' in support of the
principle that the safety of the state depended on the exclusion of the
catholics from political power, and its adherents included about a score
of peers, the same number of M.P.s, over twenty-four baronets and
some leading professional men. That many poorer protestants also
flocked into the society is indicated by the regulation limiting the expenditure on liquor at a local club meeting to 2d. per head per night.[1]

The Brunswick clubs were wound up after the great disaster of 1829,
but at the general election of 1830 the *Dublin Evening Mail*, the organ
of ultra-protestant toryism, derived intense satisfaction from the defeat
of 'placemen', 'renegades' and 'hacks' (even if their successors were
possibly liberals). And in a few constituencies anti-government tory

[1] For the Brunswick clubs see *DEM*, the *Star of Brunswick* and Brunswick club
MSS.

feeling manifested itself. But, as in Great Britain, the downfall of the Wellington ministry, the arrival of the whigs in power and the production of the reform bill drove the ultras back into association with more moderate conservatives. Though it would probably be safe to say that in Ireland the more extreme element played a greater part in determining the general tone of the party.

Irish toryism in the early nineteenth century was undoubtedly distinguished by its crudity of outlook and expression. The *Westminster Review* once remarked when dealing with a conservative pamphleteer 'that even Irish toryism is not too shocking a thing for him', and when the *Edinburgh Review* declared that 'truly the ravings of insanity are tame and reasonable compared with the eloquence of faction' it had Irish toryism in mind.[1] These were the opinions of hostile critics, but a fastidious convert to Irish toryism was constrained to excuse its style by explaining that while English conservatives knew party warfare only in its softer aspects, the Irish conservative had to struggle with men of the lowest moral and intellectual standards—'the rabid eye of a bloody-handed mob, trained in lies and lying maxims scowls in our path'.[2] Irish tories in fact were political frontiersmen, regarding their religion and their politics as different aspects of the same cause, convinced of their own moral and social righteousness, fighting tenaciously for every article of their narrow creed and every scrap of their extensive material privileges and possessions. The nature of their outlook is shown by the three names which, according to the *Dublin University Magazine*, the organ of intellectual Irish toryism, had been applied to the 'great party which embraces all the estated wealth, rank, worth, character and true loyalty in Ireland—the English interest, the protestant interest, the conservative interest'. These terms indicate how closely three aims, the preservation of the union and of existing institutions and the promotion of protestantism were related, since, as a conservative journalist put it, it was 'the vulgarest of all popular errors' to assume that the protestant ascendancy meant only a religious ascendancy. 'The true principles of the protestant ascendancy' he explained 'are allegiance to the British king, obedience to the British government, the preservation of the British connection, the maintenance of the laws and constitution of Great Britain in church and state.' Strictly speaking, he contended, it should be termed the 'British ascendancy'.[3] On another occasion 'protestant ascendancy' was defined as 'the just dominion of light over dark-

---

[1] *Westminster Rev.*, xxv. 282; *Edinburgh Rev.*, lviii. 101.
[2] *DUM*, ix. 140.
[3] *DUM*, v. 370, *DEM*, 20 Apr. 1832.

ness, of truth over error, the ascendancy of liberty and reason over despotism and arbitrary power, the supremacy of the religion, the arts, the civilization of protestant Britain over the fanaticism, the ignorance and barbarism of Rome'.[1] Very rarely was the possibility of there being catholic conservatives mentioned, though once the *Dublin University Magazine*, in a fit of generous enthusiasm, discerned in the bearing of a catholic barrister who voted the straight conservative ticket in both the university and the city constituencies, 'a calm and resolute virtue . . . which reminded us of Sir Thomas More'.[2] The superiority of protestantism to catholicism was continually insisted on, and existing institutions, lay and ecclesiastical, were defended, defects and all, if they appeared to be bastions of protestantism. In some ways it is easiest to comprehend Irish conservatism in reverse, since much of the party's controversial energy was expended in attacks on its opponents rather than in the defence of its own tenets. During this period the Irish conservatives saw themselves menaced by a monstrous, ugly and dangerous combination of radicals and catholics. Now catholicism, it was said, when it acted with its depraved energies upon the mass of society, had in every case degraded the human mind, and enslaved the human conscience, while as for the 'democratic demon' it was only another term for the progress of crime.[3] As for the whigs their behaviour was almost as exasperating as culpable. Though occasionally Irish conservatives denounced them for trying to establish a democratic ascendancy with the aim of turning Ireland into a popish country, usually they blamed them for dishonest weakness. For the sake of place the whigs were prepared to sacrifice the constitution to O'Connell.[4]

> '*Lord Grey reforms the patronage,*
> *Lops petty situations,*
> *But all the while does not forget*
> *To place his own relations.*'[5]

wrote a poetaster in the *Dublin Evening Mail*, dwelling on that well-worn theme in political satire, the inordinate appetite of the whigs for place.

But what shocked the tories, during the thirties deprived of the sweets of office, was whiggish irresponsibility. There was always, it was said,

---

[1] *SNL*, 10 Jan. 1840.
[2] *DUM*, x. 531. Sir F. W. MacNaghten argued that Irish conservatives should recognize that there are 'many catholics as well as ourselves who have property to preserve' (*Some observations upon the present state of Ireland* (1837), p. 10).
[3] *DEM*, 11 Dec. 1833.
[4] *DEM*, 28 Mar., 27 June, 4 Nov. 1833.
[5] *DEM*, 15 Feb. 1832.

something 'shuffling, indirect, and tricky in the political operations of the whigs', but by 1833 it seemed as if they had at last gone too far in gratifying the tiger, and 'the tusks of their pet savage are now flashed in their own entrails'.[1]

During the early thirties the Irish conservatives presented the ludicrous and pathetic spectacle of propertied persons in a panic. A sudden series of defeats and surrenders rattled them badly. Catholic emancipation left them overwhelmed with surprise and dismay that the government should have yielded to 'the demands of menacing rebels'.[2] The reform bill left 'the ark of civil and religious liberty to be desecrated by the impure touch of the liberals and trodden under the obscene hoof of infidelity and radicalism'. And once the bill was through, the *University Magazine* soberly surveying the political future could see ahead 'nothing but a series of ignorant, presumptuous, mischievous innovations, under the name of "judicious reform" beginning with the church and going through every great institution of the nation, which our new-fangled, conceited rulers and legislators will set down as wrong, because they were not arranged according to the superior lights of modern wisdom.'[3] All that remained for conservatives was to put their trust in the house of lords.

On occasions during the reform era the Irish conservatives showed signs of having developed a persecution complex. As early as 1831 Lord Roden, a leading evangelical and an indefatigable tory orator, referred to the 'torrent of despotism and tyranny which is pouring out against the protestant population of Ireland'.[4] About a year later it seemed as if resentment might make protestants into repealers. Boyton, the leading spirit in the Protestant Conservative Society, declared at a meeting that the opposition to repeal was based entirely on religious grounds, and that they would oppose it only so long as protestant property and protestant influence were supported by the government against indigent numbers. He admitted they were no match for the Roman catholic party and the English government combined, but he was confident that if England were sunk in the ocean, they could (admittedly after a struggle) reduce Ireland to peace. And his colleague in Trinity College, Dr Prior, in a pugnacious speech, warned the government that the Irish protestants, who were quite capable of looking after themselves, might dissolve the union, if the government failed to protect their lives and

[1] *DUM*, xvi, 108, *DEM*, 6 Nov. 1833.
[2] This view is expressed energetically in a letter from Gregory to Peel dated 4 Feb. 1829 (Add. MS. 40334).
[3] *DEM*, 7 Mar. 1831; *DUM*, i. 116.
[4] *DEM*, 25 Apr. 1831.

property. A little later sheer irritation with the whigs made the *Dublin Evening Mail* call for subscriptions to assist Barrett, the editor of O'Connell's organ, when he was facing a government prosecution, and a Derry conservative newspaper argued that if repeal was won they would have a protestant house of lords and a predominantly protestant house of commons.[1]

The strength of Irish conservativism was derived from several sources. Most of the peers, the bulk of the landed gentry, the great majority of the clergy of the establishment, and a large section of the bar, were conservatives by nature, interest or conviction. The party held a substantial number of seats in the commons, it had a strong press, comprehending, it was estimated in 1831, three Dublin and eighteen provincial journals,[2] an able monthly, and several vigorous political organizations. As might be expected from its strongly protestant character, the only Irish university was closely identified with the conservative cause. University toryism was as strong and fervent in Dublin as in Oxford, and the fact that the university was in the centre of the capital made it harder for the Dublin don to develop a cloistered conservatism. A few indeed of the fellows were liberals, including Crampton, the whig solicitor-general, and Sadleir, a strong whig who became a member of the Board of National Education, and who was accused by the *Dublin Evening Mail* of making the college pulpit 'a rostrum for the sprouting of whiggery' in his ostentatious efforts to secure promotion.[3] The delight of Irish conservatives at his failure to get a bishopric in 1836 was only equalled by their disgust when he was made provost of Trinity in the following year. But the great majority of the fellows were tories, and several of them sallied out to play a prominent part in extra-mural politics. Hodgkinson, a college pluralist, and Prior, a disappointed aspirant to the provostship, made strong speeches at conservative gatherings, Martin contributed letters to the press marked by energetic vapidity,[4] and on one occasion the most distinguished professor in the university, William Rowan Hamilton, was enticed down from Dunsink Observatory to the Conservative Society to make a short speech to the effect that it was evident that a design was on foot to establish the Roman catholic church upon the ruins of the establishment. No member of his audience, he said, should delude himself into thinking that 'the seclusion of our libraries shall afford us effectual protection' for they would continually be afraid

[1] *DEM*, 18 July, 1 Aug. 1832, 20 Sept. 1833, 21 Feb. 1834.
[2] *DEM*, 4 Apr. 1831.
[3] *DEM*, 23 Mar. 1832.
[4] In 1831 Martin published a pamphlet, *Reform considered*, attacking the Reform bill.

of hearing 'the step of the inquisitor upon the stairs'. After which he retreated to discuss optics with the professor of natural philosophy.[1] By far the most outstanding of the college conservatives was Boyton, the most popular of the tutors, a genial man, liked even by his opponents, whose forcible originality of mind redeemed his robust rodomontades from absurdity. The younger men in college though equally tory had more intellectual liveliness than their seniors, and a small group, accustomed to chatting round the fire together, founded in 1833 the *Dublin University Magazine*, which expressed crude prejudices in decent prose and tried to combine narrow and aggressive toryism with the literary enthusiasms of the romantic movement. Under Stanford, its first editor, it devoted a considerable amount of space to the unceasing and acrimonious defence of the rights of the establishment. But under the successive editorships of Butt, a lawyer and an economist, and Lever, more space was given to *belles lettres* and general politics. The magazine's outlook remained decidedly tory, but it reflected the rather muddled outlook of Irish protestantism in its denominational zeal, devotion to the union, intense interest in local affairs and sectional pride merging at times into a kind of qualified nationalism. Its approach to Irish matters is sharply illustrated by its description of the peasantry of Meath: 'as we look on their shrewd and daring countenances, their light energetic tread, and frames so well fitted for endurance and exertion, we feel a mingled pride and apprehension—a pleasing dread—a glow of congratulation that we are the countrymen of such spirits as these men could furnish in a good cause—a thrill of anxiety that these very men at the moment they delight us by their vivacity as by their urbanity may perhaps be engaged in secret designs the most formidable and atrocious'.[2]

Irish conservatism in its more pugnacious and less refined forms expressed itself through various political organizations. Of these the Orange order, 'a politico-religious' body uniting Irish protestants in 'a defensive combination,' attracted most attention. Its lodges, which were in some way analogous to the conservative working men's clubs that later became a feature of English political life, had sprung up during the stormy years at the end of the eighteenth century, and by 1835 they numbered about 1,500, the great majority being situated in the north.[4]

---

[1] *DEM*, 20 Aug. 1834; Hamilton to Wordsworth, 20 Aug. 1834 (R. P. Graves, *Life of Sir W. R. Hamilton* (1885), ii. 101).

[2] For an account of the magazine see M. Sadleir, 'The Dublin University Magazine' in *Proc. Irish Bibliog. Soc.*, v. 59-82.       [3] *DUM*, viii. 667.

[4] For the Orange order see the four reports of the select committee of the house of commons appointed to inquire into the Orange institution in Great Britain and Ireland.

They were co-ordinated by a series of elected district and county committees, and the writings and ritual of the order invested existing politics with an air of heroic romance by treating them as a continuance of the great seventeenth-century struggle which reached its climax on the banks of the Boyne. For the ordinary Orangeman his lodge was a political and social club. It provided him with some security against sickness and indigence, gave him an opportunity to decorate himself with a sash, to participate in its observances and private business, to meet his social superiors, to discuss—at least occasionally—religious topics, and to enjoy convivial political dinners and suppers. Critics of the order pointed with disapproval to its exclusively protestant character, and to the strong probability that it interfered with local patronage and the administration of justice by jobbing its members into the police and by biasing juries and justices of the peace in favour of their brethren. Moreover the lodges were charged with encouraging by their existence as well as their processions communal bad feeling, scuffling, singing and even bloodshed. The catholic peasantry also had their drum-beating societies, the Ribbonmen. And sectarianism, along with the land hunger, long memories, and contempt for the law which characterized Irish rural life, explains the strife between the two organizations. To what extent the Orange order nourished ill-will or by its discipline discouraged drunkenness, and acted as a restraining influence, is hard to say, since the truth about every episode in which the Orangemen and their opponents were involved is smothered in masses of conflicting contemporary testimony. For instance, when at a meeting of the Armagh magistrates, Lord Mandeville proposed to discuss the outrages committed at the Armagh races, 'another magistrate said you must go back to the races of Clantilew for what happened at Armagh grew out of what happened at those races; then another magistrate said you must go back to the Blackwater races for what happened at Clantilew grew out of what happened at Blackwater, upon which another magistrate observed you may as well go back to the battle of the Boyne.'[1] During the thirties moderate men in England, to whom large-scale political machinery was as yet unknown and who were only slowly growing aware of the peculiarities of Irish politics, were startled to learn of the activities of the order in both Great Britain and Ireland and particularly of its penetration into the army. Radicals naturally seized the opportunity to

[1] *Report from the select committee appointed to inquire into the . . . Orange Lodges, associations or societies in Ireland*, H.C. 1835 (377), p. 290, xv. 294. A conscientious magistrate trying to allocate responsibility for sectarian rioting in Maghera counted and divided denominationally the broken panes of glass, 615 were catholic, 605 protestant (H.O. 100/209).

try to push the tories into the incongruous and embarrassing position of having to defend a popular semi-secret society. In 1835 Hume secured the appointment of a select committee by the house of commons to investigate the workings of the institution. When the committee reported in 1836 an address was carried in the commons asking the crown to discourage the order's activities. The conservatives in the house kept remarkably quiet, the Grand Lodge of Ireland decided to dissolve itself,[1] and for the next ten years the order was inconspicuous.

Another prominent body for a time was the Irish Protestant Conservative Society, founded in 1831, a tory imitation and at times parody of O'Connell's associations. Its membership was open to conservatives from all over Ireland. At its weekly meetings in Dublin impassioned harangues were delivered on the problems of the hour, it raised 'a protestant rent' which in one week amounted to nearly £2,000, took steps to register voters, assisted tory candidates, distributed propaganda, prepared—for comparative purposes—lists of catholic and protestant subscribers to charities, and lists of conservative newspapers, and arranged for the defence of 'innocent, inoffensive but persecuted, Orangemen.[2] When the society was informed that protestants who had voted for protestant candidates were exposed to economic pressure, it decided to protect their humbler brethren from the effects of exclusive dealing by arranging for protestants to deal only with protestants. Fortunately the necessity of applying this grim measure seems to have vanished with the excitement of the election.[3]

In one respect the Conservative Society was handicapped in comparison with its radical equivalents. The latter could easily manufacture business by discussing the radical alterations required by most existing institutions, while the conservatives were reduced to duller defensive tactics. However attempts were made to evolve a positive programme. The question of protestant emigration was referred to a committee which reported that many protestants were leaving the country because of the conversion of tillage to pasture, the decay of manufactures, the persecution of the protestant peasantry by their neighbours, and the readiness of landlords to prefer high bidders to solvent tenants. Also protestants were discouraged by the belief that the government were abandoning the country to the catholic party. They saw their ancient customs and processions prohibited, the withdrawal of government support from the protestant schools, the promotion of a new, unscrip-

---

[1] By 92 votes to 62 (*DEM*, 15 Apr. 1836).
[2] *DEM*, 21 Mar., 11, 25, 31 July, 12 Sept. 1832.
[3] *DEM*, 31 Oct., 7 Nov. 1832.

tural system of education, and 'deference on every occasion evinced towards the demagogue'. Some of the remedies were obvious. In addition the society recommended that parliament should be petitioned to authorize a plan of protestant colonization, non-interest-bearing loans should be made to protestants, protestants should be encouraged by their landlords to enfranchise themselves, they should be given permission to carry arms, and they should receive their 'just portion' of legitimate patronage.[1] It is a pity that Boyton, the most vigorous thinker in the society, expounded his political ideas only in a fragmentary form. Social insecurity in Ireland, he asserted, was caused by neither popery, disaffection, nor democracy, but by 'the unlimited multiplication of poverty and wretchedness'. For the contrast between 'the bustle, the activity, the busy hum of man' in England and 'the spiritless and solitary aspect of Ireland' he blamed the absentees, who had failed to do anything to raise the Irish peasants' standard of living. He also attacked the *laissez-faire* system for failing to check the inherent disposition of capital to accumulate unduly in one part of the empire to the detriment of Ireland, and he demanded that something should be done to encourage Irish industry.[2]

In April 1833 the Conservative Society, to avoid falling under the lord-lieutenant's ban, dissolved itself, though the staff was kept up and occasional meetings held.[3] It was succeeded by local societies, including two in Dublin, the Metropolitan Conservative Society, founded in 1836 to 'maintain by every means in our power protestantism in Ireland', and the Conservative Registration Committee for the city of Dublin, set up in July 1835 which employed lawyers to appear at the registration sessions, agents to discover unregistered conservatives, and 'respectable surveyors' to examine and inquire into the value of tenements from which the lower order of radicals claim to register'.[4]

But though vocal and obstreperous the Irish tories during the thirties shared in the conservative slump, and for the whole decade (with the exception of a few months) the Irish administration was under whig control. The whigs, in the words of Jeffrey 'a small but respectable band —the friends of liberty and order with the best intentions and the best talents',[5] with their combination of aristocratic pride and intellectual

---

[1] *DEM*, 11 Apr., 9 May 1831.

[2] *DEM*, 11 July, 15, 22 Aug. 1832, 15 Aug., 15 Oct. 1834. In 1836 Boyton accepted a college living in county Donegal and ceased to play much part in politics. Before his death he courageously defended tractarianism in the north of Ireland.

[3] Crampton to Hobhouse, 13 Apr. 1833, Gossett to Hobhouse, 15 Apr. 1833 (Add. MS. 36467).      [4] *Report of the Conservative registration committee* (1837).

[5] *Edinburgh Rev.*, xv. 504.

superiority, their cliqueishness, their careful progressiveness, their complacency, their cold, self-conscious adherence to high principle and their determination to cling whenever possible to power, provided obvious material for their critics. But they had important virtues which outweighed their defects. They believed in 'common justice and common sense'. They were generous and unflinching upholders of civil and religious liberty, and ready to advocate reasonable reform. And at their best, they were governed in their approach to political problems by intelligent humanitarianism and an undoctrinaire respect for efficiency.

During their long exile from power in the early nineteenth century, free from the trammels of official routine, they had ample opportunities both to advise and warn the government of the day and to evolve their own programme. Since many of the leading whigs had Irish connections, and since the catholic question lay athwart the party's return to power, they naturally devoted a good deal of attention to Irish problems. The critical attitude of the Grenville administration to the rights of the establishment has already been referred to, and out of office the whigs in parliament continued to attack the tithe system. Tithe, the *Edinburgh Review* argued, was not the property of the clergy, any more than the taxes raised for the army were the property of the troops, and it should be abolished or at least commuted. The revenue of the episcopal estates would amply suffice for the maintenance of the establishment if it were reduced to a reasonable size and the incomes of its clergy put on a reasonable basis.[1] But putting the establishment in its place was only one item in the whig programme for Ireland. Catholic emancipation, it need scarcely be said, was needed to improve feeling, clear the ground, and deprive the agitators of employment. Once the last remnant of the penal laws was gone the catholic clergy might be induced to accept a provision from the government which would identify their interests with the state's. The government was also advised to adopt a bold, sympathetic educational policy. The Maynooth grant should be greatly increased, the charter schools should be abolished, and parochial schools set up for the education of catholics, under the direction of the catholic clergy but subject to the inspection of gentlemen of both religions. Grattan, the most outstanding Irish whig, enunciated with forcible clarity some of the principles on which he thought Irish primary education should be based. Since one great object of national education was to unite the inhabitants of a country, and since 'diversity of language and not the diversity of religion constitutes a diversity of people' English should be taught in all schools—though he would have been sorry if Irish should be

[1] See T. R. McCulloch's article in *Edinburgh Rev.*, xli. 356 ff.

forgotten. As for religion, Christianity, but 'no particular description of it', should be taught along with the four great duties of man—to God, to one another, to his country and to the government.[1]

Above all, the whigs asserted, Ireland required 'a national, not a partisan government'. The office of lord-lieutenant might be abolished, but lords-lieutenant responsible for the selection of J.P.s should be appointed in every county. The magistracy should be purged, and neither clergymen nor gentlemen worth less than £1,000 per annum in landed property should be placed on the bench. More care should be taken in selecting sheriffs and grand jurors, the civil bill courts should be reformed, and stipendiary magistrates appointed to preside at petty sessions. These measures it was believed would both increase the efficiency of the law in Ireland, and win for it the confidence of the public. Then, with the growth of tranquillity, English capital would flow into the country to promote prosperity. The theory that administrative and legal reform would have direct economic results strengthened the inherent caution with which the whigs approached Irish economic problems. The *Edinburgh Review* called on its readers 'to steadfastly oppose any scheme for providing employment for the poor of Ireland by granting money or by bounties on any particular article'. It was convinced that an Irish poor law, which might have to support seven-eighths of the population, would destroy Ireland's capital resources and eradicate what little prudence was left in the people. But the *Edinburgh Review* was strongly in favour of renewing taxes on articles of consumption and for sweeping away the 'union' duties which both prevented the Irish enjoying cheap manufactured goods and hindered the English from availing themselves of cheap Irish labour. Finally steps were to be taken to check the growth of population. Subdivision of farms was to be prohibited, and the erection of cottages with less than five or ten acres of land attached, prohibited.[2]

Though owing to the course of events at Westminster, the whigs were in control of Irish affairs for ten years between 1830 and 1841, the party was a great deal weaker in Ireland than in Great Britain. There were of course a number of whig peers, such as Leinster, Charlemont, Leitrim, Headford, Wicklow and Rossmore who had remained faithful to the party through the long years of adversity. And there were plenty of liberal country gentlemen and lawyers. But the Irish political climate was

[1] *Appendix to the fourteenth report of the commissioners of the Board of Education in Ireland*, H.C. 1812-13 (21), p. 336, vi.
[2] See articles by Sidney Smith, T. R. McCulloch, T. Mackintosh, *Edinburgh Rev.*, xxxiv. 320 ff, xxxvii. 63 ff, xli. 356 ff, lxxii, xx. 347 ff.

unfavourable to cool moderation and cautious reform. Sectarian and social tension encouraged extreme views both on the left and on the right; the old eighteenth-century rational liberalism of the protestant north was declining; in the south O'Connell's repeal movement offered a well-advertised alternative to toryism. The repealers held *vis-à-vis* the Irish whigs a similar position to that occupied by radicals in Great Britain. But O'Connell's reputation, towering personality, and political skill made Irish repeal relatively a far stronger movement than British radicalism.

As a result of his success in organizing catholic opinion and guiding it to victory, O'Connell had become a personal political force of the first magnitude. Until shortly before his death his vitality was terrific. Before 1829 he had managed to build up a huge practice at the Irish bar and to conduct the affairs of the Catholic Association, not only playing a leading part on the platform, but coping with much of the detailed drudgery of a large-scale agitation. Admittedly on entering parliament he dropped his practice, but he managed to be an active member of the house of commons, in both general debate and committee, to look after his Kerry estates, to hold a directorship of the National Bank, to produce a wordy volume on Irish history,[1] to compose a continuous stream of long contributions to the press, often commenting in close detail on proposed legislation, to found, organize and manage a series of political associations, to attend to the personal concerns of innumerable individuals, and to be an incessant, indefatigable and always entertaining speaker at an amazing variety of meetings all over the south of Ireland. A burly body, high spirits, strong convictions, an optimistic temperament, and abundant genial good nature kept him going. In addition he was a gifted organizer and orator. When planning a political campaign, he devoted careful attention to the constitution of whatever association he was running at the time, to arranging for the collection of funds and the dissemination of propaganda through meetings and newspapers, to collecting a general staff of journalists and other assidious followers and to flattering the vanity of potential supporters. His oratory was rugged, vigorous, flexible and impassioned. He had the lawyer's capacity for rapidly assimilating information on a wide variety of subjects, and this, combined with his many interests and amazing experience of Irish life, gave him a vast store of material which he could, when he was at his best, marshal with devastating ability. But his ready fluency was not an unmixed blessing. He could easily be swept off his

---

[1] *A memoir on Ireland, native and Saxon 1172-1600*, i (1843). Only the first volume was published.

feet by his own emotional oratory, so that his political animosities and alliances—sometimes of a temporary nature—were announced with astounding and unqualified vehemence. Also in an age of hard-hitting and even brutal controversy, O'Connell was outstanding for his readiness to attribute malignant motives to his opponents and for splattering them with scurrilous and sometimes silly abuse. Moreover his speeches and writings are characterized by flamboyant compliments to his supporters and himself, by repetition and over-elaboration, by gossipy anecdotes, by a monotonous use of cherished quotations, satisfactory statistics and telling historical allusions, and as a result of all this, by frequent digressions and parentheses. These stylistic tricks which harsh critics fastened on, sprang at least partly from the fact that O'Connell was addressing enthusiastic and highly sympathetic popular audiences to which he gave what they wanted with cheerful familiarity. Normally his vivid if rambling commentaries on the political situation, a number of which he delivered every year at a series of meetings and dinners usually held during the parliamentary recess, were received with delight by his audience, and were punctuated with ringing cheers and rousing responses to his rhetorical questions. And on the rare occasions when he met with opposition he usually got his way by a mixture of bullying and blarneying.

Admittedly he adopted a more restrained and serious tone when he spoke in the house of commons, only, naturally enough, to provoke the jibe that there must be another Mr O'Connell speaking outside.[1] From his entry into political life he worked under the handicap of being the first leading parliamentary figure who strove to keep continuously in touch with the public out of doors. While his contemporaries were content to appeal to their constituents every few years from the hustings, O'Connell, who, after all, had served his apprenticeship in a great popular agitation, ran a series of Midlothian campaigns and employed the methods of organizing and appealing to public opinion, later developed by Cobden and Joseph Chamberlain. Naturally then, his tactics were disliked for their novelty and criticized as vulgar. Moreover as Grattan expressed it, an oak should not be translated at fifty, the very age at which O'Connell entered the commons, and while all his distinguished parliamentary contemporaries had been to some extent educated in the House, he arrived a formed and vehement personality. Surrounded at

---

[1] *Parl. Deb.*, 3 series, ii. 816. Referring to O'Connell's early parliamentary speeches the then chief secretary unsympathetically remarked, his 'profession is ruffianism and he is wrong in my opinion to attempt to depart from a line in which he is a proficient' (Leveson-Gower to Greene, 8 Feb. 1830, Leveson-Gower letter-books).

Westminster by hostile or bored British M.P.s, he was often exasperated by his powerlessness to force the decision on Irish issues which he thought right and urgently requisite. And when he addressed the house he was far less sure than in Ireland of securing an encouraging and unquestioning response. Nevertheless he became a force to be reckoned with in parliament, and at a time when the debating level was high and the outcome often uncertain he frequently intervened effectively. He also took part in the blended social and political life of the London clubs. At Brooks' (from which his critics made two unsuccessful attempts to expel him on the grounds that his political manners were ungentlemanly) he was a conspicuous conversationalist, and his nomination by Ellice, the whip, to the first committee of the Reform Club was 'a bitter pill' to many whigs.[1]

But he was in the anomalous position of being a leading parliamentary figure without party ties and without the experience or the expectation of office. He of course lacked family or traditional connections with either of the two main parties, and though he sympathized and frequently acted with the British radicals, his independence, preoccupation with Irish questions, and his long cross-channel vacations separated him from the liberal left in the thirties and early forties. Having no official responsibility for the past and little or no prospect of enjoying direct political power in the immediate future, he could freely indulge in thorough-going criticism of the executive and in the production of simple and sweeping solutions for the problems of the day. His qualities as a statesman remained untested, while his fertile and imaginative intellect, uninhibited by contact with the realities which beset executive action, merely supplied material for his unflagging and reckless loquacity.

Considering his immense output both verbal and written it is amazing what a high degree of coherence and consistency in his opinions O'Connell managed to maintain. Catholicism, nationalism and radicalism were the three chief elements in his thinking. Brought up in a keenly catholic environment, a member of a family which had suffered during

[1] Leveson-Gower to Singleton, 29 Apr. 1830 (Leveson-Gower letter books); Littleton diary, 3 May 1835 (Tedderly MSS.); Sir W. Molesworth to Lady Molesworth, Feb. 1838 (Fawcett, *Life of Sir W. Molesworth* (1901), pp. 74-9; *Life and correspondence of T. S. Duncombe* (London 1868), i. 54, 146-7. In November 1830 Ellenborough noted that O'Connell had a cold reception at Brooks', the members turning their backs on him. Six years later a liberal politician said it was quite disgusting to see how O'Connell was 'fawned on in Brooks's' (Ellenborough, *Diary*, i. 409, C. S. Reid, *Life and letters of the first earl of Durham 1792-1840* (1906), ii. 103-4). These different reports probably indicate a change in O'Connell's political status. They may also reflect varying reactions in a club to a talkative member.

a century for its faith, he was all his life, with the exception of a short phase tinged with scepticism which he passed through while a law student in London,[1] a staunch, convinced and fervent catholic. A statesman with strong, religious convictions is always faced with a difficult moral issue, to what extent is he justified in attempting to use the political power at his disposal to compel others, some of whom may not share his principles, to behave in accordance with them? How far, in fact, is he entitled to impose his own moral standards by legislation? O'Connell never discussed the question in such general terms, but during the long struggle for catholic emancipation he evolved a theory of the relationship which should exist between church and state on which he based his attacks on the penal laws and the privileges of the establishment. Every Christian man had the right to worship 'the adorable Creator and Redeemer' in the form his conscientious conviction tells him to be the true one. 'The obligation of belief is not to our fellow-man but to the Creator of all. And the awful responsibility of which I speak relates to an eternity of weal or woe; and to nothing which human government can give or take away.' On these premisses he contended that the church should be free from state control, rejected with abhorrence all ideas of persecution and argued that no Christian should be compelled to contribute to the support of a church to which he did not belong. No man, he declared, should 'be compelled to support another man's clergyman any more than he would another man's lawyer or doctor'. These theories enabled O'Connell to be one of the small band of nineteenth-century politicians who managed to combine liberalism and catholicism. Convinced of the supreme importance of the catholic faith, of the value of political democracy, and of the social utility of most of the proposals advocated by British liberals, he rejoiced at the separation of church and state in France which followed the revolution of 1830, and he believed that if the rational freedom, which was the aim of the true liberal party, 'the party of peaceful movement', was attained, all the differences between the various Christian bodies might be left to free discussion— 'and from contests of that description the catholic church would have everything to hope for and nothing to fear'.[2]

O'Connell held these views sincerely and presumably intended to apply them fairly. But his case in the eyes of his opponents was rendered suspect by two factors. Firstly, his theory, though meant for general

[1] *Daniel O'Connell, his early life and journal*, ed. A. Houston (1906), pp. 110, 116, 118.
[2] *Pilot*, 23 Sept. 1833, *Observations on the corn laws . . . in the shape of a meek and modest reply to the second letter of the earl of Shrewsbury* (1842), pp. 99-114.

application, like most theories enunciated by busy practising politicians, had decidedly partial results in existing Irish conditions. For it told heavily against the protestants, implying as it did, catholic emancipation, the abolition of tithe, disestablishment and disendowment. Secondly, when O'Connell's intense pride in his religion, his long services to the catholic cause, and the fact that the bulk of his followers were catholic were taken into account, it was difficult not to regard any movement he might be leading as a denominational one. After 1829 O'Connell repeatedly denied having any sectarian aims, as shall be seen he positively courted the Irish protestants, and he frequently pointed out that one of the proudest boasts of Irish catholics was, that on the two occasions when they were in possession of power, in the reigns of Mary and James II, they had rigorously abstained from persecution. Probably most Irish protestants in the thirties and forties were impervious to argument or blandishment. They would naturally be biased in favour of preserving the political unit in which they formed part of the majority group. But their dislike of repeal must have been accentuated by O'Connell's readiness to plunge into theological controversy, a predilection which he shared with nearly all his Irish contemporaries, and which he indulged with his customary bluntness, verbosity and forensic vigour. At times too, excusably perhaps, considering his long battle for emancipation and the composition of his audiences, he seems to have treated catholics and Irishmen as synonymous. He frequently spoke of the catholic people of Ireland, and he referred to the catholic clergy, who often acted as his local lieutenants, as the clergy of the people. In one of his most eloquent appeals to Irish protestants to co-operate in the struggle for repeal, he tried to lull their fears of clericalism by pointing out how at a recent election in Newfoundland the catholic bishop and clergy had used their influence over their flock in favour of a protestant, who as a result was returned. Again, when, during a debate in the house of commons over some legal appointments of which he disapproved, it was pointed out that the officials referred to were at any rate Irishmen, O'Connell blurted out 'they are foreigners to us since they are of a different religion'.[1] In short, on these matters O'Connell's thinking was swayed by contradictory currents: affection and admiration for his protestant countrymen as fellow Irishmen, exasperation at the political pig-headedness of the protestant community as a whole on repeal, and an intense realization of the solidity, sufferings, and virtues of the great catholic community of which he was the leading layman.

O'Connell's nationalism was so instinctive and rooted in his being,

[1] *Pilot*, 13 Jan. 1834; *Parl. Deb.*, 3 series, xv. 325.

that he never bothered to analyse and expound it systematically. For the people of Ireland and its countryside which he knew so well and where he spent such an active, many-sided life, he cherished a deep-seated, vehement affection. 'There is not', he once said, 'on the face of the globe a more fertile country than ours . . . no country so well circumstanced for general commerce . . . our green island is indented by spacious roadsteads, magnificent bays and estuaries and capacious harbours . . . sheltered from every wind, secure from every tempest. . . . The streams that rush from our majestic mountains or sweep with abundant and rapid courses through our green and glorious valleys, give a superabundance of mill sites . . . our climate is genial and conducive to long life and manly vigour . . . inhabited by a people as brave as they are patient, as generous as they are hardy, good-humoured as they are laborious . . . above all they are a people deeply impressed with the sincerity of religious belief, differing as they do upon various points of faith they detest infidelity.' The Irish people, on another occasion he declared, were 'active, industrious, shrewd, intelligent, moral and religious'. And amongst his other *obiter dicta* on this subject were that the Irish had founded the great seats of learning, Paris, Oxford and Padua, and that if Scotland were obliterated from the earth, it could be replaced by a few Irish counties.[1]

That Ireland was a distinctive entity was to O'Connell axiomatic, and from that his immediate deduction was that it ought to have self-government. As he put it in 1830 at the beginning of his repeal campaign, 'I look for repeal because I know that no individual will have his affairs well managed if he leaves them to another.' 'Ireland', he wrote some years later, 'is too great, too powerful, too magnificent for a state of tutelage.' And one session of the reformed parliament convinced him that 'Firstly Irishmen lose much of their value by transportation, and secondly there is an anti-Irish feeling so predominant amongst the English members as to render them totally unfitted to legislate for Ireland'.[4] And speaking to a bucolic audience he explained the advantage of having a domestic parliament in simple terms. 'Instead of sending a bit of parchment to London to be heedlessly thrown under the table, three or four hundred of you could proceed in a body to Dublin and boldly state the wrongs of which you complain.'[5] Though O'Connell continually referred with exaggerated emphasis to the existence of dis-

[1] *DEP*, 7 Jan. 1832.
[2] *Pilot*, 6 July 1836, 6 Sept. 1837, 23 Sept. 1840; *MR*, 19 Oct. 1831.
[3] *FJ*, 19 Oct. 1830; *Pilot*, 12 Aug., 1 Nov. 1833; *DEP*, 20 July 1830.
[4] *FJ*, 19 Oct. 1830; *Pilot*, 12 Aug., 1 Nov. 1833; *DEP*, 20 July 1830.
[5] *DEP*, 20 July 1830.

tinctive Irish characteristics, unlike most nineteenth-century nationalists he did not attempt to buttress his demand for political independence by dwelling on the existence of a valuable national culture expressing itself through its own historic language. The materials for such an attempt lay ready to hand; there were the vast stores of Gaelic literature and tradition, and a large number of the peasantry still habitually spoke Irish. But O'Connell was not an antiquarian, nor, though he used historical material in composing his indictment against English rule, does he seem to have had a keen historical sense, and though he frequently used his fluent knowledge of Irish to get a laugh from an appreciative audience by throwing out a quip in Gaelic, he did not bother to associate repeal with cultural nationalism. Furthermore, when detailing the beneficial results of repeal, O'Connell talked in economic and social rather than cultural or spiritual terms. An Irish parliament, he prophesied, would impose an absentee tax and moderate tariffs, adjusted so as to protect Irish manufactures without eliminating the stimulus of foreign competition. The church lands would be taken over, a portion of them sold in small-holdings for eleven million, and the remainder subject to a quit rent producing a quarter of a million a year. The national debt and the grand jury cess would be abolished, local services being provided for out of the central revenue. The taxes on wine, tea, sugar and tobacco 'not a necessity but the poor man's luxury', would be removed or abolished. Indeed 'an almost total annihilation of taxes would follow repeal'. Irish money would no longer leave the country in taxation and remittances to absentees; the pressure of taxation and the prospects of a political career would bring the absentees back, resident landlords would spend their incomes at home, Ireland's resources would be developed, rack-rents would be reduced, labourers would secure employment, and jobbery and vestry cesses would be swept away.[1]

O'Connell's conceptions of the lines on which an independent Ireland would develop illustrate strikingly to what a great extent his ideas were derived from the general stock of British radicalism. As a young man he soaked himself in Godwin, and sometime later he became a political utilitarian, in 1829 avowing himself on the Ennis hustings, 'to be a Benthamite'. The aged but ever-enthusiastic Bentham, to whom O'Connell's words were 'like a gulp of intoxicating gas', strove hard to induce the great agitator and advocate to place himself at the head of a crusade for legal reform. For a while he bombarded O'Connell with draft schemes, tried to get an article out of him for the *Westminster*, begged him not to abuse the liberals, invited him to stay in his 'hermitage' with

[1] *MR* 3 Jan. 1831, 21 Nov. 1832; *Pilot*, 13 Jan. 1834.

its regular hours and rationed conversation, suggested he should start on a tour of the British Isles as a missionary for legal reform, and rather crudely assured him that law reform would not harm his professional income—for a faster and cheaper procedure would mean more cases and less spent on attorneys.[1] O'Connell for his part treated Bentham with effusive respect, and though he failed to place himself completely at the philosopher's disposal, when he entered the house of commons he spoke in favour of a codification of the law, local courts of equity, the abolition of the law terms, and an improved bankruptcy code.[2] A close friend thought indeed that at this time law reform had for the moment taken entire possession of his mind.[3] Early in his parliamentary career O'Connell also pressed for the abolition of flogging in the army, sinecures, the Jewish disabilities and the blasphemy laws. He strongly supported the emancipation of the slaves, referring on one occasion to the West Indian planters as 'sitting dirty and begrimed over a powder magazine', and he fought hard against the apprenticeship period imposed on slaves in the emancipation bill introduced by his old foe Stanley in 1833. When Indian affairs were being discussed in 1833 he declared he supported the government's policy whenever it tended to promote the diffusion of Christianity and the establishment of a solid basis for the future liberty and independence of India.[4]

Radicalism was the predominant element in the first political programme he produced after emancipation was a certainty. His manifesto to the electors of Clare in May 1829 advocated parliamentary reform, the enfranchisement of every tax-payer, the repeal of the act disfranchising the forty-shilling freeholders, an equitable redistribution of the property of the established church between the poor and the working protestant clergy, the repeal of the vestry act, removal of the restrictions on the monastic orders, a charitable trusts act which would enable catholic parish priests to acquire parochial houses and glebes, the repeal of the sub-letting act, reform of grand jury assessments, a codifying and cheapening of the law, improved internal communications, the abolition of the monopoly of the East Indian company, and free trade (he implies that Irish agriculture and English industry are complementary; later he

---

[1] For relations between O'Connell and Bentham see *The works of Jeremy Bentham* ed. T. Bowring, x. 594-603, xi. 12, 20-1, 27-38, 62-3, and Bentham to O'Connell, 25 Aug. 1829 (O'Connell MSS. U.C.D.).

[2] *Parl. Deb.*, 2 series, xxiv. 235, 280, xxii. 675, xxiii. 63.

[3] Notes of a conversation between Staunton and R. R. Madden 1864 (Madden MSS.).

[4] *Parl. Deb.*, 3 series, xvii. 53, 2 series, xxiv. 793, 3 series, xv. 679, v. 200, xiii. 77, xviii. 314; *Pilot*, 11 Oct. 1833.

declared Irish industries required protection). On the hustings he added to this pretty full programme, the abolition of tithe, universal suffrage and the ballot, and repeal was mentioned incidentally at a meeting to raise election funds.[1]

His approach to economic problems was generally speaking dominated by economic liberalism. As a young law student he had read Adam Smith, and in the early thirties, in spite of the protests of some of his followers, he urged the repeal of the corn laws, and the abolition of the usury laws—since it was absurd for the legislative to try and fix the price of a commodity. Also like many radicals he thought that the return to gold had been managed so as to benefit unduly the moneyed interest, and he suggested that the national debt should be scaled down. In constitutional matters he was a thorough-going democrat, favouring manhood suffrage, annual parliaments, the ballot (for which he used in the house of commons the *argumentum ad hominem* that in the London clubs gentlemen were willing to shelter behind it), and, when the house of lords proved an obstacle to liberal measures, an elected second chamber.[2]

This paraphernalia of principles and projects would not in itself have sufficed to turn O'Connell into a force to be reckoned with in British politics. His strength lay in his combination of intellectual receptivity, originality and oratorical power with an extraordinary aptitude, developed by experience, for mobilizing and directing public opinion. He was an expert and innovator in the whole technique of popular political management. From 1824 he always had at his disposal an organization through which he could marshal his supporters, spread his ideas, display the weight of popular sentiment behind him and influence the constituencies. Between 1830 and 1840 he floated about a dozen political societies. Early in 1830, with the catholic question out of the way, he began in a modest, business-like way by opening the Parliamentary Intelligence Office at 26 Stephen's Green, a sort of political clubhouse, with a plentiful supply of newspapers, where petitions to parliament could be prepared. The annual subscription was £1 and O'Connell hoped that the subscribers would form the basis of a great repeal society.[3] Within a few weeks the subscribers turned themselves into the Friends of Ireland of all Religious Persuasions, which was proclaimed in May 1830. Then there emerged in rapid succession the Irish Volunteers for the repeal of

[1] *DEP*, 30 May, 4 June, 1 Aug. 1829.
[2] A. Houston, *Daniel O'Connell, his early life and journal*, pp. 126-7; *Parl. Deb.*, 3 series, xvii. 1375, xxi. 1570, 2 series, xxiv. 60; *FJ*, 30 June 1830.
[3] *Parl. Deb.*, 2 series, xxiv. 1204 ff; *Pilot*, 14 Sept. 1835.
[4] *DEP*, 7 Jan., 30 Mar., 13, 15 Apr. 1830.

the union, the Irish Society for Legal and Legislative Reform, the General Association of Ireland for the prevention of unlawful meetings, and the Subscribers to the Parliamentary Intelligence Office, each essentially the same society as O'Connell struggled by changing the label to evade the government's legal offensive.[1] The National Political Union, which was founded in November 1831 and lasted until the beginning of January 1833, aimed at combining all reformers in support of Grey's ministry (with the exception of Stanley, the chief secretary, whom even as a reformer O'Connell could not stomach).[2] With reform through, the society, renamed the Volunteers of Ireland, was revived, to carry on the fight for repeal. It was suppressed in April 1833 and in November 1834 on Peel returning to power O'Connell again formed a comprehensive organization, the Anti-tory Association, in which repealers and anti-repeal liberals could unite to drive the conservatives from office.[3] It was replaced at the beginning of 1836 by the Reform Registry Association, which also had a comprehensive liberal membership,[4] and this was succeeded after a few months by the New Reform Association[5] which, having christened itself the National Association, in deference to O'Connell's desire that the name be reserved for a later occasion, renamed itself the General Association of Ireland. After the general election of 1837, having no immediate business to transact, it wound itself up.[6] Nearly a year later it was succeeded by the deliberately ambiguously named Precursor Society—which 'preceded' justice to Ireland or a repeal agitation, as circumstances would dictate.[7] This society lasted just a year, and on its dissolution in 1839 under government pressure, a new Reform Registry Association was formed in which whigs and repealers co-operated. Finally in April 1840, the National Association for full and prompt justice and repeal came into being, and in July, dropping the alternative from its title it emerged as the National Repeal Association which remained in existence until some years after O'Connell's death.

All these bodies were constituted on much the same basis. Membership was open to subscribers paying £1 per annum, there might be a committee in which contentious issues could be thrashed out in private, a public weekly meeting at which the progress of the organization was indicated by the election of new members and the receipt of subscriptions, lengthy speeches were made on current topics, reports read and

---

[1] See proclamation, *DEP*, 15 Jan. 1831.  [2] *Pilot*, 24, 26 Nov. 1834.
[3] *Pilot*, 24, 26 Nov. 1834.  [4] *Pilot*, 16 Jan. 1836.
[5] *Pilot*, 23 May 1836.  [6] *Pilot*, 4 July, Sept. 1836, 3, 19 July, 1 Nov. 1837.
[7] See pp. 174.

discussed, and strong resolutions passed. In retrospect, a substantial pro-portion of the proceedings seem humdrum, inflated and futile. But the meetings offered companionship, opportunities for self-expression and self-advertisement obviously appreciated by prominent local politicians, a public demonstration of the party's power, and for O'Connell a con-venient theatre in which to display his oratorical and social gifts. In all these societies he was the dominant figure, they were most active when he was in Dublin, and their proceedings flagged whenever he left for Westminster or the country.

In addition to the societies that have been mentioned, from November 1831 there was the Trades Political Union, composed of 'tradesmen', which met fairly regularly in Dublin, and which had branches in Cork and Belfast. The Dublin Trades Political Union began by quarrelling with O'Connell. He proposed that one-third of their council should be composed of persons paying £1 per annum, and that they should hold their meetings at 2 p.m. The Trades Union leaders pointed out that this would mean discrimination between the honest operatives and their wealthy brethren. O'Connell retorted by declaring that it was impossible to hold weekly meetings of working men. If they took place in the after-noon they would interfere with work, if they were held at night, 'I say the man that works by day should sleep by night or if he does not must take refreshments that render him unfit for deliberation.' After a fort-night's acrimonious arguing, agreement was reached. Tradesmen, certi-fied by the secretary of the Trades Political Union, were to be admitted to the National Political Union, and O'Connell proposed building a hall for the Trades to meet in. At the same time he suggested that the Trades Political Union should appoint two persons in each parish to take charge of petitions to parliament.[1] From then on the radical tradesmen of Dublin, full of bustling political self-importance, were of the greatest use to the liberal cause. They not only discussed at their meetings subjects such as the poor laws, the bank of Ireland monopoly, railroads, and the quay wall nuisance, but they attended to the drudgery of getting voters on the register and canvassing the city.[2]

Stirring and interminable verbosity, if for a time inspiring, is apt to become soporific, but O'Connell, though he obviously revelled in the picturesque aspects of agitation, kept steadily in view the main aims of his organization, the marshalling of public opinion in an imposing array behind his policy and influencing the return of Irish M.P.s. The horrors of the French Revolution and '98, his first-hand knowledge of the con-

[1] *DEP*, 3, 17, 24 Nov., 17 Dec. 1831, 5, 7 Apr., 1832.
[2] *Pilot*, 14 Nov. 1836, 12 July 1837, 9 Dec. 1840; *FJ*, 11 Sept. 1839.

sequences of agrarian strife, his reading of Godwin, his legal training, his success in winning catholic emancipation through propaganda, his natural kindliness and perhaps a realization of the fact that a successful middle-aged lawyer was not likely to cut much of a figure as a soldier, gave him a deep and genuine abhorrence of violence in politics. According to his daughter he was accustomed to say that 'Every man has a tendency to become a ruffian when he has arms placed in his hands, and it is only the strict restraints of discipline and the long habits of military obedience that control the soldier and render him patient and forbearing.'[1] 'Once you stain a revolution with blood', he declared, 'you render the edifice insecure.' No useful political change could, he thought, in the existing state of society take place through violence. 'Every outbreak of that kind necessarily increases tyranny, changing what may be hard to bear into a despotism not long to be endured.' He could justify his refusal to consider appealing to arms by his belief that there was a better alternative. With knowledge increasing and democracy making steady progress their weapons could be 'moral means, reasoning, peaceable combination, the electricity of public opinion'.[2] And during the heady days of the early thirties when radicals and revolution were often connected, he hammered home his theory at meetings and in manifestos. And there is no doubt that between 1830 and 1840 peaceful agitation secured considerable successes in both Great Britain and Ireland. Nevertheless O'Connell's theory is open to one or two obvious criticisms. It was not always as easy as he implied to draw a line between moral action and violence. In the case of a great mass movement it is sometimes difficult to see the distinction between vigorous pressure and intimidation, and the latter can degenerate into violence. Further it can be argued that it was the very possibility that this transformation might take place which was an important factor in enabling peaceful agitation to win its victories. On the other hand there was always the danger that the prestige of the movement might be seriously damaged if it failed to produce quick returns, particularly as O'Connell was inclined to stimulate enthusiasm by injections of reckless optimism. The danger was peculiarly acute in the case of repeal, when both the great parliamentary parties seemed bent on maintaining the union, and O'Connell's course, as shall be seen, fluctuated. At times he was prepared to put it to the touch and go all out for his main objective, but there were also periods when he was prepared to bargain, and to be temporarily content with

[1] Fragment of life of O'Connell in O'Connell Fitz-Simon MSS.
[2] *Pilot*, 11 Jan., 21 Oct. 1831, 20 Nov. 1833; W. J. Fitzpatrick, *Correspondence of Daniel O'Connell*, ii. 156.

limited if definite concessions. Neither policy was altogether satisfactory. If he pursued the first the ineffectiveness of his methods might be strikingly demonstrated, if he chose the second he had to abandon publicly his agitation and disappoint his more advanced followers. Fortunately for himself O'Connell was not an introspective pessimist, but a confident politician with an eye to practicalities. And so he cheerfully threw himself in turn into both courses, using his power out of doors and in parliament as circumstances demanded.

O'Connell's parliamentary power can best be assessed against the background of a survey of the working of the Irish electoral system. The Irish reform act of 1832 was a highly complex measure, the aim of its framers according to Stanley being to provide 'a competent and respectable constituency',[1] and this they thought could best be attained by creating a *pays legal* of £10 freeholders. But the whigs' respect for property in all its manifestations, and (when possible) for vested interests, led to the creation and preservation of about a score of franchises in which value, duration and type of tenure appeared in different combinations which were presumed to be socially equivalent. A system of representation based on legal equations invited attack and the defects of the Irish representative system became part and parcel of the repeal case. O'Connell, taking population as the basis on which representation should rest, complained that Ireland should have at least twenty more members,[2] secondly he argued that the electorate, which in 1841 was under 100,000, was far too small, finally he pointed out a number of technical defects in the registration arrangements. On this last point both tories and whigs agreed with him, but this unusual unanimity did not lead to the production of a generally acceptable remedy, since registration, along with the qualification issue with which it soon became joined in debate, were matters in which legal niceties and political power were inextricably mingled. The reform act having fixed a qualification for the franchise which the Irish radicals considered unreasonably high, had left uncertain how the value should be ascertained, and in 1837 a majority of the Irish judges (each member of the bench arriving on legal grounds at an opinion which strikingly coincided with his known political convictions) laid down that the higher of the two criteria employed should be used.[3] Between 1835 and 1841 no fewer than nine bills, none

---

[1] *Parl. Deb.*, 3 series, lx. 598.

[2] The Irish reform act of 1832 gave Ireland five additional members.

[3] The two criteria of 'a clear yearly value of £10' suggested at the time, were either (1) that a solvent tenant without collusion could pay that sum as an additional rent over and above all charges, or (2) that in estimating the value, what a tenant by profitable occupation might acquire should be taken into account. The second was

of which reached the statute book, dealing with these two subjects were introduced into the house of commons by either the government or the opposition. When the whigs attempted to combine a tighter system of registration with a reversal of the judges' decision or a strictly ascertained £5 franchise, the conservatives declared indignantly that by taking population instead of property and intelligence as the basis of representation, they would 'demoralize and democratize Ireland', and that they might as well introduce universal suffrage straight away. On the other hand when Stanley, after a briefing by Jackson, a hard fighting tory barrister with a special knowledge of Irish electoral problems, introduced a measure which he boldly declared was unconnected with party politics, to improve the registration system, he was accused of trying to prevent fraudulent voting by making registration unnecessarily difficult.[1] The subject sprawled across parliamentary life for nearly a decade,[2] and it was not until 1850 that the Irish franchise was placed on a scientific footing by the adoption of the poor law valuation as its basis.

The first general election to be held after the passing of the reform bill resulted in Ireland in a landslide to the left. Throughout the county the liberals, who included for obvious reasons the great bulk of the catholic gentry and clergy, were flushed with triumph and organized in local clubs with a central co-ordinating body in Dublin. In about a dozen counties the great established interests which had so long dominated the scene were violently dislodged, and in several erstwhile nomination boroughs the newly enfranchised electors chose a candidate of a decidedly radical hue. Amongst the Irish county members were Lalor, distinguished for his outspoken opposition to tithe, a son of O'Connell's, and Feargus O'Connor, an outstanding member of a family noted for political extremism and personal eccentricity. In Dublin, long dominated by an aggressively protestant corporation, O'Connell and his friend Ruthven, both standing as repealers, were returned. Drogheda returned Dwyer, a young catholic barrister standing as a repealer, Dundalk returned another catholic barrister, O'Reilly, whose attitude to repeal was ambiguous, his address stating that he no longer hesitated to declare that he considered it a paramount duty 'to secure for that momentous and all-absorbing question the fullest and freest discussion'.[3]

definitely a more liberal test. For the whole question see W. Mears, *A treatise on the law and practice relating to elections . . . in Ireland* (1847).

[1] *Parl. Deb.*, 3 series, lvi. 309, 833, xxx. 950; T. D. Jackson to Peel, 28 Sept. 1837, Stanley to Peel, 16 Jan. 1841 (Add. MSS. 40424, 40467).

[2] In 1844 Peel's government introduced still another abortive registration bill.

[3] *M.R.*, 30 Nov. 1832; *DEP*, 20, 27 Dec. 1832.

The cities of Cork, Limerick, and Galway each returned two repealers, in Armagh, long the primate's preserve, a large group of electors nominated and returned Dobbin, a local banker, on a radical programme, in Cashel the shopkeepers put in Roe, a small landowner, who, according to an unfriendly critic, was a miserable public speaker, Clonmel returned O'Connell's cousin Ronayne, a barrister with a satirical pen, and in spite of the efforts of the tories led by Maurice Fitzgerald, on behalf of Sir Edward Denny whose family for a century had controlled the borough, the trading class of Tralee elected O'Connell's son Maurice.[1]

Taking Ireland as a whole the conservatives in 1832 fared badly, securing only twenty-seven seats. Of the remaining seventy-eight Irish M.P.s at least thirty-eight were pledged repealers, and of the other forty (who labelled themselves whigs, reformers, or radicals) at least five were pledged to adopt repeal if justice was not speedily secured for Ireland. In August the Trades Political Union resolved to support only candidates pledged to repeal;[2] this attitude was imitated by several local organizations, and a number of prominent liberals, such as Lord Killeen in Meath, Wallace at Drogheda, Leader at Kilkenny and Pierce Mahony at Limerick who refused to take the pledge, had to withdraw from the field. Still, admittedly O'Connell met with a few setbacks. Wallace having been rejected by the Drogheda radicals whose battle he had long fought, was returned by the efforts of the Independent Club for County Carlow,[3] Walker, a keen liberal who refused the repeal pledge got in for Wexford,[4] and at Mallow O'Connell's secretary, O'Neill Daunt, was finally beaten by Jephson, whose family had controlled the borough since the end of the seventeenth century. Significantly enough it was in Belfast that Irish liberalism in its triumphal year met with a severe though disguised check. For years the citizens of Belfast had seen themselves theoretically represented in the house of commons by a nominee of the marquess of Donegall. The reform act however created a comparatively large constituency of about 4,000 voters, returning two members. In the summer of 1832 the heads of the liberal party, victorious at length, and, as they incautiously labelled themselves, 'the natural leaders', set to work to pick suitable candidates. Emerson Tennent, a cultured and ambitious young banker, connected with several of the leading radicals of the previous generation and the author of an enthusiastic work on

---

[1] *DEP*, 8, 10 Dec. 1832; M. Fitzgerald to Wellington, 6 Dec. 1832 (Wellington, *Despatches . . . 1819-32*, viii. 477-9).
[2] *DEP*, 31 Aug. 1832.
[3] *DEP*, 27 Nov., 4 Dec. 1832.
[4] Wallace refused to take the repeal pledge (*DEP*, 9, 18 Oct. 1832).
[5] *DEP*, 15 Dec. 1832.

Greece, intimated that he was willing to stand. But the liberal committee, riding 'roughshod over the liberties of Belfast behind closed doors', selected instead R. J. Tennent and William Sharman Crawford who pledged themselves to a strongly radical programme. Whereupon a number of citizens—probably after some canvassing by the disappointed candidate—asked Emerson Tennent to stand. He readily came forward as an independent member, emphasizing the need for church reform and economy, and attacking O'Connell as 'a capricious and remorseless demagogue'. Strong attacks were made by his supporters on the liberal caucus, which was blamed for every minor instance of municipal mis-management as well as for political insolence. The Belfast tories, who were not strong enough to run a candidate of their own, voted for Emerson Tennent, who along with the earl of Belfast, a moderate whig, was returned over the two liberal candidates. Moreover, it was noted with pain by the discomforted *Northern Whig*, the organ of northern liberalism, that while nearly all the 350 catholics on the register had voted for both Crawford and R. J. Tennent, only 200 protestants, nearly all 'new-light presbyterians', had voted for both these candidates.[1]

O'Connell's parliamentary strength was at its apogee after the general election of 1832. In the next election (1835) both the conservatives and the liberals who were not associated with repeal improved their position, winning thirty-seven and forty seats respectively, while the repealers won only twenty-eight. And, since gains and losses cancelled out, the position was practically the same after the general election of 1837.[2] In 1841, however, the repealers won only eighteen seats, while the liberals won forty-seven and the conservatives forty. And it may be added that in 1841 out of the eighteen Ulster county seats the conservatives held sixteen as well as eight out of the eleven borough seats.[3] The causes of this shift are easily discernible. That whigs or liberals tended to replace repealers was a consequence of the slackening of the repeal agitation after 1834, and the formation of a united reform front at the three following elections. In these circumstances the territorial and personal influence of the liberals was bound to assert itself, and with the disappearance of the repeal pledge, the number of parliamentary repealers fell. As for the tories they seem to have trusted with some success to Mr Taper's policy and kept a staff of local agents to watch the

[1] See *BNL* and *NW*, Aug. to Dec. 1832; *Belfast election: Mr Emerson Tennent's claims and conduct* (1832).

[2] The results in 1837 were, conservatives 34, liberals 43, repealers 28.

[3] The figures for the general elections of 1832, 1835, 1837 and 1841 are compiled from the material in *Dod's parliamentary companion*. At the end of 1844 twenty-two M.P.s were members of the Repeal Association (*FJ*, 31 Dec. 1844).

registries. Tory landlords were said to show political discrimination in giving qualifying tenures, and in the north some converts seem to have been made. The great house of Downshire, long the mainstay of whiggery, in the north, passed over to the conservative camp, and Lords Ranfurly and O'Neill, who had at least supported the reform bill, became conservatives in the later thirties. According to Emerson Tennent, who by 1836 had himself become a conservative, the only supporters of the Melbourne ministry in Belfast were 'the Roman catholics almost to a man, the lower order of mechanics, very, very few merchants, one banker, and not a single landed proprietor worth £100 per annum'. 'The partial distribution of patronage and the almost impossibility of extorting a shilling from the treasury for a harbour or public works' had weakened the liberals, and a new anti-radical registration club had been formed in Belfast, containing men of several religious persuasions, including even some catholics, which was careful to abstain from the Orange toasts and songs at its dinners. Tennent seems to have rather exaggerated the weakness of his opponents, for in 1837 the liberals temporarily triumphed in Belfast, according to Tennent owing to the superior financial resources surprisingly produced by the bankrupt marquess of Donegall, and the partisan conduct of a catholic assistant barrister.[1]

The varying size of the repeal contingent shows that O'Connell's influence over the constituencies created by the reform act was limited. Nevertheless at a time when party organization still functioned on a local basis, and when the rudimentary central machines interfered only slightly and secretly in the constituencies, O'Connell played blatantly and to a degree effectively the role of a national political leader. Frequently he addressed open letters to constituencies urging the claims of a candidate.[2] In 1837 he secured the return of the celebrated English radical, Joseph Hume for Kilkenny, by prevailing on the citizens to keep the poll open until it was clear that Hume had lost his contest at Middlesex.[3] In 1834 he offered the radicals of Dundalk a candidate willing to pay all legal expenses, Colonel Evans, a thorough radical.[4] But the local liberals selected and returned Sharman Crawford.[5] In 1835 his efforts to secure a candidate who could afford to contest Carlow

---

[1] E. Tennent to Peel, 22 Jan. 1836, 9 Aug. 1836, 10 Oct. 1838 (Add. MSS. 40422, 40493).

[2] For example see *Pilot*, 21 Jan., 19 Nov. 1834, 13 Apr. 1836; *DEP*, 5 May 1831.

[3] *Pilot*, 27 Jan. 1837.

[4] *Pilot*, 1 Aug. 1837.

[5] O'Connell to W. Brett, 19 Dec. 1834 (W. Brett, *Reminiscences of County Louth*, p. 45).

received unpleasant publicity. He pointed out to Raphael, a London business man with political aspirations, who was both a catholic and a liberal, that he would 'never again meet so safe a speculation'. Raphael with O'Connell's backing was returned, had to face a petition which would probably prove expensive, felt himself swindled, and published the whole story. O'Connell had merely acted as an honest broker for the liberals of Carlow, but his sudden discovery that his chosen candidate was 'the most incomprehensible of imaginable vagabonds'[1] was rather ludicrous, and the arrangements for the financing of Raphael's campaign, and the possibility of O'Connell's good offices securing him a baronetcy, though all part of the common form of political life, read badly in cold print.

Occasionally O'Connell held up to opprobrium sitting M.P.s. For instance in 1834 he stated that he believed human nature was scarcely degraded enough to endure that Talbot, Lambert and O'Reilly should remain M.P.s, and all three were compelled to relinquish their seats at the following election.[2] In 1837 he denounced Smith O'Brien, the member for county Limerick, for differing with him over the payment of catholic clergy and the ballot, and he publicly urged the electors of Limerick to put pressure on him to amend his ways. Two years later he made it quite clear that he would be glad to see O'Brien, who was being criticized for not co-operating closely enough with O'Connell, out of parliament. O'Brien however was not overawed, explained that he did not consider himself to be in the smallest degree controlled by Mr. O'Connell, and secured a vote of confidence from his constituents.[3] In 1840 O'Connell attacked Brabazon, Fitzgibbon and Pierce Butler, the county M.P.s for Mayo, Limerick and Kilkenny, for neglecting their parliamentary duties, and shortly afterwards he published the correspondence between himself and Butler, relating to allegations that the latter was trying by abstaining from critical divisions to blackmail the government into giving appointments to his relations. Brabazon died before the general election of 1841, Fitzgibbon retired, but Butler was unabashed. He declared that O'Connell had acted dishonestly in publishing the correspondence, bluntly avowed that as a ministerial supporter he had asked for patronage for relations in the church and the navy, 'two professions where promotions could not be obtained by purchase', and that he was aggrieved by the government's refusal to meet his wishes. And at the general election he held his seat.[4]

---

[1] *Pilot*, 9 Nov. 1835.     [2] *Pilot*, 23 Mar. 1834.
[3] *Pilot*, 11 Jan. 1837, 3, 12 Jan. 1837; W. J. Fitzpatrick, *O'Connell's correspondence*, ii. 183.     [4] *Pilot*, 13 Apr., 9, 20, 30 Oct. 1840.

It is not of course possible to assess precisely O'Connell's influence in the constituencies. He certainly could at times influence *blocs* of voters. According to himself, he was to his regret, responsible for Damer—who turned out to be a tory in whig's clothing—not being opposed at Portarlington. Two years later Dawson, Peel's brother-in-law, attributed his defeat at Derry to O'Connell ordering the catholic electors, who numbered eighty in a constituency of four hundred and sixty, to vote against him (though the vigour with which O'Connell's views were expressed by a local catholic politician almost deprived the successful whig candidate of protestant votes).[1] If O'Connell's ubiquitous activity entitled him to be termed 'the M.P. for Ireland'[2] it aroused fear and distaste in his opponents, who continually pictured him as an unscrupulous, overbearing colossus, struggling to monopolize power in Ireland and appear at Westminster with a 'tail' of servile, discreditable Irish M.P.s. But as will be seen O'Connell by no means exercised dictatorial control even over the repeal members, and in spite of conservative sneers, taking the group as a whole it was a fair cross-section of the reformed parliament, excepting the representatives of the great landed families. It had admittedly its black sheep, such as Valentine Blake, a shameless and dishonest careerist,[3] and Dillon Browne, a tippling and witty spendthrift, and it might be argued that several of O'Connell's family were in the house on their father's reputation rather than their own merits; but the repeal group also included respectable landowners such as Ruthven and the O'Conor Don, Henry Grattan, the Whites, the heirs of Luke White, said to have died the richest man in Ireland, and Vigors, the first secretary and one of the founders of the Royal Zoological Society.

[1] *Pilot*, 16 Jan. 1836; Dawson to Peel, 16 Aug. 1837 (Add. MS. 40424); G. R. Dawson's diary of Derry election.

[2] *Greville Memoirs* (1938), ii. 350.

[3] In 1845 Blake offered to test Irish feeling on Peel's policy by offering himself to his constituents for re-election. A necessary preliminary to this, however, was to be his appointment to an office compatible with a seat in parliament (V. Blake to Peel, April 1845, Add. MS. 40564).

# 6

# O'CONNELL AND THE WHIGS, 1830–41

Catholic emancipation created a great gap in Irish politics. Though sectarian animosity was not quenched and questions concerning the relationship of the catholic body to the community at large were still to arise, the disappearance of the principal catholic disabilities meant that the channel down which nearly all Irish political controversy since the union had flowed was at length closed. However within a short time a number of new issues had come to the fore. Catholic emancipation was scarcely on the statute book when O'Connell started a drive towards his next major political objective, the repeal of the union, and the passing of the great reform bill a few years later inaugurated in both Great Britain and Ireland, a constructive, exciting and highly complex political era.

Compared with the emancipation movement in its hey-day the repeal agitation was at first rather a political flop. Several of O'Connell's old associates failed to join him. O'Gorman Mahon had quarrelled with him over election matters, Wyse, the talented historian of the emancipation movement, gave up his opportunity of winning a seat in his ancestral city of Waterford, rather than identify himself with repeal.[1] Pierce Mahony, a well-known solicitor, whose shrewdness and hospitality— his home was known as 'the Holland House of the Irish whigs'—made him a force in Irish politics, took steps to organize a widely signed declaration against repeal.[2] And Sheil, after O'Connell the most powerful and sparkling advocate of emancipation, stood aloof from the new agitation. In speeches delivered at the end of 1829 he attributed the best intentions to the government, but emphasized that emancipation im-

---

[1] D. Gwynn, *The O'Gorman Mahon* (1934), pp. 110 ff; J. J. Auchmuty, *Sir Thomas Wyse, 1791-1862* (1939), chap. ix.
[2] *FJ*, 21 Jan. 1853.

plied that the catholics should have their fair share of patronage in the future. Privately he was trying to secure an immediate instalment of this policy by pressing the government to support his candidature for county Meath, because, he explained, 'if I am left to the resources of demagogy I must do much against my will in getting into the house of commons'. The chief secretary, Hardinge, was eager to assist him on the ground that 'the lawyers in Dublin from the absence of the aristocracy have an unnatural ascendancy and power', but Peel and Wellington, having 'no confidence in the discretion of Irish orators', decided not to risk a connection with Sheil.[1] Conway, the editor of the *Dublin Evening Post*, which was said to have double the circulation of any other Irish newspaper, thought Repeal impracticable and fought against O'Connell *à outrance*.[2] The government regarded the agitation with tolerant contempt, Peel about this time remarking *à propos* the suggestion that O'Connell should be made a K.C., 'he is so great a blackguard and so low at present that I should be very unwilling to see him in possession not of a silk gown but of a legitimate grievance from the refusal of it.'[3] However the prime minister, himself an Irishman and an ex-chief secretary, had shortly after emancipation laid down the principle 'that we must contrary to the usual practice in Ireland, closely examine every transaction that itself tends to a breach of the peace'.[4] And O'Connell's organizations were too suggestive of a substitute for parliament to be permitted to function for long. In addition after the July days and their repercussions in the Netherlands, which were hailed with noisy delight by the Dublin radicals, the government seems to have been afraid of an outbreak in Ireland. According to the lord-lieutenant the idea was in the air 'that what the youth of Bruxelles have effected the boys of Dublin can surely perform', and the chief secretary, though he believed that the mass of the people were in too hopeless a state to effect anything, and that O'Connell was too wary and timid to risk his life, nevertheless was afraid 'of an explosion resulting from large public meetings after the rabble had been excited'. Since he believed that the danger would be considerably lessened by taking the fearless line rather than by concession (which with a Dublin mob would inevitably lead to disaster), he turned his professional experience to account by elaborating tactical schemes for coping with a rising in Dublin, and in planning for the

---

[1] Hardinge to Peel, 13 Oct. 1830, Peel to Hardinge, 16 Oct. 1830 (Add. MS. 40313); *DEP*, 20 Sept., 24 Oct. 1829.

[2] Hardinge to Peel, 22 Oct. 1830 (Add. MS. 40313).

[3] Peel to Leveson-Gower, 11 Apr. 1830 (Add. MS. 40338).

[4] Wellington to Northumberland, 16 July 1829 (*Wellington Despatches, 1819-1832*, vi. 19-21).

coastguards to hold points where in the event of a rising loyal men might rally.[1]

In April 1830, as soon as O'Connell was safely out of Ireland on his way to Westminster, the government commenced hostilities by proclaiming the Friends of Ireland an illegal organization. This marked the beginning of a long campaign, conducted strictly in accordance with the rules of legal warfare, the government producing proclamations as fast as O'Connell founded societies.

The fall of Wellington's government in November 1830 did not make an essential change in the Irish situation. For by a political accident Ireland fell largely under the control of the more conservative section of Grey's variegated reform ministry. Anglesey's liberal ideas, experience, and popularity—won admittedly by a blazing indiscretion—when he left Ireland in 1828, may have justified his appointment as lord-lieutenant. But these advantages were balanced by his political naïveté, impetuosity and tory connections. The chief secretary, Stanley, was highly competent, courageous, zealous, self-assured and a superb if showy debator. However, an acute judge remarked after he had been a couple of years in office, 'Stanley with all his talents makes a mess of everything but this comes from his being half a tory'.[2] And from the outset of his political career, his latent toryism was revealed by the vehemence with which he maintained the value and defended the rights of the establishment. Stanley's attitude on ecclesiastical affairs was bound to annoy many of the Irish liberal members. In addition his manners were not conciliatory. He was too impatient, the duke of Leinster noticed, to display the necessary 'official humbug' by listening at interviews to what he knew already; and his own account of how he handled Pierce Mahony, a prominent if recent recruit to whiggery, shows his lack of political affability. When he arrived in Ireland he found Mahony 'a pushing impudent fellow but with great cleverness . . . always at the Castle and the Irish office and meddling with everything'. Stanley, in his own words, 'contrived to keep him at a distance, and having broken these habits should not be sorry now to buy him'.[3] During his short term of office Stanley inaugurated an era of constructive reform, antagonized O'Connell, irritated intensely several of his colleagues, including the lord-lieutenant, and rendered himself by his connections and eloquence a minister whose departure from office

[1] Northumberland to Wellington, 31 Oct. 1830 (*Wellington Despatches 1819-1832*, vii. 312-13), Hardinge to Peel, 12, 20 Oct. 1830 (Add. MS. 40313).
[2] *Greville Memoirs* (1938), ii. 383.
[3] Leinster to Hobhouse (Add. MS. 36467), Stanley to Anglesey, 7 Dec. 1831 (Plas Newydd MSS.).

threatened the cabinet's existence. In Ireland legal appointments were always scrutinized closely, partly because of the social status of the bar, and partly because in many instances political issues and legal cases were entangled. Now, the first law appointments made by the new government aroused a storm of radical criticism. Joy and Doherty, the attorney- and solicitor-general of the late tory administration, were, admittedly after some delay, turned out of office—by being promoted to the bench. Their successors were Blackburne, who according to his biographer did not hold strong political opinions but had strictly conservative views, and who refused to abandon his lucrative practice at the Four Courts to carry out his parliamentary duties, and Campion, an ex-fellow of Trinity, of mildly whig opinions, of whose professional capacity O'Connell had the lowest opinion.[1]

To Lord Grey and his colleagues Ireland proved a *damnosa hereditas* and their well-intentioned efforts to grapple with its problems constituted a minor political tragedy. A country whose political life was distinguished by bitterness, stridency and violence, did not offer an easy field for the practice of liberal principles. Grey became utterly despondent when he saw 'the high protestants on the one hand contending for the re-establishment of an odious and expensive power, and the leaders of the catholics on the other aiming at nothing else than the total subversion of the protestant establishment and the repeal of the Union'. And he complained that 'an observation of the *juste milieu* is no easy task'.[2] The ministers, overwhelmed, frustrated, forced into the distasteful role of coercionists and assailed with criticism from both the right and the left, soon became disheartened and irritated. At the outset Holland, the most philosophic (or at any rate the least officially burdened) member of the cabinet, reflected that 'to govern Ireland by force and yet preserve the semblance of a free government there and the reality of it here is impossible'. Something, he argued, must be done to secure the support of O'Connell or at least of a substantial section of the catholics. And he threw out a number of suggestions as to how this might be accomplished, the appointments of lieutenants in the Irish counties, a peerage or two for leading catholic landowners, grand jury reform and the discontinuation of grants to the Kildare Place Society. 'Would', he wondered, 'the dispersal of some legal patronage in the colonies among Irish barristers, especially catholics, would the secret consultation of some catholic

[1] E. Blackburne, *Life of the Rt. Hon. F. Blackburne* (1874), p. 62; *Life of John, Lord Campbell* (1881), ii. 27-8; W. E. Fitzpatrick, *Correspondence of Daniel O'Connell*, i. 474.

[2] Grey to Anglesey, 11 June 1832 (Plas Newydd MSS.); Grey to Newport, 2 Oct. 1832 (Newport papers).

bishop, facilitate you in obtaining for the government and for English connection, and withdrawing from O'Connell and the separationists, the co-operation of any large portion of the native and catholic Irish?'[1] Melbourne, who had begun his career as a tory, and who was still inclined to think that it was only through the protestant party that Ireland could be governed, was less fertile in suggestions, but he too advocated the appointment of lieutenants in the counties, on the ground that it would strengthen the local administration and enable the government to conciliate 'on the one hand persons of weight and influence by conferring upon them the appointments, and on the other the mass of the people by the character and popularity of those upon whom such appointments were conferred.' But he added pessimistically, there would be 'the difficulty of finding in Ireland individuals sufficiently free from local partialities and prejudices'.[2] Stanley, who unlike Melbourne was well endowed with self-confidence and driving power, managed during his short tenure of office to produce an extensive Irish programme. At the outset he was delighted to discover that the cabinet had decided to make generous grants for public works in Ireland. 'If we can only effect this', he declared, 'we may laugh at O'Connell.' In addition he was anxious to hold an inquiry into the state of the law relating to roads, which was 'very complicated and various and leads like everything else to endless jobbing'. He set up a commission to inquire into the Shannon navigation, he discussed the possibility of getting rid of market tolls, and he pushed forward civil service reform, reorganizing and reducing the staff of his own office.[3] In two and a half years he constituted an Irish board of works, initiated a national system of elementary education, reorganized the revenues of the establishment and regulated the administrative functions of the grand juries.

But if Irish conditions urgently demanded a programme of constructive reform, they created distracting difficulties for its architects, since before the whigs could put their good intentions into practice the position of the establishment involved them in a series of prolonged, intricate and angry discussions. To Irish farmers tithe at the best was an onerous legal obligation. At the worst it was an iniquitous impost, and from time to time there were refusals to pay. The excitement aroused by catholic emancipation and the general election of 1830, the critical attitude of the catholic clergy to the claims of the establishment, the noisy

---

[1] Holland to Anglesey, 3 Jan. 1831 (Plas Newydd MSS.).
[2] Melbourne to Anglesey, 28 Dec. 1830 (Plas Newydd MSS.). For Melbourne's general outlook on Irish affairs see Littleton diary, 10 Aug. 1835 (Teddesley MSS.).
[3] Stanley to Anglesey, 31 Jan., 29 Mar., 21 June, 23 Sept. 1831 (Plas Newydd MSS.).

missionary activities of the 'biblicals' and the spread of literacy, exacerbated the situation.[1] Some of the clergy refused to attempt to recover their tithes at the risk of bloodshed; others displayed a Hildebrandine determination to preserve the rights of the church, and occasionally showed a latent talent for guerilla warfare when devising schemes for the defeat of their recalcitrant parishioners. The complicated machinery prescribed for bringing a tithe defaulter to book was quite inadequate for coping with a widespread, collective refusal to pay. A process had to be secured, served and moved, a decree obtained and executed, and the whole procedure bristled with hampering technicalities. Cattle could be seized only between sunrise and sunset. If under lock and key they could not be touched, for the law did not empower the driver to force a door or a bolt, or even to raise a latch. When cattle were seized in a hostile country it was difficult to feed or sell them, and so they had often to be escorted to the coast for export. Under these circumstances, with the tithe-owners compelled by the nature of their case to act in a punctiliously legal fashion, passive resistance could achieve a lot, particularly as there was often the possibility that it might be the forerunner of less gentle methods, and the anti-tithe agitation was marked by a few horrible episodes when reckless or panic-stricken police or yeomanry clashed with embittered peasants.[2]

Not only was tithe withheld over a wide area, but in the west, in parts of Galway and Clare, rent was also challenged. Drilling, nocturnal raids, threatening notices and stock driving on a large scale led the gentry to abandon their homes, the magistrates to call for an insurrection act, and the peasantry to believe that they might divide the land amongst themselves, each man having ten acres in perpetuity. The system seemed to one indignant landowner, 'to combine in awful array all those who have nothing to lose against all the property and respectability of the country'. In Donegal the peasants assembled in thousands and 'vowed to pay neither rent nor taxes until O'Connell got new laws for them'. And O'Connell it may be added, visited the west in the summer of 1831 and denounced tithe and 'the Terryalt' system with equal vehemence.[3]

The case against tithe was expressed most forcibly and logically by

[1] Stanley to Anglesey, 27 June, 28 July 1831 (Plas Newydd MSS.).
[2] A vast amount of information relating to tithe and the opposition to its collection is to be found in the reports and minutes of evidence presented by the select committees of the house of lords and house of commons during the session 1831-2.
[3] D. H. Kelly to ——, 20 May 1831, A. St. George to E. G. Stanley, 30 May 1831, Meeting of Galway J.P.s, 4 July 1831, W. Fitzgerald to ——, 16 Apr. 1831, Meeting of Clare J.P.s, T. Mahon to Gosset 14 Apr. 1831, H. W. Ronan to Gosset, 15 Apr. 1831, Warburton to Gosset, 20 May 1831 (S.C.P. 53); *DEP*, 7 June 1831; *Report from the select committee on tithe in Ireland*, p. 125, H.C. 1831-2 (177), xxi.

Bishop Doyle, in his nervous, glittering and at times over-emphatic style. He argued that tithes were first held by the clergy for the benefit of religion and the poor, that at the reformation the catholic clergy had been ousted from the trusteeship, that their protestant successors, being allowed to marry, 'yielded to flesh and blood, and appropriated as soon as they could the whole of the church property to their personal use; they ceased to be the instructors of the people since the people did not change their religion . . . they did not relieve the widow or the orphan, they did not instruct from schools or from the pulpit the rising generation, they did not fulfil one single duty of those that were imposed upon the trustees of that fund originally', therefore it was the duty of the state to intervene, take over the trust and use the funds produced by tithe to provide for the poor and possibly to some extent for all the ministers of religion in Ireland.[1]

In Dublin a small group of young intellectuals, founded in 1831 a a weekly newspaper, the *Comet*,[2] to advocate radical opinions, and especially to keep 'a steady, scrutinizing and uncompromising eye upon ecclesiastical hypocrisy, humbug and cant'. In practice the contributors, who were both protestants and catholics, concentrated on denouncing and ridiculing the established church, its wealthy prelates and 'peasant shooting' parsons. The parson's progress was detailed in rhyme:

> *Behold him in his boyhood, sullen, dull,*
> *With well-filled belly but with empty skull,*
> *Ten thousand souls, his parish books declare,*
> *Are under his most sole devouring care,*
> *He takes, to teach them patience, from their pelf,*
> *What would support a thousand, for himself,*
> *Fish, flesh and fowl, with floods of costly wine,*
> *Are swallowed for his holiness must dine;*
> *When asked for some as cordial for the sick,*
> *He cures the ailment with a pious kick.*

and his activities were described in cruel and swinging verse:

> *Brave peelers march on with the musket and sword,*
> *And fight for my tithes—in the name of the Lord,*

---

[1] Doyle set out his views at some length when giving evidence before parliamentary committees on tithe. (*Report from the select committee on tithe in Ireland*, H.C. 1831-2 (177), pp. 290-341, xxi; *Report from the select committee of the house of lords to inquire into the collection and payment of tithe in Ireland*, H.C. 1831-2 (271), pp. 78-103, xxii.)

[2] For the writers in the *Comet* see *Gentleman's Magazine*, new series, xiii. 685-701.

*Make a corpse of whoever appears in my path,*
*And seize all each peasant in Skibbereen hath.*[1]

The *Comet* was a radical and repeal paper, but its attitude to the establishment was reproduced in soberer tones by the leading moderate liberal journals, the *Dublin Evening Post* and the *Northern Whig*; and the general dislike of the dissenter for the privileged church and 'the pride, pomp, and glorious circumstances of legal religion'[2] found an easy target in the arrangements for maintaining the state church.

The tithe war called attention to three problems—the privileged status of the church of Ireland, the distribution of its revenues, and the sources from which these revenues were derived. The Irish liberals led by O'Connell of course openly aimed at disestablishment and disendowment. O'Connell's programme was that the existing incumbents were to receive their incomes for life, but tithe was to be abolished and replaced by a land tax (from which properties worth less than £100 per annum were to be exempt). This, together with the revenues of the church lands, was to be used for charitable and religious purposes. Every clergyman with a flock of five hundred was to be provided with a house and glebe, and the clergy of the establishment were to be paid in strict proportion to the number of their protestant parishioners.[3] At the other extreme the Irish conservatives backed up by the English ultras refused to yield one iota of the church's rights and scrutinized suspiciously all suggestions for its internal reform. Between these harsh, contending factions, Grey's government was in an absurd and tragic predicament. A liberal cabinet, they found themselves from the moment they took office committed to protecting an institution which could evoke the enthusiasm only of strong conservatives. Simultaneously they had to perform the distasteful and sometimes ludicrous task of demonstrating to those that would not pay tithe that the law could not be defied with impunity, manœuvre the reform bill through parliament in the face of an outraged and determined tory opposition, and try to arrive among themselves at an agreed policy on the Irish church question. Russell, Althorp and Wellesley believed that the establishment was shockingly disproportionate to the religious needs of its members, and resented having 'to govern by military law in order that the revenues of the church should be devoted exclusively to the use of one tenth of the population'. The chief whip of the party crudely spoke of the necessity of 'throwing the Irish

[1] *Comet*, 1 May, 26 June, 31 July, 21 Aug. 1831.
[2] *Parl. Deb.*, 3 series, xxiv. 119.
[3] *MR*, 17 July 1832.

lumber overboard'.[1] As for the lord-lieutenant, shortly after arriving in Ireland, he revealed himself in his private correspondence to be in some respects a fiery radical. While fighting the repeal agitation with the impetuous zeal of a first-class cavalry commander, he threw himself into drafting sweeping schemes of social and ecclesiastical reform. He dinned into the ears of every Irish gentleman he met that they could not expect a whole people to starve submissively; employment must be provided either by the landlords or through an Irish poor law. As for the establishment, he considered it to be preposterously out of proportion to the protestant population, and with Sadleir (a future provost of Trinity), Blake and Griffith he elaborated a scheme of ecclesiastical reform which from February 1832 he pressed on the cabinet.[1] There was to be a compulsory tithe composition, the state was to take over the revenues of the establishment and dole them out to the different denominations in proportion to their needs, and any surplus was to be used along with a poor-rate to provide for the destitute, including the able-bodied unemployed.[2] Stanley's approach to the problem was utterly different. He sincerely believed that the establishment—to which he was devotedly attached on religious grounds—was one of the most beneficial social forces in Ireland, its clergy supplying the country with a resident landed gentry. Though he advocated drastic ecclesiastical reorganization and wished to replace tithe by a landed endowment, he would not countenance any diversion of the church's income to secular purposes. And he considered that the anti-tithe campaign might prove the beginning of a servile war, 'a war of those who have no property against those who have'.[3]

When it came to deciding what to do, the cabinet as a whole was largely influenced by practical considerations, the amount of parliamentary time available, the reaction of British opinion, and the attitude of the lords, where as Grey said 'we do not possess the usual powers of government'. And Anglesey, a man of action, was, as he heartily regretted, heavily handicapped by his inability to express himself effectually in discussion.[4] Grey reminded him that though there were many

[1] S. Walpole, *Life of Lord John Russell*, i. 188-90; Ellice to Graham, 7 Feb. 1833 (C. S. Parker, *Life of Graham*, i. 182); Littleton diary, 3 June 1834 (Teddesley MSS.).
[2] Anglesey to Holland, 20 Apr. 1831, 18 Jan., 12 Feb., 27 Oct. 1832, 9 Mar. 1833, Anglesey to Grey, 18 Jan., 9, 12 Feb. 1832 (Plas Newydd MSS.).
[3] Stanley to Anglesey, 26 Feb. 1831 (Plas Newydd MSS.).
[4] 'In situations where I have to control, to command, and to decide and to act from my own judgment I do well enough. I cannot persuade people I am clever for I am not, but they know I am honest. I cannot debate in the house and at council I have not the power to express my views' (Anglesey to Holland, 21 Jan. 1833 (Plas Newydd MSS.)

differences between the English and Irish establishments, they were legally united, so that any measure relating to the one had to be considered in regard to its bearing on the other, and that a proposal to take from the church any part of its revenues for catholic purposes was bound to have an effect on public opinion in Great Britain which might prove fatal to the ministry. Grey and Melbourne combined to dismiss politely two of Anglesey's suggestions. They agreed that an Irish poor law and the payment of the catholic clergy by the state were probably desirable, but they felt that both points needed careful consideration and could not be tackled in the immediate future.[1] During 1832 the cabinet settled on a programme of moderate ecclesiastical reform. The tithe act of 1832 enforced a permanent composition all over the country and began the process of commutation. The ecclesiastical temporalities act of the following year suppressed ten Irish bishoprics, uniting them with neighbouring dioceses, set up an ecclesiastical commission empowered to divide livings, suspend appointments and use the revenues of the suppressed bishoprics and the produce of a graduated income tax on all livings worth more than £200 per annum to build and repair churches and augment poor livings.

Many liberal M.P.s, though they felt these measures tended in the right direction, considered them too limited in scope, and O'Connell and the radicals, including Durham, who were strongly opposed to the continuance in any form of tithe, were deeply disappointed when clause 147 of the church temporalities bill, which they thought implied that a surplus in the establishment's revenues might be used for secular purposes, was, for the sake of avoiding a clash with the lords, dropped.[2] On the other hand devoted anglicans were shocked by the bill. Newman lamented that half the candlesticks of the Irish church had been extinguished without ecclesiastical sanction. Keble spoke of the church being betrayed into the hands of libertines for the sake of a little temporary peace. An excitable Irish clergyman, complaining that Lord Grey annihilated a bishop's jurisdiction 'with as little scruple or ceremony than when he disfranchised a rotten borough', called on Irish churchmen at the risk of praemunire to elect and consecrate bishops for the suppressed sees.[3] And Irish tory M.P.s attempted to prove by complex calculations on the yield of first fruits, church rates and bishops'

[1] Grey to Anglesey, 16 Aug. 1831, 17 Feb., 12 Sept., 24 Oct. 1832, Melbourne to Anglesey, 30 July 1832, Anglesey to Holland, 21 Jan. 1833 (Plas Newydd MSS.).

[2] Durham to Grey, 30 July 1833, C. S. Reid (*Life and letters of the first earl of Durham* (1906), i. 329-30). Holland to Anglesey, 22 June 1833 (Plas Newydd MSS.).

[3] H. P. Liddon, *Life of E. B. Pusey* (1893), i. 266-7; R. T. McGhee, *The last stand for the church* (1833).

leases, that the bill tended to exterminate the protestant religion in Ireland. In the end the minority on the third reading of the bill in the commons, though mainly composed of tories, included a sprinkling of repealers and radicals. Getting the bill through the upper house was naturally a nerve-racking process for the ministry, and at one point Anglesey at the suggestion of Holland seems to have warned the king that a tory ministry would not be able to secure from the commons the emergency powers and the troops it would need to control Ireland.[1] Fortunately Wellington and Peel, the tory leaders, realized the dangers inherent in a Pyrrhic victory won in the lords, and, throwing their weight on the side of moderation, allowed the bill to pass.

Anglesey was bitterly disappointed by the caution with which the cabinet acted, and the limited solution which it finally adopted. He begged it to accept 'the plan, the whole plan and nothing but the plan' which he had put before it, and he resented being left to carry 'at the point of the bayonet an obnoxious measure [the 1832 act for the recovery of the tithe] against which I have strenuously protested'.[2] Holland in a series of letters which display both his persuasive powers and the whig approach to Irish ecclesiastical problems, tried to soothe the angry viceroy. Holland, whose general attitude to theological matters is illustrated by his assertion, that 'any learned man in the church who is accused by the highflyers of having a Socinian trait and of nothing else is a moderate sensible man and fit to be entrusted with ecclesiastical power', loathed the old Orange protestant ascendancy and had no desire to maintain the establishment if he could see a way of honestly and quietly getting rid of it. Naturally he agreed with Anglesey's views on the tithe question, and he quite realized that the viceroy would 'be apt to consider every hesitation or inquiry an unnecessary and squeamish scruple and every delay an evasion or procrastination, all of which will fret you'. But he was afraid of encouraging Anglesey in his endeavours to obtain the impossible. After all Stanley's tithe bill was 'a wedge', the foes of the Irish church must remember '*chi va piano va sano*', and in any case 'despatch and large cabinets, houses of parliament, bishops and lords are hardly compatible terms'. On the whole, he thought the government had handled the tithe business better than might have been expected 'with the Orange high church party in the lords, and O'Connell in the commons both equally reckless of the injury they might do'.[3]

[1] Holland to Anglesey, 12, 14 July 1833 (Plas Newydd MSS.).

[2] Anglesey to Holland, 10 Feb. and 21 Oct. 1832 (Plas Newydd MSS.), *The Paget brothers* (London 1918), pp. 355-6.

[3] Holland to Anglesey, 13 June 1828, 21 Feb., 25 June, 22, 24, 25 Oct. 1832 (Plas Newydd MSS.).

While the government was shoving its ecclesiastical legislation through parliament, agrarian direct action and crime, stimulated by the tithe troubles and perhaps to some extent encouraged by the vehemence with which repeal orators denounced the establishment, had produced over wide areas in the south of Ireland conditions which, Stanley declared, could scarcely be credited in the nineteenth century.[1] Combined action to resist the law, intimidation and outrage were rife, and Melbourne prophesied that if tithe were swept away by force 'the violence which has been successful will certainly be extended further—it is according to human nature and common sense that it will be so. Rents, taxes, etc. may be very well paid now, probably the better because the country is released from the tithe—but the Irish who are the most conspiring people upon the face of the earth have sagacity enough to fight one point at a time.' That the authority of the law should be trodden underfoot, Melbourne added, filled him 'with great humiliation and despair.'[2] As early as the spring of 1831 Stanley, who had emergency legislation ready, was alarmed at the prospect of a dissolution which would leave him in charge of Ireland for six weeks without any possibility of securing additional powers.[3] And when parliament reassembled in the summer of 1831 he secured an amended Whiteboy act and an act regulating the import of arms. Over the latter however he sustained a sharp rebuff. The bill which was drawn up by a couple of law advisers, contained a clause rendering any person found with unregistered arms in a proclaimed district liable to transportation. Neither the viceroy nor the Irish lord chancellor had been consulted, and since Melbourne neglected to bring the bill before the cabinet, the clause came as 'a clap of thunder' to many of the ministers. Grey, Althorp, Holland, Anglesey and the English attorney-general 'were appalled and disgusted' by it; Wyse and O'Connell loudly protested in the commons and Stanley was finally compelled to drop the obnoxious clause.[4] For the next eighteen months the government managed anxiously to carry out its functions without asking for additional powers. With the reform struggle in full swing it would have been hard to find time for a special powers bill, it was inexpedient to offend the Irish liberal M.P.s, and the whigs were by temperament and principle averse to coercion. Grey, himself, trembled at the idea of increasing the powers exercised by the Irish magistrates, Holland dreaded extraordinary laws which were bound to give one party

[1] Stanley to Anglesey, 17 June 1832 (Plas Newydd MSS.).
[2] Melbourne to Anglesey, 30 June 1832 (Plas Newydd MSS.).
[3] Stanley to Anglesey, 22 Mar., 12 Apr. 1831 (Plas Newydd MSS.).
[4] Holland to Anglesey, 6, 11 July 1831, Grey to Anglesey, 19 July 1831 (Plas Newydd MSS.); W. M. Torrens, *Memoirs of . . . Viscount Melbourne* (1878), i. 370.

a triumph over the other. 'I prefer', he once remarked, 'soldiers, I prefer even illegal acts of vigour, I prefer almost anything to insurrection acts and arms bills,' which in the event only aggravated the evils they were meant to check by weakening respect for the law and bringing it into contempt. Anglesey, having argued that it would be easy enough with a coercion bill to subdue the Irish people for 'they and their leaders *par excellence* are poor, pitiful swaggering cowards, and a few bloody days will settle them', went on to ask, 'But what then? The gentry will have their triumph and a pretty use they will make of it. And how is it all to end?' And even Stanley was reluctant to renew the insurrection act, hoping in the summer of 1831 that the disorder would be checked by strengthening the peace preservation force.[1] Nevertheless by the close of 1832 conditions had convinced the government of the necessity for stringent measures, and when the first reformed parliament met early in 1833 the first major measure laid before it was a drastic bill for the suppression of local disturbances in Ireland which gave the lord-lieutenant power for a year to suppress public meetings and specify areas in which certain offences might be tried by court-martial. With the passing of this act, as a consequence partly of the government's repressive measures and partly of its ecclesiastical reforms, 'a singular tranquillity succeeded a singular agitation'[2] and Irish agrariand isorder subsided to about its usual level.[3]

As has been seen on two important issues, coercion and ecclesiastical reform, there were acute differences between the viceroy and the chief secretary, and while the former naturally resented being compelled to let the public think that 'the narrow and futile' policy of the government, represented his 'courage in legislation', the latter by 1833 was sick of his task and not even on speaking terms with most of the Irish M.P.s whom he regarded as cowardly and capricious.[4] Early in September 1832 Grey was playing with the idea of replacing Anglesey by the placid and peace-loving Melbourne, and in December Brougham was so impressed with the need for a new Irish administration, and for the removal of Stanley, that he hinted he would resign if nothing were done, and rather officiously offered to bustle over to Dublin and talk things over

---

[1] Grey to Anglesey, July 1832, Holland to Anglesey, 5, 7 Jan. 1833, Anglesey to Holland, 16 Jan. 1832 (Plas Newydd MSS.), *Parl. Deb.*, 3 series, vi. 21.

[2] Anglesey to Grey, 30 Aug. 1833 (Plas Newydd MSS.).

[3] The successful prosecution for seditious libel of several anti-tithe newspapers may have also have had some effect in checking the agitation (B. Inglis, 'The freedom of the press in Ireland' Gosset to Lamb, 21 May 1833 (H.O. 100 244).

[4] Littleton to Anglesey, 29 June 1833, Stanley to Anglesey, 10, 17 May 1833 (Plas Newydd MSS.).

with the lord-lieutenant and chief secretary.[1] Finally in March 1833 Stanley, sickened by the interminable debates on Irish affairs, went to the colonial office, in the hope that 'the saints and the niggers cannot be worse than the *parsons* and the *tail*',[2] and a few months later Anglesey, who, in spite of ill-health, had at the request of his colleagues held on to office to cope with the disturbances, was replaced by Wellesley.

The bitterness generated by the tithe war acerbated relations between O'Connell and the whigs. His attitude to Grey's government from the start was complex and varying. He and the cabinet shared common objectives, but they differed in their approach to a number of issues, for the whigs were not prepared to disestablish the church, and were determined to maintain the union. Several of the cabinet too were shocked by O'Connell's style, Grey indeed being convinced that his aim was to stir up the people to revolution and rebellion.[3] On the other hand the mechanism of British politics makes it difficult for any M.P. or small group to remain for long detached from both the great parties, particularly if the party which he or it tends to favour is in precarious possession of office. Secondly, some influential supporters of the government were anxious to secure O'Connell's assistance.[4] Almost immediately after taking office, Anglesey, who of course had met O'Connell when he was previously in Ireland, had a talk with him, but a day or so later Doherty—still Irish attorney-general—sharply challenged O'Connell's accuracy or veracity in the commons, and the latter, regarding this as 'a most wanton assault', sent an exceedingly stiff note to Anglesey, emphasizing that nothing he had said at their meeting was to be constructed as a pledge to support the new administration. Duncannon, who was amicable and sensible, and who, as a liberal Irish landowner, was trusted by O'Connell, intervened, and on the following day O'Connell again wrote to the viceroy in a far more friendly tone, and two days later, overcome by Anglesey's reply, he poured out his feelings to the man whom earlier in the week he had snubbed. No man had ever been so misunderstood, and from Anglesey alone he had received anything like justice. Convinced that the new viceroy would smash the old administrative faction, he was anxous to co-operate with him.[5]

---

[1] H. Brougham, *The life and times of Henry Brougham* (1871), iii. 242–9; W. M. Torrens, *The Memoirs of Viscount Melbourne* (1878), i. 428.

[2] Stanley to Anglesey, 20 Jan., 28 Mar. 1833 (Plas Newydd MSS.).

[3] Grey to Anglesey, Jan. 1831 (Plas Newydd MSS.).

[4] It was even rumoured at the end of 1830 that O'Connell was going to be appointed chief justice of Calcutta (J. J. Auchmuty, *Sir Thomas Wyse*, p. 139).

[5] O'Connell to Anglesey, 20, 24, 26 Nov. 1830 (Plas Newydd MSS.); Anglesey to Cloncurry, 15 Dec. 1830 (Cloncurry, *Recollections*, p. 411). Holland was exceeding keen that Anglesey should keep in touch with O'Connell. 'Nothing', he wrote, 'pleases

The legal appointments seem to have shattered his never very firmly grounded belief in the whigs' good intentions, and three weeks later, when Anglesey met him again he was bent on agitation. He informed the Irish people that whig policy was characterized by delusion, humbug and quackery. When Duncannon stood for re-election in County Kilkenny, O'Connell issued a manifesto against him, in which with the exaggeration customary at by-elections, he compared the contest to the Clare election of 1828.[1] And just a month after the new government took office a group of Irish liberal M.P.s, including O'Connell, the O'Conor Don, Jephson of Mallow, and Alexander Dawson who had won Louth against the great landed interests in 1826, met and decided to introduce an Irish reform bill early in the new session.[2] The government for its part was determined to teach O'Connell that 'he has to deal with a government that will not shrink from its duty',[3] and in February 1831 a successful prosecution was launched against him for promoting an illegal organization. But at this very moment the situation was abruptly changed, for in March 1831 the whigs by the introduction of the great reform bill, revealed themselves to be genuine reformers, albeit by radical standards slow and timid ones. O'Connell, who immediately grasped that the bill destroyed the political influence of the old Irish corporations and might enable him to stand successfully for Dublin,[4] like some of the English radicals, had to decide what was the maximum he could profitably and realistically press for. The whigs obviously would not grant repeal, but they seemed to be paving the way towards it, and they might be persuaded or pushed into implementing other portions of O'Connell's programme. Helping the tories to dislodge them from office because of their imperfections might be heroic, but it was not in O'Connell's opinion, sound political tactics. So immediately the bill was introduced he issued a manifesto to the people of Ireland, calling on them to support it, and while not abandoning repeal, for the sake of unanimity to concentrate on reform. A month later he blessed Sir Henry Parnell's candidature in Queen's County.[5] At the general election of 1831 he advised the electors to return, free of expense, every M.P. who had voted for the bill. He himself stood for Kerry on

vain men and Irishmen particularly so much as unreserved communications with men in power'. (Holland to Anglesey, 1830; Plas Newydd MSS.)

[1] *Pilot*, 16 Feb. 1831.

[2] *FJ*, 16 Dec. 1830.

[3] Grey to Princess Lieven, 29 Dec. 1830 (*Correspondence of Princess Lieven and Lord Grey* (1890), ii. 129).

[4] O'Connell to his wife, 2 Mar. 1831 (O'Connell Fitz-Simon MSS.).

[5] *Pilot*, 7 Mar. 1831; *DEP*, 7 Apr. 1831.

a limited programme with a wide appeal, reform and the abolition of slavery,[1] and he bombarded the Irish administration through Duncannon with expert advice on how the government's influence could be employed to assist liberal candidates.[2] He also indirectly intimated to the government that he would drop repeal if the government would drop the prosecution against himself, and sponsor measures for the peace and prosperity of Ireland. The government did not accept these overtures, and Stanley, when O'Connell's friends interviewed him, assumed 'quite as high a tone' as the viceroy could wish (though indeed he dropped a hint that the government would not oppose a postponement of the trial). Each side could honestly deny that there was a compromise, but the cabinet decided to allow O'Connell to make full play with the law's delays, which meant that by the time he had to come up for sentence, the act under which he was convicted had expired.[3] And in the long reform bill debates O'Connell heartily supported the government, 'playing' as Stanley put it 'good boy'.[4]

While the reform bill was slowly making its way to the statute book O'Connell began to feel tentatively towards closer relations with the government. In October 1831, two days after the lords threw out the bill, he dined with Burdett, the radical baronet, and Anglesey's brother Arthur, the diplomatist. The latter assured O'Connell he would win immortal honour if he would forget his grievances and come forward in support of the government; and the following day when Ebrington moved his celebrated vote of confidence, O'Connell declared that people of England, Scotland and Ireland had bound themselves together to win reform, called on the house to back up the ministry, and suggested a remedy adequate to the emergency—a wholesale creation of peers.[5] During the autumn of 1831 he vigorously pressed through Duncannon for 'a change of system' in Ireland, which would make the whigs the Irish party. He asked for liberal legislation on ecclesiastical matters, lamented that the whigs were promoting their enemies and had neglected their friends, and demanded that appointments should be given to reformers and that 'the snappish impertinent, overbearing, high church Mr. Stanley' should be removed. To be fair to O'Connell, he was not thinking in terms of an opportune introduction of the spoils system. Appointments to the magistracy and the central administration at

---

[1] *Pilot*, 2 May 1831.

[2] W. J. Fitzpatrick, *Correspondene of Daniel O'Connell*, i. 254-60, 266-7.

[3] *Parl. Deb.*, 3 series, ii. 490, 611, 1006 ff; *Lord Melbourne's papers*, ed. L. C. Sanders (1889), pp. 180-1; Stanley to Anglesey, 9 Feb. 1832 (Plas Newydd MSS.).

[4] Stanley to Anglesey, 29 Mar. 1831 (Plas Newydd MSS.).

[5] *The Paget brothers*, p. 325, *Parl. Deb.*, 3 series, viii. 443.

Dublin Castle represented power and were visible signs of the government's outlook.[1]

But in spite of O'Connell's remonstrances Stanley remained in control of Irish affairs, and suggestions that O'Connell should be given office came to nothing. At the close of 1831 Sir Henry Parnell pressed the government to try and conciliate—and politically immobilize—O'Connell by making him chief baron or master of the rolls. Six months later Holland admitted to the lord-lieutenant that 'the idea had trotted through my head' that O'Connell, who, it could not be denied, 'was one of the best speakers in the house of commons and daily acquiring more and more the ear of the house', should be offered a legal appointment in England. In the autumn of 1831 Parnell reached the point of sounding O'Connell through Bishop Doyle. But the government's (or Parnell's) proposals were so indefinite and tentative that they merely irritated O'Connell. And Holland summed up the matter at the close of the year by remarking 'we have mismanaged O'Connell—we should have had no flirting or gone further'. There is no doubt which alternative Grey would have chosen. He wanted no dealings with O'Connell, direct or indirect. In 1834, when Burdett discovered that O'Connell was prepared, if his tithe bill was accepted, to take office as attorney-general, Grey, although 'willing to give a limb to pacify Ireland', promptly made it clear he was not going to have negotiations with O'Connell.[2] Nor were Grey's relations with the Irish liberals very happy. When after the general election of 1831 about a score of Irish liberal M.P.s, including O'Connell, Lord Killeen (who acted as their spokesman), Sheil and Wyse, waited on Lord Grey to offer the government an Irish programme, and to request the immediate disbandment of the Irish yeomanry, the prime minister declined to discuss in detail the Irish bills which he assured them were in preparation, declared it was impossible to dispense with the yeomanry, and warned the deputation that for the Irish liberal M.P.s to go into opposition or press the government too hard might merely open the way to a less friendly cabinet.[3] Later at the beginning of January 1832 some liberal M.P.s met in Dublin, termed themselves, the National Council, and among other business decided that Ireland

---

[1] W. J. Fitzpatrick, *Correspondence of Daniel O'Connell*, i. 271-7.

[2] Melbourne to Anglesey, 18 Dec. 1830, Grey to Anglesey, 29 Jan. 1833, Holland to Anglesey, 27 Aug., 5 Dec. 1831 (Plas Newydd MSS.); Bishop Doyle to Sir H. Parnell, 10, 17 Oct., 23 Dec. 1831 (W. J. Fitzpatrick, *Life, times and correspondence of Rt. Rev. Dr Doyle* (Dublin 1861), pp. 334-6), M. W. Patterson, *Sir Francis Burdett and his times* (London 1831), ii. 586-9, 596, 622-3; T. C. Hobhouse, *Recollections of a long life* (London 1910), iv. 339-40.

[3] *DEP*, 10 Aug. 1831; Grey to Anglesey, 18 Aug. 1831 (Plas Newydd MSS.).

should have 125 members of parliament and that the forty-shilling free-holders should be enfranchised.[1] They must have been sorely disappointed by the government's Irish reform bill which granted only five additional members to Ireland. According to O'Connell, when he met Althorp, Lord John Russell and Stanley to discuss the bill, he managed to convince the first two of the justice of Ireland's claim, but Stanley was obdurate.[2]

Thus it is easily understandable that even before the reform bill was on the statute book O'Connell was busy gearing up his organization to fight for repeal. The victory of reform as well as catholic emancipation had shown what public opinion could do. And O'Connell put his trust in the return of repeal members, steady petitioning, and the inevitable speedy victory of radicalism over whiggery in England. His reading of the situation was highly optimistic. There were only two parties left in Ireland, the Angleseyites or the moderate reformers and the popular party, the repealers. All the decent members of the old ascendancy party were flocking to the popular standard.[3] Influenced by this last assumption, which seems to have been completely baseless, he tried to get Boyton the leader of the Conservative society, and Sheehan, the editor of the *Dublin Evening Mail*, the leading conservative newspaper, to co-operate with him against the whigs, whom they were attacking with a virulence equalling his own. He briefed his faithful supporter, Fitzpatrick, for conversations with the conservatives, instructing him to ram home when talking to Boyton, that 'as a partisan he would be worse off than as a repealing Irishman since the policy of the administration was English domination over the Irish of all parties'. Fitzpatrick was to emphasize that if repeal was secured there would be perfect religious equality, and vested interests would be respected. There would be 'no social revolution, no social change'.[4] In his efforts to conciliate protestant opinion, O'Connell was prepared to offer constitutional guarantees. The repeal of the union, he explained, would not mean separation, but a domestic legislature in Dublin, independent of or subordinate to the Westminster parliament. An independent legislature was more commensurate with Ireland's claims, but he would if necessary accept a local parliament for merely local objects, if to do so would conciliate the Irish protestants. He further suggested that it should not be within the competency of the Irish parliament to infringe the equality of civil rights which should be enjoyed by persons of every religion, and he

---

[1] *MR*, 10, 12 Jan. 1832.
[2] *Pilot*, 23 Jan. 1833.　　　　　　　　　　[3] *MR*, 25 May 1832.
[4] W. J. Fitzpatrick, *Correspondence of Daniel O'Connell*, i. 324-8.

added that these rights should be protected by the British parliament.[1] At the election of 1832 he tried without success to secure a repeal candidate for Dublin from the protestant ascendancy party in the corporation, and he hoped that a coalition between the repealers and the conservatives would destroy the government's chances of obtaining a favourable jury in political cases. 'The lancers and the artillery', he remarked with professional bias, 'are nothing compared to the jurors.' Some months later when Barrett, the editor of the *Pilot*, was being tried before a tory jury for libel, he returned to this theme. Writing to Fitzpatrick he pointed out that 'if we could get a fair and impartial jury, Barrett would be acquitted'. Therefore he wanted Fitzpatrick to remind the tory leaders that Barrett's acquittal would be a decisive blow to the ministry.[2] All these manœuvres came to nothing. A few Irish protestants, who were extreme liberals, worked with O'Connell. Others co-operated with him from time to time. But the Irish tories remained unionists, and a repeal schism did not divide their ranks.

When at the beginning of 1833 O'Connell contemplated the struggle for repeal confronting him, he admitted to his secretary that he felt like a man about to plunge into a cold bath.[3] He started in January 1833 by summoning a meeting attended by about thirty M.P.s, the National Council, which spent some days in Dublin discussing Irish affairs and listening to complaints about industrial decay from the Dublin trades.[4] During the first session of the new parliament O'Connell did not bring repeal before the house. He defended his policy of procrastination on two grounds. Firstly, it was possible, though highly improbable, that a reformed parliament, even in London, might cure Ireland's ills. Secondly, careful preparation was required before repeal was brought before parliament. Petitions had to be sent in with as many protestant signatures as possible. The registry had to be attended to so that repealers would be returned, 'for the first element and leading principle of this plan is the proper use of the elective franchise'. It had to be arranged that the parliamentary debate on the repeal question would be properly

---

[1] *Pilot*, 12 Aug. 1833, 13 Jan. 1834. The idea that federalism might provide a solution for the Anglo-Irish question was already in the air. The author of *The federalist . . . a series of papers* (1831) wanted the relationship between the two countries to be that of states in the United States of America. In 1833 W. S. Crawford in *A review of the circumstances connected with the past and present state of the protestant and catholic interests* advocated an Irish assembly, subordinated to the imperial parliament, to deal with local affairs.

[2] W. J. Fitzpatrick, *Correspondence of Daniel O'Connell*, i. 302-3, 308, 310, 314, 353.

[3] W. McN. Daunt, *Personal recollections* (1848), i. 19.

[4] *Pilot*, 21, 23 Jan. 1833.

reported (O'Connell complained that some of his best speeches had been 'burked' by the press). And finally the people of Great Britain had to be shown that repeal did not mean separation and would reduce competition in the labour market.[1]

It would be a mistake to think that O'Connell at this time was the unchallenged leader of the Irish liberal M.P.s. Apparently when he summoned a meeting at his house early in the session of 1833 to discuss the whig coercion bill only twenty-six members attended, and at a larger gathering of fifty-six which met in Palace Yard his proposal that they should employ organized obstruction to defeat the bill was turned down, Wallace, an independently-minded man, saying that though he considered the bill unconstitutional, he did not object to the section dealing with dangerous societies.[2] On the other hand O'Connell's policy was too Fabian for some of his supporters. Feargus O'Connor, who had won Cork in a whirlwind campaign, and whom O'Connell at first hailed as 'boy after my own heart', and six months later characterized as 'a calculating and coarse-minded fellow', announced his intention of bringing the repeal question before parliament, a decision which received a certain amount of support in the Irish press.[3] Early in June the Irish repeal M.P.s met to discuss what course should be taken, and decided by twelve votes to ten in favour of postponement. O'Connor was dissatisfied and summoned another meeting at which this decision was confirmed by seventeen votes to seven.[4] O'Connor, who had his own views on the tithe and poor-law questions, was showing signs of becoming a dangerous competitor to O'Connell, and clashed publicly with him at a dinner in Cork. On O'Connell declaring that he wished the government would start competing with him to see if by its measures it could make converts from repeal, O'Connor interrupted him vehemently, and later in the evening, after comparing O'Connell and repeal to Frankenstein and his monster, called on Irishmen to fight for 'repeal, the whole repeal and nothing but repeal'.[5]

[1] *Pilot*, 8, 15 Apr., 3 July 1833.

[2] Stanley to Anglesey, 19 Feb. 1833 (Plas Newydd MSS.). Though Stanley is a biased witness when speaking of O'Connell, the *Sun* quoted in the *Pilot*, refers to opposition from the Irish liberal M.P.s to O'Connell's policy (*Pilot*, 6 Feb. 1833).

[3] *Pilot*, 21 Jan. 1833; W. J. Fitzpatrick, *Correspondence of Daniel O'Connell*, i. 370–71; *FJ*, 3 June 1833. Newspapers in Cork, Tipperary and Waterford are quoted by *FJ* during May and June as favouring the immediate discussion of the repeal question.

[4] *FJ*, 13, 22 June, 9 July 1833. Baldwin and Finn who were related to O'Connell were for bringing the question forward immediately (*FJ*, 20 June 1833). After this split in O'Connell's following he was referred to in London as the pasha with two tails (Littleton to Anglesey, 15 June 1833, Teddesley MSS.).

[5] *Pilot*, 8 Nov. 1833. O'Connor lost his seat in the general election of 1835. In the following year he vigorously attacked O'Connell as a political dictator and—as his

In April 1834 O'Connell brought the repeal question before parliament for the first and last time, and after a debate in which both he and Spring Rice for the unionists made long speeches, the motion was rejected by an overwhelming majority. This marks the end of the first repeal agitation. If the house of commons was hostile, Ireland was apathetic. And O'Connell, though he had declared just before he introduced his motion that 'the moment we are defeated I will reorganize the repeal agitation on a new plan,[1] did not settle down to bang his head against a brick wall. In a series of letters to an intimate friend, written in the months following his defeat, he explained that though he had not 'in thought, word or deed' abandoned repeal, he was 'playing the proper game of conciliation'. His aim he explained was to '*get what I can* and use repeal *in terrorem* merely until it is wise and necessary to recommence the agitation'. And he hoped either to secure solid advantages for Ireland, or to show that 'quietness, humility of deportment, and irresistible argument are all put aside by the fell genius of despotic domination over our miserable country'.[2] And there seemed in 1834 a reasonable possibility of securing both tithe and corporate reform from the government.

The corroding influence of the Irish question on the ministry made it easier for O'Connell to consider co-operation with the whigs after 1833. In May 1833 Stanley at length escaped from the chief secretaryship to the colonial office. In September Anglesey, to whom O'Connell was 'that bad man',[3] left Ireland. In May 1834 the dissensions in the cabinet concerning the finances of the Irish church, which had been smothered for three years, were revealed in debate, and four cabinet ministers, including Stanley and Graham, resigned, rather than agree to the possible appropriation of a hypothetical surplus for temporal purposes. Then a couple of months later Grey, who had 'a childish dislike of O'Connell',[4] resigned in disgust on discovering that several of his colleagues, wanting evidence to justify their view that the peace preservation bill could be modified, were trying to persuade the lord-lieutenant to alter the opinion he had already officially expressed. Stanley was succeeded as chief secretary by Hobhouse, who only held office long enough to lose his seat. He was succeeded by Littleton, a modest and industrious country

support of an attempt to modify the factory act of 1833 showed—an enemy of the working classes (*A series of letters from Feargus O'Connor . . . to Daniel O'Connell* (London 1836)).

[1] W. J. Fitzpatrick, *Correspondence of Daniel O'Connell*, i. 423-4.
[2] Ibid., i. 432-4.
[3] Anglesey to Hobhouse, 5 Apr. 1833 (Add. MS. 36467).
[4] *Life of John, Lord Campbell* (1881), ii. 49.

gentleman, whose chief political failing was the common one, an undue confidence in his own tact. At the beginning of June 1833 O'Connell defended the cabinet's Portuguese policy in the house of commons, and used this intervention in debate to introduce himself to Littleton. Within a month he was convinced that Littleton was 'a famous fellow', who would act in an anti-Orange spirit in Ireland; and he was solicitous to prevent the *Pilot* praising him, since 'Lord Anglesey reads the *Pilot* . . . and he was just the man to counteract the good intentions of Littleton if he be *put forward*'.[1] To make up for this public reticence he assured Littleton that he would find the lord-lieutenant vain and jealous, and that he was the first chief secretary 'who ever evinced a disposition to afford publicity and inquiry into Irish abuses'. Littleton, while feeling that the compliment was deserved, shrewdly—and correctly—believed that O'Connell's 'coaxing' was connected with his desire to get Barrett's prosecution withdrawn.[2] In August 1833 when the question of tithe arrears was being discussed, the chief secretary 'skipped across the house and said to O'Connell, "There is much in that [Littleton's own speech] which you will disapprove of but there is also much that you will like. Have the goodness therefore to answer Peel on those points on which you will differ with him."' He did so and said little against the measure. After recording this incident Littleton reflected that 'notwithstanding that the result of our intercourse has hitherto been very much in my favour, inasmuch as he has lent himself to me on several occasions, I have no doubt that he will go over to Ireland and apologize for his silence and the unpopular part he has sometimes taken by saying, "Oh, I have never done so much for you heretofore and I have the new chief secretary in my pocket".'[3] A little later O'Connell tried to get Littleton to get rid of some Irish officials, telling him that the dismissal of an Orange assistant barrister or a dozen Orange justices of the peace would do more to strengthen the union than anything else.[4] Littleton's contacts with O'Connell resulted in a catastrophic misunderstanding, which damaged both men's reputation and led to Grey's fall. On Grey's resignation, Melbourne, who was said to have believed that Ireland could only be governed through the protestant party, moved from the home office to the premiership and was replaced as secretary of state by O'Connell's old acquaintance and correspondent, Duncannon. At once, in conversation and in a series of open letters, O'Connell set to work to

[1] W. J. Fitzpatrick, *Correspondence of Daniel O'Connell*, i. 357, 373, 380.

[2] Littleton, diary, 24 July 1833 (Teddesley MSS.); W. J. Fitzpatrick, *Correspondence of Daniel O'Connell*, i. 357.

[3] Littleton, diary, 5 Aug. 1833 (Teddesley MSS.).

[4] Daniel O'Connell to Littleton, 9 Oct. 1833 (Teddesley MSS.).

shoulder the whigs on to the right path. If the ministry would only abandon Lord Grey's wretched policy, discountenance the Orangemen and do justice to the popular party, they would have eighty parliamentary supporters from Ireland. He was trying to put the best face he could upon the government's intentions, but he warned Duncannon, if the whigs did not 'change the agency . . . by which they had hitherto conducted the Irish branch of the administration', they might count on opposition in parliament and agitation in Ireland.[1]

Before O'Connell's mixture of flattery and threats (the latter decidedly predominating) could bear fruit, the whole political situation was suddenly altered by Melbourne's dismissal early in November 1834. Not only were the whigs deprived of power, but Peel's acceptance of office marked the revival of toryism as a serious political force. The predominant feature of English political life since the reform act, had been the struggle between the whigs and the radicals, with the discomfited tories lurking in the background. Now the conservatives—as the rebaptized party tried to be termed—came forward in menacing strength. O'Connell's reaction showed his quick appreciation of the realities of a situation. He heard the news of the ministry's fall in Cork. Within a few days he had dashed up to Dublin, and assembled a gathering of 'reformers' at the Corn Exchange which he addressed on the need for a united front against the tory oligarchy, the foe of European liberty. After all, the whigs, he admitted, had done a little for Ireland, and he was not going to keep the Duke in office, by inopportunely advocating repeal. As a result of his efforts, the anti-tory association was formed, with an election committee.[2] But O'Connell's energy and managing ability were as irritating as they were inspiring. Within a week the moderate reformers in Dublin were trying to run their own campaign, the 'more respectable liberals' being alarmed both by O'Connell's violence and by his taking into his own hands the conduct of elections all over Ireland. Two well-known barristers, O'Loghlen, a catholic, and Perrin, a protestant, tried to get up a whig meeting, and the latter tried to persuade the presbyterian merchants of Dublin to come forward in support of the whigs. But he was handicapped by the unpopularity which the whigs had almost automatically accumulated from having been in power for some years, the Dublin presbyterians grumbling that the government had given an additional M.P. to Trinity College and not to the city, and that the treasury has treated them badly over customs matters. Perrin, a dour, upright man, and a steady liberal and unionist, when pressed by More O'Ferrall, a leading catholic whig and landed gentleman, to join the

[1] *Pilot*, 27 Aug., 10, 17 Sept., 17, 24 Oct. 1833.    [2] *Pilot*, 24, 26 Nov. 1834.

Anti-Tory Association, refused, on the grounds that he was afraid their proceedings were unconstitutional, and that anyone joining would be regarded as an O'Connellite. Apparently he might have added that More O'Farrell had himself abstained from joining. Perrin had personal reasons for disliking the repealers. He believed that O'Connell, in spite of voluble professions of friendship, was trying to ruin his chances in his constituency (County Monaghan) 'on the principle that no liberal person shall come into parliament who shall not be bound hand and foot by him'.[1] And Spring Rice, though he preferred O'Connell to the Orangemen, thought he was playing an artful game. His aim, according to Rice, was to manœuvre the whigs into such a position that later he could be ungrateful to them 'if they do not to some extent make themselves joints of his tail'.[2] These disagreements however were hidden from the public, and whigs and repealers co-operated freely, the former, as has already been said, gaining from this as well as other factors in the situation. For instance O'Connell's son, John, tactfully described himself as 'a reformer', when trying to secure the Devonshire interest in Youghal, and O'Connell, when considering candidates for county Carlow, a difficult constituency, offered to adopt Duncannon's son.[3] Even Perrin was prepared to negotiate with O'Connell for the purpose of patching up an understanding between him and Lambert of Wexford who had incurred O'Connell's enmity by supporting the whig coercion bill of 1833 and opposing O'Connell's repeal motion—though presumably Perrin's efforts were dictated by his wish to save Lambert's seat.[4] And Conway of the *Evening Post* and O'Connell became reconciled after tremendous and typical efforts on the latter's part. First he sent a couple of friends to try and patch matters up, Conway replied that though he bore no ill will to O'Connell he would not shake hands with him. So finally O'Connell early one morning went to Conway's office, installed himself in the editor's chair, and greeted him with 'Well, Conway, here I am among your household gods and I'll never leave until you shake hands with me.' As a result of these shock tactics they shook hands, but 'thereafter Conway was never more than a very cool friend' to O'Connell.[5]

[1] R. D. Craig to Littleton, 30 Nov., 1, 12, 15, 16 Dec. 1834 (Teddesley MSS.).

[2] Spring Rice to Lansdowne, 7 Dec. 1834, and to Sir John Newport, 18 Jan. 1835 (Monteagle papers).

[3] John O'Connell to Littleton, 20 Dec. 1834 (Teddesley MSS.), W. J. Fitzpatrick, *The correspondence of Daniel O'Connell*, i. 512.

[4] R. D. Craig to Littleton, 1 Dec. 1834 (Teddesley MSS.).

[5] McCoy to R. R. Madden, 26 Apr. 1885 (Madden MSS.). The episode is undated but probably occurred about this time.

The results of the general election of 1835 were at first obscure. It was obvious that the government and the opposition forces were closely balanced. And the heterogeneous nature of the latter, composed as it was of 'all descriptions of parties, whigs, moderates, ultra-whigs, radicals, ultra radicals, etc.,'[1] together with the fact that Peel was busy appropriating portions of his opponents' programme, made it difficult to discern which group had a majority. In the whig camp Grey was rather querulously emphasizing that their differences with the radicals and O'Connell were 'no less decided and ought to be as strongly marked as with the tories',[2] and Spring Rice was speculating on a combination of Peel, seeking protection from his own ultras, Stanley, and the old whigs who would have to break with O'Connell, Hume and Whalley. Only 'the odious Irish church question' separated Spring Rice and his section of the whigs from Stanley.[3] But before parliament met, the leading members of the late cabinet, Melbourne, Lord John Russell and Althorp, decided to try and drive the tories from office, and to begin operations by opposing the re-election of Manners Sutton as speaker. Casting round for a suitable candidate they selected Abercromby, one good reason against Spring Rice, the other possible whig candidate for the chair, being that he might be regarded as *persona non grata* by O'Connell's following.[4] O'Connell himself during this time was mainly in touch with the radicals. Henry Warburton, a leading philosophical radical who had frequently acted with O'Connell in the previous parliament, was a successful business man with wide interests who seems to have managed to combine high ideals with (when requisite) crude practice—a keen reformer, it was rumoured he had used bribery to get into parliament. About the middle of January he wrote to O'Connell asking him whom would he support as speaker, and urging that if the tories hoped to play on the divisions of the opposition, the radicals and the Irish should disappoint them by appointing 'a whig leader'. At the end of the month, when he wrote to O'Connell to tell him that Abercromby was going to be nominated, he suggested a federal party organization, whigs, radicals and Irish, each having their own chairman and co-operating for common objects. A few days later an awkward point of political etiquette cropped up. Warburton discovered that there were some Irish M.P.s who expected a personal letter from Lord John soliciting their support for Abercromby. He thought the idea improper and absurd,

[1] S. Walpole, *Life of Lord John Russell*, i. 214.
[2] Grey to Melbourne, 1 Feb. 1835 (Russell papers).
[3] Spring Rice to Coleman, 19 Jan. 1835 (Monteagle papers).
[4] S. Walpole, *Life of Lord John Russell*, i. 215; W. M. Torrens, *Memoirs of . . . Viscount Melbourne* (1878), ii. 86.

but he wanted O'Connell to give him their names so that their wishes could be gratified.[1] All this correspondence prepared the way for a decisive action by Warburton. In the middle of February, just before parliament met, he received from Russell some circulars summoning liberal M.P.s to a meeting at Lichfield House for distribution amongst his friends. Warburton promptly sent a bundle of them to O'Connell, who not only turned up at the meeting, but in an effusive letter thanking Lord John for the invitation, assured him that he would have the loyal co-operation of the Irish popular party 'until the tories are routed'. Russell, cold and cautious, and surrounded by whig magnates, drafted a damping and formal reply, but Duncannon intervened energetically, pointing out that if the whigs began their campaign by 'trembling at shadows, and quaking at the name of O'Connell and every other radical who may tender you assistance our prospects of success will not be very promising'. Russell then altered his letter, so that it implied that to some extent at least, O'Connell and the whigs had a joint policy.[2] Duncannon himself had already early in January been in touch with O'Connell, on what lines it is impossible to say, but Lansdowne had at once registered his protest against such negotiations, 'should they in any degree assume the character of party concert and alliance'.[3]

Circumstances favoured the whigs, for a common hostility to the tories united the opposition groups behind the whig leaders, and, as Spring Rice complacently explained to the absent Macaulay, 'the repealers smarting under the Orange lash were at once outraged and alarmed. The radicals gave us a confidence as martyrs they would have refused us as ministers. They submitted, took us on our own terms and only asked us to guide them with spirit and resolution.'[4] In the series of debates which drove Peel from office, O'Connell made it clear that if the whigs amended the Irish reform bill, reformed the Irish corporations, and appropriated the surplus revenues of the Irish establishment for charitable purposes he would suspend the repeal agitation. Lord John's speeches showed that the whigs intended to meet his wishes, at least on the last point, and O'Connell was so satisfied that he let it be known that he was quite ready to take office in the new administration. But though a distinct asset to the whigs in the division lobby he was an embarrassment when it came to forming a government. A number of in-

[1] Warburton to O'Connell, 20, 30 Jan., 3 Feb. 1835 (O'Connell MSS., U.C.D.; W. J. Fitzpatrick, *Correspondence of Daniel O'Connell*, i. 520).
[2] S. Walpole, *Life of Lord John Russell*, i. pp. 219-24.
[3] Lansdowne to Russell, 1 Feb. 1835 (Russell papers).
[4] Spring Rice to Macaulay, 26 Sept. 1835 (Monteagle papers).

fluential whigs and the king were strongly averse to having anything to do with him. Young, Lord Melbourne's indiscreet confidential secretary, talking to Littleton a couple of days after Peel's resignation, admitted that O'Connell was a stumbling block. Parties in the house were so nearly balanced that if he resented his exclusion from the government nothing could be done, and 'who could trust him in it? Would it be possible to make such a scoundrel a privy counsellor?' In fact exclusion was speedily decided on, and O'Connell, who seems to have for a moment regarded the Irish attorney-generalship within his grasp, promised to support the government on the basis of Russell's declaration that tithe reform with appropriation would be one of the first measures of the new government. Russell at least regarded O'Connell's behaviour as exceedingly generous, and informed O'Connell that he was willing to decline office on the grounds of his exclusion.[1]

Three years later it was suggested that O'Connell might be retired from politics in a lucrative and dignified way by being made master of the rolls in Ireland. The chief secretary was strongly in favour of it, and Lord John Russell was not averse, but the lord-lieutenant, while acknowledging O'Connell's deserts, pointed out that the prejudice against him was not confined to tories and that his promotion would have a bad effect on Lord Grey's circle. Nevertheless the offer was made and refused, O'Connell preferring, or feeling it his duty, to remain in the hurly-burly of politics.[2] O'Connell's failure to obtain a ministerial post must have irked him, and it is a pity that from his alliance with the whigs he gained only indirect power, instead of a share in the responsibility for the government's policy. He had, however, the wry consolation that no English radical was invited to break the whig monopoly of office, and he could congratulate himself not only on the exclusion of the Irish tories from power but on the fact that the new whig administration was definitely more liberal than Lord Grey's. During the next six years the most significant factor in Irish politics was the existence of a whig ministry which, hesitantly, and amidst complaints from its friends and virulent abuse from its tory opponents, introduced liberal principles into Irish administrative life and carried through some constructive measures which reflected the practical idealism of the period. An attempt will be made to assess this work, but before doing so something must be said

[1] S. Walpole, *Life of Lord John Russell*, i. 233-4; Littleton, diary, 10, 11 Apr. 1835 (Teddesley MSS.); W. M. Torrens, *Memoirs of . . . Viscount Melbourne* (1878), ii. 117-18.

[2] Ebrington to Russell, 11 June, Morpeth to Russell, 7 June, Russell to Ebrington, 14 June 1838 (Russell papers); W. J. Fitzpatrick, *The correspondence of Daniel O'Connell*, ii. 142-4.

about O'Connell's position both in relation to the government, to radicalism and to Irish opinion.

Though throughout this period O'Connell was a useful ally and on the whole a eulogist of the whigs, his contact with the government was intermittent rather than continuous, and he does not seem to have been on intimate terms with any member of the cabinet—with the possible exception of Duncannon—or of the Irish administration. The whigs appreciated his fighting powers in the house, but his independence, exuberance and unpredictability, particularly when he was down at Darrynane surrounded by his family, made them exceedingly cautious in dealing with him, Mulgrave, when viceroy, even having 'some scruple about writing direct' to him over appointments.[1] The only important government bill that he seems to have had a hand in drafting was the unsuccessful registration bill of 1835,[2] and though he once compelled the government to withdraw a fairly important Irish measure, he did so by exercising parliamentary pressure. In 1839, near the close of the session, Spring Rice, the chancellor of the exchequer and a prominent Irish whig, introduced a bill confirming for a lengthy period the bank of Ireland's privileges. O'Connell, whose temper must have been sharpened by his belief that the bank was 'an Orange confederacy', and by memories of a business dispute with its directors and of his debating clash with Spring Rice on the union, considered that the bank's guaranteed special status constituted a gross violation of sound economic principles. Announcing that he was going to take 'every fair step to prevent the measure passing into law', he began to practise obstruction, or as the indignant chancellor of the exchequer termed it, 'a mechanical opposition'. For a moment Spring Rice contemplated trying to defeat O'Connell by substituting an adjournment for the normal prorogation. But in the end he yielded, and withdrawing his bill replaced it by a temporary measure preserving the bank's rights for a short period.[3]

O'Connell's active good nature and his anxiety to see the government's patronage being used to strengthen the liberal cause, impelled him to intervene frequently over patronage matters—with varying success. For instance, writing to Drummond, the under-secretary, he pressed the claims of an ex-sheriff of Dublin (to whose impartiality he

---

[1] Ebrington to Tavistock, 10 Jan. 1836, Mulgrave to Russell, 20 Aug. 1837 (Russell papers); Mulgrave to Morpeth, 24 Mar., 8 July 1835 (Castle Howard MSS.).

[2] Littleton, diary, 2 Sept. 1835 (Teddesley MSS.).

[3] *Parl. Deb.*, 3 series, xlix. 887, 1. 454; W. J. Fitzpatrick, *The correspondence of Daniel O'Connell*, ii. 195-202; Spring Rice to Lansdowne, 30 Aug. 1839 (Monteagle papers); F. G. Hall, *The Bank of Ireland 1783-1946* (1949), p. 165.

owed his return as M.P. for the city) to an auditorship under the poor-law board; he pointed out that a Youghal business man, ruined on account of his exertions for the liberal cause, wanted a paymastership in the police; he drew attention to the fact that the catholic chaplain to the house of industry wanted apartments; he severely criticized the chancellor, Plunket, for leaving 'all the filth of the magistracy' on the bench; he regretted that a sometime 'vetoist' had been chosen as the catholic peer to receive the St Patrick; he demanded the dismissal of an obnoxious police officer; and he remonstrated vehemently when it was rumoured that Greene, a conservative who had been law adviser to the Irish government was to be placed on the bench. 'The tories', he said, 'had filled the bench with men who distorted justice.' So then 'why should I suffer the obloquy of a moment in supporting a government treading in the most vital points in the foul footsteps of their enemies'? Though the government was on the whole anxious to oblige him, O'Connell was by no means always successful in his applications, and he was occasionally discontented at the treatment he received. On one occasion, peeved by the refusal of a grant for a harbour at Tralee, he wrote a stiff note in the third person to the chief secretary withdrawing some requests he had made, since he was not prepared to have direct communication with a government which persisted in heaping insults on him. The lord-lieutenant however was unruffled, believing that 'Dan' would soon be propitiated by the appointment of his son-in-law Nicholas French, who was hard up, to a stipendiary magistracy. A couple of months earlier O'Connell had pushed his son-in-law's interests in a rather devious fashion. Having written to the under-secretary expressing his anxiety that his son-in-law should be given an appointment he asked Drummond's 'friendly advice' whether he should write to the viceroy, adding, 'It would be perhaps well to be able to say I asked for no such situation for anybody'.[1]

After 1835 relations between O'Connell and the radicals were definitely less cordial than in the exuberant days of the first reformed parliament. As early as April 1835 Grote noted in his diary an episode which reveals a distinct lack of enthusiasm for O'Connell amongst the English parliamentary radicals. 'The plan for brigading the opposition has been effectually discomfited by Hume, who, set on by Brougham, has insisted on comprehending the Irish "tail" on the pact. This not being compatible with the objects in furtherance of which the project was taken up, viz.

---

[1] O'Connell to Drummond, 16 Mar., 20 June, 13 Oct. 1836, 25 Sept., 1 Nov. 1837, 8 Apr., 30 July 1839 (Drummond-O'Connell MSS.); O'Connell to Morpeth, 24 June 1836, Mulgrave to Morpeth, 27 June 1836 (Castle Howard MSS.).

consultation and communication amongst the English radicals, our gentlemen have to abandon the design.'[1]

Admittedly on a number of occasions with a varying number of Irish liberal M.P.s O'Connell voted against the government on issues raised by the radicals such as the ballot, flogging in the army, the remission of the sentences on the Dorchester labourers, the revision of the pension list, the abolition of the newspaper stamp duty, and the Canadian question. In all these instances there was of course practically no danger of a government defeat, since the tories were bound in principle either to abstain or vote with the whigs. No one could have been more indignant than O'Connell when Hume by a tactless display of independence brought about a government defeat.[2] The radicals for their part grumbled that while O'Connell and a few of his party usually voted with them, the bulk of the Irish liberal members either stayed away or went into the government lobby. And we know that on at least one occasion O'Connell was 'nobbled' by the government. Early in 1838 when a series of debates on the embarrassing Canadian question was impending, the lord-lieutenant assured Russell that O'Connell had been spoken to and would not make mischief over Canada, and that he had promised to stay away for the first few days of the session. He seems to have kept his word for his name does not appear in the debates and divisions on the Canadian bill, and later in the session Roebuck publicly rebuked him for failing to defend the oppressed people of Canada.[3] On several points of Irish policy the radicals differed sharply from him. O'Connell detested the very suggestion of a poor law, they argued that the new English poor law ought to be extended to Ireland. He continually deplored absenteeism, they doubted if it had any ill effects. And when he accepted the whig settlement of the tithe question, a group of English radicals led by the effervescent Harvey attacked it as violating the voluntary principle. There was, too, a divergence of outlook between O'Connell and the radicals during these years on a fundamental matter. They were thoroughly dissatisfied with the whigs and hankered after the unattainable—a radical administration, rapidly pushing through a progressive programme. Shortly after Melbourne returned to office they were sourly talking of ceasing to support the whigs and fighting boldly on their own, even if that meant the destruction of the whig party and a temporary tory victory.[4] O'Connell on the other hand considered it well worth

---

[1] H. Grote, *The personal life of George Grote* (1873), p. 99.
[2] W. J. Fitzpatrick, *Correspondence of Daniel O'Connell*, ii. 176-7.
[3] Mulgrave to Russell, 6 Jan. 1838 (Russell papers); *NW*, 26 May 1838.
[4] *Westminster Rev.*, xxvi. 279-318.

while to keep the whigs in office. And in 1836 Francis Place, a shrewd if disgruntled commentator on events told Hume that O'Connell, 'who from the sympathy of the people with their distressed and oppressed Irish brethren had obtained factitious popularity has foolishly become the mouthpiece of ministers and their chief assistant in the attempt to delude the people of England.[1]

As can often happen with the most intelligent contemporary observer, O'Connell's estimate of the general situation was askew, for generally speaking he both overrated the strength of radical opinion to the left of the government and underrated the power of the tories. In March 1837, a few months before the liberals received a set-back at the polls, he confided to Fitzpatrick that 'actual examination' of the constituencies showed that if there was 'an election to-morrow the reformers would gain a large majority even in the English constituencies'. In May 1839, after the whigs had just managed to retain office, he was 'in the greatest spirits', on learning that the ministry and the radicals were reconciled on the understanding that the former adopted a more liberal programme, 'a rational reform system'. The country, he declared, was 'with us to a man' or (with an unusual burst of caution he added) 'all that is desirable to have'. As for the tories he was sure a little over a year before Peel became prime minister that they would never again regain power. The extreme and moderate tories were at loggerheads. Peel was ill, and Wellington was dying.[2] In any case a tory administration would mean a revolution. Thus O'Connell could justify his support of the whigs on the grounds that they were gradually becoming more liberal, and that in the meantime their Irish policy was, from his point of view, yielding at least limited dividends. And as for the parliamentary radicals, by reluctantly backing the whigs whenever they were in danger, they were playing sulkily the same rôle as he performed enthusiastically. It may be added that one amongst the many factors retarding the advance of English radicalism during this period was the failure of the English radicals and the Irish repealers to combine effectively.

If O'Connell's friendship was of some parliamentary value to the whigs it was an immense help in Ireland. If between 1835 and 1841 Ireland remained a breeding-ground for administrative and economic problems, it at least ceased to be a constant tax on the government's nerves. One result of O'Connell's alliance with the whigs was that repeal was put into cold storage. A few days after the new ministry took office he confessed that he had two reasons for embarking on a new course:

[1] Place to J. Hume, 11 June 1836 (Add. MS. 35150).
[2] W. J. Fitzpatrick, *Correspondence of Daniel O'Connell*, ii. 83-4, 184-6, 221-6.

he wanted to overthrow the Orange system, and to convince the most sceptical that not even a friendly ministry, but only a domestic legislature could do justice to Ireland.[1] As time went on his attitude mellowed. In 1837 he said that Mulgrave was behaving as well as if there was a parliament in College Green, and at the general election which occurred later in the year, O'Connell's General Association resolved that all the supporters of the ministry should be returned and that an opponent of any of them was to be regarded as an enemy of the country.[2] And after the election O'Connell moved the dissolution of the Association, for with a liberal ministry in power the time had come to see if Ireland could be governed by the imperial legislature. If there was a perfect equality of rights, laws and liberties, Ireland was ready 'to amalgamate with the entire empire'. 'And who', O'Connell asked, 'is the man who does not desire to be a member of the great and glorious British empire?'[3] Two years later, when after the debates on the Jamaican bill a dissolution seemed likely, O'Connell hesitated over raising the repeal issue. 'I will not', he wrote to a close friend, 'give the premature raising of that cry as an excuse by any alleged friends of reform to desert us at this moment.'[4]

O'Connell's power, or the personal nature of the repeal agitation, was indicated by the absence of criticism when he shifted from opposition to alliance with the whigs. In the south hardly a word was said, and Thomas Reynolds, a Dublin radical who attacked him at the Trades Political Union for dropping repeal, had to make a humble apology.[5] It was from the north, with its own historic, firmly grounded liberal tradition, that there came sustained, acute and acid criticism of O'Connell's political moves in this period. The *Northern Whig*, the Ulster newspaper with the largest circulation, and Sharman Crawford, a large landowner, an intelligent, progressive, crotchety man, with a strong predilection for taking a line of his own on most issues, adopted towards O'Connell a tone of candid friendship, with the candour predominating. Like the English radicals they regarded the whigs as *fainéant*, and they wanted the Irish liberal M.P.s to act as an independent 'ginger group', which would strongly oppose any attempt to appease the tories.[6] In the autumn of 1837 O'Connell was criticized pretty sharply by the *Whig* for supporting ministers rather than measures. And about the same time Sharman Crawford argued in a series of letters to the press commenting

[1] W. J. Fitzpatrick, *Correspondence of Daniel O'Connell*, ii. 20.
[2] *Pilot*, 27 Mar., 5 Apr. 1837.
[3] *Pilot*, 1 Nov. 1837.
[4] O'Connell to Bennett, 8 May 1839 (Letters to Councillor Bennett, NLI).
[5] *Pilot*, 12 Oct. 1836.　　　　　　[6] *NW*, 31 Aug. 1837, 19 Oct. 1838.

on O'Connell's conduct, that the primary object of the Irish liberal M.P.s should be to obtain desirable legislation, not merely to keep the whigs in office. O'Connell, delighted at being permitted to dispense patronage, had become 'a courtly flatterer of the ruling powers'. In spite of 'his vapouring gasconades' he had done nothing to protect the poor from ejectment. He had opposed the introduction of a poor law, and he had supported—against Crawford's opposition—the Peace Preservation act of 1835, which menaced the liberty of the subject.[1] was over the handling of the tithe issue that the northern liberals were most noisily and heartily dissatisfied with O'Connell. In 1835 the new government brought in a tithe bill which converted tithe into a rent charge, scaled down the amount to be paid, and provided that any surplus left over after the needs of the establishment were met would be appropriated to public purposes. Though the surplus was highly hypothetical, the appropriation clauses were regarded on both sides of the house as involving an important principle and the lords summarily hacked them out. The liberal majority in the commons refused to yield, and the bill was lost. The performance was repeated in the following two sessions. Finally in 1838 the government reluctantly dropped the obnoxious section and the bill passed. O'Connell's attitude during the debates was somewhat involved. He emphasized his disapproval of a system by which the community was taxed to support the church of a small minority, but he voted steadily with the ministry, thus as the English radicals did not fail to point out, resanctioning the existence of tithe, and during the year the bill was finally struggling on to the statute book he concentrated his efforts out-of-doors on a boisterous anti-poor-law agitation. The northern liberals throughout these years stuck to their demands for the complete abolition of tithe, and, Sharman Crawford was consistent enough to add, *regium donum*. When Crawford tried to sweep away tithe by moving an amendment to the 1835 bill, O'Connell taunted him with hypocrisy. Later he retorted by accusing O'Connell of leaving the poor heavily burdened and bribing the catholic gentry by giving the landlords a bonus. And the *Whig* dwelt with gusto on O'Connell's inconsistency in attacking tithe one day, and voting for a bill which sanctioned the rights of the establishment the next.[2]

Up to 1838 the rift between O'Connell and the northern liberals could be described as a dispute between a practical politician and his doctrinaire critics. During the next few years the roles were reversed. In the early summer of that year O'Connell took the initial steps towards

[1] *NW*, 9 Sept. 1837; *Pilot*, 27 July 1836, 28 Aug., 1, 11, 15, 20 Sept. 1837.
[2] *Pilot*, 11 May 1838; *NW*, 19 Jan., 2 Feb. 1837, 7 July, 16 Aug. 1838.

starting a fresh push for repeal. An Irish legislature, 'one of the proudest dreams of his youth',[1] was always at the back of his mind, and the slightest discouragement, the smallest political check, made him hanker after repeal. Then at times he felt the whigs to be unsympathetic and apathetic—'the senate of Petersburg or the divine of Constantinople', he felt, 'would be as ready to attend to the grievance of Ireland as the British house of commons'.[2] In any case the house of lords was blocking the whigs' Irish programme, and the danger steadily grew that Melbourne's ministry might be driven from office. In these circumstances a strong propagandist organization generating public opinion in favour of repeal would both assist O'Connell in prodding the whigs, and by providing an alternative policy, insure him against a tory victory. With some inconsistency then, he started to take the preliminary steps to set on foot an agitation for repeal, while continuing to support an administration whose object was to kill repeal by kindness. This being so, it is understandable why O'Connell's handling of the repeal agitation in the late thirties was exceedingly slapdash. In August 1838 he founded the ambiguously named 'Precursor Society', which was to 'precede' justice for Ireland obtained through the united parliaments, defined as an equalizing of the British and Irish franchise, a due proportion of M.P.s for Ireland, corporate reform and the extinction of tithe. Should these demands not be obtained in a reasonable time the society was to transform itself into a repeal association. The possibility that repeal might become the society's main objective prevented many liberals, who did not wish to be turned into repealers, joining, and in October O'Connell directed the society to modify its constitution. It promptly dissolved, and then, reconstituting itself with the same membership, declared that should its objectives (which remained the same) not be attained quickly, the sincere friends of Ireland could form a repeal association. This conciliatory formula was so tactless, that ten days later there was a fresh dissolution and reconstitution. The ballot, the extension of the suffrage and shorter parliaments were added to the original programme, and it was stated that if the society failed to achieve its aims, the friends of Ireland who favoured repeal would form an association. Finally in December still another effort was made to win liberal recruits. A fresh dissolution and reconstruction of the society was carried through, the new society's aims remaining unaltered, but every reference to repeal was omitted from its programme.[3]

[1] *Pilot*, 25 Jan. 1836.
[2] W. J. Fitzpatrick, *Correspondence of Daniel O'Connell*, ii. 169.
[3] *Pilot*, 20 Aug., 12, 15, 26 Oct., 19 Dec. 1838.

O'Connell's faithful following docilely obeyed his directions. But this ill-managed reversion to agitation failed to impress the whigs and disgusted the northern liberals. Spring Rice assumed that O'Connell did not intend to change his course but wanted to secure a good 'rent',[1] and Sharman Crawford turned up at the first meeting of the new society to demand an immediate break with the whigs and an alliance with the English radicals directed against the corn laws. As might be expected, before he sat down he was involved in a personal wrangle with O'Connell over the tithe bill.[2] The *Whig* adopted at this time a hypercritical tone towards O'Connell's activities. In an editorial entitled 'What is to be done next?' it insisted O'Connell should refrain from raising the repeal issue and should specify exactly what he meant by 'justice' for Ireland. Naturally it resented his disregard of its advice on repeal, and when he met the second point by issuing his programme, rather petulantly complained that it was too long. According to the *Whig* the ballot, corporate reform, and tithe extinction, would have sufficed. In any case it was clear that the whole agitation had been started to prevent the public thinking about O'Connell's retreat on the tithe question. A year later the *Whig* was boldly arguing that repeal was merely a Dublin question, and that the northerners would struggle 'as for existence' against any project which might jeopardize free trade between Great Britain and Ireland. 'We are not devoid of national feeling as Irishmen', the *Whig* explained, 'but as an industrious and enterprising people we are a thousand times more closely bound up with Liverpool and Glasgow, with Lanarkshire and Lancaster than with all Munster taken together. No doubt the *Trades* in the *national* enthusiasm for the good of *Dublin* will treat all this as unpatriotic, but as it so happened we have bridged the channel, considerations of profit and loss press heavily upon us, and we cannot disregard them if we would.'[3]

In the event the Precursor Society did remarkably little, and O'Connell continued to support the ministry. Pigot, a leading catholic lawyer, who was liberal enough to join O'Connell's association in 1837, and sufficiently in sympathy with the whigs to become solicitor-general in 1839, was certain early in 1839 that O'Connell was quite ready to drop repeal if he could do so without loss of face. And since O'Connell was constitutionally incapable of abstaining from agitation, Pigot argued that the best course would be to provide him with an organization under liberal or whig control. To effect this, Pigot tried to get up a comprehen-

[1] Spring Rice to Phelps, 11 Dec. 1838 (Monteagle papers).
[2] *Pilot*, 20 Aug. 1838.
[3] *NW*, 16, 21 Aug., 22 Sept., 30 Oct., 22 Dec. 1838, 17 Oct. 1839.

sive reform association with a central fund, which would muster Irish liberals of all shades behind the government. Discussions were held between William Murphy, Pigot, Cloncurry and Thomas Drummond. But since Drummond had a strong objection to any association, and O'Connell considered the proposed programme to be too narrow, the projected united front which the government and Pigot regarded as a means of gently putting O'Connell in a respectable strait jacket, failed to emerge.[1] Still, a month after the negotiations collapsed, O'Connell, having dined with the viceroy, Drummond and the Irish law officers, addressed a great Dublin demonstration in favour of the ministry, and at the end of August the government provided him with a dignified excuse for dissolving his society and 'cushioning' the repeal question, by announcing that no repealer would be a recipient of government patronage.[2]

During 1839 and 1840, though O'Connell continued to assure his followers that repeal was now the main object of his political life and would be achieved 'as sure as the sun rises', he did nothing to weaken the whig alliance which he compared to an old hat used by a cottager to stuff a broken window. From the summer of 1838 to the middle of 1841 he vigorously exerted himself in a wide variety of directions, supporting the whigs in parliament, organizing the Repeal Association (set up in April 1840), advising the English radicals, co-operating with the liberals in fighting Stanley's registration bill, and attending to the registries, taking part in the anti-corn law agitation, and encouraging a movement to promote the use of Irish manufactures.[3]

During this period he was embroiled in a fresh series of misunderstandings with the northern liberals. At the beginning of 1840 there was a nasty newspaper squabble in Belfast. The *Vindicator*, which had been founded as the organ of Belfast catholicism with an enthusiastic, fluent young editor, Gavan Duffy, alleged that the Belfast liberals had failed to give the catholics a fair share of the municipal offices. The *Whig* resented this and produced an effective statistical reply. O'Connell, who was delighted that the *Vindicator* had given a tone and temper to the honest and independent catholics of Ulster which had made them 'shake off their miserable subserviency to pretended friends and enabled them to act manfully for themselves', plunged into this Eatonswill

---

[1] Pigot to Morpeth, 10 Feb. 1837, 4, 10 Apr. 1839, Ebrington to Morpeth, 7 Apr. 1839 (Castle Howard MSS.), *Parl. Deb.*, 3 series, xxxvi, 206 ff.

[2] Spring Rice to Lansdowne, 14 Sept. 1839 (Monteagle papers); *FJ*, 30 Aug. 1839.

[3] *Pilot*, 4 Sept., 30 Aug., 25 Oct. 1839, 27 Apr. 1840.

brawl, characterizing the editor of the *Whig* as 'one of the most hollow, slippery and delusive hypocrites' in existence.[1]

A few months after this commotion had died down, leaving the *Whig* obviously sore, a number of Ulster noblemen and gentlemen of liberal views pulled themselves together and founded the Ulster Constitutional Society, which was to attempt to obtain for Ireland equal rights with Great Britain, in the belief that 'by complete incorporation the system of imperial legislation will be rendered permanently beneficial'.[2] A few weeks later, the Repeal Association published an address to the Ulster society pointing out that both bodies had common objectives, and suggesting that the Ulster Society should as soon as possible organize a large-scale protest against Stanley's bill. Crawford and Ross, the Ulster association's secretaries, replied indignantly that they were not prepared to discuss their Society's affairs with any outside body. They also issued an address to their own members pointing out that Lords Gosford and Charlemont had informed O'Connell the Ulster Society was being set up, 'simply as a manifestation of courtesy . . . but not for the purpose of asking Mr O'Connell's guidance'. The repeal agitation, Crawford and Ross went on to argue, both divided Irish liberals and tended to separate them from their British countrymen. O'Connell retorted that the Ulster liberals had not much to boast about when the great majority of the Ulster M.P.s were tory. And he 'respectfully' asked them, how they expected to obtain their aims except by repeal, 'the only topic that can animate the entire mass of the population'. Shortly afterwards at a meeting of the Ulster association, repeal was definitely repudiated, and the *Whig* asked how did O'Connell (assuming that he would not risk bloodshed) hope to win repeal when he did not expect to gain 'justice'.[3] At the beginning of the new year (1841) he met some of his critics, when, at the invitation of the local repealers, he paid his first and last political visit to Belfast. It looked as if he would have a hostile reception, and the viceroy believed that he was anxious at the last moment to find an excuse for backing out. However, by travelling two days before he was expected, he disappointed the tougher tories in the Ulster towns *en route*, and in Belfast he stayed most of the time in his hotel while parties of military and police patrolled the town. Only a few protestant liberals attended the dinner in his honour, though its promoters described it not as a 'Repeal' but as a 'Reform' dinner, and he had to meet a critical deputation of three leading Ulster liberals, who pointed out they were

---

[1] *NW*, 12 Mar., 7, 18 Apr. 1840; *Pilot*, 20 Apr. 1840; W. J. Fitzpatrick, *Correspondence of Daniel O'Connell*, ii. 234.     [2] *NW*, 30 June 1840.
[3] *Pilot*, 20, 24 July, 19 Aug. 1840; *NW*, 30 July, 13 Aug. 1840.

not repealers. Admitting that the *Whig* had perhaps been 'too persevering and acrimonious in controversy', they regretted that O'Connell had countenanced the *Vindicator* and had visited Belfast on the invitation of a small group actuated by sectarianism. O'Connell with typical good humour made the best of an awkward situation, declaring himself much gratified by the conversation and offered voluble and unnecessary advice on registration problems.[1]

In the wider field of national politics the alliance between O'Connell and the Whigs moved towards its dissolution as the Melbourne ministry tottered towards its fall. But until its resignation O'Connell was a fervent supporter of the administration, while keeping repeal in being in reserve. He even reconciled the two lines by arguing that the repeal agitation would be of help to the whigs by frightening the tories away 'from attempting the government'.[2] And just after the whigs left office he supported Morpeth, the ex-chief secretary, who it was thought would make the best liberal candidate, in a by-election for Dublin.[3] But in the summer of 1841 he declared that repeal alone 'is and must be, the grand basis of all future operations, hit or miss, win or lose'. As for the whigs, their day was probably past, for unless the party could undergo an immense change, and 'popularize' itself, it could never form a third force between the chartists and the tories.[4] The *Citizen*, the organ of intellectual Irish radicalism was even inclined to think that the fall of the whigs was on the whole to be welcomed. Whiggery, after all, aimed at giving Ireland and Great Britain identical laws, yet the Irish were a dissimilar people from the English.[5] The whigs for their part, once out of office, were quite ready to terminate their association with O'Connell. Russell, after some consideration pronounced he could not possibly act with a man professing O'Connell's political creed on reform and repeal. Palmerston saw that relations with O'Connell would be a problem. To act with him frequently would be impossible, to break with him openly would be damaging. Palmerston therefore was for letting the matter solve itself. 'To receive and thank him for his support when he chooses to give it us, and never to give him our support when we disapprove of the step he is about to take.'[6]

---

[1] Ebrington to Morpeth, 7, 8 Jan. 1841 (Castle Howard MSS.); *NW*, 12, 19, 21, 23 Jan. 1841. B, A. Kennedy, 'Sharman Crawford's federal Scheme for Ireland'. In *Essays in honour of James Eadie Todd*, 1949.

[2] W. J. Fitzpatrick, *Correspondence of Daniel O'Connell*, ii. 256-8.

[3] *FJ*, 4, 25 Jan. 1842.

[4] W. J. Fitzpatrick, *Correspondence of Daniel O'Connell*, ii. 266, 274.

[5] *Citizen*, iv. 108-9.

[6] Russell to Lansdowne, 12 Nov. 1841, Palmerston to Russell, 12 Oct. 1841 (*Later correspondence of Lord John Russell*, i. 47, 49).

# 7

# THE WHIGS AND IRELAND, 1835–41

If the whigs were obdurate on repeal they at least tried to offer a substantial substitute, and the government which took office in 1835
was more popular in Irish catholic and liberal circles than any administration since the union. Mulgrave, later marquess of Normanby,
the lord-lieutenant, energetic and flamboyant, saw politics as a romantic
drama in which he thoroughly enjoyed playing the part of a popular
viceroy. And when, in 1839, he was moved to the home office he was
replaced by Viscount Ebrington, another strong liberal. By a curious
chance Mulgrave has been historically overshadowed by his under-
secretary, Thomas Drummond, whose knowledge of the country, largely
acquired when working on the ordnance survey, contacts with Irish
politicians, downright directness of expression, and prodigious working
powers inspired by dour determination and clear-cut liberal principles,
made him an outstanding figure in Irish administrative life.[1] Admittedly
he had his faults, his sympathies if well directed, were restricted, and at
times he could be rather too brusque. Spring Rice once remarked that
Drummond should remember that political power had its duties as well
as its rights.[2] Moreover tradition has perhaps over-emphasized his importance at the expense of his superiors. Mulgrave was not a nonentity,
and flung himself enthusiastically into grappling with administrative
detail, and Morpeth, who, throughout the whole period 1835 to 1841
was chief secretary, had invaluable reserves of level-headed good nature,
which his colleagues greatly appreciated.

[1] In May 1839 Drummond decided that, though his position was usually considered to be a permanent one, he would resign if there was a change of ministry. The
day after he came to this decision he was asked to be a liberal candidate for Belfast
T. Drummond to Russell, 10 May 1839, and James Gibson to T. Drummond, 11
May 1839 (Russell papers, Castle Howard MSS.).
[2] Spring Rice to Morpeth, 15 Aug. 1839 (Monteagle papers); see also Morpeth to
Russell, 17 Mar. 1838 (Russell papers).

M

The new government's programme was based on the premises that, given a policy of reform and administrative fair play, the union was desirable and workable, and the goodwill of large sections of the Irish public could easily be won. Ireland was to share the advantages of the new era in British politics inaugurated by the reform bill, and with the breaking of the virtual monopoly of official power possessed by the protestant party, the full implications of catholic emancipation would be realized, and the gulf which was felt to exist between the administration and the majority of the Irish public closed. A severe critic might condemn this approach as inspired by a facile optimism derived from an inadequate grasp of the situation. The well-intentioned liberal, incapable of comprehending the strength of the forces he is trying to cope with, is an easy subject for ridicule. But it should be taken into account that Irish national feeling did not at this period express itself with the passionate intensity it attained in the forties, that O'Connell was cooperative, and that the whigs' interpretation of Irish economic history gave them grounds for believing that in the future conditions would improve and social tension diminish. It seemed indeed that the most serious obstruction the whigs had to negotiate was the stubborn and strong resistance of English and Irish toryism. The conservatives after 1835 were a large and pugnacious minority in the commons and controlled the lords. They disapproved of many of the whigs' Irish measures, they were naturally irritated—in spite of being sincere unionists—at seeing a weak whig ministry maintained in power by the Irish liberal vote in defiance of the decision of the English constituencies, and they appreciated the opportunities for attack provided by the government's Irish policy and Irish allies—not to speak of the chance of appealing to vulgar anti-popery. Graham, a recent convert to conservatism, in a letter, wisely marked 'confidential', to Bonham, a well-known tory wire-puller, put the party line bluntly. 'Protestantism is the only weapon with which we can encounter republicanism, and we have the staff in our hand and we must lay about us, upholding the church both in England and Scotland against O'Connell and his tail. And as in Ireland he is the strength of the government we must make him their bane.'[1] Consequently each of the government's major Irish measures, police, tithe, and municipal reform, the Irish poor law, and the railway grant had a dreary parliamentary history, and a series of unproductive stalemates was only avoided by the cabinet's resolution to plod on with its Irish programme, together with the fact that Peel's intellectual integrity and Wellington's bursts of clear-headed opportunism, prevented the conservative leaders

---

[1] Graham to Bonham, 2 Jan. 1839 (Add. MS. 40616).

playing the party game to the bitter end. Nevertheless the delays imposed by the opposition seriously handicapped the whigs. Timing is a vital factor in policy and concessions halted and haggled over lose half their value.

Fortunately for the government there was one sphere in which it could disregard the opposition when carrying out its Irish policy. By the deliberate and systematic bestowal of official posts on catholics and liberal protestants it could to some extent demonstrate its ideals and obtain its objectives. All the six judges placed on the bench between 1835 and 1841 were liberals (four had been liberal M.P.s), and three were catholics. During the same period the attorney—or solicitor-general was always a catholic, and his colleague a liberal protestant, and religio-political considerations played a part in a wide variety of appointments, including stipendiary magistrates, legal officials and police inspectors. There was of course a double justification for this. After a long period of tory domination the time had come to redress the balance, and, what was more important, it was the intention of the whigs to identify the administration with the community. Elevating patronage into an instrument of policy of course has its dangers. To a tory it would appear simply an attempt to sanctify jobbery, and a decade or so later Irish radicals were to sneer at Normanby's policy as a 'mere affair of place-giving', which debased 'the baronet who intrigued for a peerage, the popular M.P. who intrigued for a place, and the peasant who ambitioned to be a policeman'.[1] A keen Irish whig pointed out another danger. Drummond, as a result of his contacts with the local liberals, was in his administration of the magistracy and the police exposed to the 'solicitations and intrigues of a clique', which was liable to become, as detestable an ascendancy in Dublin as that which it is striving to replace'.[2] Drummond himself, however, after a few years of office, boldly declared that Mulgrave and Morpeth were in the proud position of being able to say that while they had been in power no man had been appointed who was incompetent or unpopular, and 'when men can say this they can hurl defiance at the devil whether he takes the shape of the recorder, the Bandon serjeant, or the preposterous Roden'. Mulgrave himself rather more realistically admitted, 'I am perfectly aware that we must job a little and that it will not do to keep too Spartan a selection while we have Irish members to manage'. But he added that he would try and exclude political considerations when appointing assistant barristers. And some time later he remarked that the first batch of magistrates appointed

[1] Cloncurry, *Personal recollections* (1849), p. 418; *Nation*, 20 Dec. 1845.
[2] More O'Ferrall to Morpeth, 22 Apr. 1840 (Castle Howard MSS.).

under the constabulary act was 'a good selection and calculated as far as is consistent with the good of the public service to satisfy those patriotic place-seekers'. As Mulgrave's comments indicate, the government was subject to considerable pressure from its supporters, 'those shabby and doubtful gentlemen' as Ebrington in an exasperated moment termed them, the liberal M.P. having replaced the territorial magnate as an intermediary between place seekers and the government. But Mulgrave, shortly after arriving, decided that M.P.s who, as a result of the reform bill represented principles rather than interests, were not necessarily the persons of consequence in their counties through whom the local liberal gentry would naturally apply to the government.[1] So he scrutinized their requests carefully, and on the whole it may be said that the whigs in making Irish appointments, while gratifying their supporters, preserved their own independence and a respect for other qualities in addition to party loyalty.

In one important sphere, municipal administration, it was impossible for the whigs to assure equality of opportunity without passing legislation. At the time of the union there were a hundred and seventeen Irish corporate boroughs, varying in size from cities such as Dublin to legal entities resembling Old Sarum. Some of them quietly vanished with the disappearance of their main *raison d'être*, returning M.P.s to the Irish parliament. The surviving corporations, which, in most boroughs were self-perpetuating bodies, filling vacancies by co-option, and in a few were elected by close guilds, generally speaking were content to do little rather badly, and in a number of instances essential municipal services were performed either by other bodies set up for the purpose by local acts or by commissioners elected by the ratepayers under the provisions of an act of 1828.[2] Naturally, in the absence of control and publicity, there was a tendency for the property and revenues to be administered with a careful respect for the private interests of the members of the corporation.[3] Finally, in spite of the Relief acts of 1793 and 1829, the corporations remained exclusively and arrogantly protestant, with the exception of Tuam where the corporation was under catholic control —and where the tolls had been set to the committee for building the new catholic cathedral.[4]

[1] Drummond to Morpeth, 26 Mar. 1839, Mulgrave to Morpeth, 23 May 1835, 3 July 1836, Mulgrave to Morpeth, 12 Mar. 1836, Ebrington to Morpeth, 23 March 1840 (Castle Howard MSS.).

[2] 9 Geo. IV. c. 82.

[3] For the Irish corporations see *First report of the commissioners appointed to inquire into municipal corporations in Ireland, with appendices*, H.C. 1835 (23, 24, 27, 28), 1836 (29), 1835, xvii, xxviii, 1836, i.  [4] Ibid., Pt. I, p. 437.

With petty peculation and jobbery, bigotry and incompetence as their outstanding characteristics, the Irish corporations were ill-fitted for survival in a reforming era. After their English equivalents had been re-modelled on severely functional lines, their doom was obviously drawing near. In 1833 thirteen young liberal barristers were appointed commissioners to report on the working of Irish municipal institutions.[1] Dividing Ireland into circuits they described with obvious gusto and damning objectivity the archaic, clumsy, and often corrupt machinery by which Irish municipal life was regulated. Fortified by their report the government in 1835 introduced an Irish municipal reform bill which became a hardy parliamentary annual for six sessions. Once it was dropped for want of time, twice it was amended out of recognition by the lords, once it was lost as a result of a dispute between the two houses over rating, once it failed to pass the commons because the lower house conceived that the lords' amendments encroached on its privileges, and finally in 1840, when Irish radicals had been tantalized almost beyond endurance and English peers were heartily sick of the subject,[2] it reached the statute book.

If the whole episode was exasperating to liberals, it severely strained the unity of the conservative party. Few were prepared to defend the indefensible, and the conservative leaders strove to discover a line of policy which would permit them to wash their hands of the old corporations and enable them to baulk their opponents. Jackson pressed Peel not to 'transfer the power and influence incident to corporations hitherto preserved in protestant hands solely to the exclusive possession of Roman Catholics'. He suggested that the conservative party should try and secure that the new corporations should be forbidden to transact non-municipal business, so that they should not become foci of general political activity, and that the municipal franchise should be fixed so as to give the catholics a share but not a monopoly of municipal power.[3] Jackson's suggestions were strongly criticized by the duke of Wellington who did not think either of them enforceable. Wellington himself, was elderly, physically shaky, testy and disinclined to experiment, but clear-headed and decided. His object at this time was to prevent the government 'doing mischief' and he thought it plainly impossible to leave 'the protestants of the Irish corporate towns to the government of those whose conduct is detailed before the intimidation committees of the house

[1] Apparently the commissioners were nominated by Perrin, the liberals in the commons being determined that only reformers should be selected (Littleton to Anglesey, 9 July 1833, Plas Newydd MSS.).
[2] Portman to Morpeth, 18 July 1840 (Castle Howard MSS.).
[3] Jackson to Peel, 31 Aug. 1836 (Add. MS. 40424).

of commons'. Still he was afraid that it was also impossible in the face of so much evidence of mismanagement for conservatives to attempt to defend the *status quo*. The only solution was to invoke the power of the crown (i.e. of the central executive), and he suggested that the Irish corporations might quiet uneasy tory consciences by offering to surrender their charters.[1] Wellington's course was followed by the party in the commons in 1836, when Peel, backed up by Stanley, argued that when the existing corporations (which they made no attempt to defend) were abolished, new corporations should not be established in Irish towns. Instead, the corporate property should be vested in a commission, the corporations' judicial and police powers should be exercised by the central government, and for the rest the Irish boroughs could use the limited powers granted to them by the act of 1828. Speakers on the conservative side of the house emphasized that in Ireland numbers were arrayed against property, and that the ministerial scheme had, from the political point of view, every fault of the old system, except that it placed power in the hands of an ignorant instead of an enlightened faction. The government's bill it was said would establish 'fifty legalized debating clubs . . . with their accompaniments of daily canvassing, yearly registration, constant elections and interminable excitement'.[2]

But the conservative party as a whole was not satisfied with this approach to the subject. In 1837 Stanley and Graham intimated that they were not prepared to oppose Ireland securing municipal corporations, and Peel, who felt both the evil of continuous conflict between the two houses on Irish questions and the strain of trying to preserve the unity of the conservative party, agreed to modify his attitude on the government's measure, 'less from love of corporations in the abstract than from the feeling that to deny them to Ireland would imply inferiority'.[3] It soon became clear that the conservatives hoped agreement could be reached on three related measures, Irish corporate reform, an Irish poor law and tithe commutation. If by the third the property of the Irish church was securely settled, the corporations' importance as a bulwark of the protestant faith would be lessened, and the rating fixed under the new poor law could be used as an objective basis for the municipal franchise. Wellington reluctantly followed Peel's lead. He thought the new corporations, created under the government's bill

---

[1] Wellington to Peel, 11, 13 Feb., 8 Sept. 1836 (Add. MS. 40310).

[2] *Parl. Deb.*, 3 series, xxxii. 658.

[3] Peel's views on Irish municipal reform and his efforts to preserve a united conservative front on the issue are illustrated by memoranda he prepared—Memorandum relating to Irish municipal reform, Paper prepared to be read at a meeting at Lyndhurst's, Memorandum on Irish municipal corporation bill (Add. MS. 40423).

unnecessary, that 'the lowest rabble of the boroughs would be the burgesses' and that the power of the corporation would be in the hands of the demagogues. Nevertheless he agreed that after Peel's conversations with Graham and Stanley they could not continue to oppose municipal reform, and, irritably yielding, he undertook to persuade Lyndhurst to accept Peel's policy.[1] Two years later, when the issue was still unsettled, though the ultimate outcome seemed certain, Wellington played with the possibility of reversing the party line. When a hitch held up the 1839 Irish corporations bill, he suggested to Frederick Shaw, the parliamentary leader of the Irish conservatives, that the lords should throw it out, 'on the point that people are getting tired of it, and that we shall attempt a better hereafter or altogether abolish the Irish corporations'. Shaw, however, did not encourage him.[2]

Shaw, who with a defiant disregard of criticism combined the lucrative judicial office of recorder of Dublin and a seat in parliament, was a practical politician in touch with English feeling. He saw from the outset that the old corporations could not be preserved, and early in 1838, deferring to the views expressed at a meeting of conservative M.P.s, he reluctantly agreed to abandon his schemes for the complete abolition of the Irish corporations. He himself favoured special legislation for Dublin, but his suggestion was almost unanimously rejected by a meeting of conservative M.P.s and peers. Above all he seems to have pressed for a speedy settlement of the municipal question since it was likely to cause dissensions between the Irish tories and their parliamentary leaders, after the latter had decided to accept in principle the government's plan. So near the end of 1838 Shaw bluntly told a deputation of Dublin aldermen that since the conservative leaders had decided to let the bill through he would not weaken the party by reopening the matter; and speaking as a lawyer, he added the unpalatable information that while the corporations bill was under consideration it would not be legal for them to allocate the corporation's funds to certain purposes in which they were interested.[3]

Naturally a section of Irish conservatives felt they had been let down by their parliamentary leaders. As late as 1839 when the municipal reform bill came up for the fifth time in the commons, in spite of Peel and Shaw emphasizing that the conservative party were bound in honour to accept it, ten Irish tories, led by Litton, a tough protestant barrister,

[1] Wellington to Peel, 31 Mar., 15 Apr., 21 May 1837, Lyndhurst to Wellington, 6 Apr. 1837 (Add. MS. 40310).

[2] Shaw to Wellington, 8 Aug. 1839 (Add. MS. 40427).

[3] For Shaw's political behaviour during this period see his speech at the Trinity College election, printed in 1841, and *DEM*, 4 Dec. 1838, 2 Jan. 1839.

voted with the minority which supported Inglis's motion for its rejection. Peel seems to have been seriously annoyed, for Litton wrote him a long explanatory letter. Inglis's Irish supporters had held two meetings in the Carlton, and though aware of the course Peel intended to take, they felt they should vote against the bill so as to strengthen the lords in their efforts to amend it, and to cheer the Irish protestants and rouse them from the state of apathy into which defeat had thrown them.[1] The Dublin corporation, whose functions, according to a eulogist, had always been 'more political than corporate',[2] fighting to the last ditch, sent Isaac Butt to plead their case at the bar of the house of lords. In the course of an eloquent address he drew attention to the clause in the Irish version of Magna Carta which declared the franchises of Dublin inviolate, and argued that the corporation had fulfilled its trust by remaining through all vicissitudes true to the throne and steadfastly attached to the protestant religion. Municipal reform meant surrendering to the catholic masses the power to tax protestant property, and the beginning of a sequence of disasters, for once the new corporations were established it would be impossible to maintain the established church, and 'when that church falls, the doom of the connection between the two countries is sealed'.[3] Back in Dublin, Butt became involved in an acrimonious controversy when he denounced Shaw for selling the pass, and ill feelings in Dublin conservative circles were exacerbated by Lyndhurst informing Butt, inadvertently or maliciously, that Shaw had advised the conservative leaders to try and settle the question quickly. The conservative press was filled with prolonged discussions over the morality of Shaw's behaviour and the rules governing the political use of private conversations. Tempers were so strained that there was a commotion at a city dinner when the health of the recorder was proposed, and John Jones, the pushing leader of the extreme right in the corporation, solaced himself after being snubbed by Peel and Wellington, by successfully suing the *Dublin Evening Mail*, the leading conservative paper, which was strongly pro-Shaw, for libel.[4] In short, over municipal reform, the right-wing Irish tories played their usual role of expostulating noisily as the course of events swept past them, and then indulging in acrimonious self-pity as their leaders in parliament abandoned untenable positions.

The whigs made no attempt to remodel drastically local government in the rural areas, and for another sixty years after the boroughs had

[1] E. Litton to Peel, 23 May 1839 (Add. MS. 40427).
[2] *Parl. Deb.*, 3 series, xxxii. 660.
[3] I. Butt, *The Irish corporation bill* . . . (1840).
[4] *EP*, 5 Oct., 5, 14 Nov. 1840; *DEM*, 9 Oct., 4 Dec. 1839.

passed under popular control the Irish landed gentry governed the counties through the grand juries as well as dispensing justice at petty and quarter sessions. Still, during the thirties their powers were somewhat curtailed. To Drummond 'the radical vice' of the existing county police system was the appointment of the constables by the justices of the peace, for as a result the force was regarded as a partisan body, an opinion justified by 'the very language the constables use in making their reports. . . . They speak of loyal inhabitants meaning thereby the protestant inhabitants'. The constabulary act of 1835, drafted in accordance with Drummond's suggestions, amalgamated the county constabulary and the peace preservation force, and placed the new force under the command of an inspector-general who was responsible for its management and for the recruitment of constables who were expected to possess 'a good character for honesty, fidelity and activity'. After being held up by the lords for a session the constabulary act reached the statute book in 1836, and under its first two inspectors-general, both Scotsmen who had fought with distinction in the Peninsula, the new force, adequately paid, and drilled and disciplined with military precision, not only acquired a reputation for vigour and aloofness from local partialities, but even, to Drummond's delight, had in a few years 'in fact become a popular force'.[1] Along with the new constabulary there was a considerable increase in the number of stipendiary magistrates appointed by the government, who were particularly useful when it came to making inquiries into incidents involving political or religious prejudice and to enforcing the law where the local magistrates were reluctant to move, as in the north against Orange processions. Naturally enough there was frequent friction between the executive and the unpaid magistracy, several instances receiving wide publicity. When the King's County J.P.s in 1836 refused to allow a newly appointed assistant barrister to preside at quarter sessions, Mulnay was only prevented by a cabinet decision from dismissing them en bloc.[2] But Colonel Verner, the M.P. for Armagh was dismissed from the commission for giving the toast of 'a lawless and most disgraceful combat',[3] the battle of the Diamond, and Langford, a county Limerick J.P., who, by the highly officious use of his position and of the police (which he ought not to have interfered with), discovered a Ribbon conspiracy which turned out to be a

[1] Drummond to Morpeth, 6, 27 Aug. 1835, 1 Apr. 1836, 26 Mar. 1839, Shaw to Morpeth, 7 Oct. 1836 (Castle Howard MSS.).
[2] Mulgrave to Morpeth, 5 Feb. 1836 (Castle Howard MSS.); Opinions of members of cabinet, c. Feb. 1836 (Russell papers).
[3] T. Drummond to Verner, 22 Aug. 1837 (R. B. O'Brien, Thomas Drummond (1889), p. 259).

mare's nest, was rewarded with a sharp rebuke from the Castle for acting *ultra vires* and on an out-of-date warrant.[1] In 1838 the executive struck a sweeping blow by taking advantage of the demise of the crown to make a general revision of the magistracy, omitting the names of agents of resident landowners, of clergymen, and of gentlemen who had ceased to reside, parted with their property, sunk in the social scale or become financially embarrassed, with the result that about 30 per cent of the justices of the peace were removed from the commission.[2]

The antipathy between the bulk of the Irish gentry and the government was increased by the belief, prevalent in government circles, that the Irish landlords were failing, during a critical period, to perform their essential social functions adequately. Ireland, liberals argued, was in the throes of an agricultural revolution. The excessive subdivision which had been going on for years, unchecked if not encouraged by landlords, had been responsible for the backward state of Irish agriculture over wide areas and for a deterioration in the living standards of many of the peasantry. Fortunately the process was being reversed, and it was expected by the consolidation of farms and the transformation of a large section of the peasantry from 'the state of pauper tenants to that of independent labourers', the foundations of a sound agrarian system would in time be laid. During the transition the Irish landlords had a double duty—to push forward and organize the necessary changes, and simultaneously to mitigate by the 'judicious humanity' with which their operations were conducted, the distress which a series of local economic upheavals was bound to inflict on the poorer peasantry.[3] But many Irish landlords had neither the patience, the resources nor the relationship with their tenantry required for such a difficult rôle, and improvement was closely associated in the peasant mind with eviction. While Drummond wrote of the Irish landlords as being 'cold-blooded and indifferent to the sufferings of their tenants',[4] the conservative gentry who, at least emotionally, associated ribbonism, catholicism and liberalism as a group of destructive forces, loudly resented the failure of the government to stamp out agrarian crime. When in 1838 the Tipperary

---

[1] *Returns respecting crimes, outrages, etc., in Co. Limerick*, H.L. 1841 (40), xviii.

[2] *A copy of a circular addressed by the lord-lieutenant to the lieutenants of counties in Ireland*, H.L. 1837-8 (292), xviii.

[3] For attitude of political and economic liberals to Irish economic conditions see *Second report of the commissioners appointed to consider and recommend a general system of railways for Ireland*, H.C. 1837-8 (145), xxxv. An important section of this report dealing with Irish economic conditions and trends was drafted by Drummond. (For the authorship of the different sections of the report, see *Life and correspondence of Field Marshal Sir John Burgoyne* (1873), i. 402-17.)

[4] Drummond to Morpeth, 21 June 1836 (Castle Howard MSS.),

magistrates requested the government to take stringent steps to suppress outrage, Drummond in his reply not only refuted their contention that conditions were abnormally bad, but going to the root of the matter, in a pungent apopthegm which delighted liberals and scandalized landlords, reminded the gentry of Tipperary that property had its duties as well as its rights. Two years later the justices of peace of King's County, when writing to the Castle, produced a gloomy apologia for an unsuccessful and handicapped ruling caste. It was, 'unquestionable' the address declared, that 'the landlords in each part of the United Kingdom act upon the same principles as far as the different habits of the peasantry and the different circumstances' permit. But in Ireland there were difficulties 'unknown in England arising from the more feeble exercise of the rights of property'. In Ireland a tenant would transfer his lease without asking the landlord's consent, the new tenant 'trusting for a title to the powers of intimidation', another tenant would cut up his farm into minute holdings against the landlord's wish, still a third type of tenant was 'idle and dishonest, he pays no rent, but he also endeavours to hold his farm relying upon the efficiency of intimidation'. But 'a landlord who submits to that system of dictation necessarily abandons the management of his property and forsakes the duties which he owes to society. And while we all feel most anxious in our respective spheres to promote the comfort and happiness of those who stand in the relation of tenants, we also feel most strongly the necessity of keeping clearly in view the broad distinction *between acts of kindness and concessions to intimidation.*'[1]

Ireland's economic problem, represented by a 'vast accumulation of human suffering',[2] still influenced and underlay all political issues. The whigs trusted to prevalent economic trends ultimately to improve Irish conditions, nevertheless during the mid-thirties they reluctantly decided that some means would have to be employed to alleviate the pains of the transition period. Though economic tendencies in Great Britain and Ireland were fundamentally different, in both countries pauperism and widespread distress were endemic, and social remedies were continually being adumbrated and argued over. As regards Ireland, discussion tended in the thirties to centre round the poor-law question. By the beginning of the nineteenth century, the English poor law, which at the close of the Elizabethan period had been systematized on clear principles, had be-

---

[1] *Letter from Lord Oxmantown . . . to the chief secretary . . . also memorial from the justices of the peace, King's county, assembled in Oct. 1840 . . . H.L.* 1841 (28), xviii.
[2] H. G. Ward, *The first steps to a poor law* (1837).

come confused and extravagant in its operations. Often administered with lazy good nature and a great lack of foresight, it seemed to critical contemporaries designed to discourage thrift and initiative, and to demoralize and defraud the poor at the expense of the overburdened ratepayer. The prevalent economic philosophy was not very favourable to any kind of poor law, which would enable an able-bodied man to eat without working, or would interfere with the important and sensitive relationships between the labour force and the wage fund. But since humanitarianism, which was at least as strong as orthodox economic theory, shrank from leaving the starving unemployed to the play of supply and demand, a compromise was reached, and in the early thirties the variable and extravagant old system was replaced by a new poor law, meant to be uniform, centralized and strict, with the workhouse test as its keystone. The discussion over the English poor law naturally drew attention to the absence of such a law in Ireland, if for no other reason, than that the two islands formed a single labour market, and during the early thirties parishes scattered throughout England petitioned parliament, complaining that they were being forced to support Irish paupers and demanding that parliament should take steps for their relief at home. Owing to the absence of a poor law in Ireland, England, it was said, was virtually being rated to maintain a great part of the Irish population. It was also sometimes alleged that in the absence of an Irish poor law, the Irish poor would swarm over and depress the wages of the English labourer. But more benevolent arguments were also employed in support of an Irish poor law. In 1830 Bishop Doyle of Kildare urged with his accustomed fervour that the state must make some provision for the indigent Irish poor, possibly at the expense of the established church.[1] The cause of the Irish poor was also taken up by Sadler, a man abounding in good will and eccentric economic theory, who, shocked at conditions in Ireland, 'that dark abyss of suffering which never abates, over which a spirit of suffering and despair is perpetually brooding',[2] vehemently asserted the right of the Irish poor to relief, and argued, both in print and in the house of commons, in favour of a system of relief which would set the indigent to work on useful projects—'for human labour was too sacred an instrument to squander'. Poulett Scrope, the geologist and economist, also, both in the house of commons and in pamphlets, argued in favour of an Irish poor law. Two parties only, he asserted, opposed the suggestion: a section of the Irish landlords who dreaded high poor-rates, and the political economists. Scrope retorted

---

[1] T. Doyle, *Letter to Thomas Spring Rice* (1831).
[2] *Parl. Deb.*, 3 series, vi. 795.

with an argument frequently employed by the advocates of an Irish poor law. What Ireland needed was capital, the want of security in the country prevented capital being invested, and that insecurity would prevail as long as the starving Irish labourer was denied relief. Moreover, it was urged that the existence of a poor law would greatly minimize the suffering which would inevitably accompany the necessary and impending Irish agricultural revolution, the replacement of small cottier tenants by large-scale, capitalist farmers. As for the fear that poor-rates would swallow the rental of Ireland, a sound system would 'extend relief only to those in want, and relieve the community from the frauds, the contortions, the knavery of imposters'.[1]

The question was also taken up by several Irish M.P.s, Wyse, the educationalist, Lynch of Galway, Sir Richard Musgrave, Sharman Crawford, and Smith O'Brien, and between 1831 and 1837 no fewer than seven Irish poor relief bills were introduced into the house of commons. The more modest aimed at providing assistance through local committees for the helpless poor; the more ambitious bills, supported by Wyse, Sharman Crawford, O'Brien and Lynch attempted to set up a central authority to supervise poor relief and find employment for the able-bodied, who were 'in danger of perishing', in public works.

Schemes for granting public assistance to the impotent poor met with comparatively little criticism, but the idea that the community should accept responsibility for the able-bodied unemployed aroused vigorous opposition. It was alleged that the suggestion emanated from selfish Englishmen, who wanted the use of cheap Irish labour but would do nothing to help the Irish poor. As for the English poor, an Irish poor law would not benefit them by diminishing Irish competition in the labour market. For the poor Irishman would be all the more ready to emigrate if he could leave his wife and family on the rates. An Irish poor law, it was declared, would both stimulate the growth of an already redundant population, encourage idleness, and prove the first step towards Owen's utopian plan for extinguishing private property.[2] This view was forcibly enunciated in the house of commons by Robert Torrens, the son of a county Derry landowner and one of the leading systematizers of orthodox economic theory, who pointed out that the factors determining wages, the profits on capital, and the value of land were all involved in Sadler's proposals. He painted a grim picture of the

[1] G. P. Scrope, *Plan of a poor law for Ireland* (1833); G. C. Lewis, *Local disturbances in Ireland* (1836); W. S. O'Brien, *Plan for the relief of the poor in Ireland* (1830); *A letter to the Rt, Hon. the Lord Mayor*, by Patricus (1830).
[2] G. H. Evans, *Remarks . . .* (1829); H. Flood, *Poor laws* (1830); *Parl. Deb.*, 3 series, vi. 849.

future if these proposals were implemented; the whole of the rental of Ireland would soon be swallowed up by a compulsory assessment, the poor would become co-proprietors of the soil, and none would 'be left at liberty and leisure to sound the depths of science and cultivate the fields of knowledge'. In time the peasantry would breed up to the point when the whole of the national income would be absorbed in their subsistence, then it would of course be impossible to purchase foreign corn in an emergency, and the country would face 'hopeless and unmitigated famine'.[1] The most powerful opponent of an Irish poor law was, however, O'Connell, who applied the prevalent principles of economic science to the situation with a disregard for popularity unusual in a demagogue and a warmth of expression rarely found in an exponent of orthodox economics. One objection to a poor law which he repeatedly urged was a religious or moral one. The spirit of charity would be greatly weakened if the opportunities for its spontaneous exercise were removed. For the rest his arguments were economic ones. Something, he thought, might be done for the impotent poor, the sick and aged, preferably through funds administered by ecclesiastical persons, but he had the greatest repugnance to granting relief to the able-bodied unemployed. A poor-rate would mean that so much less was available for wages and might easily swallow one-third of the rental of Ireland. 'No philanthropy', he once remarked, 'was more easy and imposing than that which vented itself in taxing other people.' In addition 'it would diminish self-reliance, paralyse industry, decrease economy' and destroy initiative. In the parliamentary discussions on the poor law in 1837 and 1838 he mentioned, as alternatives to such a law, well-managed emigration schemes and productive public works (though he also denounced the latter as implying slavery). If O'Connell's contributions to the discussions on the Irish poor-law were vehement and voluminous they were not outstandingly helpful, for his belief in *laissez-faire*, his conviction that Ireland's misery was mainly due to political causes such as the catholic disabilities and the union, and his long-standing familiarity with the political issues involved, meant that he paid comparatively little attention to economic factors.[2]

As for the government, Stanley in 1831 persuaded the cabinet to assent to a bill raising a compulsory poor-rate for the support of the Dublin Mendicity Institution. This he was convinced would prove the

---

[1] *Parl. Deb.*, 3 series, v. 1112, vi. 818 ff.

[2] *Parl. Deb.*, 3 series, xv. 1149 ff., xvii. 871 ff., xxvi. 1212 ff., xxxviii. 360 ff., xl. 947 ff, 1030, 1276 ff.; *FJ*, 14 Nov. 1830; *MR*, 4, 13 Jan. 1832; *Pilot*, 14 Nov. 1836. About this time O'Connell was vigorously criticizing from the standpoint of an economic liberal trade union activities in Dublin (*Pilot*, Jan. 1838).

thin end of a wedge preceding the introduction of a general system of poor laws.[1] But, presumably owing to the pressure of reform on parliamentary time, the bill never even reached a first reading, and for several years when the question of any Irish poor law was raised, the government's spokesmen fell back on the time-worn arguments for caution and delay. Finally in May 1833 Althorp, after being badgered by a group of pertinacious advocates of an Irish poor law, accepted a suggestion of Peel's, and agreed to appoint a commission of inquiry into the relief of the Irish poor. Though one M.P. suspected that by adopting this device the government 'hoped they might slumber on in their own places doing nothing',[2] the commission was a strong one. Its twelve members included the two archbishops of Dublin, three leading catholic laymen, two liberal divines (the dean of the Chapel Royal and Carlile of the national board), and five amateur economists. Highly conscious of the important nature of their task, for they were sure that 'no commission could be entrusted with a more complicated subject for investigation than ours', they set to work to survey the field with microscopic thoroughness, circulating 7,600 questionnaires and sending out a number of assistant commissioners to tour the country to collect information respecting the social and economic condition of the Irish poor and the working of local charities.[3] The assistant commissioners were drawn in equal numbers from Great Britain and Ireland and conducted their investigations in couples, since the commission believed that the only mode of combining local knowledge with impartiality was by joining in the inquiry an Irishman with a native of Great Britain. Since the assistant commissioners visited many parishes, encouraged the inhabitants (brought up in a voluble country) to express their views on a wide variety of topics and recorded them often almost verbatim, they amassed evidence on a Brobdingragian scale. This took time, and at the beginning of 1836 after the commission had been at work for more than two years, Lord John Russell announced his intention of winding it up if nothing definite was produced within a few weeks.[4] This may have acted as a spur; at any rate just a month later Russell was informed by one of the commissioners that though it was doubtful whether the report would give general satisfaction, nevertheless they had recommended some pretty strong measures.[5] The recommendations which were laid before parliament in April 1836 were decided and comprehensive. The new English

---

[1] Stanley to Anglesey, 27 June 1831 (Plas Newydd MSS.).
[2] *Parl. Deb.*, 3 series, xvii. 879-80.
[3] See the commission's report and appendices.
[4] Russell to Morpeth, 4 Jan. 1836 (Castle Howard MSS.).
[5] Killeen to Russell, 5 Mar. 1836 (Russell papers).

poor law was decisively rejected, the commission estimating that in Ireland 585,000 labourers were unemployed for thirty weeks of the year. In any case the workhouse test would be useless and absurd when no work was available. The commissioners recommended a bold, constructive alternative to the English scheme, the creation of a board to plan and supervise wide schemes of national improvement. The board was to partition and improve waste lands by drainage, road building and fencing on a large scale, and was to be empowered to permit tenants for life to grant long leases if they included improvement clauses. The expenses incurred in carrying out the board's projects were to be met by loans from the board of works and by a local rate, and there was to be a special court of review and record to settle summarily the legal disputes bound to arise from the board's operations. There was also to be an Irish poor law commission supervising local boards which were to be responsible for the care of the infirm, sick, aged and lunatic poor. The organization of emigration from Ireland was to be the joint responsibility of the colonial office and the poor law commission, and the guardians were to have power to compel vagrants to emigrate, the expenses of the operation being met partly by a national rate and partly by the landlords of the locality from which the emigrants went. Not content with handling purely economic questions the commissioners suggested that the fiscal powers of the grand juries should be transferred to elected county boards and that an involved and comprehensive tithe commutation scheme, which would satisfy the tithe payer and the clergy as well as putting £313,000 per annum at the state's disposal, should be passed.

Taken as a whole the report was an intelligent and comprehensive document and its recommendations offered a positive and possibly feasible plan for dealing with the problem of Irish poverty, and for redressing by bold political action Ireland's economic maladjustments. Unfortunately it was also almost certain to dismay a cabinet of average calibre when it contemplated putting the report's proposals into legislative form and pushing them through parliament. In addition, possibly on account of the commission's size and the reluctance of its members to curb one another's enthusiasm, the report was diffuse and over-inclusive. Furthermore the commissioners do not seem to have been in close touch with the government, while Whately, who was generally taken as being responsible for the report, carried little weight in official circles. The Irish administration, busy with routine duties, paid little attention to the report, Mulgrave's first reaction being that it would not satisfy the English landowners who wanted an Irish poor law.[1] Russell was un-

[1] Mulgrave to Russell, 1 Feb. 1836 (Russell papers).

sympathetic and soon showed that he preferred to rely on a more conventional approach to Irish economic problems. He began by requesting
a couple of experts to review the report confidentially for the government.
Nassau Senior's comments were friendly, as he considered the report
contained many valuable suggestions. Cornewall Lewis, the son of
Frankland Lewis, was thoroughly hostile.[1] To try to restrict poor relief
to certain categories (i.e. the impotent poor) as proposed by the commission, would lead, he argued, to a series of illogicalities and administrative
absurdities, and would prevent a poor law fulfilling its primary purpose,
which was to induce the poor, by offering them the prospect of a maintenance in the event of absolute need, to loosen their hold upon the
land. A poor law, strongly guarded by the workhouse test, would restore
to the Irish landlords the power of doing what they would with their
own. He argued that the commissioners grossly exaggerated the number
likely to seek relief, and to the argument that the workhouse test would
not function in Ireland, since conditions in the house would be superior
to those usually enjoyed by the Irish labourer, he retorted, that 'the
lowering of the diet was not the keystone' of the system, but compulsory
labour, discipline and classification. After all the English poor had
christened the new institutions 'not starving houses but bastilles'.

Another well-known poor-law expert also pulverized the report. In
January 1836 Nicholls, an able and experienced administrator fanatically
devoted to the principles of the new English poor law, though 'he did
not pretend to any personal knowledge of the state of Ireland, feeling
that his views would receive a favourable reception' sent Russell a
memorandum arguing that the English poor law should be extended to
Ireland. At the end of August Russell sent him to Ireland to discover
what system of relief was most adapted to the country's needs. Nicholls
scarcely required the indications as to the lines his report was to follow
contained in his instructions. After being in Ireland for a few weeks,
energetically travelling and talking, he was able to pronounce that the
general opinion was in favour of the English poor law, and that he had
seen nothing to show that it could not be extended to Ireland. By the
middle of November he was back in England and had his first report
drafted, and a month later he was directed to prepare a bill embodying
its conclusions.[2] It was easy to ridicule the rapidity with which his
foregone conclusions were confirmed. Whately, who had 'poohpoohed'

---

[1] *A poor law for Ireland: letter from Nassau Senior 1837*, and C. C. Lewis, *Remarks
on the third report of the Irish poor inquiry commissioners* (1837.) Printed in H.C.
papers.
[2] G. Nicholls, *Poor laws—Ireland* . . . (1837); G. Nicholls, *History of the English
poor law* (new ed. 1898), i. xliii-lix.

Nicholls's mission, wrote bitterly a little later, 'so Mr Nicholls is sent to get one bottle of water from the Liffey and one from the Shannon, and then to persuade the English people that he can give them a better poor law than we who have been three years considering it'.[1] But he recognized his competitor's strength when he wrote to an old friend expressing his apprehensions on hearing the 'simplicity and practicality' of Nicholls's proposals contrasted with 'the complexity and onerous machinery of the commissioners'. 'Nothing', Whately added, 'ever exceeded the simplicity of bad legislation except the simplicity of those who admire it.'[2] Nicholls's reports, as the archbishop implies, were distinguished by lucidity and self-assurance. He was convinced that a sound poor law, using the workhouse test as a basis, offered the best palliative for Ireland. He believed that the commission had overestimated the number who would probably demand relief under normal conditions—his own figure being about 80,000—and in any case he protected his system by recommending that no right to relief should be granted, so that the guardians' obligations would cease once the workhouse was filled. He believed that the poor law would not work miracles, but that it would carry Ireland through the transition period from the system of small allotments and extensive subdivision to the sounder practice of the labourer being paid money wages. Admittedly it was impossible, to make 'the lodgings, clothing and diet of the inmates of an Irish workhouse inferior to those of the Irish peasantry'. But Nicholls was confident that the restrictions and discipline imposed would render it irksome enough. He was careful to point out that a famine was a contingency 'altogether above the power of a poor law to provide for'. If it was general, there would be an actual deficiency, so to assess the ratepayers would only shift the suffering. If it was local, 'the public and private exertions of the opulent and charitable' would be available to assist the afflicted districts. But he foresaw that in the future 'as habits, intelligence and forethought of the people improve', famines would be provided against and avoided. His suggestions met with a mixed reception from the government. Russell obviously was in favour of following his advice, but Lansdowne thought they should begin by building a few workhouses as an experiment. Rice agreed, with the addendum that the experiment would be a miserable failure, Mulgrave wanted a special poor law commission for Ireland, and Melbourne typically accepted rather than approved the plan.[3]

[1] Mulgrave to Russell, 26 Sept., 5 Oct. 1836 (Russell papers).
[2] E. J. Whately, *Life and correspondence of Richard Whately* (1866), i. 394-405.
[3] Spring Rice to Lord John Russell, 16 Mar. 1837, Melbourne to Lord John Russell, 4 Sept. 1837, Mulgrave to Lord John Russell, 4 Dec. 1836 (Russell papers).

In the session of 1837 a bill based on Nicholls's recommendations was introduced into the commons and had reached the committee stage when parliament was suddenly dissolved. In the following session it was introduced again and passed. The debates on the two bills, which were marked by muddled goodwill, revealed divergences of opinion that cut across party lines. For instance O'Connell accepted the first bill only as part of the experiment he was making to see if the whigs could give good government to Ireland; when the second bill came up he resolutely opposed it. He was supported by his old opponent Shaw, the Irish conservative leader, who denounced charity by law, and advocated instead of the government's suggestions indoor relief for the impotent and aided emigration for the able-bodied. On the other hand Smith O'Brien and Sharman Crawford, with qualifications, supported the measure. Crawford demanded a greater degree of administrative flexibility, O'Brien wanted some outdoor relief—'domiciliary relief would be most effectual and grateful', and with Poulet Scrope he tried to insert a provision empowering the guardians to pay the wages of destitute labourers under their care if they were engaged on public works. Russell firmly quashed this suggestion as admitting the dangerous principle of outdoor relief. In the final division on the bill in the commons the minority of sixty-two against it was composed of a few English liberals, about twenty Irish liberals and repealers, and for the rest English and Irish conservatives in about equal numbers. Rather more than twenty Irish members voted for the bill (including one conservative and about equal numbers of repealers and liberals), which received overwhelming support from both sides of the house. When the bill arrived in the lords Wellington announced his intention of supporting it on the grounds that it might make Irish landlords manage their properties properly and pay some attention to the poor on their estates. Lyndhurst however broke away from his leader and violently attacked the bill as heralding a new despotism. It was, he complained, full of blanks, which the commissioners were empowered to fill up. To invest a certain number of individuals 'with absolute authority' to carry a measure into effect, 'however convenient it may be for the government of the day', was in Lyndhurst's opinion, outrageous.[1] But after opening his batteries Lyndhurst abandoned the attack, and the bill went through against the futile opposition of the Irish representative peers.

As soon as the bill received the royal assent the poor law commission set to work with hard driving determination to extend its system over Ireland. The country was divided into poor law unions, a hundred and

[1] *Parl. Deb.*, 3 series, xliii, 31–4.

thirty workhouses were erected, severe disciplinary codes were promulgated, and elected boards of guardians, which the commissioners (as circumstances dictated) chivied, rebuked or encouraged, constituted. The commissioners, as can be seen from their reports, viewed with intense satisfaction the progress of a system which they believed not only provided for the genuinely destitute on efficient, economical lines, but was bound to exercise a bracing influence on Irish life by training the poor to be prudential and the better-off to be business-like. Admittedly, to posterity the system's inherent limitations are glaringly obvious, and just after it began to function in its entirety it temporarily collapsed under the strain of an unprecedented catastrophe. But at least it was the first effort to cope with Irish poverty on a nation-wide basis, and, by contemporary standards, a striking instance of large-scale administrative planning.

A year or two later, Melbourne's ministry fumbled with a more positive measure for Ireland's economic improvement. While in England railways were being rapidly built, admittedly with speculation and muddle, in Ireland by the middle of the thirties there was only a short strip six miles in length, and in October 1836 the government appointed a strong commission, including Drummond and Burgoyne, to discover the best way of promoting railways in Ireland. Rather less than two years later this commission produced a report which from a lucid survey of social conditions in Ireland argued that the construction of railways on a large scale would be of the greatest value in both developing the country's resources, 'extending civilization with its attendant lights and benefits' and in affording employment to many of the labouring poor at a time when it was urgently needed. Since it was certain that private enterprise would undertake the work slowly in a piecemeal fashion, concentrating on the portions likely to yield quick returns, the commission boldly recommended that the state should step in and construct and manage a well-planned railway system linking Dublin with Cork and Limerick.[1] Drummond urged this scheme, his 'hobby and pride',[2] on the cabinet with his natural ardour, writing to Russell, that 'it is impossible to look at the magnificent district of country through which our lines to Cork and Kilkenny run—it is impossible to think of its present state, its great capacities, and now imperfectly developed resources, without an ardent desire to see these lines executed as a national work'.[3]

---

[1] *Second report of the commissioners appointed to consider and recommend a general system of railways for Ireland*, H.C. 1837-8 (145), xxxv.

[2] Morpeth to Lady Carlisle, 5 Mar. 1839 (Castle Howard MSS.).

[3] T. Drummond to Russell, 20 Mar. 1838 (Russell papers).

The report was severely criticized by the directors of the projected Great Munster and Leinster railway, and at a meeting held in Dublin to protect 'the numerous body whose vested rights and paid up capital are threatened' by the commission.[1] On the other hand a gathering in London of Irish proprietors, after long, rather muddled discussions between the advocates of state intervention and private enterprise, agreed that if the government was prepared to undertake to build simultaneously three main lines, they would back up its efforts to obtain parliamentary support for a state-constructed and controlled railway system.[2] The cabinet, as might be expected, were divided and hesitant, torn between the strict ideals of *laissez-faire* and the feeling that Ireland should perhaps be treated as a special case. And Spring Rice pessimistically told the chief secretary, 'If you have any hope of reconciling the Irish at once to a centralization of railways which will put down local jobbery, that will deprive attorneys of fees on private bills, engineers of their costs of surveys, and country gentlemen of their expected compensation, and that in addition to energy to counter these difficulties you can devise and reconcile Ireland to a general local tax there is somewhat of a probability that parliament would adopt the railway project.'[3] But the Irish executive managed to get its plan adopted by the cabinet, and in March 1839 Morpeth asked the house to sanction a loan of two and a half millions to be used by the board of works for constructing an Irish railway system, the sum so advanced to be secured on the profits of the lines, and, if there was a deficiency, on an assessment levied on the areas through which they ran. The Irish members were pleased, but Peel, basing his case on the prevalent economic canons, delivered an impressive attack on the government's proposal 'which', he thought, 'must inevitably disparage native intelligence, industry and enterprise besides being a most unfair interference with the capital already in the field'. And though the government secured a majority in a small house they dropped the matter for the session.

At the time they left office the whigs had achieved little for Ireland in the economic sphere. But in another field where results are less ponderable they had at least begun a striking if controversial piece of work.

---

[1] *Railroads (Ireland); copy of all resolutions and memorials presented to the lordlieutenant or chief secretary of Ireland or to the chancellor of the exchequer respecting railroads in Ireland*, H.C. 1839 (154), xlvi.

[2] *A report of the proceedings at two public meetings held at the Thatched House Tavern . . . for the purpose of taking into consideration the necessity of providing railways . . .* (1839); *Irish railways proceedings of the deputation* (1839).

[3] S. Rice to Normanby, 23 Nov. 1838, 2 Jan. 1839, S. Rice to Morpeth, 26 Sept. 1838 (Monteagle papers).

For years the urgent need of providing education for the poor had been acknowledged but there had been interminable and inconclusive discussions over the machinery to be employed. Giving large grants to organizations dominated by the establishment had proved to be futile and wasteful; and to subsidize separately the schools provided by each of the main denominations would invite bickering and complications and put a premium on disunity in Irish social life. Stanley, who on taking office courageously decided to cope with the problem, therefore adopted the formula of combined secular and separate religious education. At the end of 1831 a board was constituted to administer an annual vote.[1] This board made grants to local schools on condition that part of the required sum was raised locally, supervised the work of the schools, supplying textbooks and trained teachers, and took steps to see that the secular instruction given in common was accepted by the most tender theological consciences and was kept rigorously separated from the denominational religious teaching. The first members of the board were all liberals by conviction or temperament. The establishment was represented by Sadleir, one of the few Irish academic liberals, the good-tempered duke of Leinster, and Whately, the recently arrived protestant archbishop of Dublin, who from the outset of his episcopal career assumed an attitude of contentious detachment from all Irish parties; the catholics on the board were Murray, the amicable archbishop of Dublin; Blake, an educational idealist and wily politician; and there were two presbyterians, Holmes representing the unitarians, and Carlile, an ex-moderator of the synod of Ulster. The members of the board, who were all from their different standpoints moderates, had two tasks to perform. They had to build up a general elementary educational system, and they had if possible to prevent it being wrecked on theological issues. The former task they accomplished; to have achieved the latter would have required superhuman dexterity. In the first decade or so of the board's existence, largely through the unsparing efforts of Carlisle and McDonnell, the first two 'resident' commissioners, two of the earliest great British educational bureaucrats, a system which comprised 3,500 schools attended by over 400,000 children was set up. And if critics could point to the board's emphasis on standardized educational techniques, its predilection for rules, regulations, returns and red tape, and its elephantine balancing when trying to handle sectarian issues, the board could claim to have produced a competent, economical and intelligent educational system which by the forties was making a definite

[1] Board of Commissioners of National Education. Its proceedings are outlined in its annual reports.

contribution to Irish life. Always working within relatively narrow financial limits the board provided cheap, well-arranged, dry, and informative little textbooks, set up model schools and tried to produce a great, graded, inspected, well-behaved, disciplined educational force.

Needless to say the board could not confine itself to mere questions of educational routine. From the outset the whole system was vehemently attacked on theological grounds, and the board's early efforts to cope with theological opposition, though well meant, were not only unsuccessful but rather absurd. Though children were to be carefully segregated for denominational religious instruction the board felt that it was possible and advisable to give some religious teaching which would be acceptable to all. For instance, the ten commandments were allowed to be displayed (but unnumbered to avoid denominational disputes over their division) and a selection of scriptural extracts was published for school use.[1] Carlile, who prepared this work, employed a method which he thought would render it acceptable to everybody. Himself a presbyterian, he took the protestant and catholic versions, made his own translation and sent it in typescript to the two archbishops of Dublin for comment.[2] In spite of these precautions his labours were violently criticized. The extracts, 'the word of God doled out to us contaminated by the presumption of man', were characterized as a work in which Rome concealed her errors and protestants omitted the truth,[3] and Carlisle's handling of the word *ipsa* (or *ipsum*) in the third chapter of Genesis was discussed at immense length before two parliamentary committees.

A strong section in each of the larger Irish denominations conducted a strenuous campaign against the board, and as so often happens these hostile groups of extremists revealed common likenesses and based their opposition to the board on much the same principles. A few months after the scheme was laid before the public, the Church of Ireland archbishops of Armagh and Tuam and fifteen bishops issued a protest against it.[4] Only five members of the bench abstained from signing this manifesto, Whately of Dublin, Laurence of Cashel (another Englishman), Jebb of Limerick, a man of piety and peace, and two bishops recently appointed by the whigs, Ponsonby of Derry, a *grand seigneur*,

---

[1] *Reports from the select committees on foundation schools and education in Ireland together with minutes of evidence*, p. 367, H.C. 1836 (630), xiii. 373.

[2] *Report from the select committee on the new plan of education in Ireland, evidence*, p. 41, H.C. 1837 (543), viii. 45.

[3] *National education . . . speeches delivered at the meeting in . . . Belfast, Jan. 1832* (1832).

[5] *Christian Examiner*, 1832, pp. 221-3.

and Knox of Killaloe who later became notorious as an episcopal absentee. In their statement the bishops complained that the government's proposal deprived the clergy of the establishment of their right to superintend national education, virtually transferring to the Roman catholic priesthood 'that preference and predominating influence, which has hitherto been assigned to the purity and authority of religious truth rather than to the numerical supremacy of the members of any communion in a single part of the united empire'. Also they protested against the principle of excluding as a source of common instruction the Bible and replacing it by a selection approved of by the Roman catholic hierarchy, and therefore unlikely 'to exhibit to the youthful mind a correct standard of faith and practice'. Some years later the church of Ireland's claims were placed on the highest grounds and set out with considerable power by Archer Butler, professor of moral philosophy in the University of Dublin. The church's spiritual Israel, 'with its threefold orders, its sacraments, its services' and with its bishops and clergy 'tracing an unbroken succession to the earliest pastors of the Irish church and teaching a doctrine the express image of the first faith of Rome, and Ephesus and Corinth', had an undoubted right to supervise education in Ireland. For education was not necessarily a blessing; to be so it had to be closely combined with religious instruction, and 'the instruction of children in the elements of religious truth is no brief and occasional task but a continual and laborious process'.[1]

During the thirties steps were taken by the clergy and laity of the church of Ireland to implement these principles. Diocesan educational societies were started to assist parochial schools and finally in 1839 the Church Education Society for Ireland was founded to co-ordinate their efforts. Schools assisted by this society had to be under the control of the incumbent and only employ teachers belonging to the Church of Ireland. Church of Ireland children attending these schools were to be taught the catechism and all children attending were to read daily the scriptures in the authorized version. For years the clergy and ecclesiastically-minded laity of the establishment were sharply divided over the educational issue, the majority struggling to maintain their own educational system, a minority accepting the rules of the national board or striving to obtain a compromise.

The presbyterians had always been eager for education and were a far poorer body than the establishment, but they were intellectually acute and had just experienced an era of theological ferment. Their first reaction to the government's proposals was naturally to secure the

[1] *Irish Ecclesiastical Journal*, i. 49-51.

grant on their own terms.[1] They viewed with disapproval two points in the government's plan: the extensive powers vested in the board and the restrictions on the use of the scripture at all times in the school, since in a Christian country the Bible 'unabridged and unmutilated' should form the basis of national education. Representatives of the synod of Ulster had interviews at which they expressed these views with both Stanley and Grey. Stanley could not forbear pointing out that their suggestions implied the 'novel and unheard of' idea 'that any child at any hour in the midst of any other allotted employment should be permitted to read the Bible'.[2] The government refused to modify the scheme in essentials, but pointed out that schools might be under exclusively presbyterian management, that the periods devoted to separate religious instruction could be arranged in any way which was convenient to all parties concerned, so that it could be claimed by presbyterians that presbyterian children were receiving their necessary theological grounding in 'school hours'. And it seemed as if the presbyterians would be satisfied. But the evangelicals in the Synod of Ulster were suspicious, and the form of the 'queries' issued by the board and the promulgation of a regulation making the clergy of all denominations *ex officio* 'visitors' of the schools in the locality, gave the presbyterians a reason or excuse for breaking off negotiations, and the Synod by a very small majority followed Cooke's lead, and, complaining that the scriptures were being banished from the schools out of deference to the Roman catholic hierarchy, advised their members to have nothing to do with the board. For a short period the Synod tried to maintain its own schools, and the ministers who supported the national system were subject to severe pressure. For instance at Ballymena a procession of evangelical presbyterians marched through the town to coerce the local minister, each man promising to carry his Bible and abstain from whiskey for the day.[3] But it was expensive to stand out, so by 1839 the presbyterians had become less intransigent, and on learning that the board had shown 'an anxious disposition to accommodate the Synod' they resumed negotiations. Though the board stood firmly by the dis-

[1] The presbyterian attitude is set out in the minutes of the synod of Ulster 1832-40, the board's in its reports. And see also R. Battersberry, 'The Synod of Ulster and the National Board', in *Irish Ecclesiastical Record*, lvi, 548-61, lviii. 16-28, lix. 61-73.

[2] *Eighth report of the commissioners of national education in Ireland for the year 1841*, p. 8, H.C. 1842 (398), xxiii. 246.

[3] *Report from the select committee of the house of lords on the new plan of education in Ireland . . .*, pp. 191-2, H.C. 1837 (543), viii. 196-7.

*Report from the select committee of the house of lords on the new plan of education in Ireland together with the minutes of evidence*, pp. 169-70, H.C. 1837 (543), viii. 173-4.

tinction between secular and religious instruction they made concessions on points of detail, which meant the presbyterians could in practice have schools with a presbyterian *ethos* and largely under their own control.

The catholic church in Ireland was also divided on the educational issue. Murray, the archbishop of Dublin, by sitting on the board gave a general sanction to its policy, and the majority of the bishops permitted the foundation of schools connected with the board in their dioceses. Admittedly they wanted modifications in the government's scheme, and in 1840 the catholic bishops in a memorial to the lord-lieutenant demanded that the catholic clergy should have power to appoint and dismiss teachers in schools attended solely by catholic children and to veto the appointment of teachers in 'mixed' schools. They also demanded that all books used in the religious and moral instruction of catholic children should be approved of by the four Irish archbishops, that the catholic representation on the board should be strengthened, and that the lecturers in the model schools who gave instruction to catholic teachers in religion, morals, or history, 'which is capable of being explained in an irreligious or offensive manner', should be catholics. The government refused to make any concessions and the hierarchy did not persist in pressing their demands.[1] But MacHale of Tuam, an outstanding personality and a harsh controversialist, opposed the system on the grounds that it set at naught the legitimate authority of the catholic bishops in educational matters and was an attempt to sap the religion of the people 'under the specious guise of a liberal education'. He complained that there was an overwhelming protestant majority on the board and he sneered at their method of compiling books—the way in which the board regarded their printing office as 'a theological laboratory in which all the asperities of creeds and confessions are to be rubbed away'.[2] MacHale and Murray set out their views in letters to the papers and both sections appealed to Rome. After careful consideration, Propaganda decided that each bishop should use his own discretion as to the attitude to be adopted to the national board, and Irish ecclesiastics were requested to refrain from newspaper contention on the issue.[3]

National schools, along with workhouses, town halls and police bar-

---

[1] For the bishops' memorial and the lord-lieutenant's answer see *The complete catholic directory for . . . 1841*, pp. 368-71.

[2] *The letters of the Most Rev. John MacHale . . .* (1847), pp. 392-423. For an *ex parte* account of the disputes between MacHale and the bishops who co-operated with the Board, see B. O'Reilly, *John MacHale . . . Archbishop of Tuam . . .* (1890), i. 473-76.

[3] The text of Propaganda's decision is printed in *The complete catholic directory for . . . 1842*, pp. 164-7.

racks, were monuments to the whig régime in Ireland. And taken together they represented a decade packed with systematic administrative activity. Nevertheless when the whigs left office the ultimate success of their policy—which aimed at devitalizing the repeal movement by removing Irish grievances—was still doubtful. For one thing the whigs were perhaps too confident that they knew better than any section of Irish opinion what were the best remedies. Russell later reflected their outlook when he remarked, 'the wants of Ireland are real and must be supplied, her wishes are transitory and intemperate'.[1] However, the whigs could argue that if the right remedies were applied the time would come when Ireland would no longer require any greater degree of special treatment than any other area in the United Kingdom. But, as a highly intelligent whig said at the close of the thirties, Ireland not only needed just laws but their just administration, 'such as they [the Irish catholics] have experienced from the whig government'.[2] Now the whigs could scarcely believe that a conservative government, even if well intentioned, could establish such relations with the leaders of Irish radical and nationalist opinion as would induce them to accept the union as the constitutional basis on which to work. And in August 1841 the whigs, on being forced to resign, had, to relinquish control of Irish affairs.

[1] Lord Russell, *Recollections and suggestions* (1875), p. 227.
[2] Sydney Smith, preface to collected works dated June 1839.

# 8

## PEEL AND IRELAND, 1841–46

---

Though the government formed by Sir Robert Peel in the summer
of 1841 undoubtedly deserved to be ranked amongst the four or
five most memorable administrations of the century, its Irish
policy was at first unadventurous. On taking office the cabinet was con-
fronted by a bewildering variety of complex and urgent problems. Compelled to cope with trade depression, social unrest, a disastrous war in
Afghanistan, a cluster of dangerous disputes with the United States, an
ill-organized and injurious tariff, and a frightening budgetey deficiency
of two and a half million, the ministry understandably avoided initiating
any important Irish legislation and was content to keep the Irish administrative machine functioning on routine lines. But it was unable to
ignore Ireland for long. The repeal movement caused concern and
alarm in the cabinet, at any rate during 1843, and even earlier Peel and
his home secretary, Graham, were sorely tried by squabbles among their
Irish colleagues. In selecting his Irish administration Peel had achieved
an inharmonious balance. De Grey, the lord-lieutenant, was an elderly,
self-confident peer, of moderate abilities connected by marriage with
the high tory protestant earl of Enniskillen. The chief secretary, Eliot,
was a young, zealous, over-impetuous liberal-conservative. Sugden, the
lord chancellor, was a great equity lawyer, not largely endowed with
political acumen. The chief secretary enthusiastically approved of the
principles of the national board. The lord-lieutenant began with a series
of ecclesiastical promotions confined to its opponents. He and the
attorney-general, Blackburne, without consulting anyone else, prosecuted the Belfast *Vindicator* for a libel on the administration of justice.
Shortly afterwards the chief secretary sent a subscription to the *World*,
a radical journal which had been successfully sued for libel by the Cashel
Reform Club. Eliot wanted to widen the franchise and increase the
grant to Maynooth. The lord-lieutenant promoted only protestants in

the police. Peel discouraged the former by pointing out that an inquiry into Maynooth would prove 'the arena for very bitter religious contests', while Graham warned the latter that his 'unbroken series of protestant appointments . . . will give rise to invidious comment if not to angry feelings'. And about the same time Peel forced De Grey to make Howley, 'a Roman catholic barrister of high character and moderate opinions', third sergeant.[1] So strained did feelings become that towards the end of 1842 Eliot bitterly complained to Peel that 'I am more or less responsible for every act of the government, and no man likes to be responsible for acts of which he does not altogether approve.' Peel poured oil on the troubled waters by assuring Eliot that he himself appreciated from experience the difficulties inherent in the relationship between the chief secretary and the lord-lieutenant, difficulties which, however, made the former office 'a most valuable preparatory course for higher duties'. Later Graham acidly reminded the lord-lieutenant that mutual concession was 'the real cement of a government' and suggested that he and Eliot might try and settle their differences without bothering Whitehall. Privately he speculated on the possibility of sending Eliot to Canada, and the probability of his being soon transferred to the lords by his father's death.[2] Finally Sugden in the spring of 1843 increased the government's difficulties by dismissing justices of the peace for attending repeal meetings. Wellington defended him in parliament, but Peel sharply reminded Sugden that Irish conditions made it 'a matter of grave consideration what particular thing should be done, at what time it should be done, and in what mode'.[1]

A divided administration with a liberal chief secretary dependent on a cabinet the essence of whose policy was cautious moderation, naturally failed to satisfy the long-deferred hopes of the Irish tories. From the outset the *Dublin Evening Mail* suspected Eliot, and at the end of May 1842 it pointed out that the drainage bill, the grand jury bill and the Irish law courts bill, all containing provisions adverse to the conservative party were progressing towards the statute book, while time could not be found for a registration bill, or an arms bill, 'or any other measure calculated to inspire hope'.[3] Two of these objectionable measures passed, but vigorous tory opposition defeated a medical charities bill, introduced by Eliot on the inspiration of Nicholls and Phelan

[1] C. S. Parker, *Life and letters of Sir James Graham* (1907); i. 365, *World*, 18 June 1842; *FJ* and *DEM*, 5 Sept. 1842; correspondence between Peel and Eliot, Oct. 1842 (Add. MS. 40480); Graham to Peel, 14 Oct. 1842 (Add. MS. 40435).

[2] C. S. Parker, *Sir Robert Peel* (1899), iii. 41-5, 50; *Life and letters of Sir James Graham*, i. 354-5; Peel to Graham, 31 Aug. 1843 (Add. MS. 40449).

[3] *DEM*, 30 May, 11 July 1842.

of the poor law board, which would have increased the powers of that body at the expense of the local gentry.[1] Furthermore in the debates arising over the efforts to hush up the Belfast election scandal of 1841 Peel and O'Connell acted together against several Irish tories. But the issue which created the widest breach between the government and the Irish conservatives was education. In 1841, as Hamilton, one of the political champions of the church of Ireland, put it, 'after a struggle of more than ten years, under circumstances of no ordinary difficulty, especially to our Irish clergy, a great political triumph has been achieved; in bringing about that triumph the established church in both countries and the friends of scriptural education in this country have aided not a little and the government of the country has passed into other and better hands.'[2] Realism, however, made the victorious churchmen reduce their demands to what they considered the reasonable minimum, viz. that the Irish system of national education should be placed on the English basis, by the state making a separate grant to the Church Education Society, and this policy was pressed on Peel by the Primate Beresford, supported by the lord-lieutenant.[3] The Church of Ireland's case was put persuasively by Leslie Foster, a veteran of the 1812 commission. He agreed that the attitude adopted by the majority of the bench was regrettable, but if it was maintained and the government did nothing, the poor who were members of the establishment, would in the future be the worst educated section in Ireland. And far from weakening the national board, competition, he suggested, would strengthen both systems.[4] The supporters of the board were naturally alarmed at the possibility that a conservative government would modify its predecessor's educational policy. Whately, who considered it 'monstrous' that a grant should be given to a particular denomination, made it clear that if such a step were taken he would leave the board, and Murray it was known would follow him. Anthony Blake wrote a weighty letter to Peel arguing that the national system 'afforded the only means of friendly intercourse between the government and the great mass of the people in Ireland . . . and the only means by which the rising generation of the poorer classes, protestant and catholic, can be purged of sectarian bile'. A separate grant to the establishment would tend to perpetuate the dissensions produced by the evil policy of former times, and 'unfortunately the popular feeling

---

[1] *DEM*, 4 Jan. 1843.

[2] See Report of the Church Education Society in Ireland, printed in *The Irish Ecclesiastical Journal* for April 1842.

[3] Peel to De Grey, 2 June, 13 Nov. 1842, De Grey to Peel, 11 Oct. 1842 (Add. MS. 40477).

[4] Foster to Fitzgerald, Mar. 1842 (Add. MS. 40462).

is rather in favour of disunion than union in Ireland'.[1] On much the same grounds the chief secretary supported the National Board system. He thought that if concessions were made to the Church Education Society the presbyterians would demand a separate grant and the National Board's schools would become exclusively catholic, so that there would be at 'the expense of the state a little Maynooth in every parish', and the attempt to bring up the youth of all denominations together would come to an end.[2] Eliot emphatically announced his adherence to the national board system in the first debate on the Irish education vote after the conservatives came to power, and since Jackson, the Irish solicitor-general, voiced the wishes of the Irish conservatives, there took place according to Macaulay, 'the very best parliamentary set-to between the secretary and the solicitor-general for Ireland which has ever been witnessed'.[3] Stanley privately defended his system by an argument calculated to appeal to a busy cabinet. Far less trouble would be incurred by refusing to comply with the demands of the establishment than by tampering with the existing system and thereby creating widespread dissatisfaction.[4] Finally in November 1842 the cabinet decided to preserve the existing system of national education. To abandon it would destroy the growing confidence of the catholics in the government and revive their fear of protestant ascendancy. In any case under the national system 'a larger number of catholic children have received a scriptural education subject to a direct control of a protestant government than in any other country in Europe'.[5]

The conservative opponents of the national board system did not accept this defeat as final, and the following year in the debate on the estimates several prominent Irish conservatives called on the government to help the Church Education Society, and show, in the words of Lefroy, 'an avowed determination not to subordinate religion to policy but to consecrate policy by subordinating it to true religion'. On this occasion Peel himself replied to his Irish supporters, telling them that if their proposal was adopted 'the polemical instruction in each of the schools might be improved but the practical effect would be not to conciliate rival sects but to produce new religious enmities and deepen those already existing'. In 1845 a third attempt was made to shake the government. At the beginning of the year the majority of the bench issued a

---

[1] Whately to the bishop of Meath, 28 Jan. 1842; A. Blake to Wellesley, 20 Sept. 1842; A. Blake to Peel, 3 Feb. 1842 (Add. MSS. 40582, 37313, 40501).
[2] Eliot to Peel, 14 Sept. 1842 (Add. MS. 40480).
[3] *Parl. Deb.*, 3 series, lxv. 207-19, lxviii. 687-726, lxx. 802.
[4] Memorandum prepared by Stanley (Add. MS. 40462).
[5] C. S. Parke, r*Life and letters of Sir James Graham*, i. 356-7.

statement condemning the national board's system. Though catholics, the bishops asserted, 'would prefer their children were taught the Bible, this desire is seldom so enlightened or so strong as of itself to arouse them to a contest with the authorities of their church'. In the past Irish catholics had realized that submission to ecclesiastical authority would have meant renouncing their only chance of getting a decent primary education, now as a result of the government's policy no such renunciation was involved. And in May the archbishop of Armagh transmitted to Peel an address from about forty Irish peers and M.P.s demanding assistance for the Church Education Society, which had over 1,800 schools. Peel, who had been informed by Whately that 'any grant great or small to any other society would involve the immediate resignation of Mr Blake and myself and the total extinction of the existing Board of National Education,' replied that the government was not prepared to encourage denominational divisions in primary education.[1] Days of his ministry Peel was also troubled by patronage questions in which personal and political issues were mixed. The prime minister's difficulties in gratifying his legal following were apparently lessened by the fact that immediately after the conservatives returned to power William Johnson, a justice of the common pleas, aged eighty, and Bushe, the chief justice of the queen's bench, who 'had struggled in ill-health to retain the chief justiceship until he could place it at Peel's disposal'[2] resigned. This enabled the government to place Pennefather and Lefroy on the bench, as well as appointing an attorney and solicitor-general and filling a sergeancy. These arrangements aroused indignation amongst the Dublin tories who felt that West, a popular barrister who had been returned for Dublin after a hard tussle with O'Connell, had been slighted. And Shaw, who was peeved because the lord-lieutenant did not consult him over legal appointments, remarked that neither Blackburne (the new attorney-general) nor Pennefather had ever sacrificed anything for the conservative cause, and complained that it was felt in Dublin that so far as government patronage was concerned past political service was a positive disqualification—adding as a shocking example that West had been informed by the comptroller of the household that the lord-lieutenant intended if possible to patronize tradesmen who had been neutral during the election. It may also be added that about this time Peel refused to interfere on behalf of an

[1] *DEM*, 10 Jan. 1842; Correspondence between Peel and the archbishop of Armagh, May and June 1845 (Add. MSS. 40568); J. G. Beresford to Peel, 13 May 1845 (Beresford MSS.).
[2] Shaw to Peel, 22, 31 Oct. 1841, Peel to Shaw, 29 Oct. 1841 (Add. MS. 40493); Peel to Eliot, 27 Sept. 1842 (Add. MS. 40480).

acquaintance of Shaw's with the right of the Irish executive to appoint
assistant barristers, and he advised the chief secretary to disregard
Shaw's suggestion that Blacker should be restored to the commission
of the peace.[1] Towards the end of 1842 Shaw got his own back, when the
promotion of Jackson to the bench created a vacancy in the university
constituency. The university tories put forward Hamilton, a strong supporter of the Church Education Society. The government candidate,
the new solicitor-general, had to withdraw, to the chagrin of Graham
who regarded the defeat as 'an evil omen'.[2]

Conservative indignation with the Peel administration mounted during 1843, the *Dublin Evening Mail* declaring that Eliot was governing
Ireland 'upon principles of mistaken expediency and upon a code of
cowardly conciliation'. The pernicious franchise remained unaltered, the
whig system of national education was neither abandoned nor amended,
the ruinous poor law remained unreformed. Admittedly at the beginning
of the session it was understood that the government intended to amend
the poor law act of 1838 and when a meeting of the Irish conservative
M.P.s held at the Carlton sent a deputation to the chief secretary, they
learned that the government intended to increase the number of *ex
officio* guardians and to exempt the smaller ratepayers from direct payment of their rates. Needless to say the deputation approved of the
former provision, but the latter struck them as 'unfair'. When, however,
the bill was going through the house the government dropped the
clause relating to the guardians, while retaining the section which
'turned the resident gentry into poor-law proctors'.[3] During the same
session, when the arms bill was being debated, Eliot showed himself
rather too ready to meet the wishes of the opposition. By the middle of
the year the *Evening Mail*, the organ of the ultras, could see little to
choose between the two English parties, for if one of them had transferred to popery the municipal power of the country, the other had
failed to give the loyal protestants, or those 'whom we may call the
English party in Ireland', the help they required. The *Mail* felt that the
time had perhaps come for the formation of an Irish party in parliament,
'distinct from politics and associated only upon subjects bearing upon
the welfare and prosperity of our country'. But it would be a mistake
to regard these ebullitions as the beginning of a protestant repeal move-

---

[1] That 'steady and consistent protestant politician', Colonel Blacker, had been
removed from the commission of the peace in 1833 on account of his attitude to
Orange demonstrations (*DUM*, xvii. 628–33; *Third report from the select committee
appointed to inquire into Orange lodges*, H.C. 1835 (476), pp. 237–42, xvi. 241–6).

[2] *DEM*, 29 Aug. 1842 and Graham to Peel, 13 Sept. 1842 (Add. MS. 40477).

[3] *DEM*, 17 Feb., 5 Apr., 31 July 1843.

ment. Simultaneously with its attacks on Peel, the *Mail* was denouncing O'Connell's repeal agitation, which by 1843 was in full swing, as 'a desperate humbug', hinting that the Tara meeting might prove a prelude to a religious war, and calling for firm measures, such as the removal of Eliot and the prosecution of O'Connell for sedition. And it was delighted when the government at last displayed energy and zeal by banning the Clontarf meeting.[1]

Unfortunately, from the narrow provincial standpoint of the Irish conservative, the government was not prepared to limit its Irish policy to a suppression of agitation by legal skill and military power. To Peel it seemed clear that 'mere force, however necessary the application of it, will do nothing as a permanent remedy for the social evils of Ireland. We must look beyond the present, bear in mind that the day may come —and come suddenly and unexpectedly—when this country may be involved in serious disputes or actual war with another power, and that it may be of the first importance that the foundations of a better state of things should have been laid.'[2] Peel's cabinet was peculiarly rich in Irish administrative experience, for its fourteen members included an ex-viceroy and five sometime chief secretaries. The prime minister himself, so far as official experience went, had acquired a knowledge of Irish affairs unrivalled amongst nineteenth-century British statesmen. He also possessed administrative gifts of the highest order, being able to grasp swiftly and analyse lucidly the main factors involved in any problem brought officially to his attention, and, that done, of producing a clear, considered, decisive solution—usually carefully tempered by caution. Determination, perseverance and vigilance, rather than inspiration, he held to be the qualities requisite for success,[3] and his enormous correspondence illustrates his well-organized administrative power, his unremitting industry, and the ease with which he could shift his attention from the issues of high politics to harassing trivialities. His talents had received early recognition, and his father's great wealth had insulated him from political careerism in its grosser forms. A minister at twenty-two, his outlook in many respects was that of a higher civil servant, with the imaginative powers less developed than a sense of duty and a grasp of detail, and he approached difficult issues more as an administrative technician than as a political theorist. If his political creed was flexible

[1] *DEM*, 20 Mar., 15, 17, 19 Apr., 5 May, 21 July 1843.

[2] C. S. Parker, *Sir Robert Peel*, iii. 65.

[3] Peel gave a revealing account of the qualities which he believed were needed for a successful and useful political career when addressing a Scottish academic audience (*A correct report of the speeches delivered by the Rt. Hon. Sir Robert Peel on his inauguration into the office of lord rector of the university of Glasgow* (1837)).

and evolutionary to a degree which startled and dismayed many of his simpler followers, his personal behaviour was marked by a self-conscious rectitude and a heavy sense of responsibility. Efficient, upright, conscientious and sedate, he was unpleasantly impressed from early in his career by the slackness, demagogy, violent sectarianism, jobbery and job hunting he found prevalent in Ireland. And from time to time testy irritation characterized his comments on Irish affairs.

His long political apprenticeship as chief secretary, at a time when the catholic question occupied the forefront of Irish politics, inclined him to try to deal with the general problem of Irish discontent by political rather than by economic measures. Moreover, although he was keenly interested in financial questions his economic outlook inhibited him from advocating drastic constructive intervention by the state in Irish life. Careful account-keeping, retrenchment and reform characterized his handling of the nation's finances. He trusted to individual enterprise, intelligent self-reliance, sturdy independence and hard work to improve conditions in Ireland, and time and again he referred to the dangers of using public money to stimulate economic advance. With state subventions went malversation, loss of initiative, favouritism and the discouragement of private enterprise.[1] 'Everybody in Ireland,' he complained towards the end of his long official connection with the country, 'instead of setting about improvement as people elsewhere do, pester government about boards and public aid. Why cannot people in Ireland fish without a board if fishing be, as Lord Glengall declares it to be, so profitable? I strongly suspect Lord Glengall is well acquainted with an excellent secretary for the new consolidated board.' When, a few months later, it was suggested that the government should make advances for drainage work in Ireland, he pointed out with some asperity that considering the grants already made for public works in Ireland and the exemption of Ireland from income tax it was 'a bit hard to call upon Great Britain to bear the charge or a considerable proportion of the charge of improvements which confer immediate pecuniary benefits upon Irish proprietors'. A few years back, he reminded the inexperienced chief secretary, the treasury had advanced considerable sums to Limerick for docks, and now just a week before the drainage suggestion had come up, a deputation had arrived from Limerick, asking for some more money and a remission of the debt 'on the ground that it is impossible to recover it'.[2] And a few months later he bluntly told 'a large and hungry deputation' which came to ask for a grant for a canal between the Erne and

[1] *Parl. Deb.*, 2 series, xix. 1044–5, 3 series, xv. 372, xvi. 82, xlv. 1085.
[2] Peel to Fremantle, 13 Mar., 12 June, 19 July 1845 (Add. MS. 40476).

the Shannon, that 'I would never ask for public money for local improvements in Ireland without being satisfied that the public as opposed to local and pecuniary interests would be really benefited and that the latter if the benefit were a joint one would contribute a fair share of the expense'.[1]

His ability and his bias can be seen in three striking memoranda on Irish affairs which he prepared for the cabinet in February 1844.[2] 'I view', he emphatically declared, 'our future position with respect to Ireland and the administration of affairs there with great anxiety.' It seemed, he thought, only too clear that the government might find itself impotent to punish sedition by the normal and proper procedure of trial by jury. Moreover Great Britain was handicapped in dealing with France and the United States by the existence of Irish discontent, and, in the event of war, if 'the whole catholic mind of Ireland be alienated' the position would be exceedingly critical. The remedy, it seemed to Peel, was to attempt to detach from the repeal agitation 'a considerable proportion of the respectable and influential Roman catholic population'. With O'Connell's prestige weakened by the queen's bench verdict, the time seemed opportune for decisive action. And so long as the union and the establishment were maintained, Peel had an open mind on the concessions required for the success of a conciliatory policy. He suggested three points for consideration, the franchise, education, and the endowment of the catholic clergy. Taking the first, a knotty and technical subject, he wondered whether freehold county franchise might not both be a reform and strengthen the protestant landlords. Education involved two questions, to some extent related, better education for the catholic priesthood and the provision of higher educational facilities for the catholic laity. The existing grant to Maynooth was insufficient and the state gained no credit 'for indulgence or liberality'. The standard of living and the habits engendered at the college produced every year 'fifty spiritual firebrands', sour malignant demagogues, instinctively from their low birth hostile to the law, living by agitation, and fitted to it, 'by our elementary but penurious system of education'. Stanley, who to the close of his political career was ready to dash at the most difficult political fences, was also keen to tackle the education question which he thought offered the best field for a conciliatory policy. He was not prepared to touch ministers' money or even the administrative defects in the ecclesiastical temporalities act, but he was in favour of setting up three provincial colleges, 'where young men destined for the priest-

---

[1] Peel to Fremantle, 19 July 1845 (Add. MS. 40476).
[2] Memoranda dated Feb. 1844, 11, 17 Feb. 1844 (Add. MS. 40540).

hood might receive a liberal ecclesiastical education, in connection with a general education they would share with others'.[1] Six weeks later Graham suggested the government should pay off Maynooth's debts and set up provincial colleges. In addition, Graham urged the appointment of a commission to inquire into the question of land tenure in Ireland. This inquiry, if conducted with ability and prudence, would, he believed, give the cabinet 'a distinct view of the causes of discontent in Ireland'. Though, he added pessimistically, 'I fear the remedies are beyond the reach of legislative power. Some palliatives may be applied, some abuses may be exposed on which public opinion may operate as a corrective, at all events sympathy with the sorrows of an entire people will be evinced by the government, and the public mind may be softened.' Graham also thought that 'a conciliatory policy would be completely ineffectual' unless some provision were made for the catholic clergy. He was also almost certain that protestant pressure would prevent any such provision being made.[2]

Graham's suggested commission of inquiry was appointed in November 1843, and during the session of 1844 the government produced two measures which it hoped would be taken as evincing goodwill towards Ireland, a registration bill and a reform of the law relating to charitable bequests. Stanley, who had for some time been attempting to cope with the Irish franchise question, was by 1844 in favour of increasing the number of voters by including the *bona fide* £5 freeholders in the counties, and Peel explained to Wellington that if they maintained the existing £10 franchise narrowed by the judges' decision, 'we shall have no connecting link between the great mass of the population in Ireland and the county franchise'. The duke as usual reluctantly yielded. He regarded a limited franchise as a 'security', but if an extension was necessary it could not be avoided. At the beginning of April 1844 a registration bill which included a £5 freehold franchise was introduced, and after a 'desultory' debate was given a second reading. A few days later the chief secretary learned that the Irish whigs had convinced their party leaders that the bill was unpopular in Ireland and ought to be opposed, which meant that the bill could only be carried if the government sacrificed the rest of their legislative programme. So the bill was first postponed and then dropped.[3]

The bequests bill substituted for the charitable donations board

[1] Stanley to Peel, 10 Feb., 20 Mar. 1844 (Add. MS. 40468).
[2] C. S. Parker, *Sir Robert Peel*, iii. 65–6.
[3] Peel to Wellington, 22 Mar. 1844 Wellington to Peel, 23 Mar. 1844, 25 Jan. 1845 (Add. MS. 40460); Eliot to Peel. 26 Apr. 1844 (Add. MS. 40480).

established in 1800, a body which was overwhelmingly protestant and which included amongst its *ex officio* membership a number of dignitaries belonging to the establishment, a bequests board of thirteen, of which at least five were to be catholics. The new board was empowered to sue for the recovery of charitable donations wrongly applied, and property might be vested in it in trust for the maintenance of catholic clergy or places of worship in Ireland. The bill had a favourable parliamentary reception, only seven Irish M.P.s voting against it on the second reading. But in Ireland it was vehemently attacked by two outstanding figures. MacHale denounced the bill in a series of letters, declaring that any catholic who became a member of the new board was a traitor to the sacred interests of the church, and O'Connell produced two condemnatory 'opinions' which displayed a confident mastery of the law, though admittedly the first was based on a garbled version of the text and the second was muddled. Critics of the bill made great play with several of its subordinate provisions, arguing that it would render it exceedingly difficult, if not impossible, for religious orders to hold property, and that it was outrageous to annul bequests for religious purposes made less than three months before the death of the testator, and above all that the bill enabled a group of government nominees to interfere in the internal affairs of the catholic church. This latter charge was supported by diffusing an absurdly exaggerated impression of the effects of the bill, which, according to O'Connell, would bring all catholic charities within 'the greedy grasp' of the board. In fact, when deciding who was the proper recipient of any donation, the board was to act merely in an executive capacity and was subject to the jurisdiction of the courts.[1]

The real cause of the uproarious hostility to the bill was that its opponents feared it might, as the government intended, conciliate or at least split Irish catholic opinion. According to MacHale its worst feature was 'the association of catholics with the old and inveterate enemies of our faith . . . detached from their brethren and acting against the interests of their religion, dependent on the crown, fearful of its displeasure, and fawning on its caresses, hearing the language of their new companions and adopting with the zeal of proselytes many of their perverse opinions'.[2] One tactical point was quickly grasped by both MacHale and O'Connell. If no catholic, or at least no prelate, would

[1] For an account of the objects and working of the bequests act and of the first reactions of Irish public opinion to it, see Most Rev. William Walsh, 'The board of charitable donations and bequests' (pts. ix, xi, xii of 'The law in its relation to religious interests', *Irish Ecclesiastical Record*, xvi. 875–94, 971–96).
[2] *The letters of the Most Rev. John MacHale* (1847), p. 583.

accept a seat on the new board, the act would be inoperative or at any rate morally ineffective, and the government would be rendered ridiculous. Immediately a vigorous and noisy agitation was set on foot the immediate object of which was to impress on the hierarchy the opinion of the country. Pamphlets appeared, there were letters in the papers, the *Freeman's Journal* conducted a sustained campaign against 'The subjection to the state of the catholic church in Ireland',[1] the archbishop of Tuam and twelve bishops produced a protest signed by numerous priests, and O'Connell, calling on the laity to tell the clergy what they thought of the bill, addressed a series of protest meetings in Dublin. Nevertheless when the catholic bishops met in Dublin at the beginning of November, though the majority seem to have disapproved of the Bequests bill, their customary caution and the influence of the minority made them decide to leave every prelate to act according to his conscience in respect to the bill.[2] Shortly afterwards MacHale wrote to Cardinal Fransoni, complaining bitterly of the libellous attacks which the episcopal opponents of the bill had to endure, and suggesting that a letter should be sent from Rome to the Irish bishops directing them not to accept seats on the board except with the consent of their brethren and the Holy See. If prelates went on the board, MacHale pointed out, 'their business will be to procure honours and places for their relations and others and the cares of worldly purposes will distract them from seeking the spiritual welfare of their flocks'.[3]

The government aimed at securing three catholic prelates as commissioners, and approached the archbishops of Armagh and Dublin and Bishop Kennedy of Killaloe. Crolly of Armagh at first peremptorily declined, but on being pressed again at the suggestion of Anthony Blake, who naturally had agreed to be one of the catholic lay commissioners, he admitted that the act was intended as a boon and after the meeting of the hierarchy he consented to serve. A quiet principled man, he believed Peel was striving to be fair, and he was annoyed rather than intimidated by the storm which was being raised, declaring, according to his biographer, that 'he would rather trample his mitre in the gutter and retire into a convent than surrender his liberty and prostitute the dignity of his office to a violent and unwarrantable attempt at dictation'. Murray of Dublin hesitated, accepted a seat, seemed about to withdraw, but in the event remained staunch. Kennedy at nearly the last moment with-

---

[1] *FJ*, 29 June 1844.

[2] *The complete catholic directory . . . for . . .1845*, pp. 105–6.

[3] Archbishop MacHale to Fransoni, 25 Nov. 1844 (O'Reilly, *John MacHale, his life, times and correspondence* (1890), i. 551–3).

drew, but his place was filled by Bishop Denvir of Down, who was recommended to the government by the other catholic commissioners. And in spite of the home secretary's fears that the wavering bishops might allow themselves 'to be bullied out of their engagement to the government to co-operate with it in the execution of a law favourable to their own church and country', the commission was gazetted on 18 December, and Graham complacently repeated Sheil's declaration that placing the names of the catholic archbishops before those of the privy councillors in the commission was 'gallantly done'.[1]

MacHale was not alone in invoking the assistance of Rome, for the government also cautiously tried to influence Vatican opinion on Irish problems and even to secure the approval of the Holy See for its Irish policy. It seemed after all there might be advantages in governing a community subject in spiritual matters to a foreign power, if that power could be persuaded to countenance the government's policy. Already at the close of 1843 the British government had, through Metternich, drawn the Vatican's attention to the political activities of the Irish clergy who publicly supported repeal. The result had only been a letter to the archbishop of Armagh advising the Irish clergy in very general terms to abstain from taking part in politics.[2] Now early in September 1844, Graham, who was afraid that the bequests act might be condemned at Rome as a result of MacHale's machinations, pressed Peel to take counter-measures.[3] Peel promptly directed the foreign office to place the government case before the Roman authorities, and requested the lord-lieutenant to prepare for use at Rome 'a clear memorandum, stripped of technical phrases' on the act. Since it was thought that the bill of rights and the act of settlement debarred the crown from having normal diplomatic relations with the court of Rome, Great Britain was represented at the Vatican only intermittently in a semi-official fashion. In 1844 Petre, a member of a well-known catholic family (though according to Aberdeen 'little of a catholic in reality'),[4] was an attaché at Florence. In October he was directed to proceed at once to Rome and to try to induce the authorities there to forbear pronouncing an opinion on the bequests act based on the *ex parte* statements of MacHale, and to explain that the bill was intended to remove catho-

---

[1] Graham to Peel, 6, 20 Dec. 1844 (Add. MS. 40450); Heytesbury to Graham, 29 Sept. 1844, Graham to Peel 28 Sept., 6 Oct. 1844 (Add. MS. 40450); Crolly, *Life of the Most Rev. Dr Crolly*, p. xciv.

[2] F. J. Broderick, *The Holy See and the Irish movement for the repeal of the union* (Rome 1951), pp. 163–91.

[3] Graham to Peel, 26 Sept. 1844 (Add. MS. 40450).

[4] Aberdeen to Peel, 4 Jan. 1845 (Add. MS. 43151).

lic grievances. He was armed with arguments and documents, the latter including an opinion from the Irish attorney-general and a letter drafted by Anthony Blake.[1] Aberdeen hoped that by a judicious use of the information supplied from Great Britain Petre would be able to assist the court of Rome to arrive at a correct judgment, and he advised him to emphasize that the dispute was between the heads of the church in Ireland and political agitators, and that 'if the democratic prevail over ecclesiastical authority the effects will not be confined to Ireland'.[2] Petre on arrival at Rome in the second half of October secured an interview with Cardinal Lambruschini, the secretary of state, to whom he expounded at length the advantages the catholics gained by the bill. The cardinal was courteous but highly non-committal, assuring Petre that no attempt had been made to influence the pope or himself against the act, 'we are untouched, *siamo vergini*'. He was, he added, well aware that 'the Comte di Aberdeen wished that the court of Rome should come forward in some more public manner—but we are sure that if we acted differently to how we have done we should embitter animosities and perhaps produce schisms'. During the next six weeks Petre kept pressing for an immediate decision, supplying Cardinal Acton, who as an Englishman wished to help Her Majesty's government, with documents, and even having an interview with the pope, who, he discovered, had only the vaguest conception of the technicalities involved in the bequests act, which he spoke of as 'the decree of the ministry'.[3] The only outcome of Petre's endeavours was an unsigned memorandum which he received at the end of November from the secretary of state to the effect that the Holy See could not entirely approve of the bequests act as several of its provisions did not conform to canon law, but that nevertheless it was very gratified 'by the benevolence by which Her Britannic Majesty and Her government declare themselves to be actuated'. It may be added that the Vatican's disapproval of the act seems from the memorandum to have been based on a misapprehension of its provisions,[4] and if Petre was disappointed so also was MacHale, who just about a month later was informed by his Roman correspondent Cullen that since the Irish synod had failed to arrive at a decision on the

---

[1] Heytesbury to Graham, 24 Sept. 1844, Canning to Petre, 7, 10, 22 Oct. 1844 (F.O. 43/38).

[2] Aberdeen to Petre, 28 Dec. 1844; Aberdeen to Petre (draft), 28 Dec. 1844 F.O. 43/38).

[3] Petre to Aberdeen, 21, 25 Oct., 2 Dec. 1844; Petre to Canning, 28 Oct., 1, 24 Nov. 1844 (F.O. 43/38).

[4] Petre to ————, 29 Nov. 1844, enclosing memorandum from the papal secretary of state (F.O. 43/38).

act it would be difficult to get anything done at Rome.[1] At the beginning of the new year the undaunted Petre was pressing the Roman authorities for a public expression of their approval of the prelates who had accepted seats on the board. But he himself realized by now that 'the court of Rome' would 'prefer as usual mild remonstrances with the refractory, particularly with Irish bishops, who are feared here for their unwillingness ever to submit quietly to authority'. And Lambruschini, when assuring Petre that the Holy See approved of Crolly and Murray, emphasized that it relied on 'time and moderation—*quelle potenti medicine*'. 'The cardinal', Petre explained, 'not infrequently asks me about Mr O'Connell but immediately I allude to the assistance and support he receives from the clergy he shrugs up his shoulders. ... If I mention Dr MacHale he is sure to turn the conversation to Dr Murray.'[2]

During the session of 1844 the government also had to introduce legislation to meet the needs of the Irish presbyterians, who were perturbed by two legal issues. In 1844 the house of lords by upholding decisions of the Irish courts determined that a marriage celebrated by a presbyterian minister was not valid if both parties were not presbyterians. Secondly there had been disputes between the non-subscribing and the orthodox presbyterians over the ownership of ecclesiastical property in which the decisions of the courts had borne hardly on the former. Irish presbyterians were enraged by the 'stigma' inflicted on their clergy by the decision on the marriage question and they demanded immediate redress from parliament. The non-subscribers were also aggrieved by what they regarded as the iniquitous consequences of applying legal principles of ownership to property held for religious purposes. In this instance, however, the orthodox presbyterians maintained that the decisions of the courts ought not to be upset by legislation. Cooke refused the chief secretary's invitation to meet Montgomery and the Irish law officers to discuss the matter, and a deputation from the general assembly proved obdurate to the pleadings of Peel and Graham when they urged the evils of litigation.[3]

The tension between the government and the main body of Irish presbyterians was intensified by the Scottish controversy over the relations of church and state. So strongly were feelings running in Ulster that at the end of 1842 when there was a by-election at Coleraine the conservative candidate, Sir Hervey Bruce, a local large landowner, was

---

[1] For Cullen's letters to MacHale at the end of 1844 and beginning of 1845 see B. O'Reilly, *John MacHale*, i. 553–60.

[2] Petre to Aberdeen, 14, 15, 21 Jan. 1845 (Add. MS. 43151, F.O. 43/38).

[3] *BU*, 27 Mar. 1843, Cook to Peel, 23 Jan. 1844 (Add. MS. 40539).

opposed by another conservative, Dr John Boyd, standing in the presbyterian interest. And after an exciting contest in which the church of Scotland and the marriage question loomed large, Boyd was returned.[1] In March 1843, Cooke, who in the previous year had 'endeavoured to stand between the government and public clamour' on the Scottish church question,[2] had to exert himself to prevent the assembly preparing for political action by forming a Presbyterian Defence Association. At the next assembly it was proposed that the Irish presbyterians should take steps to return M.P.s who would truly represent them. This, however, was watered down to a resolution urging Irish presbyterians to use the franchise for the benefit of their religion and liberty, after a fervent speech from Cooke, who warned the assembly that should it alienate the people from their landlords 'the peaceful fields of Antrim and Down would be converted into the blood-stained fields of Tipperary'.[3]

These ebullitions showed that Irish presbyterianism was still a political force to be reckoned with, and the government after strenuous negotiations with a deputation from the general assembly[4] passed an Irish registration act which placed presbyterian ministers in an analogous position to that of the Church of Ireland clergy in respect to marriages. The government also disposed of another issue—in a way less gratifying to the orthodox presbyterians. The dissenters' chapels bill of 1844 laid down that in the case of a religious trust when the founders' intentions were not clearly expressed, the usage of the previous twenty-five years should be taken as deciding conclusively what doctrines it should be used to maintain.

By the bequests bill the government had tried to remove one of the catholics' grievances. In the following year (1845) a more positive step was taken towards conciliating the Irish catholics. As Peel said, the annual grant to Maynooth was insufficient for the college's needs, and it was in financial straits, professors' salaries being 'below the allowances for reputable clerks' and the president being frequently compelled to save on catering by sending students home for a couple of months. In 1841 and in 1842 the bishops privately approached the government to see if the grant could be increased, but in 1844 the government took the initiative, the lord-lieutenant beginning negotiations with several moderate and influential catholics, including the inevitable Anthony Blake.[5]

---

[1] *BU*, 28 Dec. 1842, 20 Jan. 1843, 17 and 19 Feb. 1843.
[2] Cooke to Peel, 15 Jan. 1842 (Add. MS. 40506).
[3] *BU*, 4 Mar., 14 July 1843.
[4] *BU*, 5 July 1844.
[5] Copy of Memorandum of catholic prelates to Lord de Grey (Add. MS. 40564);

And at the beginning of the session of 1845 the government introduced a bill raising the annual grant from about £9,000 to £26,000 and giving £30,000 for capital expenditure.

The cast of his mind as well as the exigencies of the situation inclined Peel to try to divert the debates on the measure from a consideration of underlying principles to matter-of-fact issues. Precedent, he thought, had granted the principle of the bill, parliament could scarcely with honour withdraw the grant, and as it was plainly inadequate to the maintenance of the college, common sense demanded that it should be increased. And he concluded his first speech on the bill by expressing his conviction that 'it is perfectly compatible to hold steadfast the profession of our own faith without wavering, and at the same time to improve the education and to elevate the character of those who—do what we will—pass this measure or reject it—will continue to be the spiritual guardians and religious instructors of millions of your fellow countrymen'. But all the dexterity of an old parliamentary hand was powerless to tone down discussion in Victorian England when theological issues were involved. Within a week of this speech, Lord Ashley noted in his diary that 'the country is becoming furious, the Free Church of Scotland, the "religious public" of England, Wesleyans, dissenters, all alike are protesting and petitioning'.[1] Even in Cambridge where whiggery had always been stronger than at Oxford, Goulburn, at the beginning of the year found the idea of increasing the Maynooth grant being deprecated, 'as putting arms into the hands of the enemy. . . . The master of Trinity who has always been of very liberal opinions, indicated that his fears had been aroused by the Maynooth suggestion. The relief bill, he said, had shown how little liberal concession could allay Roman catholic hostility.'[2]

Outside academic circles the opposition to the Maynooth bill was more crudely expressed. A number of active if undistinguished ecclesiastical politicians at a meeting in Exeter Hall on 18 March set up the Central Anti-Maynooth Committee to fight the public endowment of popery by pamphlets, meetings, 'the free and intelligent use of the press', petitions to parliament, deputations of indignant constituents to M.P.s and a national day of prayer.[3] Admittedly the opponents of the scheme

---

Eliot to Peel, 18 Nov. 1842 (Add. MS. 40480); Memorandum of Sir J. Graham's marked 'confidential', dated 18 Nov. 1844 (Add. MS. 40525); and J. Healy, *Maynooth College . . .* (1895), pp. 406–10.

[1] E. Hodder, *The life and work of the seventh earl of Shaftesbury* (1886), ii. 101.
[2] Goulburn to Peel, 6 Jan. 1845 (Add. MS. 40445).
[3] *Proceedings of the Anti-Maynooth conference of 1845* (1845).

did not completely agree in their premises. There were those who were shocked at the state endowing error, and there were those who disapproved of it subsidizing any form of religious teaching. Sir Robert Inglis, the M.P. for Oxford, who was always ready 'to take part in the defence of our ancient institutions in church and state'[1] found himself in the same lobby as John Bright, the quaker radical. Inglis would not pay anyone to teach what he thought wrong—though by an ingenious argument he demonstrated that dissenters were morally bound to pay tithe. Bright was against state churches, and feared that the bill might be used as a precedent later for establishing the catholic church in Ireland. Outside parliament the Anti-Maynooth committee fought the bill on the ground that since the Roman doctrine was superstitious and idolatrous, and opposed to the best interests of society and the welfare of immortal souls, for the state to countenance it was to invite Divine punishment. But a number of the protestant dissenters on the committee met separately and produced a friendly address to the Irish catholics, telling them that the anglican establishment in Ireland was an unjustifiable offence.[2] In spite of their divergencies of outlook the opponents of the bill exercised considerable pressure on parliament, and Peel's position was also weakened by internal dissensions in the conservative party. Croker, who, in retirement, kept his fingers on the party's pulse, told Peel that the majority of the tory opponents of the Maynooth grant would have voted for it 'had it not been for the timber duties', and Peel himself said that 'the tariff—drought—forty-six shillings a quarter for wheat quicken the religious apprehension of some—disappointed ambition and the rejection of applications for office of others'.[3] At one stage at least the chief whip envisaged a serious government defeat, for it was rumoured in the clubs that the conservatives who were opposed to the Maynooth grant might abstain on Ward's motion that the grant to Maynooth be taken from the funds of the establishment, and so place the government in a minority. Blake, who came to warn the whip, was 'in quite a fright'[4] but the conservative recalcitrants, presumably aware that playing with fire might be a costly way of beating Peel, turned up in force to protect the property of the establishment. Three factors, moreover, were in the prime minister's favour, his indomitable determination once he had chosen his course, the support of the liberal wing of his own party, and the attitude of the whigs. Naturally they did not fail to rub in

[1] *Gentleman's Magazine*, new series, xliii. 640.
[2] J. Blackburn, *The three conferences held by the opponents of the Maynooth endowment bill* (1845), pp. 21–4.
[3] Croker to Peel, 25 Apr. 1845; Peel to Croker, 22 Apr. 1845 (Add. MS. 40565).
[4] J. Young to Peel, 25 Mar. 1845 (Add. MS. 40563).

how contemptuously Peel was disregarding the passions and prejudices of his own party, but they agreed with Macaulay that it was 'infinitely better that the Irish peasantry should live and die Roman catholics, than indulge their passions without any religious restraints, bear the calamities of life without the consolation of religion and die at last without religious hope'.[1] And the bill was finally carried by the consolidated centre, whigs and liberal conservatives in approximately equal numbers voting in its favour against a minority of which five-sixths were conservatives, and the remainder doctrinaire radicals. Of the thirty-seven Irish conservative M.P.s who took part on the division on the bill, ten supported and twenty-seven opposed it. In Ireland it aroused less excitement than might have been expected. Lord Clare remarked to Peel that protestant Ireland was quiet on the question, the great protest meeting in the Rotunda, though attended by two hundred protestant clergymen of various kinds, was a tame affair, and Henry Montgomery, the liberal presbyterian divine—not admittedly an unbiased witness—was probably correct when he assured Peel that while there had been some murmurings amongst 'the clergy who call themselves evangelicals, the low Orange mechanics and the labourers', the dignified members of the established church both lay and clerical, were quiescent, and that, though some of the Calvinist presbyterians had been inclined to protest against the increased grant, 'there was however a general cry of "Shame! Shame!" against the graceless pensioners'.[2] Two reasons may explain this comparative calm. The strength of Irish protestant feeling on the Roman question was such that it would be hard to intensify it, and secondly that there was something to be said—though not publicly—for giving the catholics an interest in ecclesiastical endowments.

Something having been done, it was hoped, towards winning the sympathies of the catholic clergy for the government, the next part of the government's programme was directed towards placating the laity. For some time it seemed as if adequate facilities for higher education were lacking in Ireland. Theological considerations apart, economic and geographical factors rendered the university of Dublin difficult of access to many who wanted an academic education. In the late eighteenth century the presbyterians of the north, who were largely dependent on the Scottish universities, had discussed the possibility of founding a university at Armagh, and early in the nineteenth century they had set up the Royal Belfast Academical Institution, in which was combined a

---

[1] *Parl. Deb.*, 3 series, lxxix. 652.
[2] Clare to Peel, 20 Apr. 1845; H. Montgomery to Peel, 21 Apr. 1845 (Add. MS. 40565).

theological college, an embryonic university and a high school. The people of Cork in 1829 had also tried to secure a college, sending a strong deputation to try to obtain a grant from the government, without success.[1] In 1838 a parliamentary committee on Irish education recommended a comprehensive scheme of elementary and secondary education crowned by four provincial colleges, providing teaching on a university level, financed by the state and the grand juries and controlled by a national education board. The committee cautiously avoided saying much about the place religion should occupy in their scheme, being content to work on the assumption that the National Board's principle of mixed secular and separate religious instruction could prevail throughout the whole system.[2] But considering the controversies generated by elementary education, the storms aroused by the Maynooth grant, and the hot disputes over the problem of providing academic accommodation for the English dissenters, it would have been utopian for the government to think that theological issues could be ignored when dealing with higher education in Ireland. There were two main lines of policy open to the government: it could found and endow colleges in Ireland under the control of the major dissenting denominations, presbyterians and catholic equivalents of Trinity College, or it could model its new foundations on University College, London. The government, apparently without any hesitation, adopted the second policy. Concurrent endowment of sectarian colleges was bound to arouse hostility and rivalry, it would antagonize those who suspected that independently endowed corporations tended to neglect their duties and above all it would accentuate the denominational divisions amongst the educated classes in Ireland, counteracting on a higher social level the work of the National Board. The government's bill introduced in 1845 provided for a capital grant of £100,000 and an annual one of £30,000 which it was thought would suffice for the endowment and working expenses of three colleges providing education on a university level. For three years the government were to appoint the officials and professors and the treasury was to keep a close watch over the colleges' finances. It was hoped to render the colleges acceptable to all shades of theological opinion by making no provision for religious instruction, though private persons might arrange for theological instruction to be given to those attending the colleges.

On the whole the bill had a favourable reception in the house of com-

[1] Leveson-Gower to Goulburn, 31 Dec. 1829 (Leveson-Gower letter books).
[2] *Report from the select committee on foundation schools of education in Ireland*, pp. 75 ff., H.C. 1837–8 (701), vii. pp. 419 ff.

mons, Gladstone reflecting the general attitude when he remarked that it was an imperfect measure but that the cause of its imperfection was the state of Ireland. The Irish conservative M.P.s for once were silent, being content to hold a watching brief for Trinity College. Several members felt that the powers given to the gove nment were excessive but the debate turned largely on the religious aspects of the scheme. Its naked secularity obviously rendered many members uncomfortable. Inglis denounced it for establishing 'a gigantic scheme of godless education'. A few Irish M.P.s pressed the government to accede to the demands put forward by the catholic bishops, and the official whig view was that the government had blundered badly by not having prior consultation with the heads of the catholic church in Ireland. Only a few radicals heartily commended the government's plan, which nevertheless, as not infrequently happens with a legislative *pis aller*, managed to reach the statute, book.

At the beginning of the year the landlord and tenant commissioners published their long-expected report along with three enormous volumes of evidence. Considered as a research unit their record was impressive—innumerable documents digested, eleven hundred witnesses examined at ninety points throughout Ireland—and justified their boast that the material they had collected would serve as a guide to all Irish social reformers. But as for the report, *The Times* rightly remarked that its most outstanding feature was the inadequacy of the remedies it suggested to the evils it described.[1] The commissioners were obviously intellectually overwhelmed by the magnitude of their task, and, only too aware of the complex balance of advantages and disadvantages inherent in any project, shied away from all drastic remedies. Except for the suggestion that tenants receive compensation for improvements, the commissioners' recommendations were a cautious if lengthy collection of minor palliatives. The legal disabilities of tenants for life wishing to improve their estates should be modified, 'persons of the highest professional eminence' should consider how encumbered estates might be sold in portions of moderate size rather than *en bloc*, leases for lives should be converted into perpetuities, the public works act should be amended to facilitate improving landlords obtaining loans, loan societies for farmers should be encouraged, agricultural schools might be founded, the lessors of cottages might be encouraged to keep them in suitable repair, though the commissioners could not conceal from themselves the danger of dealing by law with such a matter, the cost of the constabulary might be transferred from the county cess to the

[1] *The Times*, 24 Feb. 1845.

consolidated fund and county officialdom reorganized, an efficient emigration system might be set on foot, the consolidation of farms should
be carried out in a humane manner, and landowners should try to fix
fair rents and acquire an intimate knowledge of their tenantry. Much
might be done, the report emphasized, by patience, perseverance, and
mutual understanding. Radical opinion in Ireland naturally gave the
report a cold reception. The *Nation*, which was comparatively friendly,
said that a 'commission composed of decent landlords and zealous im-
perialists had reported modestly, plausibly and to some effect'. But of
course what Ireland wanted was the extension of Ulster tenant right
guaranteed by law to the whole country. The *Pilot* and *Freeman's Journal*
both announced they were not disappointed—they had expected nothing from the commission, and sneered at its homilies and the failure to
recognize tenant right.[1] What is rather more surprising is that the Irish
conservatives were seriously disturbed by 'extravagances' in the report
which foreshadowed a return to the feudal system. They also complained that the commission had failed to grapple with the real problems—the prevalence of agrarian crime, which by creating insecurity
checked investment, and the need to raise the moral standards of the
people, which could be done only by building schools and churches and
providing 'an enlightened, scriptural and painstaking clergy'.[2]

The government, intensely concerned with the fate of its educational
scheme, did not seem to find the report particularly inspiring. Still at
the beginning of June it attempted to implement the most striking of the
commission's recommendations by bringing forward a compensation
for improvements bill. Stanley, who introduced the bill in the lords, in a
thoroughly competent speech argued that what was needed in Ireland
was capital to bring waste land into cultivation and thus redress the
balance between population and employment, and that the easiest way
to secure the requisite capital was to encourage tenants to improve their
holdings. The government proposed that a tenant if ejected should receive compensation for building, draining, and fencing (i.e. levelling the
high unsightly bulky banks, primitive boundary marks which zigzagged
over many Irish fields). An improvement commission in Dublin with
local assistant commissioners throughout the country would decide
disputes arising over the value or the suitability of improvements.
Though the government carried the second reading of the bill, Wellington, who himself thought it impracticable to include yearly tenants within
its scope, described the debate as 'uncomfortable'. Several peers ob-

---

[1] *Nation*, 22 Feb. 1845; *Pilot*, 21 Feb. 1845; *FJ*, 19, 24 Feb. 1845.
[2] *DUM*, xxv. 471 ff. 616 ff; *DEM*, 26 Feb. 1845.

jected strongly to 'act of parliament improvement' and to civil servants intruding between landlord and tenant. A number of peers connected with Ireland sent an indignant deputation to Stanley, and Salisbury, a prominent if intellectually insignificant conservative peer, sent a remonstrance to Wellington pointing out that if the bill was passed it would soon be extended to England and Scotland. And even Devon was annoyed by the bill's departure in some matters of detail from the recommendations of his commission.[1] The bill went to a select committee of the house, and after some weeks the government announced that as it would have to be modified considerably and as it was late in the session, it would be postponed until the following year. In the autumn Devon sent Peel a list of bills which he had caused to be prepared, and which he optimistically believed embodied reforms which involved no party question. The list included bills for amending the registration law and the laws for the recovery of rent, to enable mortgagees to grant leases, to enable tenants of corporations to acquire estates in fee simple, for facilitating the sale of encumbered estates, for compensating tenants and for registering births, deaths, and marriages.[2] But before the government made up its mind to adopt this programme the forces of nature began to operate on the economic structure with startling rapidity.

It is difficult to measure the success of Peel's Irish policy, since within the next few years the famine, Peel's own fall from power, the death of O'Connell and the schism in the repeal movement were to alter drastically the Irish situation. His policy during 1844 and 1845 certainly made it easier for a catholic to be a conservative and an anglophile and so facilitated the growth of a quiet but influential body, the catholic unionists. One immediate effect of his policy however is clearly discernible, the alarm and anger generated amongst the Irish tories. The *Dublin Evening Mail* in 1845 complained that his policy was one of 'unlimited, unconditional, and complete concession'. The *Dublin University Magazine* also sneered at Sir Robert's 'coaxing system', his endeavour 'to chain the repeal mania down by such soothing syrup and sugar plums as the surrender of the established church, and the large and liberal endowment of the Romish clergy', which it compared to the efforts of wretched factory women to quiet their children by doses of opium. By the close of the year the *Mail* was talking about the government driving loyal Irishmen into rebellion, and the *University Magazine* was calling on the Irish conservatives to consolidate their strength, to form an association, to

---

[1] Wellington to Peel, 2 Jan. 25 June, 1845; Salisbury to Wellington, 20 June 1845 (Add. MS. 40461); *DEM*, 20 June 1845.

[2] Devon to Peel, 14, 17 June, 29 Nov. 1845 (Add. MSS. 40568, 40580).

act independently of all English parties, and to use the power derived from having M.P.s at Westminster to defend their own interests.[1]

Protestant exasperation was not only expressed in print. In the south, in both the city and county of Dublin, conservative voters during 1845 were apathetic over registering.[2] In the north protestant resentment was shown in a less passive form. At the end of August the Orange society was formally reconstituted, after a meeting in Fermanagh with the earl of Enniskillen in the chair, and a strong committee was set up to arrange, after securing counsel's opinion, that the new society's rules would be in conformity with the law. When the government dismissed James Watson from his deputy lieutenancy for presiding at an Orange gathering, a huge protest meeting, presided over by the marquess of Downshire and attended by about twenty J.P.s, was held; and when Archdale, a J.P., was removed from the commission for moving a resolution at a great Orange meeting in Enniskillen, he was toasted at a large protestant meeting in Belfast. Early in September a printed handbill was circulated through Cavan drawing attention to 'a Jesuitical placard' summoning a catholic gathering at Killeshandra on the anniversary of Ballinamuck and calling all loyal protestants to assemble on the same date at the same place. A serious clash was only averted by the strenuous efforts of the local magistracy backed by five companies of foot and four troops of horse.[3]

All this left Peel and Graham exasperated and baffled. If a proclamation were issued against Orange meetings, and it were set at defiance, the government would be bound to prosecute, and this of course meant relying on the willingness of juries to convict. If Lord Enniskillen, a deputy lieutenant, was dismissed for countenancing the revival of Orangeism, most of the protestant J.P.s in the north might resign. Yet if the government spared Orange magistrates after dismissing repeal ones, it would be accused of partiality. But if it treated both parties equally it would be 'compelled to uproot the unpaid magistracy throughout Ireland'. By the close of 1845 irritable pessimism was the prevalent note in Graham's comments on Ireland. Quoting Wellington's remark that 'conciliation without coercion will be ridiculous', he added, 'I fear

[1] *DEM*, 7 Feb., 6 Oct. 1845; *DUM*, xxvi, 74, 77, 731 ff, 601 ff.

[2] *DEM*, 10 Jan. 1845 and 'Proceedings of the aldermen of Skinners' Alley' (a conservative club), 17 Mar., 4 June 1845 (RIA MSS.). The chief secretary, however, felt at the end of the year that he had restored the party's spirits by giving £200 to the Dublin registration fund and securing appointments for a couple of keen conservative barristers (Fremantle to Peel, 3 Dec. 1845, Add. MS. 40476).

[3] *DEM*, 23, 27 June, 3 July, 11, 20 Aug., Sept. 1845; Printed handbill enclosed in Heytesbury to Peel, 7 Sept. 1845 (Add. MS. 40479); *Laws and ordinances of the loyal Orange institution* (1845).

that conciliation without coercion will be impossible and coercion has long been tried in Ireland with what success history will record.' The only concessions which he believed would satisfy Irish catholics were those which Great Britain was not prepared to grant and which Irish protestants would resist to the last. Peel, who was equally disappointed, felt at the end of the year that conditions in Ireland seemed 'to preclude honest and impartial government'.[1]

While Peel and Graham were gloomily surveying the tempestuous buffoonery of Irish political life, a sudden catastrophe delivered a staggering blow to the Irish social and agrarian system. The potato was the staple, almost indeed the sole food of a large section of the people and not infrequently a poor harvest had inflicted severe distress over wide areas. The crop of 1845 was not merely bad, but mysteriously blighted by an infectious disease which rapidly turned potatoes all over Ireland into a black, putrid mass. By the beginning of October, Peel, though 'impressed with the necessity of not taking for granted that Irish reports must be well founded', realized that the government should be prepared to take drastic action to deal with the impending emergency. And the bent of his thought was shown by the first remedy he suggested—the removal of the duties on foreign corn.[2] For, by a complicating coincidence, the failure of the Irish potato crop occurred just at the moment when Peel, whose thinking was conditioned by a cautious receptivity, had finally decided that agricultural protection was unsound. Consequently his major measure for meeting the Irish crisis marked a momentous turning point in British economic policy, and during the session of 1846 the Irish problem was overshadowed by vehement debates on Great Britain's future fiscal policy and the prime minister's past behaviour.

But the government did not rely solely on the repeal of the corn laws to meet the Irish crisis. Though Peel, as might be expected, was afraid that 'a prodigality of benevolence' might discourage local exertions, and demoralize the people by teaching them to look to the state for 'that which is a moral duty for themselves to perform',[3] steps were taken to provide both food and employment in Ireland. As early as the beginning of December 1845 a treasury minute authorized the purchase of £100,000 worth of Indian corn. This operation was carried out secretly, so as to raise neither the market price nor Irish expectations, and later the corn

[1] Graham to Peel, 22, 23 Aug., 2, 30 Oct. 1845, Peel to Graham, 25 Aug. 1845 (Add. MS. 40451).
[2] Peel to Goulburn, 8 Oct. 1845 (Add. MS. 40455).
[3] *Parl. Deb.*, 3 series, lxxxiv. 991.

was sold from local depots, 'at the very lowest price'. Advances were made for building harbours and piers, local relief funds for providing employment were supplemented by government grants, and grand juries were encouraged by loans to embark immediately on extensive public works. Owing to the financial factor involved, ultimate control over these schemes rested with the treasury, and Trevelyan, the assistant secretary, an ardent administrator whose decided views, terrific organizing ability and driving force are reflected in a series of purposeful minutes, supervised and directed the commissariat department's arrangements for the distribution of food and the board of works's plan for providing employment. Trevelyan was anxious that the Irish public should 'learn to depend upon themselves for developing the country instead of having recourse to the assistance of the government upon every occasion', and from the start he braced himself to make a firm stand against the tendency, which he was sure existed, to take advantage of the crisis to break down all barriers and use public money 'to secure the interested views of private individuals'. He began by laying down that landowners and ratepayers in each locality were primarily responsible for the relief of the destitute, and that the government's efforts were merely meant to supplement their endeavours. And he saw that every effort was made by the board of works to secure as much local support as possible from either charitable subscriptions or the rates for schemes providing emergency employment. Also, he held the government's food stocks in hand as long as he could and then doled them out slowly in the most distressed districts. For he hoped that the existence of these reserves would check speculative price increases, and he feared that 'if we open our stores for the general sale of meal, we shall have the whole country dependent on us, and the supplies of different kinds of food in the hands of private persons will be exported'. Nevertheless Trevelyan believed that '*coute qu'il coute* the people must not *under any circumstances*, be allowed to starve', and he and his assistants and their subordinates worked unsparingly within the limits laid down.[1] Given the absence of a large experienced staff, a remarkable piece of emergency social engineering was accomplished and by August 1846 after £850,000 had been spent on Irish relief, it looked as if the crisis had been surmounted and a note of justified complacency can easily be detected in official correspondence.

[1] For the working of the government's relief schemes see *Correspondence explanatory of the measures adopted by Her Majesty's government for the relief of distress arising from the failure of the potato crop in Ireland*, H.C. 1846 (735), xxxvii. For Trevelyan's approach see particularly, pp. 25, 27, 39, 81, 84, 101, 107, 124-5, 291-3. This selection of letters, minutes and documents forms a brilliant anthology illustrating benevolent bureaucratic action.

# 9

# O'CONNELL AND YOUNG IRELAND,
## 1841–46

At last, twelve years after winning catholic emancipation, O'Connell began a sustained, well-organized effort to secure repeal. The new agitation was planned on his usual pattern. There was the Loyal National Repeal association with three types of member, volunteers paying £10 annually, members who paid or collected £1 and associates paying a shilling a year. There was the repeal rent, the produce of these subscriptions, 'the most useful practical embodiment of the national enthusiasm',[1] the amount of which was reported weekly as a mathematical index of the movement's growth. And there was the general committee of the association, 'the popular privy council',[2] in which business was thrashed out in advance. Members of O'Connell's staff were selected to tour the country, encouraging the local branches whose officers were the repeal wardens, 'men of industrious habits and good character', nominated either by the parochial clergy or at a parish meeting, and appointed by the association. They were expected to arrange for petitions to parliament, watch the registries, help to keep the peace and collect subscriptions. As time went on there were founded in many areas repeal reading-rooms, subsidized by the association, which were both working-men's clubs and propaganda centres. A public meeting of the association was held every week in Dublin, at first in the Corn Exchange and later in a specially constructed hall, at which new members if present were welcomed, subscriptions acknowledged, reports and correspondence read, and an immense volume of oratory delivered on the principles and progress of the movement, together with long-distance rejoinders to the parliamentary speeches of the previous week.

[1] O'Neill Daunt at the association (*Nation*, 12 Nov. 1842).
[2] G. Duffy's phrase in *Thomas Davis* (1890), p. 64.

The most striking feature of the new agitation was the number of intelligent young professional men, who, convinced of the supreme value of national independence, joined the association. In October three of them, Duffy an experienced catholic journalist, Dillon a barrister, and Davis a protestant barrister and pamphleteer of ardent temperament, 'a patriot philosopher' who believed that Ireland's moral and intellectual energies had been enfeebled by the union,[1] founded a weekly newspaper, the *Nation*, which, like the celebrated *Examiner*, combined news, literary criticism, poetry and leaders on social and political questions. Carefully produced, with an attractive layout, a clear-cut style and definite convictions, the *Nation* quickly attained a large circulation and attracted a talented array of contributors many of whom expressed themselves in verse, employing the imitation ballad, popularized by Scott and Macaulay, with its swinging metres and simple values.[2] Irish history was ransacked for episodes which could be romanticized, and contemporary politics were expounded in martial songs with a lavish use of military metaphor. If much of the verse now seems artificial and hollow it nevertheless caught the mood of many Irishmen, who, dissatisfied with the ordinary round of party politics, hankered after some dramatic form of political activity and ardently hoped for a crisis which would transform Irish public life.

The nationalism of the *Nation* was derived directly from Grattan and O'Connell, but it was more intellectual, comprehensive and explicit. And it contained latent elements which were not included in their outlook. A shrewd critic put his finger on these, when, on being asked what was the 'tone' of the *Nation*, he replied 'Wolfe Tone'.[3] Grattan's nationalism was largely an expression of the *esprit de corps* of the Anglo-Irish, O'Connell's was to a great extent compounded of his religion and his experience of life. But the nationalism of Davis and his circle was a typical product of the early nineteenth century. Living in an age of unresting, systematized activity, they saw nationalism as a great constructive force, and in reaction from the business-like, bourgeois sobriety of their day they romanticized the past and looked forward expectantly to an heroic future. Dressed in chimney-pot hats and toiling in committee rooms they saw themselves as the successors of Rienzi in the forum and the Swiss foresters charging at Morgarten.[4] The drabness of nineteenth-century life was accentuated in Dublin by a consciousness of departed

[1] *Nation*, 27 Sept. 1845.
[2] For identifications of the authors of many of the articles in the *Nation*, see K. M. MacGrath, 'Writers in the "Nation"', in *IHS*, vi. 189–223.
[3] T. W. Moody, *Thomas Davis, 1814–45* (1945), p. 36.
[4] G. Duffy, *Thomas Davis*, p. 110.

greatness which prevented many young and ardent Irishmen accepting with resignation the place of provincials. Towards the close of the eighteenth century Ireland had been exhilarated by gaining independence, and Dublin had seen the flowering of a proud, privileged civilization based on the protestant landed interest, which had left easily perceptible monuments in the massive public buildings, the private palaces and upright squares of the capital. By the forties the eighteenth century was already evoking admiration as an age of famous men, vigour, generous enthusiasm, and achievement. Even the violence and eccentricities of the period provided material for anecdotage and contributed to the traditional picture of the Irish eighteenth century as a time of high spirits and good taste. To young men starting their careers in Dublin the contrast between this brilliant, creative, classical world and the dowdy, pretentious, and in places slightly seedy society of a provincial capital was bound to be disheartening and exasperating, and they bitterly regretted the 'absenteeism of the Irish mind', the emigration of the wit, wisdom and power of the land which had followed the union, and resented 'absorption into that cold and pulseless imperial heart of our genial nationality which ought to have made Irish art and Irish literature the glory of modern civilization—the degrading feeling of provincial inferiority which makes us turn our worshipping eyes to London as a Mussulman turns to Mecca'. Not only did the *Nation* deplore the workings of 'the demon of centralization,' but Davis was infuriated by the philosophy of efficiency which underlay it. 'Utilitarianism,' he wrote, 'the creed of Russell and Peel, as well as of the radicals—this thing, call it Yankeeism or Englishism which measures prosperity by exchangeable value, measures duty by gain, and limits desire to clothes, food and respectability, and which, having come into Ireland under the whigs, had become "the very Apostles' creed" of the professions and [threatened] to corrupt the lower classes who are faithful and romantic.' Thus though Davis and many of his political associates were in agreement with the radicals they were not prepared to subscribe to the 'Benthamy' which despised nationality as a vulgar superstition and considered a general European trades union followed by a universal republic as the final aspiration of 'all enlightened men'.[1] To the writers in the *Nation* 'nationality' (defined as 'the application of all the forces of a country to improve its physical comfort, enlarge its powers and ennoble its soul') meant to a nation 'what prudence and great desires mean to an individual' and could only be secured by 'self-respect, self-rule and self-

---

[1] *Nation*, 17 June 1843, 28 June, 15 Nov. 1845, 23 May 1846; G. Duffy, *Thomas Davis*, p. 83.

reliance'. That Ireland had the 'notes' of a nation was taken as axiomatic, and that a nation required political independence for its healthy development seemed clear—as the *Nation* put it, 'the English parliament cannot feel for us the ceaseless sympathy that Irishmen could'.[1] Were Ireland independent a resident parliament would see that the resources of the country were developed to their fullest extent, the absentees would spend their money at home, Irish industry would be fostered by wise and moderate tariffs, and Irishmen would see 'an Irish navy sweep the seas, an Irish flag float from our ships, an Irish commerce penetrate both hemispheres, and Irish art rise like an awakened angel, Irish diplomacy strengthen us with the free nations of the old and new world, liberal tenures and growing manufactures create an Irish middle class, and a native militia guard our shores'. Ireland would be a land of political and religious freedom, 'a moral, faithful and religious land', with democratic principles steadily progressing not to the detriment of the aristocracy but to the advantage of the people.[2] Davis and his followers displayed unwearying pertinacity in discovering new activities which could be pulled into the campaign for national independence, and a surprising variety of subjects was discussed and evaluated in the *Nation* from one aspect—their value to the Irish cause. Agricultural improvement, archaeology, art, history, industrial development, literature, music and temperance, were all to be studied and encouraged for the sake of Ireland. The nationalism of the *Nation* was comprehensive in another respect. It was not based on a limited section of the community or a narrow tradition. Both cultures, the powerful and predominant Anglo-Irish, and the rich and indigenous, if declining, Gaelic, were to be appreciated and nourished.[3] Irish nationalism was to 'contain and represent the races of Ireland'. It was not to be Celtic nor Saxon, but Irish. And the *Nation* in 1845 was delighted to see the races of Ireland 'about to become harmonious and related with intimacy sufficient for combined and single-ended action without any race losing its special propensities and special powers'.[4] Conciliation was to be one of the watchwords of their movement and Davis disposed of religious dissension which had played so prominent a part in Irish politics by declaring that religion was an affair between each man and his God, perfect

---

[1] *Nation*, 23 Aug. 1845.

[2] *Nation*, 11 Feb. 1843, 4 July 1846.

[3] There began about 1830 an active and productive era in Gaelic scholarship. And during the thirties and forties a group of great antiquarians and editors were devoting themselves to early Irish history and drawing attention to the wealth of available material.

[4] T. Davis, *Essays*, p. 222; *Nation*, 12 July 1845.

religious equality and liberty being every man's right. Religious questions should not be introduced into public affairs since Ireland's sole hope lay in the union of all denominations in the national cause.[1] As shall be seen these formulas, while expressing Davis' ideals, did not suffice to solve the problems presented to the association by educational reform in 1845. Finally the teaching of the *Nation* was marked by a strong note of moral earnestness. Self-government was spoken of not only as a way of improving material conditions but as a means of ennobling the soul. 'Nationhood', the *Nation* declared, 'is a great trust as well as a great blessing, and in a new state demands a race of men not alone religious, gallant, enduring and laborious, but full of knowledge and fertile in resource.' They must continually try by teaching and example to lift their neighbours, 'to that pitch of industry, courage, information and wisdom necessary to enable an enslaved, dark and starving people to become rich, free and rational'.[2]

At the outset the contributors to the *Nation* were sincere and ardent adherents of O'Connell whom they regarded as the patriarchal leader of the national cause. But early differences of opinion, and, what was at least equally serious, differences of tone, began to emerge.[3] To begin with there were journalistic rows between the *Nation* and the *Pilot*, the semi-official repeal organ conducted in a slap-dash fashion by O'Connell's old crony, Barrett. The *Pilot*, which could scarcely have welcomed the birth of a vigorous rival, hinted that Duffy's apology in a libel action had let down the liberal press, and later attacked the *Nation* for its business arrangements with the *Monitor*.[4] O'Connell, who for years had been surrounded by admiring and submissive adherents, had grown unused to criticism from the ranks. But his new followers, young, quick-witted, hard-working and independent, openly differed from him on several issues. O'Connell thoroughly disapproved of the poor law; the *Nation* argued that though it required amendment it was necessary.[5] O'Connell abused on the score of their politics Mahony, Maginn and the *Dublin University Magazine*, while the *Nation* commended all of them for their literary ability.[6] O'Connell, a fervent anti-slavery man, frequently denounced slavery in America; the *Nation* implied that considering the value of American sympathy to Ireland it would be better

---

[1] *Nation*, 15 Feb. 1845.
[2] *Nation*, 11 Nov. 1843, 4 May, 26 Oct. 1844.
[3] See R. Clarke, 'The relations between O'Connell and the Young Irelanders' in *IHS*, iii. 18–30.
[4] *Pilot*, 21 Nov. 1842, 30 Jan. 1843.
[5] *Nation*, 31 Dec. 1842.
[6] *Nation*, 25 Feb. 1843, 12 Oct., 7 Dec. 1844.

to be quiet about the matter.[1] And if O'Connell sneered in public at the poor rhymed dullness of the *Nation* ballads, Davis in private referred to the miserable style of O'Connell's work on Irish history.[2] Finally there were two fundamental issues on which one can perceive from an early date a difference of emphasis which might easily develop into a clash of principles. At the first glance it might appear that O'Connell and the writers on the *Nation* shared a common standpoint when considering the place of religion in Irish politics. Both proclaimed the need for union amongst Irishmen of all creeds, both dwelt on what Ireland owed to the catholic faith. But while in O'Connell's mind catholicism and nationalism were inextricably blended, the contributors to the *Nation* were quick to depreciate sectarianism and called on men of every religion to work together in building up the Irish nation. Again, though the *Nation* repeatedly endorsed O'Connell's doctrine that only moral force should be employed in the repeal struggle, it continuously printed ringing verse glorifying the soldierly virtues and enlivened its comments on the political situation by analogies drawn from military science. Moreover there were differences in age, background, experience, standards and temperament between O'Connell and 'Young Ireland', as the group round the *Nation* came to be called. He was impulsive, rather haphazard, genially overbearing, and ready, after forty years in politics, to adapt his course to circumstances. They were earnest, hard-working, high principled and doctrinaire. Soon in the councils of the association there were sharp clashes. O'Connell was shocked at the 'wild impracticality' of some of their projects, and must have been annoyed by their readiness to run things; they were irritated by his undiscriminating affection for his family and henchmen, and his reluctance either to 'prearrange or allow others to prearrange a *decided* policy'.[3] It would, however, give a false impression of the repeal movement in the early forties to dwell on the differences between O'Connell and the new generation of his supporters. It was not until the close of 1844 that a serious open conflict of opinion occurred, and it is only by diligently searching the files of the *Nation* that one can discover traces of the tendencies which led to the great split in the association in the summer of 1846. Between 1841 and 1844 all sections in the repeal movement co-operated heartily in a vigorous effort to attain repeal and the other objectives of the agitation.

The programme adumbrated by O'Connell was a full and attractive

[1] *Nation*, 9 Aug. 1845.
[2] *Nation*, 24 June 1843; G. Duffy, *Davis*, p. 107.
[3] G. Duffy, *Davis*, p. 109; G. Duffy, *Young Ireland*, pp. 308, 314; J. O'Connell, *Recollections* (1849), i. 222.

one. Not only was he striving to obtain repeal but he hoped it would be accomplished or followed by the return of the absentees, the abolition of the poor-rate, the diversion of tithe rent charge to the support of the poor, the abolition of county cess, the transference of the cost of upkeep of roads and bridges to the central exchequer, household suffrage, the ballot, a further instalment of municipal reform, fixity of tenure, elective justices of the peace, a satisfactory financial settlement with Great Britain which would mean the disappearance of the Irish national debt, and a drastic scaling down of indirect taxation with a reduction of the tax on tobacco.[1]

Two points in this programme, repeal and agrarian reform, require some further attention. Generally it seems to have been taken for granted that repeal meant a return to the constitutional position secured in 1782, but during the early forties the Irish federalists, a small but vocal and respectable group, influenced by the example of the United States and recent Canadian developments, advocated as the best solution of the Anglo-Irish problem, a local parliament for Ireland's domestic needs and a central assembly in which both Ireland and Great Britain would be represented to deal with common concerns.[2] O'Connell usually implied that his goal was the restoration of Grattan's parliament (though in the early thirties he seemed to have played with a scheme on federal lines) but he avoided inconvenient detail when discussing the post-repeal constitutional position, and emphasized that the repeal association was open to all, including federalists, who sought the repeal of the act of union. In the autumn of 1843 a pertinacious Birmingham radical, Sturge, who was sympathetic to the repeal movement demanded a precise definition of the association's constitutional aims. O'Connell replied that being convinced that England and Ireland if separated would lack 'that cordial strength they must possess by continuing united', he believed that while the Irish parliament should alone legislate on all Irish matters the crown should form the link between the two islands, with the royal prerogative in respect to the forces, the colonies, treaties, peace and war remaining undiminished. Sturge, unsatisfied, returned to the attack, pointing out that the royal prerogative in fact was only exercised on the advice of responsible ministers, and he wanted to know to which parliament the ministers were to be responsible. O'Connell promptly replied that 'for Irish administrative functions the Irish parlia-

[1] O'Connell's programme can be found in the speeches he delivered at the mass meetings held between April and October 1843.

[2] For federalist schemes see T. Fitzpatrick, *Outline of a plan for an Irish parliament* (1844); J. G. Porter, *Some calm observations upon Irish affairs* (1844), and letters of Sharman Crawford in *FJ*, Nov. 1844.

ment would have control within Ireland, and that for all other administrative functions the British parliament would have control'. In short the control of the royal prerogative in imperial matters was to be vested in the British parliament. After all, he emphasized, the Irish parliament would have power to exercise a salutary check by refusing supplies. Sharman Crawford, always a swift critic of O'Connell, complained that these proposals admitted Ireland's inferiority by denying her a voice in imperial matters, and would inevitably lead to a collision between the English and Irish administrations.[1] The *Nation* on the other hand, while ostensibly criticizing Crawford's federalism, explicitly repudiated O'Connell's desire to preserve the British connection. Ireland should have nothing to do with an empire which cumbered the earth and whose ruin would be a blessing to humanity.[2] And a year or so later Barry, one of the most eloquent of the Young Irelanders, in his pamphlet on repeal argued that the existence of the common crown should only mean a personal union, analogous to that between Great Britain and Hanover, Ireland having her own fleet, army, diplomatic service and foreign policy.[3]

During the thirties it began quite suddenly to be suggested that the Irish agrarian system should be modified in the tenant's favour by legislation. In 1835 Sharman Crawford for the first time introduced a bill providing that on the termination of his lease a tenant should receive compensation for improvements he had made.[4] The *Citizen*, an advanced liberal journal, in many respects a precursor of the *Nation*, enunciated that a great change was needed in the law of landlord and tenant in Ireland, drew attention to the Norwegian and Swiss agrarian systems, and suggested that when an estate worth more than £10,000 per annum was sold the tenants should be given an opportunity to purchase their farms at a reasonable figure.[5] In widely separated corners of Ireland two obscure men simultaneously advocated drastic remedies. In Newry John Jackson printed a small tract in which he violently attacked the pernicious influence of the landed aristocracy, bloated by sinecures, and owing to their monopoly of the soil and the operation of the corn laws, 'revelling in all the pleasures of the senses at the expense of the agricultural, the commercial and the mechanical interests'. Jackson advocated

---

[1] *Nation*, 27 Oct., Nov. and 9 Dec. 1843.

[2] *Nation*, 9 Dec. 1843.

[3] M. J. Barry, *Ireland, as she was, as she is and as she shall be* in *Repeal prize essays: essays on the repeal of the union* (1845), pp. 77–86.

[4] *Parl. Deb.*, 3 series, xxix. 218.

[5] *Citizen*, i. 75, ii. 443–7; *Dublin monthly magazine* (a continuation of the *Citizen*, 1842, pp. 218–37. The article in the *Dublin monthly magazine* was by Thomas Davis.

that the tenant should be granted compensation for improvements and a perpetual property in the soil at a fixed rent. This, he prophesied, would 'fertilize our lands, reclaim our wastes, and treble the agricultural produce of the island—it would civilize and refine the people, destroy intemperance and add to our strength as a nation by keeping at home the flower of our youth'.[1] Somewhat similar views were propounded by William Connor of Mountmellick who urged that 'the evil of the non-increase of land', should be counteracted by a sworn jury in each parish valuing farms and fixing fair rents, the payment of which should give perpetuity of possession. Connor not only wrote pamphlets but expounded his scheme at public meetings, with the result that in 1842 he was prosecuted for seditious libel. After conducting his own defence in an irregular and highly excitable fashion, he was sentenced to six months' imprisonment.[2]

Early in 1843 O'Connell, arguing that 'the landlord's right was a mere creation of the law which society might alter as it saw fit', suggested that the repeal association should take Connor under its patronage and assist him in securing petitions for fixity of tenure. But a little later, having compared Connor's scheme with Sharman Crawford's, O'Connell definitely pronounced in favour of the latter, on the grounds that Connor's scheme would only shift the monopoly in land from the landlords to their tenants.[3] It was not, however, until a year and a half later that the association produced an agrarian programme. Then, in the early part of 1845, stimulated by the labours of the Devon commission, the parliamentary committee of the association published three reports on the land question. The third of these, which seems to have been largely the work of O'Connell himself and William Smith O'Brien, made a series of thirty-five recommendations as a basis for remedial legislation. The committee was greatly struck by the way in which the development of Ulster had been influenced by tenant right, 'but impressed by the difficulties which surround any attempt to interfere between landlord and tenant', it was unable to agree on a scheme for enforcing the custom throughout the whole country. There were, however, four important points in its programme. A heavy income tax—it was to be at least two shillings in the pound—was to be imposed on absentees. Tenants were to receive compensation for improvements; a series of modifications of the law of ejectment were suggested, which would both improve the

---

[1] T. Jackson, *Ireland vindicated from tyrannical oppression.* . . . (1840).

[2] William Connor, *The prosecuted speech delivered at Mountmellick.* . . . (1842); *A letter to the Rt. Hon. the earl of Devon . . . on the rack-rent system in Ireland.* . . . (1843); *FJ*, 16 and 17 Mar. 1842.

[3] *Nation*, 11 Feb., 15 Apr. 1843.

tenant's position and induce landlords to grant twenty-one-year leases, and some modest proposals were advanced for promoting the creation of a peasant proprietary. It was suggested that estates sold under the authority of a court and crown estates should be disposed of in small lots, the occupier being given a right of pre-emption, and that poor families should be settled on reclaimed waste lands, under a scheme which would enable them eventually to become freeholders.[1]

However agrarian reform and constitutional forms were bound to be academic questions until repeal was won, and the problem which faced O'Connell and the repeal movement from 1841 was how this was to be achieved. For a time the question could be shelved. During 1841 and 1842 O'Connell was busy spreading his organization, beating up recruits, producing propaganda and arranging for a steady revenue to finance the fight. But by the beginning of 1843 the repeal association was functioning admirably (if a trifle monotonously), and O'Connell's followers were ready for the next move. On one point O'Connell was adamant. He emphatically insisted nearly every week that he would use only legal means in the struggle and that under no circumstances would he risk bloodshed. He was certain that 'the electric power of the entire national will' was bound to prevail; 'the man knew nothing of history who said the reasonable request of three million people could be refused.'[2] But though he continually eulogized with confident vehemence the ethical and practical superiority of moral force, he never bothered to analyse deliberately the methods by which politicians were influenced by public opinion. Catholic emancipation and the reform victory in 1832 proved, it could be argued, little, since in each case not only was there a substantial section of the whole community behind the measure, but there was a distinct possibility that moral pressure might be supplemented by physical force. In 1843, however, British opinion was almost solidly opposed to repeal, and important sections of Irish opinion, the landed interest, the industrialists of the north, the established church, were hostile. O'Connell must have realized this, and at the first glance it is hard to see how he expected to gain his objective. Admittedly he may have played with the idea of passive resistance—he once pointed out that the people could refuse to cut the harvest and abstain from the consumption of excisable articles[3]—but as often happens his policy was

---

[1] *Nation*, 17 May 1845; *Reports of the parliamentary committee of the Loyal National Repeal Association of Ireland*, ii. 295-9, 317-27; and Printed preliminary resolutions submitted for the consideration of the parliamentary committee (Gavan Duffy papers).

[2] *Nation*, 6, 20 May 1843.

[3] *Nation*, 9 Sept. 1843.

fundamentally Micawberish. The forties were a disturbed period in Great Britain and difficulties with France and America suggested that at any moment a situation might arise when it would be vitally necessary for the British government to conciliate the most powerful and best organized party in Ireland. After all it was Yorktown which had set the stage for Grattan's victory in 1782. This implied that winning repeal might be a prolonged progress of indefinite duration. Nevertheless, carried away by the impetus of agitation and oratorical exuberance, O'Connell proclaimed 1843 to be repeal year,[1] and a new manifestation of the movement, the 'monster meetings', seemed to his enthusiastic followers to justify his boast. Early in the spring of 1843 there began a series of these meetings which were held at suitable points over the three southern provinces and on the borders of Ulster. The Irish country people were gregarious and ready to travel, the meetings, with attendances counted in tens of thousands, were not only impressive demonstrations of the strength of the cause, but great social gatherings. If the gentry were poorly represented the catholic clergy were present in force, and O'Connell with unflagging vigour and optimism always delivered a rousing address at both the open-air meeting and the banquet which usually followed it. Throughout the spring and summer excitement mounted. 'The great national question', the *Pilot* declared in May, 'travels at railroad speed.' And in August it reported that repeal was virtually won.

As the situation grew more tense, some of the young men gathered round the *Nation*, affected by the fiery enthusiasm of the day, felt that 'a time was at hand when this country would negotiate best with arms in hand'.[2] And even O'Connell and the *Pilot* began to explain in bellicose terms how they would react to an attempt by the government to interfere with their legitimate rights, though they were careful to make it quite clear that they would not strike the first blow. As for the Irish administration, having at first treated the repeal movement with contempt, by the summer of 1843 it was seriously alarmed. De Grey, the lord-lieutenant, who was elderly and excitable, complained that the repeal wardens and the enormous meetings might paralyse the ordinary machinery of civil life, and he asked for extraordinary powers.[3] But Peel refused to be stampeded into strong measures which might prove ineffectual. At the beginning of May he reminded the viceroy that if the ordinary legal forms were to be observed 'we are dependent on the willingness of juries to convict'. Five weeks later the cabinet met to

---

[1] *Nation*, 27 May 1843.  [2] G. Duffy in *Nation*, 18 July 1846.
[3] De Grey to Peel, 6 May 1843 (Add. MS. 40478).

decide before the recess whether emergency legislation should be proposed for Ireland. Peel himself had little faith in coercion. He saw immense technical difficulties in suppressing a widespread movement, however great were the powers vested in the lord-lieutenant. It would be hard to distinguish, he argued, between religious and political meetings held on a Sunday, and it would be difficult to deal with municipal corporations if they became centres of repeal agitation. Above all, a coercion bill would be opposed by the whigs, radicals, chartists, the anti-corn law league, and all 'who were in favour of democracy or mischief and confusion'. And in Ireland the cry of anti-coercion could be substituted for repeal. For these reasons Peel and the cabinet decided to trust that 'the sense of danger, not to the maintenance of the union, but to the security of property, to the regular payment of rent, to the freedom of opinion and action will alienate men of moderate opinions or men actuated by self-interest from the cause of repeal and democracy'.[1] Discretion was obviously the best policy for the government and as the autumn drew on without any perceptible weakening in the union, O'Connell was in danger of looking ridiculous. Admittedly he had an alternative to the monster meetings to tide him through a month or so, the assembling of a council of three hundred influential men who would deliberate on the best means of carrying out the repeal programme. Even this would have been an unimpressive climax to his campaign, but at this point the government rescued him, by proclaiming the meeting which was to be held at Clontarf on 8 October, which it was thought could be proved to be an illegal assembly. O'Connell at once deferred to the proclamation and called off the meeting, and though some of his younger followers such as Davis were 'painfully discomposed by the retreat',[2] they did not suggest an alternative course of action. Defiance of the authorities would scarcely have produced on the spur of the moment a successful rebellion and might have caused an uglier Peterloo. A week later the contest was transferred to a sphere in which O'Connell was completely at home, for the government charged him and seven other leading repealers with taking part in a seditious conspiracy. The ensuing legal proceedings straggled over a year; the trial in the king's bench lasted nearly four weeks and with its sharp technical wrangles, periods of factitious cross-examination, 'incidents' and bursts of glowing oratory, aroused intense interest, and like so many of O'Connell's activities provided nearly all the glory and excitement of civil war with none of the guilt and less than 25 per cent of the danger. The crown's case was weak. It rested almost

[1] Peel to De Grey, 8 May, 12 June 1843 (Add. MS. 40478).
[2] G. Duffy, *Davis*, p. 185.

entirely on the speeches and writings of the accused, and these, though they offered interesting material to anyone interested in political semantics in their fusion of constitutional agitation and martial terminology, failed to provide an adequate basis for a charge of sedition. Moreover the conduct of the trial was not calculated to raise the reputation of Irish courts as tribunals for deciding political issues. To the intense annoyance of the British government the jury panel, through negligence or worse, was defective, and the possibility of a catholic being picked was so reduced when the crown had struck off repealers, that, to the chief secretary's regret, the jury was composed solely of protestants.[1] Then the Irish attorney-general made, in Peel's words, 'a sad exhibition of himself',[2] by challenging in open court one of the counsel for the defence at a time when feeling against duelling was running high in England. And finally the chief justice during the proceedings referred to the counsel for the defence as 'the gentlemen on the other side'. And though Peel accepted his explanation that the remark merely contrasted two sides of the court house, he was not prepared to offer it to the house of commons.[3] The verdict of guilty carried little weight and it is not surprising that the house of lords quashed the sentence and O'Connell and his associates, after eight weeks' imprisonment in comfortable conditions, were released.

Though O'Connell finally won on legal points, for the first time in his life he had been jailed, and the temporary defeat and long-drawn-out tension of the proceedings were a trying experience for a man of nearly seventy. On being released he contented himself with recuperating and criticizing the government's moves. Having been saved by the prosecution from being involved in an anti-climax, he wisely refrained from setting on foot another series of large-scale demonstrations. The *Nation* also realized that winning repeal would necessitate a long-sustained effort. From early in 1844 it began to preach the need for organization and above all for education. 'The carnival of agitation was over; now they were in the year of work.' The repeal reading-rooms were to replace the mass meetings, the association was to become the schoolmaster of the Irish people. Repealers were to study all aspects of Irish life, literature, history and statistics. And it was boldly asserted that if Ireland was dotted over with centres of intellectual co-operation it would be impossible to refuse any concessions demanded by the Irish people.[4]

---

[1] C. S. Parker, *Life and letters of Sir James Graham*, i. 402–3.
[2] Peel to De Grey, 2 Feb. 1844 (Add. MS. 40478).
[3] Correspondence between Peel and Pennefather, Feb. 1844 (Add. MS. 40540).
[4] *Nation*, 13 April, 17 Aug. 1844, 8 Feb. 1845.

Writing to Smith O'Brien, a county M.P. who had recently become a repealer, Davis, early in 1844, pronounced that popular education was the only moral force in which he had any faith. 'Mere agitation', he added, 'is either bullying or a preparation for war. I condemn the former, others of the party condemn the latter. But I suppose we all agree on the policy of education.'[1]

But disappointment and the discouraging prospect of a long struggle before success could be attained, was bound to effect the cohesion of the repeal party which had been maintained for the previous two years largely by the seeming momentum of the advance, and during the next year or so tempers were to be badly racked by disputes over policy.

The first of these arose in the autumn of 1844 over the attitude to be adopted towards the federalists who remained an uncertain element in Irish politics. Since they had neither an organization nor an organ of opinion it was difficult to gauge their strength, but several outstanding figures, Crawford, O'Hagan, Caulfield (Lord Charlemont's brother), and Grey Porter, an ex-high sheriff of Fermanagh who joined the repeal association in April 1845 and resigned the following month, were avowed federalists, and it was assumed that federalism as a compromise would probably attract many of the leading Irish whigs. The association, as has been said, was open to federalists, and in June 1843 the *Nation* avowed its willingness to co-operate with them as a step to independence.[2] Davis went even further, his attitude being more typical of a student of politics than of a hard-bitten party man, for he thought that federalism, though it could not provide a final settlement, deserved a fair trial, and he was willing to encourage it as a means whereby moderates, to whom 'mere repeal' was 'raw and popular', could be gradually won over to the nationalist cause.[3] And in the autumn of 1844 when the repeal cause was sagging he went north to discuss matters with the local federalists. Simultaneously O'Connell, isolated at Darrynane, had decided that 'a strong federal display made by and with men hitherto non-repealers would induce the ministry to strike and canvass the terms on which the Irish legislature should be re-established'.[4] Before leaving Dublin he had seen signs of a 'powerful and influential rally for federalism'.[5] At the beginning of October he issued a diffuse manifesto in which he declared

[1] Davis to W. S. O'Brien, 22 Mar. 1844 (G. Duffy, *Young Ireland*, p. 673 and O'Brien papers).

[2] *Nation*, 3 June 1843.

[3] G. Duffy, *Davis*, p. 111, and Davis to W. S. O'Brien, 18 Oct. 1844 (O'Brien papers and G. Duffy, *Davis*, p. 262).

[4] W. J. Fitzpatrick, *Correspondence of Daniel O'Connell*, ii. 332.

[5] O'Connell to W. S. O'Brien, 1 Oct. 1844 (O'Brien papers).

his preference for federalism—that is to say 'a congressional parliament for imperial affairs in addition to local parliaments in Great Britain and Ireland'—over simple repeal.[1] And he hoped that once the federalists came forward, a conference could be held between them and the repealers, the latter refusing to entertain any compromise which would 'render precarious the right of Ireland to legislative self-protection'.[2] Considering the timid or limited nature of the federalists' schemes, it is doubtful whether a joint policy could have been hammered out. Still, given the hard fact that the repeal cause after three years of agitation had made no headway, a new departure, offered by an alliance with the federalists, was advisable, at least for the preservation of O'Connell's reputation as a political strategist.

But the quick, slapdash, imperative mode in which he broached his new policy produced unfortunate repercussions. The Young Ireland group were incensed by O'Connell's precipitancy and intellectual imprecision. And the *Nation* publicly and emphatically dissented from his manifesto, arguing that federalism would perpetuate Ireland's 'moral and intellectual subjection to England', and firmly asserting that the repeal association was not entitled to abrogate its constitution.[3] It was very unusual for O'Connell's autocratic handling of his organization to be challenged publicly, and a vigorous debate began in the press on the merits of federalism and simple repeal. O'Connell waited impatiently for a response to his gesture, and even tried through Pierce Mahony to stimulate the Dublin federalists into issuing a declaration. But according to a severe critic, 'not one influential federalist would go into the same room' as Mahony,[4] and all O'Connell received was a draft scheme, the production apparently of a group of Dublin liberals, which envisaged increased Irish representation in the imperial parliament which would continue to control foreign, commercial, ecclesiastical and general financial policy, and a local assembly for Ireland responsible for 'local taxation, the relief of the poor, and the development of the natural resources of the country'.[5] And a federalist meeting at Belfast at the end of October, which O'Connell looked forward to expectantly, failed to make a public pronouncement.[6] So four weeks after his first

[1] *Nation*, 12 Oct. 1844.

[2] O'Connell to W. S. O'Brien, 1 Oct. 1844 (O'Brien papers).

[3] G. Duffy in *Nation*, 19 Oct. 1844. Also G. Duffy, *Young Ireland*, bk. iii, chapter iii and *Davis*, chapter vii; T. Davis to W. S. O'Brien, 18 Oct., 3 Nov. 1844 (O'Brien papers), partly quoted in *Davis*, p. 262, *Young Ireland*, p. 616.

[4] T. Davis to W. S. O'Brien, 3 Nov. 1844 (O'Brien papers).

[5] Paper printed in W. J. Fitzpatrick, *Correspondence of Daniel O'Connell*, ii. 329–30. See also G. Duffy, *Young Ireland*, pp. 608–9.

[6] O'Connell to W. S. O'Brien, 21 Oct. 1844 (O'Brien papers). The meeting

manifesto O'Connell issued a second statement in which having rebuked the federalists for not producing a plan, and the anti-federalists for attacking what they had not yet seen, he emphasized that he himself would not consent to receive less for Ireland than she had before. The *Nation* seized on this indefinite statement as satisfactory and closed the crisis with a leader entitled 'Cordiality and conciliation'[1] but O'Connell was left resenting the way in which in his opinion he had been opposed by half his friends and deserted by the rest.[2]

The bequests bill increased the strain within the repeal party. While O'Connell led the fight against it, the *Nation* was silent, and Davis, who was irritated by O'Connell's autocratic efforts to settle the wording of the section of the second general report of the parliamentary committee of the association,[3] complained to O'Brien that O'Connell with his attack on Bellew, and Dr Cantwell with his fourteenth-century threat of excommunication to anyone in his diocese who acted under the bequests act, were doing horrible injury to the cause.[4] About the same time it began to be alleged that the influence of the *Nation* tended both to undermine O'Connell and weaken the authority of the priesthood. It was also said that indifference in religious matters was one of the characteristics of the Young Irelanders, a party of 'great ambitions and small morality'.[5] The *Pilot* not only warned the people against 'utilitarian' educational schemes, but emphasized that repeal was essentially a catholic movement. 'O'Connell, the clergy and the people of Ireland' were one and indivisible. If language was a mark of the distinction between Milesian and Saxon, 'still better defined, more positive and unmistakable is the distinction created by religion'. The catholic church was the only organization which could 'preserve the confederacy of the Irish mind', and peaceably win concessions from Great Britain. Protestants, of course, it was added, could join the repeal movement. But there was no reason why protestant converts to repeal should be treated like demigods.[6]

Davis was naturally bitterly disturbed by the attacks on the *Nation*

which was attended by S. Crawford and H. Caulfeild, was held at the Royal Hotel, Belfast. It was said that a declaration was sent to the Dublin federalists, but no public statement was issued (*NW*, 5 Nov. 1844).

[1] *Nation*, 9 Nov. 1844.
[2] O'N. Daunt, *A life spent for Ireland*, p. 43.
[3] J. O'Connell to W. S. O'Brien, 6, 10 Nov. 1844; T. Davis to W. S. O'Brien, 13 Nov. 1844 (O'Brien papers).
[4] T. Davis to W. S. O'Brien, *nd* (O'Brien papers).
[5] *Waterford Chronicle* quoted *Pilot*, 8 Nov. 1844, and *Belfast Vindicator* quoted in *Pilot*, 1, 20 Nov. 1844.
[6] *Pilot*, 29 Nov., 9 Dec. 1844, 5, 19 May 1845.

which he regarded as 'part of a system for stopping the growth of secular education and free discussion'. 'I would prefer', he wrote to O'Brien, 'a military to a theocratic government.'[1] And he urged O'Brien to request O'Connell to put a stop to the newspaper attacks on the *Nation* and its supporters.[2] O'Connell, whose skin had been toughened by years of political battling and who privately thought Davis dangerously erastian,[3] replied confidentially to O'Brien minimizing the significance of the whole business. Newspapers, he pointed out, would take up any topic for the sake of circulation, and he was anxious that the association should steer clear of their squabbles.[4] O'Connell also wrote Davis a long, shrewd, bantering letter, which was scarcely likely to have a soothing effect, pointing out that he had no influence over the press and that in any case catholics were entitled to state their views.[5] Though Davis failed to check the hostile press campaign he scored one small success. John O'Connell had prepared a repeal dictionary, containing, in Davis's opinion, highly objectionable matter, including a short article on 'ignorance' in which it was asserted that 'no people are really ignorant who understand and practise as the Irish do their religious, moral and social duties', and that the Christian faith of the Irish people was endangered by 'the theories we now hear broached about "a general system of popular education"'. Davis successfully insisted that the work should be prefaced by a statement that though it was printed by the association, O'Connell was solely responsible for its contents.[6]

Early in 1845 while accusations and insinuations of bigotry and theological laxity were breeding bickering and distrust, Peel's scheme for extending higher education brought to the forefront an issue bound to inflame already irritated feelings. In February both Dillon Browne, the bankrupt M.P. for Mayo, and the *Pilot* pronounced in favour of separate university education on denominational lines, though the latter added a demand for the opening of Trinity College, that is to say the admission of all denominations on an equal footing.[7] O'Connell himself

[1] T. Davis to W. S. O'Brien, 3 Nov. 1844 (O'Brien papers), partly quoted, G. Duffy *Young Ireland*, p. 615.

[2] T. Davis to W. S. O'Brien, 27 Oct., 3 Nov. 1844 (O'Brien papers), partly quoted, G. Duffy, *Young Ireland*, pp. 614–5.

[3] John O'Connell wrote that his father said 'Davis is quite led away by his fondness for church and state connection and state control' (J. O'Connell to W. S. O'Brien, 10 Nov. 1844, O'Brien papers).

[4] O'Connell to W. S. O'Brien, 9 Nov. 1844 (O'Brien papers).

[5] O'Connell to T. Davis, 30 Oct. 1844 (G. Duffy, *Davis*, pp. 274–6).

[6] J. O'Connell, *A repeal dictionary*, Pt. I (1845), p. 110; T. Davis to J. O'Connell, 2 Jan. 1845 (Gavan Duffy papers) and T. Davis to W. S. O'Brien, *n.d.* (O'Brien papers).

[7] *Nation*, 15 Feb. 1845; *Pilot*, 19, 24 Feb. 1845.

publicly announced that he would be bound by the opinion of the hierarchy, and privately wrote to the archbishop of Tuam requesting the bishops not to attack Peel's plan until its details were published—lest precipitancy should weaken the effect of their condemnation.[1] In the following month the *Nation* revealed its attitude in a long and courteous review of a pamphlet which argued that catholics and protestants should receive academic education separately.[2] The review pointed out that though the author dwelt at length on the danger of religious laxity he omitted to notice the danger of religious acerbity. 'Shall the British minister', it asked, 'be petitioned to immortalize our weakness by fostering our disunion?'[3] Later the *Nation* stated clearly its opinion of Peel's bill. The scheme was based on two principles, mixed education and government nomination of the collegiate staffs. The *Nation* was as resolute for the first as it was against the second.[4] And at a meeting of the association Davis declared himself emphatically in favour of 'combining the education of youth in order to secure the union of men'— particularly in a country such as Ireland where dissensions were rife. The *Pilot* on the other hand dismissed the government's education scheme as a fraud with a tendency to breed religious indifference, and O'Connell and his son John, both of whom favoured higher education in separate establishments for each denomination, condemned the government's scheme as savouring of the anti-catholic, not to say anti-Christian spirit which inspired the educational policies of the French and Prussian governments.[5] Two conflicting conceptions of education faced one another, but after a vehement and at times painful and personal debate in the association a formula which permitted apparent agreement amongst repealers was found. The catholic bishops met in May and suggested the amendments to the government's plan which they considered necessary for the protection of the faith and morals of catholics. A fair proportion of the professors and other officers in the new colleges were to be catholics whose moral conduct should be certified by their prelates. There should be catholic professors of history, logic, philosophy, geology and anatomy, and catholic chaplains to look after catholic students. Both the opponents and supporters of mixed education expressed their approval of this statement, each interpreting it as being fundamentally in agreement with their own standpoint.[6] The

---

[1] *Nation*, 15 Feb. 1845; O'Connell to Archbishop MacHale, 19 Feb. 1845 (W. J. Fitzpatrick, *Correspondence of Daniel O'Connell*, ii. 350–1).
[2] *Thoughts on academical education.* By A catholic priest (1845).
[3] *Nation*, 29 Mar. 1845.       [4] *Nation*, 29 Mar., 17 May 1845.
[5] *Nation*, 17, 31 May, 14 June 1845; *Pilot*, 19 May 1845.
[6] *Nation*, 31 May 1845.

*Nation* optimistically declared that an outspoken discussion within the association was a healthy sign, and would undoubtedly lead to a better understanding and warmer co-operation in the future. But the issue remained alive and irritating. The *Nation* welcomed the bill in its final form and while admitting there were strong reasons for having separate professors of history and philosophy added that it would be inconvenient.[1] On the other hand the O'Connells continued violently to attack the colleges bill, considering that it would poison the springs of knowledge from which the youth of Ireland were to be supplied and turn them out into the world foetid monsters, conscienceless, creedless, without religious feelings and ready to sell themselves to whomsoever was in power.[2]

Davis, on his part, though he had endeavoured at first to avoid an open clash on the colleges question, strongly condemned 'the mad bigotry' with which the measure was opposed, and he even at one point spoke of quitting the country. He felt that O'Connell surrounded by a 'lying, ignorant, lazy clan' who wanted 'the uncensured handling of public money in their gluey claws' was trying to drive the supporters of mixed education into secession from the association. And he was amazed at the 'evil influence such little creatures can exercise over so great a mind.[3] A month or so before he died he remarked that 'between unaccounted-for funds, bigotry, billingsgate, Tom Steele missions, crude and contradictory dogmas, and unrelieved stupidity any cause and any system could be ruined'. Nevertheless he saw on the credit side 'a sincere and humorous people, a rising literature, an increasing staff of young, honest, trained men'.[4]

Towards the end of 1845 there began to loom up the danger of a schism in the repeal movement over a question which would put its principles to an immediate practical test. So long as the conservatives were in office O'Connell's course was easily plotted, and he could devote himself whole-heartedly to repeal. But if the whigs were to come in, his position would become more delicate, since, after all, a whig administration could grant immediate if limited concessions. Admittedly from the summer of 1841 the whigs and O'Connell had drifted steadily apart, and the former, while naturally making party capital out of their successors' trouble with the repeal revival, emphatically asserted their determination

---

[1] Ibid., 28 June 1845.    [2] Ibid., 7, 28 June, 12 July, 30 Aug., 13 Sept. 1845.
[3] T. Davis to W. S. O'Brien, several undated letters (O'Brien papers); G. Duffy, *Davis*, pp. 302, 304-5.
[4] T. Davis to W. S. O'Brien, 26 July 1845 (O'Brien papers), printed G. Duffy, *Davis*, p. 311.

to uphold the union. Furthermore the whigs' efforts to hammer out a positive Irish policy were not very impressive. To Irish economic problems their approach was unadventurous. Howick admittedly advocated a national system of industrial education and the employment of the able-bodied poor on public works until sufficient private capital was available. But Russell, though he thought that the law governing the relationship of landlord and tenant should be amended, was unable to specify the modifications required. Nassau Senior, one of the party's economic experts, modestly deferred making any suggestions on the matter until he could see the Devon report. Macaulay, referring to fixity of tenure, uncharacteristically declared, 'I would rather be a learner than a teacher', and Palmerston, an improving Irish landlord, bluntly stated that for parliament to interfere between landlord and tenant would be 'to establish the principle of confiscation—to interfere with the rights of property, the foundation of all human society'. And he trusted to the pressure of public opinion to prevent Irish landowners abusing their rights.[1] The main plank in the whigs' Irish programme was the necessity for fair play and impartiality such as had been shown during Melbourne's administration. And this, they argued after 1841, demanded drastic steps to level the inequalities which existed between the establishment and the catholic church in Ireland. An increase in the grant to Maynooth, the abolition of tithe, disestablishment, partial disendowment, proportioning the revenue of the establishment to the needs of its adherents, disestablishment and concurrent endowment were all mentioned.[2] The last received the most concentrated attention. In the early thirties Grey, Holland and Littleton, had all referred to the desirability of the state making payments to the Irish catholic clergy. Later, at the close of 1837, Mulgrave had momentarily favoured the idea. But after consulting Archbishop Murray, the leading 'moderate' amongst the catholic bishops, he had advised his colleagues to refrain from immediate action.[3] Now, during the early forties, Nassau Senior and Charles Buller both advocated in the *Edinburgh* state payment of the catholic clergy. Such a measure, it was urged, would both provide for the spiritual wants of the majority of the population, relieve the

---

[1] *Parl. Deb.*, 3 series, lxx. 1837 ff., 1001 ff., 798 ff., 1064 ff., 281 ff.; *Edinburgh Review*, lxxix, 249.

[2] *Parl. Deb.*, 3 series, lxx, 60–3, 886–9, 807–9; *Edinburgh Review*, lxxiv. 474–97, lxxlx. 189–266. For the evolution of the articles in the *Edinburgh* see M. Napier, *Selection from the correspondence of McV. Napier*, pp. 370, 448–57.

[3] Grey to Wellesley, 20 Nov. 1833; Holland to Wellesley, 1 Dec. 1833; Littleton to Melbourne, 18 Nov. 1833 (Add. MS. 37306); Mulgrave to Russell, 11, 23, 27 Dec. 1837 (Russell papers).

peasant of a heavy burden, and rescue the clergy from a dangerous dependence on their flocks. Ellice, the whig whip, was an enthusiastic supporter of this policy, and explained to Russell that the funds required could be secured partly from the establishment and partly through a land tax. But he begged Russell not to mention the last point to Lansdowne and Bessborough, for the very idea of taxing Irish landlords even on the most equitable grounds, would 'blow up the party'. Curiously enough Lansdowne was also a fervent advocate of a provision for the catholic clergy, though he felt that the scheme should be financed from the imperial exchequer. As for Bessborough he was afraid the conservatives would take up the idea and give O'Connell another subject to dilate on, for 'nothing would give so great a spruce to his agitation as a religious question'. Palmerston's feelings were divided. He looked upon the catholic religion as a bad political institution, 'unfavourable to morals, industry, and liberty', but he was anxious to improve the condition of the catholic clergy. Macaulay was thoroughly pessimistic and in a resounding letter pointed out that any proposal to pay the catholic clergy would be opposed by 'all the zealots of the high church and all the zealots of the low church, Oxford and Exeter Hall, all the champions of the voluntary system, all the English dissenters, all Scotland, all Ireland both Orange and papist'. Admittedly all the statesmen, whig and tory would be in favour, 'but no combination of statesmen is a match for a combination of fools'.[1] Even the advocates of the scheme agreed that it would only be accepted in Ireland if put forward by a government which had the confidence of the leaders of Irish catholic opinion—an additional argument for restoring the whigs to power.

Such a temperate, not to say timid, approach to Irish problems was unlikely to form a basis for co-operation with O'Connell, and during the sensational summer of 1843 the whig leaders turned down a request of their Irish followers for a great demonstration of the party's sympathy with Ireland. Nineteen Irish M.P.s persuaded Lord John Russell to convene a party meeting at the Reform Club, to consider organizing English public opinion behind a demand for a just and conciliatory Irish policy. Palmerston, Wood, and Bernal argued vigorously against such a step, since the government was moving rapidly towards a 'break up' and the matter was shelved.[2] The Irish liberal M.P.s had to fall back

[1] Ellice to Russell, 31 Mar. 1845, Bessborough to Russell, 10 Dec. 1845 (Russell papers); Palmerston to Russell, 22 Oct. 1843 (*Russell Correspondence*, ii. 67) and Macaulay to McV. Napier, 25 Nov. 1843 (*Selections from the correspondence of McV. Napier*, pp. 449–50).

[2] *DEP*, 25 July 1843; Russell to Lansdowne, 19 July 1843 (*Russell Correspondence* ii, 64–5).

on the less impressive course of issuing a manifesto, drafted apparently by Smith O'Brien, who in a few months' time was to declare himself a repealer, demanding a series of concessions, such as disestablishment and a larger representation in parliament, which would give Ireland perfect equality with England, 'the only secure and legitimate foundation upon which the union can permanently rest'.[1] And during the period Peel was in power the Irish liberals who were not repealers played an inconspicuous part, in spite of the efforts of Wyse to build up an active Irish parliamentary opposition.[2]

Towards the close of the year Palmerston, who could not forgive O'Connell his 'wicked endeavours to get up hatred of race between the Irish and the Saxon as he calls us', warned Russell that Melbourne was very much against acting in any way with O'Connell. In any case, Palmerston stressed that Russell and himself were precluded by their statements on the union from becoming O'Connell's 'bottle-holders'.[3] And in the autumn of 1844 Russell warned the duke of Leinster as head of the Irish whigs to have nothing to do with federation since the party was committed to the defence of the union 'as a fundamental part of our political system'.[4] O'Connell, for his part, even in the rather subdued mood which followed his release, loudly proclaimed his unhalting devotion to repeal and his contempt for the whigs. He derided Russell's appeal for justice for Ireland, declared he would have no compromise, no half measures, no palliatives, and during the summer emphasized that at the next general election they would only support repeal candidates whose principles were guaranteed by their membership of the association.[5] Nevertheless as early as January 1844 he had written to Charles Buller, an active young whig politician, listing the measures—religious equality (each denomination paying its own clergy), municipal reform, extension of the suffrage, the ballot, absentee tax, a restoration of the law of landlord and tenant to its condition at the union, and consideration at least of fixity of tenure—which he thought 'would mitigate the present ardent desire for repeal'. On reading this letter Clarendon, one of the most sagacious of the whigs, pronounced that were they back in office they could soon bring O'Connell to terms, and 'by doing what was strictly just quash the cry for repeal'.[6] In December 1845, when Peel

---

[1] NW, 8 Aug. 1843. See correspondence for August 1843 in O'Brien papers.
[2] T. Wyse to W. S. O'Brien, 24 Nov. 1843 and Jan.–May 1844 (O'Brien papers).
[3] Palmerston to Russell, 22 Oct., 22 Dec. 1843 (Russell papers).
[4] Russell to Leinster, Sept. 1844 (Russell papers).
[5] Nation, 25 Jan., 7 June, 16 Aug., 13 Sept. 1845.
[6] O'Connell to Buller, 9 Jan. 1844 (Russell papers); Clarendon to Russell, 25 Jan. 1844 (Russell Correspondence, i. 69).

resigned, O'Connell showed how his mind was working. As soon as the news reached Dublin he told the repeal association that he would support Russell in his battle to give cheap food to the people, and he informed Pigot, a leading Irish whig, that he was going to call on the repeal members to attend at Westminster in support of 'the anti-corn law ministry'. Admittedly he also declared at the association that 'repeal and no compromise would be the toast at each convivial meeting of repealers', but Pigot was inclined to think that the whigs would soon see 'those who have hitherto seceded from parliament . . . once more voting cordially with us upon imperial ground'.[1] O'Connell had scarcely shown his hand when dissensions amongst the whig leaders forced Peel to resume office, and during the early months of 1846, backed by a heterogeneous and precarious majority, he swept away the restrictions on corn. O'Connell naturally found himself in the same lobby as the whigs. What was more, at the beginning of the parliamentary campaign he turned up at a meeting at Russell's house, and at the beginning of June at a meeting of members opposed to the government's coercion bill, also held at Russell's house, O'Connell expressed his gratitude to Lord John for having decided to oppose the bill.[2]

At the end of June when Russell replaced Peel, O'Connell began bombarding Pigot with notes concerning 'details which will conduce much to the popularity of the new government'.[3] He suggested names for legal appointments, pressed for the reappointment of J.P.s dismissed as repealers, demanded that something should be done about 'the infidel colleges', put forward a scheme for the reorganization of the Registry of Deeds which would incidentally lead to the promotion of his son Morgan, successfully urged the government to drop their arms bill, and pointed out the importance of selecting catholics as tradesmen to the lord-lieutenant. When Bessborough arrived as viceroy O'Connell called and had a confidential conversation in which he asked the government not to raise the Irish church question and to tackle the university question, transferring the new colleges to catholic control.[4] Thus O'Connell's behaviour implied a resumption of the relations between himself and the government which had existed from 1835 to 1841, and as usual when he altered his course he had to push his organization into the new groove. This in the past had been an easy operation, amounting almost

[1] *Nation*, 20 Dec. 1845, Pigot to Russell, 15 Dec. 1845 (*Russell Correspondence*, i. 92–3).

[2] *Nation*, 14 Feb., 13 June 1846.

[3] O'Connell to Pigot, 8, 12 July, 4, 13, 14, 15 Aug. 1846 (W. J. Fitzpatrick, *Correspondence of Daniel O'Connell*, ii. 377–84).

[4] Bessborough to Russell, 11 Sept. 1846 (Russell papers).

to a mere formality. But now, in the association he had founded, there was a determined group, representing, they believed, 'the young intelligence of Ireland'[1] who were determined to prevent it taking any steps which could be construed as foreshadowing a whig alliance. They were a high-minded and eloquent band, but their oratorical powers, developed in the rather enervating atmosphere of unanimous and appreciative audiences, were greater than their political acumen. And if they were not out-argued they were certainly out-fought by O'Connell's staunch supporters in Conciliation Hall. As early as December 1845 the *Nation* defined precisely the attitude for the repeal movement to adopt in the event of Peel's resignation. The new government should be supported only if it was 'a whig ministry with a national democratic basis' which would hand the administration of Ireland over to repealers.[2] Some months later, in May 1846, the existence of divergent tendencies in the association was clearly revealed by the bickerings over Smith O'Brien, who had been imprisoned by the house of commons for refusing to serve on a committee. Though the association passed a vote of confidence in him, it carefully avoided commenting on the correctness of his attitude. And this restraint irritated both the *Nation* and the fiery Meagher, a brilliant young rhetorician who suddenly came to the front early in 1846. Shortly afterwards Meagher began to trounce the whigs. In the past, he argued, they had really done very little for Ireland, though a whig government might be 'a relief committee for Irish political mendicants' who described themselves as 'moderate catholics' and 'enlightened protestants'. Nevertheless, he warned the association 'the whigs were the most effective enemies the disseminators of the national sentiment were destined to encounter', for as their policy worked on 'the less exalted passions of society', servitude entered the country's very soul.[3] The *Nation* too, warned nationalists that once the whigs returned to power they would play the old game of trying to catch repealers with sprats. 'We demand', declared the *Nation*, 13 June 1846, 'nationality, not Noodle or Doodle.' On the other hand while Steele, O'Connell's faithful squire, complained that all these warnings were unnecessary, Fitzpatrick, another of O'Connell's supporters, dwelt on the benefits the whigs in the past had conferred on Ireland, and John Reilly argued that to say down with the whigs was tantamount to saying up with the tories, adding, 'that if I can't vote for a repealer I shall vote for a whig'.[4]

Naturally tempers became exacerbated by imputation of easily im-

---

[1] A phrase of Smith O'Brien's (see *Memorandum of General T. F. Meagher. . .* ed. by M. Cavanagh, pp. 47–8).     [2] *Nation*, 20 Dec. 1845.
[3] Ibid., 21 Mar., 20 June 1846.     [4] *Nation*, 13, 20, 27 June 1846.

agined ugly motives. The Young Irelanders who had the advantage of being political puritans, could hint that gratitude to the whigs was mixed with a lively sense of favours to come. Their critics retorted by denouncing them as a small, noisy clique intent on belittling O'Connell. The *Nation*, though it lavished tributes on O'Connell, pointed out in what must have been a highly irritating tone of objectivity that Irish politics had been marked by progressive change. At one time there had been little more in the repeal movement than O'Connell and the multitude, and at times the agitation had been 'too low, too timid, occasionally too sectarian, and on the whole much too lawyer-like'. Now a new generation with a fresh outlook was coming to the fore.[1] The *Nation's* doctrine of development could be illustrated by a contrast of attitudes on several issues. When O'Connell praised Peel's government for its efforts to cope with the famine, the *Nation* a few days later referred contemptuously to the inadequacy of its legislative and administrative measures.[2] While O'Connell continued to advocate 'a coercion law against landlords' to compel them to grant compensation for improvements, the *Nation* declared that a revolution in the Irish agricultural system, slow or rapid, peaceful or bloody, was at hand. Only the landlords benefited from existing conditions which seemed designed to augment and perpetuate the degeneration of the people. And the *Nation* pouring scorn on the 'contented lumper eater', the exploited peasant whose submissiveness tempted 'the needy, greedy, jobbing gentry', argued that every effort should be made to convert the tenant into a proprietor, perhaps by the foundation of a company to purchase Irish estates and sell them in small lots to tenants.[3] Finally, as might be expected, the vehemence with which the *Nation* group approached social and political problems prevented them from being enthusiastic adherents of O'Connell's continuously enunciated doctrine of moral force. 'Its singular fitness', the *Nation* suggested, 'for the era in which it sprang up, almost implies a particular not a general truth'. To treat it as a political absolute would be 'a profanation of the holy struggles which oppressed nations even in our day have made for liberty'. Later the *Nation* summed up the issue by explaining that its contributors differed from O'Connell regarding the relative value of national liberty and individual life; 'we think scarcely any amount of the latter equivalent to the former, Mr O'Connell thinks each priceless.'[4]

[1] Ibid., 30 May, 20 June 1846.　　　　[2] *Nation*, 18 Apr. 1846.
[3] The D.L. whose scheme, published in *The Times* 11 Apr. 1846, was commended by the *Nation* seems to have been David Leahy (*Post Office, London Directory 1846*).
[4] *Nation*, 11 Apr., 27 June 1846.

It was with this subdued but swelling chorus of criticism in the back-ground that O'Connell had to explain to the association his attitude towards the Russell administration. His explanations were prolix and flamboyant rather than illuminating. He emphatically asserted to 'take away some claptraps from juvenile orators', that while he lived 'the repeal cause will never be abandoned, postponed or compromised—to support a party or a faction'. He had nailed his colours to the mast. But after repeating all the reasons he had so often reiterated why repeal should be granted and listing the grievances, agrarian, educational and administrative, the new prime minister would have to redress, if 'he bids for the people of Ireland', O'Connell dropped a pregnant comment on the situation; 'there is now a pause—there is a period arrived propitious to all who desire good government for every part of the empire.'[1]

From his manifestos it was plain that the prospect of a partnership with the whigs, involving a temporary easing off of the repeal agitation but producing immediate benefits, was making a strong appeal to the shrewd pragmatism which was such an important element in O'Connell's character. It would be hard to define a policy which rested on an implicit understanding, but a test of what O'Connell's new course meant was immediately provided when Sheil, his old ally and rival, who had distinguished himself in the debates preceding Peel's fall by the fervour of his whiggery, offered himself for re-election at Dungarvan on appointment to office. The committee of the association considered starting a repeal candidate against him, but O'Connell, by producing strong if rather unconvincing technical reasons for doing nothing on this occasion, secured Sheil's unopposed return.[2] Then with unflagging vigour and dexterous if blatant tactical ability, he set to work to drive his critics out of the association. Selecting the point, possibly at issue, on which he was least vulnerable, he produced, first in the committee,[3] and then in the association a series of resolutions pledging the association to the principle that peaceable, legal, and constitutional means alone should be used to promote political amelioration. Mitchel protested that the question was an academic one, raised to distract attention from O'Connell's dealings with the whigs. 'Nobody', he said, 'is the least afraid of physical force but there are some of us mortally afraid of whiggery. . . . It is their [the whigs'] principle that the country may be governed under the present system, it is our aim to prevent their governing the country at all.' The Young Irelanders might have tried to foil O'Connell by accepting his resolutions—on the ground that leaving abstract principle and hy-

[1] Ibid., 27 June, 4 July 1846.    [2] *Nation*, 18 July 1846.
[3] M. Crean to W. S. O'Brien, 9 July 1845 (O'Brien papers).

pothetical cases aside, they agreed that moral force was the only method to be used in the existing Irish situation. But they were not in a submissive or conciliatory mood, and O'Brien refused to subscribe to the doctrine that in no circumstances was a country justified in resorting to force for its amelioration, attacked the whig alliance, and accompanied by several leading members of the *Nation* group, withdrew from the association.[1]

Immediately the committee, by implementing with summary vigour the principle that anyone who had in any way indicated his disapproval of the moral force resolutions *ipso facto* ceased to be a member of the association, expelled a number of sympathizers with the seceders. Steps were taken to damage the circulation of the *Nation*, statements were secured and published from catholic bishops condemning 'the schoolboy philosophy' and 'jacobin impiety' of the Young Irelanders, and O'Connell, overwhelming his critics with contemptuous ridicule, earnestly explained that as 'counsel for Ireland' it was his duty to preserve the association from any taint of illegality.[2]

For the moment it seemed as if O'Connell had managed to get his own way and that his opponents would silently acquiesce in their expulsion. Though a fair number of repealers in both Dublin and the country withdrew from the association, and though local protests against the proceedings in Conciliation Hall were made, the leaders of the secession at first seem to have regarded the breach as a temporary one and to have intended to restrict themselves to educational work, planning the publication of a series of instructive, uplifting essays on Irish topics in the *Nation*.[3] This would scarcely have competed seriously with O'Connell's activities, but soon the beginnings of a new repeal organization emerged. The politically conscious sections of the Dublin working class were accustomed to express themselves, and a month after the secession a group denominating itself the Friends of Freedom drafted a remonstrance attacking the whig alliance, the administration of the association, and the new test which was driving honest men out of the national movement.[4] This remonstrance was contemptuously disregarded by the association, and at the beginning of November the remonstrants held a large meeting attended by members of the *Nation* group, which set up a committee.[5] About this time some of the seceders had come to the conclu-

[1] *Nation*, 1 Aug. 1846.
[2] *Nation*, 8, 15, 22 Aug. 1846.
[3] Smith O'Brien to his constituents (*Nation*, 5 Sept. 1846); *Nation*, 21, 28 Nov. 1846; J. Mitchel to W. S. O'Brien, 11 Nov. 1846 (O'Brien papers).
[4] *Nation*, 3 Oct. 1846.
[5] Ibid., 7 Nov. 1846.

sion that a newspaper, however ably conducted, would never be a match for O'Connell and his machine. But they thought that the repeal association was declining and that in a short time there would be room for 'a new and honest organization'. The remonstrants were waiting to be led and 'a moderate, forward course' was imperatively called for.[1]

At the end of the year an attempt to reconcile the two wings of the repeal movement merely led to a display and definition of their differences.[2] Early in December O'Connell suggested that a small conference of leading repealers from both sections should be held so that they might at least know what they were quarrelling over. That was in fact all the negotiations achieved. The Young Irelanders felt they had to respond to O'Connell's appeal, since many of their supporters regarded his offer as 'a magnanimous act done in defiance of the parasites who surround him', and expected the seceders to save his face. The leading seceders, with the exception of Smith O'Brien who was in the country, decided after some hesitation to formulate the conditions on which they would return to the association. Counsel's opinion was to be secured as to whether or not the rules of the association were sufficient to protect it from prosecution. In the future the association's accounts were to be audited and published, paid officials were not to sit on its committees, members were to be expelled only by the association after due notice had been given, religious topics were to be excluded from its proceedings, and an election committee was to be set up to secure the return of repealers.[3]

These conditions pointed to a constitutional revolution in the association to which O'Connell, after twenty years of masterful control would have found it hard to submit. Even before he met the seceders' deputation he announced that he considered that the only matter which the conference ought to deal with was the first, viz. whether the association would be legally immune if the seceders rejoined it. If the answer was in the negative, he argued, further discussion would be a waste of time, and if the seceders could be safely readmitted, then they could propose in the association the changes they thought necessary. And referring to one of their conditions, he at once flatly refused to 'listen to a proposal to prevent the shield of the association being thrown over the catholic people of Ireland'. Neither O'Connell nor the deputation would give way, and the preliminary discussion failed to find an agreed

---

[1] W. Griffith to W. S. O'Brien, 3 Dec. 1846; R. O'Gorman to W. S. O'Brien, 27 Nov. 1846 (O'Brien papers).
[2] For these negotiations see *Nation*, 12, 19 Dec. 1846.
[3] J. Dillon to W. S. O'Brien, 10, 19 Dec. 1846 (O'Brien papers).

basis for negotiations, Smith O'Brien whom O'Connell had approached, summing up the seceders' position by declaring that he would not discuss the physical force question, but only the policy of the association.[1]

A few days after these embittering and futile conversations broke down Mitchel wrote 'most fervently I hope we have done with Dan for ever'[2] and about the middle of January 1847 a new repeal organization, the Irish Confederation, was formally founded at a meeting in the Rotunda. Though at first it might, as a savage critic suggested, be only 'a decently conducted Conciliation Hall, free from its open and brazen professions of meanness, falsehood, cowardice and corruption, but essentially just as feeble, inefficient and ridiculous',[3] relieved from the domination of an over-mighty leader it proved a forcing house of nationalist opinion. Many of its members, impregnated with the fervent nationalism of the early forties, developed an intense loathing of the union and of British influence in Ireland, and accepted that they might have to resort to physical force to win Irish independence—which would probably be accompanied by sweeping agrarian changes. Constitutional agitation having proved fruitless, as well as, in the opinion of its critics, morally enervating, the tradition of '98 revived to become a long-enduring force in Irish politics. O'Connell in his prime might have dealt with this new movement by devising a compromise or taking vigorous counteraction. But now he was old, breaking up and dispirited by the horrible consequences of the famine. To the end he was prompt in producing plans. As early as October 1845 he suggested that distilling, brewing and the export of provisions to foreign countries should be forbidden, supplies purchased abroad, and the import duties on food removed. A little later he urged the government to raise a loan of £40,000,000 for Irish relief and called on the landlords of Ireland to form an association which might advise and direct the executive. And in one of his last speeches delivered at a great gathering of Irish landlords he energetically advocated the formation of an Irish party, 'a party that without any individual sacrificing any of his political opinions would make all bring to the altar of our country our prejudices and bad passions, and sacrifice them to the object of rescuing Ireland from misery'.[5] But cut off from the centres of decision, where policy was

---

[1] *Nation*, 19 Dec. 1846.

[2] Mitchel to Martin, 23 Dec. 1846 (Dillon, *Life of John Mitchel*, i. 141).

[3] *James Fintan Lalor, patriot and political essayist* ... ed. L. Fogarty, 2nd ed., p. 5.

[4] *FJ*, 29 Oct. 1845. The chief secretary sourly complained 'his [O'Connell's] business is to suggest every remedy he knows the government *cannot* adopt' (Fremantle to Peel, 28 Oct. 1845, Add. MS. 40476).

[5] *Nation*, 3, 10 Oct. 1846; *Pilot*, 15 Jan. 1847.

settled, he could only plead in parliament for 'a great act of national generosity, calculated upon a broad and liberal scale'.[1] He had no longer the energy to formulate and press a programme, for during the terrible winter of 1846–7 his health had steadily declined. In March 1847, with flagging vigour he set out for Rome, and, moving slowly southwards, on 15 May he died at Geneva. His death meant the disappearance of the only Irish politician who might conceivably have exercised a decisive influence over the government's Irish policy. There was abundant diffused goodwill in Ireland, and drastic remedies were being urgently advocated. But there was no commanding figure to seize and express imperatively the country's feelings and demands. While normal economic and social life collapsed over wide areas the government's good intentions were vitiated by timidity. Overwhelmed by the magnitude of the catastrophe, inhibited by caution and treasury tradition, and relying on economic principles evolved in a robust, expanding society, the government failed to display the imaginative boldness which might have enabled it successfully to surmount the Irish crisis.

[1] *Parl. Deb.*, 3 series, lxxxix. 943.

WANDSWORTH PUBLIC LIBRARY

# BIBLIOGRAPHY

## Synopsis

---

## A. Original Sources

### I. MANUSCRIPT MATERIAL

LONDON

*British Museum*

Aberdeen papers (Add. MSS. 43151).

Broughton papers (Add. MSS. 36455–36483). Vol xii (Add MSS. 36467) contains the correspondence of J. C. Hobhouse when chief secretary.

# BIBLIOGRAPHY

Hardwicke papers (Add. MSS. 35701–35779).
Liverpool papers (Add. MSS. 38237–38372).
Peel papers (Add. MSS. 40344–40429).
Place papers (Add. MSS. 35142–35147).
Correspondence of Nicholas Vansittart (Add. MSS. 31229–31237). Vols i and ii (Add. MSS. 31229, 31330) contains Vansittart's correspondence when chief secretary.
Wellesley papers (Add. MSS. 37274–37318). Vols xxv–xxxiv (Add. MSS. 37298–37307) contains Wellesley's correspondence when lord-lieutenant.

*Public Record Office*

Records of the Home Office relating to Ireland (H.O. 100).
Records of the Foreign Office relating to negotiations with the papacy (F.O. 43/38, 79/76, 43/7, 8).
The Chatham papers (G.D.).
The Russell papers (G.D.).


DUBLIN

*Public Record Office*

Leveson-Gower letter books.

*Irish State Paper Office*

State of the Country papers, 2nd series, 1790–1831.
Government correspondence books (iv. 6).
Private official correspondence books (iv. 16).

*Library of Trinity College*

Major H. C. Sirr's papers (N. 4. 4–13).

*Library of University College*

Letters of Daniel O'Connell.

*National Library of Ireland*

Brunswick Club papers.
The Monteagle papers.
The Newport papers.
The O'Brien papers.
O'Connell, Daniel, letters to Councillor Bennett.
O'Connell, Daniel, Correspondence with his constituents, etc.
O'Connell-Drummond correspondence (MS. 2150).
Richmond papers.

262

# BIBLIOGRAPHY

*Royal Irish Academy*

Aldermen of Skinner's Alley, ledger and minute book (23 H. 51–2).
Diaries of Mr Justice Day (12 W. 14–17).
Gavan Duffy papers (12 P. 15–17).

*Public Library, Pearse Street*

Materials for a history of Irish newspapers and periodicals collected
by R. R. Madden (Gilbert collection MSS. bundles 263–74,
276–85).

BELFAST

*Public Record Office of Northern Ireland*

Drennan letters (typescript).
Foster papers.
G. R. Dawson's diary of Derry election, 1837 (typescript).

MANUSCRIPTS IN PRIVATE OWNERSHIP

*Castle Howard MSS.*

Correspondence of Lord Morpeth (later tenth earl of Carlisle), chief
secretary, 1835–41.

*Plas Newydd MSS.*

Correspondence of the first marquess of Anglesey, lord-lieutenant
1828–9, 1830–3.

*Teddesley MSS.*

Correspondence of the first Lord Hatherton, chief secretary, 1833–4.

*O'Connell Fitz-Simon MSS.*

A large collection of O'Connell family letters.

*Papers in possession of Mr Maurice O'Connell*

O'Connell family letters and letters relating to the Repeal Association.


# II. PRINTED MATERIAL

1. COLLECTIONS OF LETTERS AND PAPERS

Abbot, Charles, Lord Colchester. Diary and correspondence. 3 vols.
London 1861.
Bentham, Jeremy. Works, *Ed.* J. Bowring. 12 vols. London 1843.
Buckingham and Chandos, Duke of, ed. Memoirs of the court and
cabinets of George III. 3 vols. London 1855.
Creevy, Thomas. Papers. *Ed.* H. M. Maxwell. 2 vols. London 1903.

Croker, J. W. Correspondence and diaries. . . . *Ed.* L. J. Jennings. 3 vols. London 1885.

Cusack, M. F. The speeches and public letters of the Liberator. 2 vols. Dublin 1875.

Drennan, W. The Drennan letters . . . 1776–1819. *Ed.* D. A. Chart. Belfast 1931.

Report on the manuscripts of J. B. Fortescue preserved at Dropmore (H.M.C.), vols viii, 1912; ix, 1915; x, 1927.

Extracts from the records of the general synod of Ulster from the year 1800 till the year 1822. Belfast 1822.

Records of the general synod of Ulster from 1691 to 1820. 3 vols. Belfast 1890–98.

Between 1822 and 1840 the minutes of the general synod were published annually in pamphlet form.

Report on the manuscripts of Earl Bathurst (H.M.C.) 1923.

Gregory, Lady, *Ed.* Mr. Gregory's letter-box, 1813–30. London 1898. Selections from the correspondence of Sir W. Gregory, the under-secretary.

Gregory, Sir William. An autobiography. *Ed.* Lady Gregory. London 1894.

Greville, Charles Cavendish. The Greville Memoirs, 1814–60. *Ed.* G. L. Strachey and R. Fulford. 7 vols. London 1938.

Grey, Charles, 2nd earl. Correspondence of Princess Lieven and earl Grey. *Ed.* G. Le Strange. 3 vols. London 1890.

George IV. The letters of George IV, 1812–30. *Ed.* A. Aspinall. 3 vols. Cambridge 1938.

Hobhouse, J. C. Recollections of a long life, with additional extracts from his private diaries. *Ed.* by Lady Dorchester. 6 vols. London 1909.

Houston, Arthur. Daniel O'Connell, his early life and journal. 1795 to 1802. London 1906.

Lalor, J. F. James Fintan Lalor, patriot and political essayist, collected writings. *Ed.* by L. Fogarty. Dublin, 2nd ed. 1947.

Lamb, William, 2nd Viscount Melbourne. Papers. *Ed.* L. C. Sanders. London 1889.

Law, Edward, earl of Ellenborough. A political diary 1828–30. *Ed.* R. C. Abbot, Lord Colchester. 2 vols. London 1881.

Lewis, George Cornewall. Letters of the Right Hon. Sir George Cornewall Lewis, Bart. to various friends. *Ed.* Rev. Sir Gilbert Frankland Lewis, Bart. London 1870.

Littleton, Edward John, 1st Lord Hatherton. Memoir and correspondence relating to political occurrences in June and July 1834. *Ed.* Henry Reeve. London 1872.

MacDonagh, M. The viceroy's post-bag. London 1904.
Largely based on Hardwicke papers.

MacHale, The Most Rev. John. The letters of the Most Rev. John MacHale, D.D., under their respective signatures of Hierophilos, John, Bishop of Maronia, Bishop of Killala and Archbishop of Tuam. Dublin 1847.

MacHale, The Most Rev. John. Sermons and discourses. Dublin 1883.

Maher, Rev. James. Letters. *Ed.* Rev. R. P. F. Moran. Dublin 1877.

Napier, McV. Selections from the correspondence of the late McV. Napier. London 1877.

O'Connell, Daniel. Correspondence. *Ed.* W. J. Fitzpatrick. 2 vols. London 1888.

Parker, C. S. The life and letters of Sir James Graham . . . 1792–1861. 2 vols. London 1907.

Peel, Sir Robert. Memoirs of the Rt. Hon. Sir Robert Peel. . . . *Ed.* Lord Mahon and E. Cardwell. 2 vols. London 1856.

Peel, Sir Robert. Sir Robert Peel from his private papers. *Ed.* C. S. Parker. 3 vols. London 1891–99.

Powerscourt, Theodosia, Viscountess. Letters and papers. *Ed.* Rev. R. Daly. London 1838.

Russell, Lord John. Early correspondence . . . 1805–40. *Ed.* R. Russell. 2 vols. London 1913.

Later correspondence, 1840–78. *Ed.* G. P. Gooch. 2 vols. London 1925.

Stewart, Robert, 2nd marquess of Londonderry. Memoirs and correspondence of Viscount Castlereagh. *Ed.* by Charles Vane, marquess of Londonderry. Vols. 1–4. London 1848–9.

Walker, Rev. J. Essays and correspondence. . . . *Ed.* W. Burton. 2 vols. London 1838.

Wellesley, marquess of. Memoirs and correspondence. . . . *Ed.* R. R. Pearce. 3 vols. London 1846.

Wellington, 1st duke of. Despatches, correspondence and memoranda, 1819–32. Ed. by his son the 2nd duke of Wellington. 8 vols. London 1867–80.

Wellington, 1st duke of. Civil correspondence and memoranda of Field Marshal Arthur, duke of Wellington. Ireland [from March 30 1807 to 12 April 1809], London 1860.

# BIBLIOGRAPHY

## 2. Newspapers and magazines

Banner of Ulster.
Belfast Newsletter.
Christian Examiner.
Citizen.
Comet.
Dublin Evening Mail.
Dublin Evening Post.
Dublin University Magazine.
Edinburgh Review.
Evening Packet.
Freeman's Journal.
Gentlemen's Magazine.
The Irish Ecclesiastical Journal.
Irishman.
Nation.
Northern Whig.
Pilot.
Quarterly Review.
Saunders's Newsletter.
Star of Brunswick.
The Times.
Westminster Review.
World.

## 3. Parliamentary debates

The parliamentary history of England from the Norman conquest to
the year 1803. 36 vols. London 1806–20.
The parliamentary debates from the year 1803 to the present time (1820).
41 vols. London 1804–20.
The parliamentary debates published under the superintendence of
T. C. Hansard . . . new series (1820–30). 25 vols. London 1820–30.
Hansard's parliamentary debates . . . 3rd series 1830–91. 356 vols.
London 1831–91.

## 4. Parliamentary papers

Papers relating to the established church in Ireland, presented to the
house of commons. Ordered to be printed 1807.

First report from the select committee on the state of Ireland, and the minutes of evidence, H.C. 1825 (129), viii.

Second report from the select committee on the state of Ireland 1825 with the minutes of evidence, H.C. 1825 (129), viii.

Third report from the select committee on the state of Ireland 1825 with the minutes of evidence, H.C. 1825 (129) viii.

Fourth report [from the select committee on the state of Ireland] viz. minutes of evidence, H.C. 1825 (129), viii.

First, second, and third reports from the select committee on emigration, H.C. 1827 (88, 237, 550) 1826–7, v.

Reports from the lords concerning the collection and payment of tithes in Ireland . . . with the minutes of evidence . . . H.C. 1831–2 (271), xxii.

Second report from the select committee of the house of lords appointed to inquire into the collection and payment of tithes in Ireland . . . with the minutes of evidence . . . H.C. 1831–2 (663), xxii.

Minutes of evidence taken before the select committee of the house of lords appointed to inquire into the collection and payment of tithes in Ireland . . . H.C. 1831–2 (271), xxii.

First report from the select committee on tithes in Ireland, H.C. 1831–2 (177), xxi.

Second report from the select committee on tithes in Ireland, H.C. 1831–2 (177), xxi.

First report of His Majesty's commissioners on ecclesiastical revenue and patronage, Ireland H.C. 1833 (762), xxi.

Copy of the correspondence between the Rev. Thomas Locke . . . and the chief or under-secretary for Ireland . . . relative to the collection of tithes. . . . H.C. 1835 (119), xlvii.

Copy of the proceedings of an investigation held at Armagh of the transactions which took place in the neighbourhood of Keady, between the police and the country people on collecting an arrears of tithe. . . . H.C. 1835 (179), xlvii.

Second report of His Majesty's commissioners on ecclesiastical revenue and patronage, Ireland, H.C. 1834 (589), xxiii.

Report of the commissioners appointed to inquire into the municipal corporations in Ireland, H.C. 1835 (23–4, 27–8), xxvii–viii, 1863 (29) xxiv.

Report from the select committee appointed to inquire into . . . Orange lodges, associations or societies in Ireland, with the minutes of evidence and appendix, H.C. 1835 (377), xv.

Second report from the select committee appointed to inquire into . . . Orange lodges, associations or societies in Ireland with the minutes of evidence and appendix, H.C. 1835 (475), xv.

Third report from the select committee appointed to inquire into . . . Orange lodges, associations or societies in Ireland with the minutes of evidence, appendix and index, H.C. 1835 (476), xvi.

Report from the select committee appointed to inquire into . . . Orange institutions in Great Britain and the colonies with the minutes of evidence . . . H.C. 1835 (605), xvii.

First report from His Majesty's commissioners for inquiring into the condition of the poorer classes in Ireland, with appendix (A) and supplement, H.C. 1835 (369), xxxii.

Reports from the select committees on foundation schools and education in Ireland together with the minutes of evidence, appendix and index (Pt. I and II), H.C. 1835 (630), 1836 (586), 1836, xiii.

Return of the several persons recommended by the judge to fill the office of high sheriff in the respective counties of Ireland for the year 1836 . . . H. L. 1836 (301), xxv.

Correspondence relating to the appointment of high sheriffs in Ireland. H.L. 1837–8 (180), xviii.

Report from the select committee [of the house of commons] on the new plan of education in Ireland, with evidence, H.C. 1837 (485), ix.

First report from the select committee on combinations of workmen, together with minutes of evidence, H.C. 1837–88 (488), viii.

Second report from the select committee on combinations of workmen, with minutes of evidence, H.C. 1837–8 (646), viii.

Circular addressed by order of the lord-lieutenant to lieutenants of counties in Ireland dated 4 May 1838, order from the hanaper office calling upon magistrates in the new commission to take out their dedimus, and lists of the old and new commissions . . . H. L. (292), 1838, xviii.

Railroads (Ireland), copy of all resolutions and memorials presented to the lord-lieutenant or chief secretary of Ireland or to the chancellor of the exchequer respecting railroads in that country, H.C. 1839 (154), xlvi.

Correspondence between T. E. Langford . . . and the Irish government on the subject of Ribbon papers found in the county of Limerick. . . . H.L. 1840 (182, 208, 227), xiv.

Report of the trial . . . on 23, 24, 25, 29 June 1840 of Richard Jones who was charged with being a member of an illegal society, H.L. 1840 (241). xiv.

Report from the select committee on medical charities, Ireland, together with minutes of evidence . . . H.C. 1843 (412), x.

Report of Her Majesty's commissioners into the state of the law and practice in respect to the occupation of land in Ireland, with evidence, H.C. 1845 (605, 606, 616, 657, 672, 673), xix, xx, xxi, xxii.

Correspondence and accounts relating to the different occasions in which measures were taken for the relief of the people suffering from scarcity in Ireland between 1822 and 1839, H.C. 1846, (734), xxxvii.

Correspondence explanatory of the measures adopted by Her Majesty's government for the relief of distress arising from the failure of the potato crop in Ireland, H.C. 1846 (735), xxxvii.

Report from the select committee on miscellaneous expenditure together with the minutes of evidence, H.C. 1847–8 (543), xviii.

Report from the select committee on outrages (Ireland) with proceedings of the committee, minutes of evidence, etc., H.C. 1857 (438), xiv.

Reports of the committees of inquiry into public offices and papers connected therewith, H.C. 1854 (1715), xxvii.

Papers on the reorganization of the civil service, H.C. 1854–5 (1870), xx.

Report of Her Majesty's commissioners appointed to inquire into the management and government of the college of Maynooth, with appendix, H.C. 1854–5 (1896, 1896), xxii.

Report from the select committee on the Grand Jury presentments (Ireland) together with . . . minutes of evidence and appendix, H.C. 867–8 (392), x.


5. CONTEMPORARY WORKS OF REFERENCE

The complete catholic directory, almanac and registry . . . compiled by W. J. Battersby. Dublin 1836–

Dod's parliamentary companion. London 1833–

The Dublin almanack and general registry, 1834–

Erck, J. C. Account of the ecclesiastical establishment subsisting in Ireland. Dublin 1830.

Lewis, A. A topographical dictionary of Ireland . . . 2 vols. London 1839.

The parliamentary gazetteer of Ireland . . . 3 vols. Dublin 1844–6.

Thom's Irish almanac and official directory, 1844–

The treble almanack, 1801–33.

Wakefield, E. An account of Ireland, statistical and political. 2 vols. Dublin 1812.

# BIBLIOGRAPHY

ts agriculture, mines and fisheries. London 1802.

Bond, Thomas. Hints tending to increase the wealth of the Irish nation. Dublin 1803.

[Burgh, William]. Essays on the population of Ireland. . . . By A member of the last Irish parliament. London 1803.

Scully, Denys. An Irish catholic's advice to his brethren. Dublin 1803.

The catholic question: correspondence between the Rt. Hon. Lord Redesdale and the Rt. Hon. the earl of Fingall. Dublin 1804.

Lauderdale, earl of. Hints to the manufacturers of Great Britain on the consequences of the Irish union. Edinburgh 1805.

A letter to the Rt. Hon. Sir John Newport, Bart. on the embarrassing situation and prospects of the present ministry. By An Irishman. Dublin 1806.

Essay on the present state of manners and education among the lower class of the people of Ireland. 3rd ed. Dublin 1805.

Resolutions passed or intended to be passed at the catholic meetings held in the repository Stephen's Green. Dublin 1806.

To the Roman catholics of Ireland [1806].

[Lidwell, George]. Lidwell's speech for the abolition of tithes and thereby meliorating the condition of the poor of this country. Belfast 1807.

An account of the petition finally agreed to at a general meeting of the catholics of Ireland. . . . Dublin 1807.

A letter to the Rt. Hon. Henry Grattan on . . . his vote on the Insurrection bill. By An Irishman. Dublin 1807.

The letters of Timoleon and the answers thereto by an Irish whig and Aristides on the late parliamentary conduct of the Rt. Hon. Henry Grattan. Kilkenny 1807.

Proceedings at a general meeting of the catholics held . . . on 18 April 1807. Dublin 1807.

Report of the committee appointed to prepare a plan of education and government for the intended Academical Institution, Belfast. Belfast 1807.

Report of a deputation from the Hibernian Society respecting the religious state of Ireland. London 1807.

A sketch of the speech delivered by Mr John Keogh at a meeting of the catholics of Dublin. . . . Dublin 1807.

270

# BIBLIOGRAPHY

J. B. Clinch. An inquiry, legal and political, into the consequences of giving to his majesty a negative upon the appointment of an Irish catholic bishop. Dublin 1808.

[Croker, John Wilson]. A sketch of the state of Ireland, past and present. Dublin 1808.

Bellew, R. Thoughts and suggestions. London 1808.

McElligott, P. Observations on the Gaelic language. [1808].

Trotter, J. B. A letter to Lord Viscount Southwell. Dublin 1808.

Woodward, Rt. Rev. R. The present state of the Church of Ireland. Dublin 1787, new ed. 1808.

A letter addressed to the late grand jury of Armagh with some observations on the subject of tithes. . . . By A Kilkenny weaver. Dublin 1808.

The present state of catholic affairs in Ireland considered . . . By Inimicus Veto. Dublin 1808.

Syllabus of the first commemoration of Carolan consisting of ancient Irish melodies as performed at the private theatre in Fishamble Street. . . . Dublin 1809.

Royal veto. By An Irish catholic clergyman. Dublin 1809.

Duigenan, Patrick. The nature and extent of the demands of the Irish catholics fully explained. London 1810.

Keogh, Cornelius. The veto: a commentary. London 1810.

Milner, Rev. John. Letter from the Most Rev. Dr Milner . . . respecting . . . a veto. . . . London 1810. An elucidation of the veto. London 1810.

[O'Conor, Rev. C.]. Columbanus ad Hibernos. Dublin 1810.

O'Flaherty, J. T. Thoughts upon the catholic question and the veto. Cork 1810.

Address of the Roman catholic prelates assembled in Dublin, 26 Feb. 1810. . . . Dublin 1810.

An address to the catholics of Ireland . . . with a few remarks upon the question of the veto. . . . By An Irish catholic. Dublin 1810.

An answer to Lord Greville's letter. By a Fingalian. London 1810.

An answer to the Rt. Hon. P. Duigenan's two great arguments. By A member of the establishment. Dublin 1810.

A method of improving the condition of the Irish poor. Dublin 1810.

Rules and regulations of the Irish harp society. . . . Dublin 1810.

A short inquiry into the causes of the present distresses of the Irish traders. Dublin 1810.

O'Mara, S. D. Repeal, or ruin. . . . Dublin 1811.

Letter to the citizens of Dublin on the convention act. Dublin 1811.

Proceedings of the catholic committee taken from their accredited papers. Dublin 1811.

A vindication of the policy and conduct of the Irish government in relation to the Roman catholics. Dublin 1811.

[O'Beirne, Rt. Rev. T. L.] A letter to the earl of Fingal. Dublin 1813.

[O'Beirne, Rt. Rev. T. L.] A letter to Rt. Hon. George Canning. . . . London 1812.

O'Conor, Rev. C. An historical address on the calamities occasioned by foreign influence in the nomination of bishops to Irish sees. [1812].

[Scully D.] A statement of the penal laws . . . in two parts. Dublin 1812.

Townshend, Rev. E. Observations on the catholic claims. Dublin 1812.

Address of the Roman catholic prelates assembled in Dublin, 18 Nov. 1812. . . . Dublin 1812.

An address to the protestants of the United Kingdom. By A citizen of Dublin. Dublin 1812.

A commentary upon the proceedings of the catholics of Ireland. Dublin 1812.

The leading speeches delivered at the city of Cork election. Cork 1812.

Catholic affairs considered in a series of letters signed A Cork catholic freeholder. Cork 1813.

Observations on a pamphlet entitled 'A report of the trial of David Morgan, John Carroll, William McMullan, and Mathew Trainer for the murder of Andrew McNarry and Hugh Grahan on the twelfth of July last in Belfast. . . . Belfast 1813.

Trial of the Belfast Orangemen. . . . Belfast 1813.

Edwards, J. The interests of Ireland. Dublin 1814.

Ensor, George. Observations on the present state of Ireland. Dublin 1814.

Fletcher, W. A charge delivered to the grand jury of the county of Wexford. London, Dublin, Belfast 1814.

Darcy, Stephen. A letter addressed to Richard Shiel. Dublin 1815.

Rice, Thomas. An inquiry into the effects of the Irish grand jury laws as affecting the industry, the improvement, and the moral character of the people of England. London 1815.

Catholic emancipation (as it is absurdly called) considered . . . Dublin 1815.

Faction unmasked, or a letter to the Roman catholics on the conduct of certain men who compose the catholic junta. Dublin 1815.

Gough, John. Account of two journies southward in Ireland. Dublin 1817.

[Gough, J.]. A tour in Ireland. By An Englishman. Dublin 1817.

Hamilton, Rev. George. Observations upon Mr O'Callaghan's pamphlet. Kilkenny 1816.

Lawless, John. A letter addressed to the proprietors of the Belfast Academical Institution. Belfast 1816.

O'Callaghan, A. Thoughts on the rendering of the Bible. Dublin 1816.

Parker, W. Observations on the intended amendment of the Irish grand jury laws. Cork 1816.

O'Callaghan, A. The Bible Societies against church and state. Dublin 1817.

The case stated: or observations on a report purporting to be the proceedings of a committee assembled to confer with the methodist conference. . . . Dublin 1817.

A history of the proceedings at the particularly interesting election for a member to represent the city of Limerick. . . . Dublin 1817.

The Irish ecclesiastical register for the year 1817. Dublin 1817.

A report of the proceedings of the general committee of the methodists in Ireland. . . . Dublin [1817].

Thoughts on the veto. By A Roman catholic. Dublin 1817.

Chichester, Rev. E. Oppressions and cruelties of Irish revenue officers. London 1818.

Coffey, A. Observations on the Rev. Edward Chichester's pamphlet. . . London 1818.

A full report of the proceedings at the election for the city of Cork. [Cork 1818].

Gamble, J. Views of society and manners in the north of Ireland. London 1819.

Parker, W. A plea for the poor and industrious: Pt. I. the necessity of a national provision for the poor of Ireland. Cork 1819.

Woulfe, Stephen. A letter to a protestant on the balance of evils. Dublin 1819.

Lees, Sir H. A cursory view of the state of Ireland. Dublin [1820].

A report of the proceedings at the election for the city of Dublin. . . . Dublin 1820.

Stokes, William. Observations on the population and resources of Ireland. Dublin 1821.

Irish priests' the great obstacles to every measure intended to promote the tranquillity, civilization and unanimity of Ireland. Dublin 1821.

A letter to the Rt. Hon. Sir John Newport. By Hibernicus. Dublin 1821.

Browne, D. Letter . . . to the Most Noble the Marquess of Wellesley on the present state of Ireland. London 1822.

Doyle, W. Ostensible causes of the present state of Ireland considered
. . . Scarborough 1822.

Ensor, George. An address to the people of Ireland on the degradation
and misery of their country. Dublin 1822.

Fraser, R. Sketches and essays on the present state of Ireland. Dublin
1822.

Magee, Most Rev. W. A charge delivered at his primary visitation.
Dublin 1822.

[Rice, T. S.]. Consideration on the present state of Ireland. . . . London
1822.

Calumny and ignorance exposed, or a refutation of Dr Magee's defence
of his late charge. . . . Dublin 1822.

Correspondence between Daniel O'Connell and the Rev. Dr Blake . . .
on the subject of ecclesiastical securities. Dublin 1822.

Emigration recommended as a means of improving the condition of the
unemployed. . . . By A retired officer. Dublin 1822.

An impartial view of the true causes of the existing misery in Ireland.
Dublin 1822.

A report of the trial of Michael Keenan. Dublin 1822.

[Doyle, Most Rev. J. W.]. A vindication of the religious and civil principles of the Irish catholics. By J. K. L. Dublin 1823.

[Elrington, Rt. Rev. Thomas]. An inquiry whether the disturbances in
Ireland have originated in tithes. . . . By S. N. London 1823.

[Emerson, J. S.]. One year of the administration of His Excellency
the marquess of Wellesley in Ireland. London 1823.

[Laurence, Most Rev. R.]. Remarks upon certain objections . . . against
the Tithe Composition bill. London 1823.

A letter containing some observations on the delusive nature of the
system proposed by Robert Owen, Esq. . . . Dublin 1823.

Practical views and suggestions on the present condition and permanent
improvement of Ireland. By Hibernicus. Dublin 1823.

A report of the British and foreign philanthropic society . . . explanatory
of Mr Owen's plan. . . . Dublin 1823.

Report of the proceedings at the several public meetings held in Dublin
by Robert Owen, Esq. . . . Dublin 1823.

Sketch of an amendment to Mr Goulburn's bill for the composition of
tithes in Ireland. London 1823.

Jebb, Rt. Rev. John. Speech delivered in the house of peers, 10 June
1824. . . . London 1824.

Miller, G. The policy of the Roman catholic question discussed. London
1824.

Ryan, P. B. Provision for the poor in Ireland without additional taxation. Dublin 1824.

Shackleton, E. Proposal of a public provision for the poor of Ireland. Dublin 1824.

Wheatley, John. A letter to the duke of Devonshire on the state of Ireland. Calcutta 1824.

An authentic report of the discussion which took place by agreement at Carrick-on-Shannon on 9 Nov. 1824 between three Roman catholic priests and three clergymen.

Glimpses across the Irish channel. By A friend not a flatterer. London 1824.

A letter to the Rt. Hon. J. Abercombie on the new Tithe bill. Dublin 1824.

South of Ireland : hints to Irish landlords on the best means of obtaining and increasing their rents. . . . By A land agent. London 1824.

Thoughts on the present disturbances. By A Resident in County Cork. London 1824.

W– T–. Plan for the improvement of the people of Ireland. Dublin 1824.

Cropper, James. Present state of Ireland with a plan for improving the condition of the people. Liverpool 1825.

Lawless, John. An address to the catholics of Ireland. London 1825.

[Doyle, J. W.]. Letters on the state of Ireland. Dublin 1825.

A letter to a British M.P. on the state of Ireland. By An Irish magistrate. Dublin 1825.

On the encouragement of the peasants in Ireland. London 1825.

Remarks on the evils of Ireland. By A Protestant inhabitant. London 1825.

Statement of some of the causes of the disturbances in Ireland. . . . Dublin 1825.

Allen, W. Colonies at home : or the means for rendering the industrious labourer independent of parish relief. . . . London and Dublin 1826.

Miller, Rev. G. The policy of the Roman catholic question. London 1826.

Winter, John Pratt. Suggestions for the regulation of the office of justice of the peace in Ireland and the powers of the grand juries in levying money. . . . Dublin 1826.

The controversial letters of the Rev. Robert Daly, and of Daniel O'Connell, Esq., on the subject of Bible societies, proselytism and the real presence. Dublin 1826.

Minutes of the proceedings and evidence, of the commission of inquiry, ordered by the Irish government into charges of proselytism and cruelty preferred against the officers of the Richmond General Penitentiary. Dublin 1827.

Report of the discussion which took place at a meeting of the Ballinasloe auxiliary of the London Hibernian Society. . . . Dublin 1827.

Report of the meeting of the Reformation Society at Carlow and the discussion which took place. Carlow 1827.

Andrews, R. C. A letter to the Rt. Hon. Robert Peel on the prevention of the re-establishment in Ireland of popery and priestcraft. London 1828.

[Blake, A. R.]. Thoughts upon the catholic question. By An Irish Roman catholic. Dublin 1828.

Bruce, W. Poor-rates the panacea for Ireland. Bristol, 2nd ed. 1828.

Burke, J. Exposure of frauds and malversations carried on in the Leinster constabulary. . . . Dublin 1828.

Sadleir, M. P. Ireland, its evils and their remedies. London 1828.

Authenticated report of the discussion which took place at Londonderry between six Roman catholic priests and six clergymen of the established church. . . . Dublin 1828.

A full and authentic report of the proceedings of the first annual meeting of the Brunswick Constitutional Club of Ireland. Dublin 1828.

A letter to the landed proprietors of Westmeath on the character and consequences of the last election. London 1828.

Statement of the proceedings of the society for the improvement of Ireland for the year 1828. [Dublin] 1828.

Daly, Rev. Robert. A letter . . . on the subject of a legal provision for the poor of Ireland. Dublin 1829.

Evans, G. H. Remarks on the policy of introducing the system of poor rates into Ireland. London 1829.

Napier, J. Brunswick policy for the amelioration of the present condition of Ireland. London 1829.

[McNaghten, Sir F.]. A view of the catholic question as it relates to Ireland. London 1829.

Wyse, Thomas. The political catechism explanatory of the constitutional rights and civil disabilities of the catholics of Ireland. London 1829.

Proceedings of the friends of civil and religious freedom in Ireland. . . . Dublin 1829.

Drummond, William Henry. The Unitarian Christian's faith. London 1830.

Flood, H. Poor Laws: argument against a provision for paupers. Dublin 1830.

McCormac, H. Plan for the relief of the unemployed poor. Belfast 1830.

# BIBLIOGRAPHY

O'Brien, W. S. Plan for the relief of the poor in Ireland. London 1830.

O'Connell, D. Letters on the repeal of the legislative union between Great Britain and Ireland. Dublin [1830].

A letter to the Rt. Hon. the Lord Mayor . . . proposing a wholesome and improved system of poor laws for Ireland. By Patricius. Dublin 1830.

The repeal of the legislative union of Great Britain and Ireland considered. London 1830.

Report of the proceedings at the town meeting held at Belfast on 2 December 1830 for the purpose of petitioning parliament for a reform in the system of representation. . . . Belfast 1830.

A statement of the management of the Farnham estates. Dublin 1830.

[Burgoyne, Sir John]. Ireland in 1831: letters on the state of Ireland. London 1831.

Clinch, James Bernard. On the spirit, nature and effects of the Irish independence of 1782 and of the act of union, 1800, with the danger of further agitating its repeal. Dublin 1831.

Doolan, Thomas. Munster: or the memoirs of a chief constable. London 1831.

Doyle, Rt. Rev. James. Letter to Thomas Spring Rice on the establishment of a legal provision for the Irish poor. . . .Dublin 1831.

M'Nevin, Thomas. Gerald: A national dramatic poem in three acts founded on the invasion of Ireland by Henry II. Dublin 1831.

Martin, J. C. Reform considered. . . . Dublin 1831.

Smith, Rev. Thomas. The Parson's horn-book examined and its concealed, cowardly author exposed. Dublin 1831.

Staunton, Michael. The case of Ireland. Dublin 1831.

Considerations addressed to the landed proprietors of County Clare. Limerick 1831.

The federalist: or a series of papers showing how to repeal the union so as to avoid a violent crisis. By A minister of peace. Dublin 1831.

Ireland vindicated. . . . By A True whig. London 1831.

Letter from the Rev. Henry Montgomery to Daniel O'Connell, Esq., M.P. 1831.

The Parson's horn-book. London 1831.

The Parson's horn-book. Pt. II. By the Comet Literary and Patriotic Club. Dublin 1831.

Plan, or the proposed system by which about fifty thousand poor in Ireland may not only be supported but lodged in comfort and made useful . . . without any additional taxation. Wexford 1831.

Darby, J. N. A letter to the Rev. Dr Singer on the opinion of his grace the archbishop of Dublin. Dublin 1832.

R. B. G. A repeal of the union the ruin of Ireland. Dublin 1831.

The repeal of the union considered. By A protestant of the established church. Dublin 1831.

Boyton, Rev. C. Speech . . . at a meeting of the Protestant conservative society. Dublin 1832.

Connor, W. The speech of William Connor, Esq., against rack-rents etc. Dublin 1832.

Darby, J. N. A letter to the Rev. Dr Singer on the archbishop of Dublin. Dublin 1832.

Hudson, W. E. A treatise on the elective franchise. . . . Dublin 1832.

Irwin, J. The triumph of the bible in Ireland. London 1832.

McBride, John. The anti-union melodist; a collection of original, patriotic poems and songs dedicated to the independent electors of Ireland. Dublin 1832.

O'Connell, D. Letters . . . on the reform bill  Dublin 1832.

Letters to the reformers of England on the reform bill for Ireland. London 1832.

O'Connor, Feargus. A letter . . . to His Excellency the marquess of Anglesey. Cork 1832.

Letter of James Emerson Tennent, Esq., to the electors of Belfast. Belfast 1832.

An appeal to Irishmen of all classes and creeds . . . on the necessity of repealing the legislative union. By A protestant. Dublin 1832.

Belfast election: a collection of squibs and songs. . . . Belfast 1832.

Belfast election: Mr Emerson Tennent's claims and conduct. Belfast 1832.

National education . . . speeches delivered at the meeting in. . . Belfast, January 1832. Belfast 1832.

A plan for improving the condition of the Irish peasantry. By A Friend to Ireland. Dublin 1832.

Transactions of the Protestant colonization society of Ireland. . . . [1832].

Atkinson, A. Ireland in the nineteenth century and seventh of English dominion. . . . London 1833.

Battersby, W. J. The repealers' manual or absenteeism; the union reconsidered. Dublin 1833.

Crawford, W. S. The expediency and necessity of a local legislative body in Ireland. . . . Newry 1833.

Crawford, W. S. A review of the circumstances connected with the past and present state of the protestant and catholic interests in Ireland. . . . Dublin 1833.

McGhee, Rev. R. J. The last stand for the church. Dublin 1833.

Martin, R. M. Ireland, as it was—is—and ought to be. . . . London 1833.

O'Connell, Daniel. Letter . . . to the people of Ireland. Dublin 1833.

Scrope, G. P. Plan of a poor law for Ireland. . . . London 1833.

Detailed report of contributions (parochial and personal) to the O'Connell national annuity for the year 1832. Dublin 1833.

Thoughts on the mixed character of government institutions in Ireland, with particular reference to the new system of education. By A protestant. Belfast 1833.

Bish, Thomas. A plea for Ireland; submitting the outline of a proposition for holding the court and parliament at occasional intervals in Dublin. London 1834.

Cloncurry, Lord. The danger of a law for promoting the pacification of Ireland. Dublin 1834.

Finlay, J. Miscellanies. . . . Dublin 1834.

Croly, Rev. D. O. An essay religious and political on ecclesiastical finance as regards the Roman catholic church in Ireland. Cork 1834.

Longfield, M. Four lectures on poor laws. . . . Dublin 1834.

McGhee, Rev. R. J. A letter to the clergy of the church of Ireland. . . . Dublin 1834.

Scrope, G. P. How is Ireland to be governed? London 1834.

The causes of the evils existing in Ireland with a plan and a simple remedy. London 1834.

Detailed report of the contributions . . . to the O'Connell national annuity for the year 1833. Dublin 1834.

A letter on the repeal of the union addressed to Sir William Gosset. Dublin (n.d. c. 1834).

A plan for the improvement of Ireland by the union of English and Irish capital. London 1834.

[Colden, R.]. England, Ireland and America. By A Manchester manufacturer. London 1835.

Broadhurst, J. A letter to Lord Melbourne on the Irish church and Irish titles. London 1835.

Doyle, M. An address to the landlords of Ireland. 2nd ed. Dublin 1835.

Hinchy, John. General observations on the state of Ireland and plans for its improvement. Dublin 1835.

Keane, J. H. An address to the young men of Ireland. London 1835.

Kennedy, J. P. Instruct; employ; don't hang them, or Ireland tranquillized without soldiers and enriched with English capital. London 1835.

# BIBLIOGRAPHY

O'Connell, D. Seven letters on the reform bill and the law of election. Dublin 1835.

O'Flynn, J. The present state of the Irish poor. . . . London 1835.

Stanley, W. The policy of a poor law for Ireland. Dublin 1835.

Detailed report of the contributions to the O'Connell national annuity for the year 1834. Dublin 1835.

Laws and ordinances of the Orange Institution of Ireland. Dublin 1835.

Three letters addressed to the Rt. Hon. Viscount Melbourne. By A conservative whig. London 1835.

Barrow, J. A tour round Ireland. London 1836.

Killarney, Frank. A letter to the earl of Mulgrave. . . . Cork 1836.

Lewis, G. C. On local disturbances in Ireland and on the Irish church question. London 1836.

McBride, J. A summary history of the law-made church and the origin of parsonical tithes. . . . Dublin 1836.

O'Connor, F. A series of letters . . . to Daniel O'Connell. . . . London 1836.

Wyse, T. Education reform or the necessity of a national system of education. London 1836.

Considerations of the case of Raphael and O'Connell. . . . By A constitutional reporter. Dublin 1836.

The inquisition in the jury box: an appeal from Irish protestants for British protection. . . . Dublin 1836.

A letter to Viscount Melbourne. . . . By A conservative whig. London 1836.

Proof of national prosperity under protestant governments and national ruin under popish rule. Dublin 1836.

Reflections on the O'Connell 'alliance' or Lichfield house conspiracy. London 1836.

Report of the proceedings at the first meeting of the Metropolitan conservative society. . . . Dublin [1836].

A report of the speeches and proceedings at the third anniversary dinner of 'The Belfast Society'. . . . Belfast 1836.

A statement of persecutions on the part of certain tory landlords in the county of Carlow. . . . London 1836.

Butt, I. The poor law bill for Ireland examined. . . . London 1837.

Crawford, W. S. Observations showing the necessity of an amendment to the laws of landlord and tenant. Belfast 1837.

# BIBLIOGRAPHY

[Davis, T.]. The reform of the Lords. By A graduate of the Dublin university. Dublin 1837.

Kennedy, J. P. Analysis of the projects proposed for the relief of the poor of Ireland. London 1837.

Lindsay, H. L. The present state of the Irish grand jury law considered . . . Armagh 1837.

MacDonnell, E. Letters . . . to the editor of *The Times*. London 1837.

Murray, Rt. Rev. Dr D. Letters addressed to the Roman catholics of Ireland. . . . Dublin 1837.

Nicholls, G. Poor laws—Ireland, report . . . published by direction of His Majesty's principal secretary of state for the home department. London 1837.

MacNaghten, Sir F. W. Some observations upon the present state of Ireland. London 1837.

O'Malley, T. Poor laws—Ireland—to Lord John Russell. [Printed sheet dated 1837].

Ward, H. G. The first step to a poor law for Ireland. London 1837.

Authentic reports of the special meetings of the Irish metropolitan conservative society. Dublin 1837.

Ireland under Lord Mulgrave. London 1837.

Letters to the north from a traveller in the south. By J. K. Belfast 1837.

Remarks on the application of the workhouse system with other modes of relief to the Irish poor. By An assistant commissioner. London 1837.

Report of the conservative registration committee. Dublin 1837.

Carlisle, Rev. James. Defence of the national system of education in Ireland. Dublin 1838.

Clements, Lord. The present poverty of Ireland. London 1838.

Hoare, E. N. Practical observations on church reform, the tithe question and national education. Dublin 1838.

Lynch, A. H. An address to the electors of Galway on the poor-law bill for Ireland. . . . London 1838.

Lynch, D. Letter to Rt. Hon. Lord Cottenham on the prerogative of the crown in respect of the appointment of sheriffs in Ireland. . . . Dublin 1838.

Mason, H. J. M. Reasons and authorities and facts afforded by the history of the Irish Society respecting the duty of employing the Irish language . . . for conveying scriptural instruction to the native peasantry of Ireland. 4th ed. Dublin 1838.

Meyler, Irish tranquillity under Mr O'Connell, My Lord Mulgrave and the Romish priesthood. Dublin 1838.

Murray, Rt. Rev. Daniel. Letters addressed to the Roman catholics of Ireland on the subject of National education. Dublin 1838.

MacNevin, Thomas. A letter to the Rt. Hon. the earl of Roden on the nature and causes of crime in Ireland. London 1838.

Ryan, John. A disclosure of the principles, designs and machinations of the popish revolutionary faction of Ireland. London and Dublin 1838.

Ryan, P. B. Provision for the poor in Ireland without any additional taxation. Dublin 1838.

Torrens, R. Plan of an association in aid of the Irish poor law. London 1838.

Irish landlords as they are and the poor-law bill accompanied as it ought to be. . . . Dublin 1838.

Justice in Ireland, exemplified in a correspondence between the Irish government and David John Wilson, Esq., which caused him to resign the commission of the peace. Ennis 1838.

Letter to the Rt. Hon. Lord Lyndhurst on the appointment of sheriffs in Ireland under the earl of Mulgrave. By A barrister. London 1838.

Necessity of combining a law of settlement with local assessment in the proposed bill for the relief of the poor. Dublin 1838.

Chatterton, Lady H. G. Rambles in the south of Ireland. 2 vols. London 1839.

Nangle, Rev. Edward. The origin, progress and difficulties of the Achill mission. Dublin 1839.

Napier, Sir C. J. An essay on the present state of Ireland. . . . London 1839.

Combinations defended, being a commentary upon and an analysis of the evidence given before the parliamentary committee of inquiry into combinations of employers and workmen. . . . By The London Trades Combination Committee. London 1839.

Letters to a parish priest on Peter Purcell and precursorism. By An Independent radical. Dublin 1839.

An epitome of the case of Irish corporations. . . . Dublin 1839.

Irish railways, proceedings of the deputation. London 1839.

A letter to the Rev. Dr Singer, S.F.T.C.D.; the objections to the plan of national education in Ireland groundless. By A graduate of the university of Dublin. Limerick 1839.

Report of the Conservative registration committee for the city of Dublin with an account of the results obtained within the four last years. Dublin 1839.

# BIBLIOGRAPHY

A report of the proceedings at two public meetings held at the Thatched house tavern, on the 18 and 20 April 1839, for the purpose of taking into consideration the necessity of forming railways throughout Ireland. . . . London 1839.

Butt, I. The Irish corporation bill. . . . London 1840.

Jackson, T. Ireland vindicated from tyrannical oppression. Newry 1840.

A plea for the protestants of Ireland . . . with proposals for modifying the national system of education. Dublin 1840.

Report on the registration and election laws of the United Kingdom as prepared by a sub-committee of the Ulster Constitutional Association. . . . Belfast 1840.

Alton, J. B. The evils of Ireland and their only remedy. Limerick 1841.

Alvaney, Lord. The state of Ireland considered. London 1841.

[Clements, E.] Report on the two bills brought into parliament by Lord Morpeth and Lord Stanley read at a meeting of the Loyal national repeal association. [1841].

Fagan, J. M. The repeal of the union would lead either to the reconquest of Ireland or the destruction of the British empire. Dublin 1841.

Neligan, Rev. W. H. A letter to a clergyman in the diocese of Cloyne on National education in Ireland. 2nd ed. Cork 1841.

O'Callaghan. The Green book or gleanings from the writing desk of a literary agitator. . . . Dublin 1841.

O'Sullivan, Rev. M. Reasons for declining to be connected with the system of national education. . . . Dublin 1841.

Shaw, Sir Frederick. Speech . . . at the election of the university of Dublin. Dublin 1841.

A letter to the earl of Charleville upon the Loyal national repeal association. By An Irish barrister. Dublin [1841].

The reign of terror in Carlow. . . . London 1841.

The repealer repulsed: a correct narrative of the use and progress of the repeal invasion of Ulster. . . . Belfast 1841.

A report upon the outrages and intimidation at the late elections with an address to the protestants of Ireland. Dublin 1841.

Rules of the Kilkenny citizens club with an explanatory introduction. Kilkenny 1841.

O'Connell, D. Observations on the corn laws, on political pravity and ingratitude, and on clerical and personal slander in the shape of a meek and modest reply to the second letter of the earl of Shrewsbury. Dublin 1842.

Connor, William. The prosecuted speech delivered at Mountmellick. ... Dublin 1842.

Anketel, W. R. The effects of absenteeism briefly considered. London 1843.

Campbell, W. I. Hints to repealers. London 1843.

Connor, William. A letter to the Rt. Hon. the earl of Devon ... on the rack-rent system of Ireland. ... Dublin 1843.

Martin, R. M. Ireland before and after the union with Great Britain. London 1843.

Napier, J. L. W. Observations on the elective franchise and fixity of tenure. Dublin 1843.

O'Brien, William Smith. Speech ... on the causes of discontent in Ireland. Dublin: printed for the Loyal national repeal association 1843.

Plunket, Hon. Edward. Address to the landowners of Ireland. London 1843.

Stapleton, A. G. The real monster evil of Ireland. London 1843.

Staunton, Michael. Speech ... on the state of Ireland ... Dublin: printed for the Loyal national repeal association. 1843.

Civil and religious liberty: Address of the Irish universal suffrage association to the Most Rev. and Rt. Rev. the Roman catholic archbishops and bishops of Ireland. Dublin 1843.

Discussion on repeal: ... report of the important discussion in the corporation of Dublin. Dublin 1843.

Instructions for the appointment of repeal wardens and collectors of the repeal fund: their duties, etc. Dublin 1843.

A letter to an English member of parliament upon the subject of the present state of Ireland. By An Irish country gentleman. Dublin 1843.

Observations and strictures on the present Irish poor law. By An Irish magistrate. Dublin and London 1843.

Suggestions for checking the repeal agitation, addressed to the landlords of Ireland by one of themselves. Dublin 1843.

Two addresses to the protestants of Ireland ... by the Dublin Protestant operatives society. ... Dublin 1843.

Barrington, Matthew. Letter to Sir Robert Peel. [1844].

Cowan, John. A letter to the Rev. Henry Woodward. Dublin 1844.

Fitzpatrick, Thomas. Outline of a plan of an Irish parliament. Dublin 1844.

Hiffernan, Rev. J. A review of the controversy on national education in Ireland. Dublin 1844.

[Keogh, William]. Ireland under Lord de Grey. Dublin 1844.

Kohl, J. G. Travels in Ireland. London 1844.

O'Brien, Thomas. A glance at parties. London 1844.

O'Callaghan, J. C. The green book. . . . Dublin 1844.

O'Neill, J. A. Ireland's case, disease and remedy. . . . Dublin 1844.

Porter, J. G. V. Ireland. London 1844.

Porter, J. G. V. Some calm observations upon Irish affairs. Letter A. Dublin 1844.

Ryland, Rev. R. H. Observations on a pamphlet by the Rev. Henry Woodward. Dublin 1844.

Shrewsbury, earl of. Hints towards the pacification of Ireland. 2nd ed. London 1844.

Staunton, M. A reply to Mr Montgomery Martin's 'Ireland before and after the union with Great Britain.' Dublin 1844.

Wyse, Francis. Federalism. Dublin 1844.

The charitable bequests act: a letter to the Most Rev. Dr Murray. By a Lay Roman catholic. Dublin 1844.

County elector's manual . . . published under the superintendence of the Loyal national repeal association. Dublin 1844.

An epitome of the grievances of Ireland emanating indisputably from a gripping landed aristocracy sustained by a hostile alien parliament. Dublin [1844].

The life and death of Lord Edward Fitzgerald with a selection of historical and biographical sketches and anecdotes of celebrated United Irishmen, to which is added Mr O'Connell's speech at Mullaghmast 1 Oct. 1843. Dublin 1844.

Rules for the establishment of repeal reading rooms, unanimously adopted at a meeting of the Loyal national repeal association. . . .

The voice of the *Nation*: a manual of nationality. 2nd ed. Dublin 1844.

Whig and tory remedies for Irish evils. Dublin 1844.

Barry, N. J. Ireland, as she was, as she is, and as she shall be. Dublin 1845.

Blackburn, J. Three conferences held by the opponents of the Maynooth College endowment bill. London 1845.

Hope, J. B. The new government scheme for academical education in Ireland considered. London 1845.

Kane, Robert. The industrial resources of Ireland. Dublin 1845. 1st ed. 1844. 2nd ed. 1845.

Miller, Rev. George. The present crisis of the church of Ireland considered. Dublin 1845.

Newland, Rev. H. Brief observations on the past and present condition of the education of the poor in Ireland. Dublin 1845.

O'Connell, John. The repeal dictionary. Pt. I. Dublin 1845.

Stopford, Rev. E. A. A report to the Lord Bishop of Meath on the state of the elementary schools in the diocese. . . . Dublin 1845.

Fitzgerald, Maurice. A letter to Sir R. Peel on the endowment of the church of Ireland. London 1845.

Correspondence with the National Board on the subject of the trust deed of the national schools. Dublin 1845.

First general report of the Trade and commerce committee of the Loyal national repeal association read at a meeting of the association 31 March 1845.

History and proceedings of the '82 club. . . . Edited by A member of the Irish press. Dublin 1845.

A letter on the Irish Colleges bill. Dublin 1845.

Repeal prize essays: essays on the repeal of the union. . . . Dublin 1845. Contains essays by M. J. Barry, M. Staunton, J. Godkin and G. Ramsay.

Report of the committee of the Loyal national repeal ossociation on the Valuation (Ireland) bill. . . .

Report of the parliamentary committee of the Loyal national repeal association on the tenants' compensation bill. . . . [n.d.].

Reports of the parliamentary committee of the Loyal National Repeal Association of Ireland. 2 vols. Dublin 1844–5.

Suggestions on the best modes of employing the Irish peasantry. By Agricola. London 1845.

Thoughts on academical education, ecclesiastical and secular. . . . By A catholic priest. Dublin 1845.

Blacker, William. An essay on the best mode of improving the condition of the labouring classes of Ireland. London 1846.

Browne, R. D. Debate on the first reading of the Protection of Life (Ireland) bill. London 1846.

Butt, Isaac. Protection to home industry . . . the substance of two lectures. . . . Dublin 1846.

Fitzgerald, Lord William. Some suggestions for the better government of Ireland. . . . London 1846.

Ray, T. M. Report on the Irish coercion bill, the causes of discontent in Ireland, condition of the people, comparative criminality with England—remedial measures, etc. Dublin 1846.

The case of the tenant farmers. . . . Cork 1846.

Soirée of the Dublin protestant association and reformation society at Whitefriars Hall, 14 Jan. 1846.

Mears, W. A treatise on the law and practice relating to elections . . . in Ireland. Dublin 1847.

Trevelyan, C. E. The Irish crisis, reprinted from the *Edinburgh Review*, No. clxxv, January 1848. London 1848.

Phelan, W. History of the policy of the church of Rome in Ireland . . . with a biographical memoir by John Jebb. 3rd ed. London 1854.

O'Donoghue, J. The summary jurisdiction of the magistrates in Ireland. Dublin 1855.


7. OTHER CONTEMPORARY WORKS

Barrow, T. A tour round Ireland. London 1836.

Brett, William. Reminiscences of county Louth. Dundalk 1913. (First edition 1857).

Brooke, Rev. R. S. Recollections of the Irish church. London 1877. Recollections of the Irish church: second series. London 1878.

Brougham, 1st Lord. The life and times of Henry Lord Brougham, written by himself. 3 vols. Edinburgh 1871.

Cloncurry, Lord. Personal recollections of the life and times with extracts from the correspondence of Valentine Lord Cloncurry. Dublin 1849.

Cobbe, F. P. Life of F. P. Cobbe. By herself. 2nd ed. London 1904.

Thomas Cromwell. My excursion through Ireland. London 1820.

Curran, W. H. Sketches of the Irish bar. 2 vols. London 1855.

Daunt, W. J. McN. Personal recollections of the late Daniel O'Connell. 2 vols. London 1848.

Duffy, C. G. Young Ireland, a fragment of Irish history 1840–50. London 1880.

Duffy, C. G. Four years of Irish history, 1845–49: a sequel to 'Young Ireland'. London 1883.

Duffy, C. G. My life in two hemispheres. 2 vols. London 1898.

Killen, Rev. W. D. Reminiscences of a long life. London 1901.

Le Fanu, W. R. Seventy years of Irish life. London 1896.

Morgan, Lady Sydney. Lady Morgan's Memoirs. 2 vols. London 1862.

O'Beirne, Rt. Rev. T. L. Sermons preached on several occasions. 3 vols. London 1799–1821.

O'Connell, Daniel. A memoir on Ireland native and Saxon. Vol. i. 1172–1660. Dublin 1843.

# BIBLIOGRAPHY

O'Connell, John. Recollections and experiences during a parliamentary career from 1833 to 1848. 2 vols. London 1849.

Plowden, F. The history of Ireland from its union with Great Britain. . . . Dublin 1811.

Ullathorne, Most Rev. W. B. From cabin-boy to archbishop: autobiography. London 1941.

Wakefield, E. An account of Ireland, statistical and political. 2 vols. Dublin 1812.

White, H. C., Rev. Sixty years' experience as an Irish landlord: Memoirs of John Hamilton, D.L. London [n.d.].

Wyse, Thomas. Historical sketch of the late catholic association of Ireland. 2 vols. London 1829.

## B. SECONDARY AUTHORITIES

The life and work of Mary Aikenhead, foundress of the congregation of the Irish Sisters of Charity 1787–1858. By A member of the congregation. London 1924.

Allen, R. 'Henry Montgomery 1788–1865'. In essays in British and Irish history in honour of James Eadie Todd. *Ed.* H. A. Crowe, T. W. Moody, and D. B. Quinn. London 1949.

Atkins, J. B. The life of Sir William Howard Russell. 2 vols. London 1911.

Amherst, Rev. W. J. The history of catholic emancipation. 2 vols. London 1886.

Anderson, J. History of the Belfast library and society for promoting knowledge. Belfast 1888.

Auchmuty, J. J. Sir Thomas Wyse, 1791–1862: the life and career of an educator and diplomat. London 1939.

Ball, F. E. The judges in Ireland, 1221–1921. 2 Vols. London 1926.

Batterberry, R. 'The synod of Ulster and the National Board' in *Irish Ecclesiastical Record*, lvi. 584–61; lviii. 16–28; lix. 61–73.

Belfast Literary Society, 1801–1901: historical sketch. Belfast 1902.

Benn, G. A history of the town of Belfast . . . 2 vols. London 1877–80.

Berens, Rev. E. A memoir of the life of Bishop Mant. London 1849.

Blackburne, E. Life of the Rt. Hon. Francis Blackburne. London 1874.

Broderick, J. F. The Holy See and the Irish movement for the repeal of the union with England, 1829–47. Rome 1951.

Cambridge Modern History, vol. x, chapters xviii, xix, xx; vol. xi, chapter i.

Campbell, A. A. Belfast newspapers past and present. Belfast 1921.

Chart, D. A. Ireland from the union to catholic emancipation. London 1910.

Clark, George Kitson. Peel and the conservative party, 1832–41. London 1929.

Clarke, R. 'The relations between O'Connell and the Young Irelanders.' In *IHS*, iii. 18–33.

Cogan, Rev. A. The diocese of Meath, ancient and modern. 3 vols. Dublin 1862–70.

Connell, K. H. The population of Ireland 1750–1845. Oxford 1950.

Crolly, Rev. G. Life of the Most Rev. Dr Crolly. . . . Dublin 1851.

Dillon, W. Life of John Mitchel. 2 vols. London 1888.

Duffy, C. G. Thomas Davis: the memoirs of an Irish patriot, 1840–46. London 1890.

Duncombe, T. S. Life and correspondence of T. S. Duncombe. London 1868.

Edwards, R. Dudley. 'The contribution of Young Ireland to the development of the Irish National idea.' In *Feilscribhinn Torna*, ed. S. Pender. Cork 1947.

Ellis, J. T. Cardinal Consalvi and Anglo-papal relations, 1814–24. Washington 1942.

Extracts from an orderly book of 1803 to 1820 of the Belfast Charitable Society. Belfast 1905.

Fagan, L. The Reform Club. London 1887.

Fawcett, H. G. Life of the Rt. Hon. Sir William Molesworth. London 1901.

Ferguson, Lady M. C. Sir Samuel Ferguson in the Ireland of his day. 2 vols. London 1896.

Fisher, J. R. and Robb, J. H. Royal Belfast Academical Institution: centenary volume, 1810–1910. Belfast 1913.

Fitzpatrick, W. J. The life, times and correspondence of the Rt. Rev. Dr Doyle. 2 vols. Dublin 1861.

Grattan, Henry. Memoirs of the life and times of the Rt. Hon. Henry Grattan. 5 vols. London 1839–46.

Graves, Rev. R. P. Life of Sir William Rowan Hamilton. 3 vols. Dublin 1882–9.

Green, E. R. R. The Lagan valley, 1800–50. London 1949.

Grote, H. The personal life of George Grote. London 1873.

Gwynn, D. The O'Gorman Mahon: duellist, adventurer and politician. London 1924.

Hall, F. G. The bank of Ireland, 1783–1946. Dublin 1949.

Hastings, Selina. The life and times of Selina Countess of Huntington. By A member of the houses of Shirley and Hastings. 2 vols. London 1839–41.

Healy, Most Rev. J. Maynooth College, its centenary history, 1795–1895. Dublin 1895.

Hincks, T. D. Notices of William Bruce. London 1843.

Historical memorials of the first presbyterian church in Belfast. Belfast 1887.

Hodder, E. The life and work of the seventh earl of Shaftesbury. 3 vols. London 1886.

Inglis, B. The freedom of the press in Ireland, 1784–1842. [Unpublished Ph.D. thesis, Trinity College, Dublin.]

Kennedy, B. A. 'Sharman Crawford on the repeal question, 1847'. In *IHS*, vi. 270–3.

Kennedy, B. A. 'Sharman Crawford's federal scheme for Ireland'. In Essays in British and Irish history. London 1949.

Kiernan, J. The financial administration of Ireland, 1782–1817. Dublin 1925.

Lampson, G. Locker. A consideration of the state of Ireland in the nineteenth century. London 1907.

Leader, R. E. Life and letters of John Arthur Roebuck. London 1897.

Lefevre, G. Shaw. Peel and O'Connell. . . . London 1887.

Lefroy, T. Memoirs of Chief Justice Lefroy. Dublin 1871.

Liddon, Rev. H. P. Life of E. B. Pusey. 4 vols. London 1893–7.

MacGrath, K. M. 'Writers in the *Nation*, 1842–5'. In *IHS*, vi. 189–223.

McCullagh, W. T. Memoirs of the Rt. Hon. Richard Lalor Sheil. 2 vols. London 1855.

McLennan, J. F. Memoirs of Thomas Drummond. Edinburgh 1867.

Madden, H. Memoir of the Rt. Rev. Robert Daly. London 1875.

Madden, Rev. S. Memoir of the life of the late Rev. Peter Roe . . . with copious extracts from his correspondence. . . . Dublin 1842.

Mant, Rev. W. Memoirs of the Rt. Rev. Richard Mant. . . . London 1857.

Massy, Rev. Dawson. The life and times of a faithful shepherd: a memoir of the Rev. Godfrey Massy. London 1855.

Mathias, Rev. W. B. Brief memorials of the Rev. B. W. Mathias. . . . Dublin 1842.

Monaghan, J. J. A social and economic history of Belfast [unpublished Ph. D. thesis, Queen's University, Belfast.]

Moody, T. W. Thomas Davis, 1814–45. Dublin 1945.

Moore, H. K. An unwritten chapter in the history of Irish education;

# BIBLIOGRAPHY

the history of the society for the education of the poor of Ireland, generally known as the Kildare Place Society, 1811–31. London 1904.

Nicholls, G. A history of the English poor law ... and a biography [of George Nicholls] by H. G. Willink. 2 vols. London 1898.

Nolan, K. B. 'Writings in connection with the Thomas Davis and the Young Ireland centenary, 1945.' In *IHS*, v. 265–72.

O'Brien, George. The economic history of Ireland from the union to the famine. London 1921.

O'Brien, R. B. Fifty years of concessions to Ireland, 1831–81. 2 vols. [n.d.]

O'Brien, R. B. Thomas Drummond ... life and letters. London 1889.

O'Connell, Mrs. M. J. Charles Bianconi: a biography. London 1878.

O'Reilly, Rt. Rev. B. John MacHale, archbishop of Tuam, his life, times and correspondence. 2 vols. New York 1890.

Owen, D. J. History of Belfast. Belfast 1921.

Palmer, N. D. 'Sir Robert Peel's "select MS. library".' In *IHS*, vi. 101–13.

Parker, C. S. The life and letters of Sir James Graham ... 1792–1861. 2 vols. London 1907.

Plunket, David. The life, letters, and speeches of Lord Plunket. 3 vols. London 1867.

Porter, J. L. The life and times of Henry Cooke. London 1871.

Reid, Rev. J. S. History of the presbyterian church in Ireland. *Ed.* Rev W. D. Killen. 3 vols. Belfast 1867.

Reid, S. J. Life and letters of the first earl of Durham, 1792–1840. 2 vols. London 1906.

Edmund Ignatius Rice and the Christian Brothers. By A Christian Brother. Dublin 1926.

Roberts, M. The whig party, 1807–12. London 1939.

Smith, Mrs. R. The life of the Rev. Mr Henry Moore ... including the autiobiography. ... London 1844.

Stanhope, Lord. Life of the Rt. Hon. William Pitt. 4 vols. London 1861.

Sullivan, G. D. 'Irish parliamentary representation, 1800–32.' [Unpublished Ph.D. thesis, Trinity College, Dublin.]

Tierney, M. *Ed.* Daniel O'Connell: nine centenary essays. Dublin 1949.

Torrens, W. M. Memoirs of the Rt. Hon. William 2nd Viscount Melbourne. 2 vols. London 1878.

Two centuries of Irish history. *Ed.* R. B. O'Brien. With an introduction by James Bryce. London 1888.

Walpole, S. The life of Lord John Russell. 2 vols. London 1889.

# BIBLIOGRAPHY

Ward, Rev. B. The eve of catholic emancipation. 3 vols. London 1911 12.

Walsh, Most Rev. William J. 'The board of charitable donations and bequests' (Pts. ix, xi, xii, of 'The law in its relation to religious interests') in *Irish Ecclesiastical Record* 3rd series, xiv. 875–94, 971–96, 1071–99.

Webster, C. K. The foreign policy of Castlereagh, 1815–22. London 1925.

Whately, E. J. Life and correspondence of Richard Whately. 2 vols. London 1866.

White, T. de V. The road of excess. Dublin 1945.

Wrottesley, G. Life and correspondence of Sir John Burgoyne. 2 vols. London 1873.

Woodward, E. L. The age of Reform 1815–1870. Oxford 1938.

# LORD-LIEUTENANTS, CHIEF SECRETARIES AND UNDER-SECRETARIES, 1801–46

## LORD-LIEUTENANTS

Earl of Hardwicke (May 1801).
Duke of Bedford (Mar. 1806).
Duke of Richmond (Apr. 1807).
Viscount (afterwards Earl) Whitworth (Aug. 1813).
Earl Talbot (Oct. 1817).
Marquess Wellesley (Dec. 1821).
Marquess of Anglesey (Mar. 1828).
Duke of Northumberland (Mar. 1829).
Marquess of Anglesey (Dec. 1830).
Marquis Wellesley (Sept. 1833).
Earl of Haddington (Jan. 1835).
Earl of Mulgrave (afterwards Marquess of Normanby)
    (May 1835).
Viscount Ebrington (Apr. 1839).
Earl de Grey (Sept. 1841).
Lord Heytesbury (July 1844).
Earl of Bessborough (July 1846).

## CHIEF SECRETARIES

Charles Abbot (May 1801).
William Wickham (Feb. 1802).
Sir Evan Nepean (Feb. 1804).
Nicholas Vansittart (Mar. 1805).
Charles Long (Sept. 1805).
William Elliot (Mar. 1806).
Sir Arthur Wellesley (Apr. 1807).
Robert Dundas (Apr. 1809).

William Wellesley Pole (Oct. 1809).

Robert Peel (Aug. 1812).

Charles Grant (Aug. 1818).

Henry Goulburn (Dec. 1821).

William Lamb (Apr. 1827).

Lord Francis Leveson-Gower (June 1828).

Sir Henry Hardinge (July 1830).

Edward Smith Stanley (Nov. 1830).

Sir John Cam Hobhouse (Mar. 1833).

Edward John Littleton (May 1833).

Sir Henry Hardinge (Dec. 1834).

Viscount Morpeth (Apr. 1835).

Lord Eliot (Sept. 1841).

Sir Thomas Francis Fremantle (Feb. 1845).

Earl of Lincoln (Feb. 1846).

Henry Labouchere (July 1846).

## UNDER-SECRETARIES

Alexander Marsden (Oct. 1801).

James Trail (Sept. 1806).

Sir Charles Saxton (Sept. 1808).

William Gregory (Oct. 1812).

Sir William Gossett (Dec. 1830).

Thomas Drummond (July 1835).

Norman Macdonald (May 1840).

Edward Lucas (Sept. 1841).

Richard Pennefather (Aug. 1845).

Thomas Redington (July 1846).

# INDEX

Abbot, Charles, 78, 85
Abercromby, James, 163
Aberdeen, George Gordon, 4th earl of, 216–7
Acton, Charles Januarius Edward, Cardinal, 217
Afghanistan, 204
Agrarian disturbances, 59–62, 144, 150–1, 187
Agriculture, Irish, 27
Alcock, Henry, 44
Aldermen of Skinners' Alley, 227n.
Althorp, John Spencer, styled viscount, 146, 150, 156, 163, 191
Anacreontic Society, 53
Anglesey, Henry William Paget, 1st marquess of, Irish policy, 147–52; 67, 70–1, 141, 159
Antrim, County, 50
Archdale, Edward, 232
Arkwright, Richard, 58
Armagh, Archbishops of, see Beresford, John George; Crolly, William
Armagh, city, 45, 64, 134
Armagh, County, 20, 33, 64, 115, 185
Arms bill, 252
Ashley, Anthony Cooper, Lord, 220
Assistant barristers, 74n., 179, 185

Bagwell, John, 104
Baldwin, Herbert, 158n.
Balfour, Arthur James, 67n.
Ballinamuck, 227
Ballot, the, 128, 172, 251
Ballymena, 201
Ballymore (Westmeath), 60
Bank of Ireland, 166
Bankes, Henry, 85
Baptist Irish Society, 30
Barrack board, 48
Barrett, Richard, 113, 157, 160, 234

Barry, Michael Joseph, 237
Bath, 60
Bedford, John Russell, 6th duke of, 21, 90
Belfast, George Hamilton Chichester, styled earl of, 135
Belfast, at the beginning of the nineteenth century, 52–9; parliamentary elections in, 134–6; 50, 62, 206, 244
Belfast Academical Institution, 53, 55–7, 222
Belfast Literary Society, 53–4
*Belfast Monthly Magazine*, 57
Belfast Natural History Society, 53
Belfast Society for Promoting Knowledge, 54
Bellew, Sir Edward, 90, 95, 100, 105
Bentham, Jeremy, 126–7
Bequests bill, 214–6, 245
Beresford, John George, 73, 206, 208
Bernal, Osborne Ralph, 250
Berwick, Edward, 21
Bessborough, John William Ponsonby, 4th earl of, relations with O'Connell, 152, 154, 160–2, 166, 252; 153, 164, 250
Bethesda Chapel, 26, 27
Blackburne, Francis, 142, 208
Blacker, William, 209
Blackwater, 115
Blake, Anthony, and Irish education, 198, 206–7; 147, 215, 217, 219, 221
Blake, Michael, 97
Blake, Valentine, 138
Bligh, Thomas, 104
Bloxham, 26
Board of commissioners of national education, 198–9, 206–8
Board of customs and excise, 78
Board of stamps, 78

# INDEX

Hawkesbury, see Liverpool.
Hayes, Richard, 97
Hazlett, Henry, 54
Headford, Thomas Taylour, 2nd marquess of, 119
Hibernian Bible Society, 30
Hill, Sir George, 55
Hipplesley, Sir James, 84
Historical Society (Belfast), 53
Hoare, John, 27
Hobhouse, John Cam, 159
Hodgkinson, Francis, 113
'Hogans', 61
Holland, Henry Richard Vassall, 3rd baron, 142, 149, 150–1, 151*n*., 155, 249
Holmes, Robert, 198
Howick, Henry Grey, styled Viscount Howick, 249
Howley, John, 205
Hume, Joseph, 116, 136, 163, 167, 168, 169
Huntingdon, Selina Hastings, Countess of, 25
Hutchinson, John Hely-, baron, 88
Hutchinson, Christopher Hely-, 104
Hutton, Henry, 27

India, 127
Inglis, Sir Robert, 221
Irish confederation, 258
Irish protestant conservative society, 112, 116–7
Irish Society, 30
*Irishman*, 58

Jackson, John, 237
Jackson, Joseph Devonsher, 133, 181, 207
Jebb, John, 199
Jeffrey, Francis, 117
Jephson, Charles Denham, 134, 153
Johnson, William, 208
Jones, John, 184
Jones, William Todd, 50
Joy, Henry, 142
Justices of the peace, 80–1, 119, 160, 167, 185, 227

Keady, 54*n*.
Keble, John, 148
Keenan, Michael, 65
Kelly, Thomas, 26

Kenmare, Valentine Browne, 1st earl of, 88
Kennedy, Patrick, 215
Keogh, John, 88, 91
Kerry, county, 20, 46, 60
Kilcoole, 64
Kildare, bishop of, see Doyle, James Warren
Kildare, 59
Kildare Place Society, 75, 76, 142
Kilkenny, city, 134, 136
Kilkenny, county, 44, 60, 61, 104, 137
Killaloe, bishops of, see Kennedy, Patrick, Knox, Edmund, Mant, Richard
Killeen, Arthur James Plunkett, styled Lord Killeen, 43, 134, 155
Killeleagh, 28
Killeshandra, 227
King's County, 46, 59
Knox, Alexander, 30
Knox, Edmund, 200

Lagan Navigation Company, 54
Lalor, Patrick, 133
Lambert, Henry, 137, 162
Lambruschini, Cardinal Luigi, 217–8
Land question, 38–40, 186–7, 224–5
Langford, John, 185
Lansdowne, Henry Petty-Fitzmaurice, 3rd marquess of, 36, 88, 194
Laurence, Richard, 22, 73, 199
Lawless, John, 55–8, 99, 100, 104
Leader, Nicholas Philpot, 134
Leahy, David, 254*n*.
Lees, Sir Harcourt, 102
Lefroy family, 43
Lefroy, Anthony, 207
Lefroy, Thomas Langlois, 27
Leinster, Augustus Frederick Fitzgerald, 4th duke of, 119, 198
Leitrim, 64
Leitrim, Nathaniel Clements, 2nd earl of, 119
Lever, Charles, 114
Leveson-Gower, Lord Francis, 77, 121*n*.
Lewis, George Cornewall, 193
Lewis, Sir Thomas Frankland, 193
Limerick, bishop of, see Jebb, John
Limerick, city, 44, 134, 211
Limerick, County, 27, 47, 59, 60, 61, 64, 137
Lisburn, 45, 62

299

# INDEX

302